CARPENTERS

CARPENTERS

The Musical Legacy

Mike Cidoni Lennox
& Chris May

with

Richard Carpenter

PRINCETON ARCHITECTURAL PRESS · NEW YORK

Published by
Princeton Architectural Press
202 Warren Street
Hudson, New York 12534
www.papress.com

Printed and bound in China
24 23 22 21 4 3 2 1 First edition

ISBN 978-1-64896-072-7

Editor: Jennifer N. Thompson
Designer: IN-FO.CO
Production Development, Image Digitization and Restoration: Jozelle May
Senior Contributing Editor: Sandy Cohen
Contributing Writer and Editor: Denise Quan
Associate Editor: Deborah Sprague
Researchers: Simon Worsley, Joe DiMaria, Stephen Richardson,
Billy Rees, Nancy Mescon
Photo Acquisition: Peter Desmond Dawe
Photo Clearances: Donavan Freberg
Administration: Brian Lennox

Library of Congress Control Number: 2021937229

Page 2: 1971

Page 6: 1970

For our spouses,
Brian Lennox and Jozelle May,
who sacrificed so much as we looked to our dreams.

And to Mary Carpenter,
who loaned us her husband for the past two years.

We're singin' this song for you.

I love you in a place
Where there's no space or time
I love you for in my life
You are a friend of mine

—Leon Russell

Contents

Los Angeles, 2021

Introduction

Hello, and welcome to our book. My name is Richard Carpenter. My late, great sister, Karen, and I constituted the pop-music duo, Carpenters, more commonly known as *the* Carpenters.

In May of 1970, A&M Records released our second single, "(They Long to Be) Close to You." This record became an overnight sensation, as well as a touchstone in popular music. It proved to have a lasting impact—not only on pop music but also, as it turned out, on pop culture.

The single changed our lives. Within weeks, the Carpenters became a household name, in demand at home in the United States and all around the world. "Close to You" was that popular. Still, it was one record, and one record does not a career make.

Karen and I shouldn't have been worried. We followed "Close to You" with "We've Only Just Begun," "For All We Know," "Top of the World," "Yesterday Once More," and many more hits. Nevertheless, the Carpenters were not just a "singles act," as a number of our detractors wished to believe. We sold many millions of albums. And they continue to sell today.

I'm not surprised by this, as Karen's warm, unmistakable voice overcomes all language barriers, and people the world over are drawn to our lush harmonies and memorable melodies. Being her sibling and spiritual twin, I instinctively realized what songs, keys, and accompaniments would best showcase her vocals.

Over these past fifty-odd years, countless words—most of them uninformed and just plain nasty—have been written about Karen and me. And documentaries of varying quality have covered our career. Yet very few have devoted time and thought to the music we made; they prefer to concentrate on our Waspish background, mainstream pop music, and personal demons.

So, I was happily surprised when veteran Associated Press entertainment reporter Mike Cidoni Lennox and musically multifaceted Carpenters expert Chris May contacted me, proposing a book that would center on the Carpenters' career. They would focus on our instantaneous and overwhelming success, hectic touring schedules, and uninspired management. And the text would be accompanied by an array of rarely seen photographs.

I agreed to become involved in the project. And involved I became.

As Mike and Chris are both, shall we say, connoisseurs of the Carpenters oeuvre, I answered (or attempted to answer) over many sessions a tsunami of questions. They asked informed questions, some that I didn't know how to answer. In addition, and with some trepidation, I ventured into the rarely visited Carpenters archives and discovered, among the large number of career-related things, items that I'd forgotten had existed but were nevertheless extant. I trust that you will find some of this arcana to be of interest. Finally, I edited reams of copy to make absolutely certain that the facts contained herein are absolutely correct.

I wish to thank my wife, Mary, for allowing the authors and me the use of her office.

And for their countless hours and passionate dedication to this book, I want to thank Mike and Chris. I believe the book has proved to be a much larger and far more complicated undertaking than any of us originally envisioned.

Richard Carpenter
February 25, 2021

Authors' Note

"You know, even I didn't know that," says Richard Carpenter, with a chuckle. He's thumbing through our book proposal on the career and musical legacy of the Carpenters, the duo he formed with sister Karen in the late 1960s.

With her timeless voice and impeccable phrasing, and his gift for writing, selecting, producing, and arranging hit singles and sparkling album tracks, their classics came fast and furiously—starting in the summer of 1970, when "(They Long to Be) Close to You" set a new gold standard for popular music.

Zip ahead a half century, and the trim Carpenter, a youthful seventy-four, continues reading in the airy and cozy sitting room of his California ranch home in a gated community forty miles west of downtown Los Angeles. In the entryway, a custom-built ceramic likeness of Brian Griffin, the boozehound from TV's *Family Guy*, holds court—and a martini. The center-piece of the sunken living room is a Steinway concert grand piano.

There's a console table dotted with statuettes, and a photo in honor of the Twenty-Fifth Grammy Awards from January 11, 1983. Here, the Carpenters stand shoulder to shoulder with other Grammy-winning luminaries including Dionne Warwick, Gladys Knight, and Burt Bacharach. It's the last professional shot of Richard and Karen together, taken just twenty-four days before Karen's death.

Richard finishes reading, looks up, and asks where we—the veteran entertainment reporter and the Carpenters historian—gleaned information concerning a song referenced in one of the chapters. It was an interview with one of the tune's two songwriters.

"Sorry, guys," Richard says. "But that isn't how it happened. When it comes to what Karen and I recorded, everything is either up here or down there," gesturing first to his head and then to the floor below, the 2,500-square-foot media underground. That area houses a massive collection of recordings, a sound room, a movie room, and, most importantly for our book, a large and meticulously organized personal assemblage of photos, memorabilia, and other media documenting his life and career.

And, just like that, our game plan changed. We boldly took the leap from merely asking for Richard's blessing to proposing a partnership with him. Who better than the duo's sole-surviving member, one with a long and keen memory, to serve as our primary source?

We felt that our odds were slim, as Richard had tried this kind of arrangement once before. Some twenty years earlier, he authorized a highly regarded music journalist to write a Carpenters biography. The result, however, was what Richard dubs, with disappointment, disparagingly "the anorexia book," referring to the disorder that took Karen at age thirty-two.

And yet Richard speaks of the writer of that book empathetically. "He was trying to figure out what was going on psychologically with Karen. He was trying to solve an unsolvable mystery."

This book is instead about the Carpenters' work legacy: their recordings. And as you're about to read, the three of us spent more time working in that sitting room than anyone would have ever imagined.

As if opening his home weren't enough, Richard offered full access to his archive. A majority of the images in this book come from his personal collection, many never previously published. We lost count of the times he went downstairs to pull an image, double-check a date, or dig up a fifty-year-old document—all for accuracy's sake.

Richard called in personal favors and gave up huge chunks of family time. And it was usually he who offered iced tea, went to the kitchen, filled the glasses, and came back with our drinks before each session.

We're grateful to Richard for generosity beyond belief, for so many things he has done and given to make this book possible. But those countless trips down to the archive and back have got to be at the top of the list.

Thanks for keeping us out of the fiction section, brother.

Mike Cidoni Lennox and Chris May

Prologue:
The Image Problem

**"We'd been hammered for so long,
and there were all those bad album covers.
It just had a cumulative effect."**

Summer, 1981: Richard and Karen Carpenter are on the A&M Records soundstage shooting a music video for their latest single, and it should be a happy occasion. After years without a major hit in the United States, the Carpenters had high hopes for their dreamy, finely crafted pop ballad "Touch Me When We're Dancing." And, initially, those hopes looked as if they would be fulfilled.

The record's chart run started strongly, entering the *Billboard* Hot 100 June 20 and flying into the Top 40 in just three weeks—faster than any Carpenters single in more than five years. For another month, the swift ascent continued. But, all of a sudden, it was done. The record was stuck at No. 16 for a month. It just wouldn't move any higher.

"Karen and I honestly thought it should be doing better," Richard remembers.

During a break in the video shoot, Jon Konjoyan makes a set visit. As a national promotion director of A&M, the Carpenters' record label since 1969, it's Konjoyan's job to address Richard and Karen's concerns about their records' success on the radio. He agrees the single has what it takes to return the duo to their Hot 100 glory days.

However, Konjoyan says there are two problems:

One is the timing of the release. Four years have passed since Richard and Karen's last Top 40 hit in the United States, "Calling Occupants of Interplanetary Craft (The Recognized Anthem of World Contact Day)."

Reflecting on the meeting some forty years later, Konjoyan explains, "1981 was light years away from 1977, in record industry terms. So to achieve the chart comeback that they did with "Touch Me When We're Dancing" in 1981 was impressive.

It would have charted even higher had all the stations played it at the same time.

"But some programmers waited," Konjoyan continues.

"They needed to be convinced. By the time some of the 'late' stations started playing the song, early stations started to drop off. You need everybody at the same time to really maximize chart position."

The other problem? Konjoyan tells the Carpenters it appears they are finally losing their long battle with an image problem that, for the most part, was not of their making.

Since Day One at A&M, Richard and Karen were inaccurately portrayed, promoted, and marketed as bland and boring, both personally and artistically. Some colleagues and contemporaries—and, especially, critics—had a field day, cruelly perpetuating that image. Konjoyan, who was new to the label in 1981, tells the Carpenters their persona has finally caught up with them.

In a business that thrives on "hip," Konjoyan explains, Richard and Karen have become radioactively square. Richard recalls, "Jon said that a number of radio programmers had told him, 'It doesn't matter if it's the greatest record in the world. If it says *Carpenters* on it, we're not going to play it.'

Looking back on that meeting, and still frustrated with the idea of "the image," Richard says Konjoyan's news came as no surprise. "We'd been hammered for so long, and there were all those bad album covers. It just had a cumulative effect."

After racking up so many US chart hits in the 1970s that they were the No. 1 American-born singles act of the decade, "Touch Me When We're Dancing" would be the duo's last time in the US pop Top 40.

But it is by no means the end of the Carpenters' success story.

Music-industry
trade ad for
Made in America,
1981

Chapter 1

From the Top

1952–1968

The Richard Carpenter Interview

Mike Cidoni Lennox and Chris May: Take us back to your hometown of New Haven, Connecticut. What's your earliest musical memory?

Richard Carpenter: Oh, getting into my father's record collection. The records were 78s, and he kept them in racks, except for the albums. Most 78s were made out of shellac and easily breakable. This turned into a problem, so Dad built a wooden grid to front the record cabinet. You have to remember that I was around three.

For Christmas of 1949, Mom and Dad bought me a Bing Crosby Junior Juke. It was patterned after the famous Wurlitzer 1015 jukebox. It lit up and had a 78 player in it. But no bubble tubes. Along with this were some vinyl 78s that RCA and other labels made for kids. There was a Spike Jones set with "Hawaiian War Chant," "Chloe," "Old MacDonald," and "Our Hour." I played these to death, especially the first two, but I still wanted to get back to Dad's records.

Tell us about your dad's library.

It was any number of things, different types of music: light classical, Dixieland jazz, a lot of vocalists and bandleaders like Bing Crosby and Glen Gray. But he also had [Pyotr Ilyich] Tchaikovsky's first piano concerto with [Vladimir] Horowitz and [Arturo] Toscanini, and [Sergei] Rachmaninoff's second piano concerto with the composer at the piano—just a number of different types of music, like Western swing and Spade Cooley. I'm very much like my father, as far as my likes and dislikes in music and automobiles. We're both the same.

Do you remember the first record you owned?

Believe it or not, the first one I asked for was "Mule Train" by Frankie Laine. This was not a children's record. I later learned that it hit No. 1 in November of 1949. So, I would have just turned three.

That's young.

Really young.

Where was your dad's phonograph in the house?

Well, originally it was in the living room. He and Mom had purchased a Zenith radio console in 1937—AM and shortwave, with a twelve-inch speaker. Dad hooked up an input in the back of it, where you flipped a switch, and you could play a record player through the radio's amp and speaker.

Ultimately Dad and Mom finished off our basement. The Zenith went down there, the records went down there, and so I went down there. I spent a hell of a lot of time in our basement, just listening to records. And, later, Karen did the same.

Was your mom musical?

She had a nice alto [voice]. Warm. Mom loved popular music and would play the radio while she worked in the kitchen. She was great at remembering lyrics and passed that gift along to Karen and me.

Who were your mom's favorite artists?

Oh, Bing, of course. Dick Haymes. And later, Perry Como and Nat King Cole, among others.

There was another family member living with you in the New Haven house, correct?

Page 16: Karen, Wes Jacobs, and Richard—the Richard Carpenter Trio, 1966

Page 18, left: Karen and Richard with their father, Harold Carpenter, New Haven, 1950

Page 18, right: Karen and Richard with their mother, Agnes Carpenter, New Haven, 1950

Left: Richard sits near his father's record cabinet, New Haven, 1949

Correct. Joan Tyrell—"Joanie"—Mom's niece, born in 1936. Mom and Dad raised her from the time she was eighteen months old. Joan's like an older sister, and she loves music as well. Right after graduating from high school, she got a good job with Bell Telephone.

Joan wanted to learn to play the piano. As there wasn't one in the house, she went to the Baldwin dealer and purchased an Acrosonic spinet. Joanie didn't kid around. So we now had a piano in our house, but the lessons didn't click with Joan. I guess she liked listening to music more than learning how to play. But there was the piano, and my folks thought I should learn to play.

My first teacher was Mrs. Florence June, from whom I learned the rudiments. I was given the Hanon book of exercises and the John Thompson piano course, book one. This was mid-'54. I'd taken lessons for about a year when Mrs. June spoke with my parents and told them I wasn't all that interested in the lessons and, in so many words, that we should stop. She was honest, and she was correct.

So that was it for lessons?

For a good couple of years, but every now and again, I'd sit at the piano and "fiddle around," as it were, and soon found I could play certain songs by ear. I became more interested, and a young chap by the name of Henry Will signed on as my teacher. I imagine he was in his midtwenties, and just a good guy. [Joanie and Henry, aka Hank, eventually married.]

We stayed with the exercises in the Hanon and Czerny books, which I actually enjoyed. But, in addition, Hank taught me how to read the chord symbols that are on the sheet music of popular songs and introduced the "fake book" [a book of songs with just basic chord sequences] to my musical life.

I had reached a degree of proficiency where Hank suggested to my parents that I should audition for the Yale music school. Technically, he said, "I've taken him as far as I can." So I auditioned and was accepted.

Just to be clear, I was fifteen and still in high school. It's not like I was accepted to Yale [University], but this enabled me to study with a staff member of the music school's piano department.

The public perception has always been "young Richard Carpenter, Yale-prodigy."

I mean [shrugs], I was good enough to be accepted. But one day I got to my lesson a little early and through the door, I heard someone just burning through some classical piece that was way beyond

my capability. And the lesson finishes. The door opens and an Asian girl about eight years old walks out. I mean, right then and there, I knew if I had any aspirations—which I didn't—toward a career as a concert pianist, the little girl shot them to pieces.

There went your career as a concert pianist. But when did you think you could actually make a living playing the piano?

I'm not quite sure of that, but not at this time. Actually, I wasn't thinking too much at all. I was a real fuck-up at school, especially tenth and eleventh grades. All I thought about was music and automobiles.

When did your family move to the West Coast?

June of 1963. My dad didn't like cold, didn't like the snow and the wet and chains for the tires, and all that. They'd been saving to move to Southern California, and around '62, they made the decision. This was a big change because Dad would have been fifty-five and Mom forty-eight. To pull up roots and say goodbye to friends of many years, as well as to sell their house—of which they were so proud—took some balls. Of course, they never regretted it.

So you get here, and…

In almost no time, things started to happen. Dad had a job guaranteed for him, so that was no

problem at all. But the job was in Vernon, one of many smaller cities in Southeast L.A. But next to nobody actually lives in Vernon. It's all industrial—like a population of eighty. So Dad asked his pal from New Haven, Ed Cox, "Where do you recommend we live, not too far from Vernon?" And Ed said, "Downey."

Downey had a population of over a hundred thousand. As we soon learned, it was named after John Gately Downey, founded in 1873, and incorporated in 1956. So we started our tour by driving down Downey Avenue looking for an apartment building where we could settle temporarily, until the house in New Haven sold, and came upon a nice place named "The Shoji" at 12020 Downey Avenue. The folks rented apartment 21, which was furnished. It needed, however, a TV, which we soon purchased, and a piano, which we rented until mine arrived from New Haven.

A few days after getting settled in, we were driving and looking for an address. I can't remember the details, but we were soon lost. We noticed a park over to the left—Furman Park—and asked the groundskeeper, whose name was Nip, I remember, "How do we get to…(whatever we were looking for)?" He gave us the directions and, noticing the Connecticut plate, asked whether we were visiting, and so on.

And my mother [sighs and rolls his eyes] mentioned the weather, but also said, "My son, the musician." And Nip replied that every Sunday afternoon the park has a talent show of sorts. "He should play." So I did. On a raised platform, and a seasoned Hamilton upright, I knocked out the "Theme from Exodus," a recent hit, and very showy. And then I prevailed on Karen to sing "The End of the World." She was only thirteen and not much interested in singing, but I thought she had promise. She sang all right. In tune. But the great voice hadn't shown itself yet.

Well, following the show, this fellow by the name of Vance Hayes came up to me and said he's the choirmaster at the Downey Methodist Church. "We're looking for an interim organist, and I think you could fill the bill." And I said, "I don't play the organ. I don't play the pedals; I can only play the piano." To which he replied, "I think you'll be fine."

To a degree, Vance was right, as long as the church didn't require actual organ music meant for actual organists. So I took the job and did a fair job of faking it.

I could play from the hymnals and quickly learned the [Richard] Wagner and [Felix] Mendelssohn wedding marches, and got fairly comfortable with the pedals. Nevertheless, I knew church elders were wanting the genuine article, and not some sixteen-year-old kid. I was shown the door in August, roughly, but not before word had gotten around about the teenaged church organist.

A reporter/photographer from our local newspaper, the *Southeast News*, interviewed me and took a nice picture of me sitting and "working" at the piano. I didn't listen to my mother and left my glasses on.

The article mentioned my playing these clubs back in New Haven, and in a day or so…knock, knock, knock.

Was history repeating itself?

Just like in New Haven. A couple of fellows in their early thirties, who moonlighted playing gigs on the weekend, needed a pianist. "*You* are the kid?" "Yes." "So, could you come over and rehearse?" I mean, he meant right then and there, and we took off in one of the guys' new '63 Thunderbird. The guys were legit, but can you imagine this happening in this day and age?

We ended up playing weekends at the Roaring 20s lounge, which was part of the Wonderbowl on Firestone Boulevard in Downey. So I had that and the church job. This was all in a matter of maybe

three weeks of being here in Downey. I have to mention that Downey's slogan at this time was "Future Unlimited."

You performed with these guys for a while.

Oh, yeah, and some others. One drummer's name was Larry Black. And he drove a '58 Chrysler.

1963

Composer and Pianist

Teenagers have varied pastimes, but in the case of Richard Carpenter of Downey it's music. Here he takes time out from composing a musical score — he has written numerous ballads and rock 'n' roll — to smile for the camera. He hopes to become a "commercial" pianist.
—Daily Signal Photo by W. R. Barnett.

Teen Gives 'Concert in Park' But Yearns for a Stage Career

By AL BUSCH
Daily Signal Staff Writer

A secretary's typographical error deprived many Southeast District residents from hearing a talented young pianist play in a Downey concert.

Because the concert was publicized as 4½-hours-long, instead of the correct 1½-hours, many persons arrived toward the end—or after completion—of Sunday's "Concert in the Park" by 16-year-old Richard Carpenter of Downey.

His concert was part of a weekly series in Furman Park by the Downey Recreation and Park District.

A native of New Haven, Conn., Carpenter moved to Downey with his parents, Mr. and Mrs. Harold Carpenter, and sister, Karen, 13, about a month ago. The family resides at Apt. 22, 12020 Downey Ave.

Popular Field

A piano student for five years, one of which was with Seymour Fink of the Yale University Music School, he presently is studying with Ronald Tarr at the School of Music, University of Southern California.

Carpenter said his career will be in piano, not as a concert pianist, but as a "commercial" pianist. He is aiming somewhat toward the radio-television field or popular stage entertainer.

He hurriedly admitted to enjoying "long hair stuff" but that he prefers to play the popular field material.

This was evident in his Sunday concert when the program included popular theme songs from movies and the stage, boogie woogie, some of his own selections, Broadway show hits and Chopin's "Fantasy Impromptu."

He also accompanied his sister who sang two original songs by a Connecticut acquaintance, and "End of the World" and "Honeymoon" from Broadway's "Anchors Away."

Carpenter became somewhat of a professional last Christmas. He formed a trio, adding bass and drums, and performed as restaurants and night clubs in the New Haven area. He was the leader" despite the fact his fellow performers were 22 and 24 years old.

Carpenter also had a rock 'n' roll combo comprised of school friends. They apparently made "beautiful music" and cut a record of his own "The Strut" and supplied the musical background for The Bari's, a vocal group, on the Josie (Jubilee) label.

Composer, Too

In all, the 16-year-old admits to writing the music for some 25 ballads and three rock 'n' roll numbers.

The young performer played at various school musical reviews and produced one show, "Rhythm Review" for the American Cancer Society in New Haven.

In addition to his popular field music, Carpenter was pianist for the Johnson Junior Symphony which performed in Woolsey Hall at Yale University, and served as a church organist for Park Methodist Church, New Haven.

Carpenter's immediate plans call for enrollment at the Earl Warren High School, Downey, to become an organist for an area church, and to form his own rock 'n' roll group and a trio to do restaurant and night club work.

Somewhere along the line he also learned how to play the accordion.

"I never took lessons on the accordion or did any specific studies on it," explained Carpenter. "I just picked it up.

"I like playing the accordion, but naturally I go more for the piano and organ."

Page 20: Richard and his Junior Juke(box), New Haven, 1949

Above: Richard and the family's Plymouth Satellite, Downey, CA, 1965

Left: Richard is profiled in the local newspaper, Downey, CA, 1963

The cars back then had large trunks, and his drum set went in there with room to spare. The electric bass player's name was Phil Manfredi.

They both had day gigs, of course, and Larry wasn't too much of a drummer, and he didn't listen to pop radio. I knew this because someone asked us to play "Wipeout," with the tom-tom breaks and all. He hadn't heard of it, and this was summer of '63, when it was a No. 1 record. So he bought the record, and tried, and tried and tried. I really felt for him.

The place we played was named Leo's, a so-called nightclub in Gardena. A real dive. But we played Friday and Saturday nights and had a good ol' time. And then President [John F.] Kennedy was assassinated, and that cast a pall on everything. We never were invited back to Leo's. But it's interesting to follow the thread of the story leading to Karen and me signing with A&M [Records].

One night at the club, Phil Manfredi, our bassist, asked me if I would accompany a friend of his, a co-worker who was an aspiring singer. The fellow's name was Ed Sulzer, and he asked me if I knew the song "Walk Away," a recent hit by Matt Monro, which I did.

Anyway, he sang it quite well. You know, a pianist is always a bit nervous in situations like this. But with ballads in particular, Eddie was quite impressive. Over the next several years, whenever there was an occasion where he could perform, he'd give me a call. Ed Sulzer. Remember the name.

All this and high school too.

There's the first day of my senior year at Downey High. I discovered that if you played in the marching band—I love this—you could get out of Phys Ed. The reason was that marching was good exercise—which was fine, but I played the piano. I thought that maybe if I waited to the end of the class, while kids were starting to disperse, I could sit at the piano and show off. Maybe it would lead to something. And damned if it didn't.

The band director, a young chap named Bruce Gifford, came over to me. First, he wanted me to know that after the Christmas break, marching band would become concert band. He'd like me to play "Rhapsody in Blue" with the band for its final concert of the school year, April of 1964.

And then he let me know that he and his brother, Rex, had a band that played weekends and they were in need of a pianist. Wow. Bruce and Rex Gifford. Sax and trumpet. Jack Dawes on drums, and Pete Perez on electric bass. We did a lot of Louis Prima stuff.

What was the band's name?

The Casuals. I said, "Bruce, there must be umpteen, I don't know how many 'The Casuals' around the country. How about The Brothers Gifford and the Mark III?" "Yes." We played any number of "casuals" for several years—mostly weekend gigs.

Left: Richard and Karen rehearsing an amateur musical, Downey, CA, 1965

Page 23: Richard is at the keyboard, far right of lower photo, on a flier for one of his gigs, mid-1960s

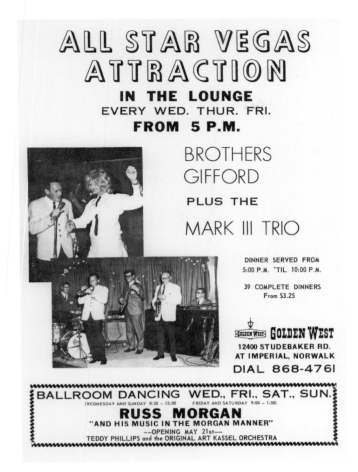

ALL STAR VEGAS
ATTRACTION

IN THE LOUNGE
EVERY WED. THUR. FRI.
FROM 5 P.M.

BROTHERS
GIFFORD

PLUS THE

MARK III TRIO

DINNER SERVED FROM
5:00 P.M. 'TIL 10:00 P.M.

39 COMPLETE DINNERS
From $3.25

GOLDEN WEST
12400 STUDEBAKER RD.
AT IMPERIAL, NORWALK
DIAL 868-4761

BALLROOM DANCING WED., FRI., SAT., SUN.
(WEDNESDAY AND SUNDAY 8:30 – 12:30   FRIDAY AND SATURDAY 9:00 – 1:30)
RUSS MORGAN
"AND HIS MUSIC IN THE MORGAN MANNER"
—OPENING MAY 21st—
TEDDY PHILLIPS and the ORIGINAL ART KASSEL ORCHESTRA

But then we ended up becoming a sort of house band, weekends of course, at a little club named the Sierra Room on Paramount Boulevard in Downey. I actually turned twenty-one at midnight of '67 while playing at the Sierra Room. This came as quite a surprise to the bartender.

We're seeing a variation on a theme: "RC knew how to land on his feet."

How about "faked his way out of many a situation." [Laughs.] Anyone who can play the piano halfway decently, play by ear and improvise if needed, is always in demand.

No drums for Karen yet?

Not at first, but by 1967, certainly. She'd shown an interest in drums for years, actually back in New Haven.

What inspired her to finally pick up the drumsticks in high school a year or so later?

Karen didn't want to go to Phys Ed, so I told her to see Bruce Gifford. Bruce put her on glockenspiel,

which was part of the drum section of the marching band. There, she met Frankie Chavez, another student, who was a show drummer—the whole Buddy Rich deal—and this impressed the hell out of her. She brought home a practice pad, and in no time she took to the rudiments, played press rolls, and was truly interested in learning to play. She asked for a drum set.

How much resistance from your parents?

Well, I'm certain they questioned her once or twice. This was out of the ordinary, but we could see the genuine interest and sense her natural talent. And they were really loving parents and generous people, at times overly generous. It's not like we were well off.

Were there many female drummers at the time?

Certainly not to my knowledge. But, right off the bat, Karen could play and had no trouble with any exotic time signatures. And her time was metronomic. She found out that the place to study was in Hollywood, the Pro Drum Shop with Bill Douglass. So the folks would drive her up, or I would, every Saturday, to her drum lesson. And back of course.

Your parents encouraged you both.

They most certainly did.

So let's go to your first meeting with Wes Jacobs at Long Beach State.

This is jumping ahead a bit, as Karen's lessons and all started in fall of '64, and I didn't meet Wes until near the end of the school year, 1965. I'd seen him in the music department over the course of the school year. He was majoring on the tuba. But on this day, he accompanied a student in my class on an upright bass. And he was good. So I introduced myself after class, adding that "my sister and I" so on and so forth. "If you have some time to come up to Downey and rehearse…" And he did, the whole summer of '65. Karen, Wes, and I really hit it off. We rehearsed a lot and laughed almost as much. And then, the following year, we heard about the Hollywood Bowl Battle of the Bands.

And suddenly you, Karen, and Wes are at the Hollywood Bowl.

Well, it wasn't exactly suddenly. We weren't familiar with this event, but we subsequently learned it had taken place for a number of years and was quite a production. It was sponsored by the L.A. Department of Recreation and Parks, and each year's finals took place at the Hollywood Bowl, with a panel of name adjudicators. I put together two arrangements, and we rehearsed like crazy. We won the quarters and the semis. These were in the combo division.

You played "The Girl from Ipanema" and one of your own tunes, "Iced Tea."

"Iced Tea," yeah, if someone has to lay claim to it. It's a crazy piece, named after the drink we consumed while rehearsing. I arranged it to showcase each member of the trio, with drum solos for Karen and for Wes, shifting from tuba to bass. The other song, "The Girl from Ipanema," I set in a variety of time signatures.

Did Wes end up stealing the show?

No. I think I stole the show, if anybody did. I was voted outstanding instrumentalist. In addition, we were named best combo,

and the Richard Carpenter Trio took home the overall sweepstakes trophy.

Was the Battle of the Bands the pivotal moment of that period?

Yes and no. Right around this time, spring of '66, Karen had an opportunity to audition for a fledgling independent label named Magic Lamp Records. As the [unnamed] A&R man/copartner of the label didn't get off work until midnight, the meeting wasn't to happen until approximately 1 a.m. at his garage studio in a neighborhood of Van Nuys. Karen and I were to meet the "money man" of the team—Don Zacklin, I believe was his name—at a little past midnight in a parking lot of Ralphs supermarket, and to look for his '66 Chrysler New Yorker: light yellow with a black vinyl top. He would drive us to the studio, as it was a bit of a labyrinthine route. Don was a pleasant chap, and Karen and I weren't the least bit nervous with how all of this was playing out. Once again, can you imagine this happening today?

At any rate, we reached our destination, walked around the back of the house, past the washer/dryer,

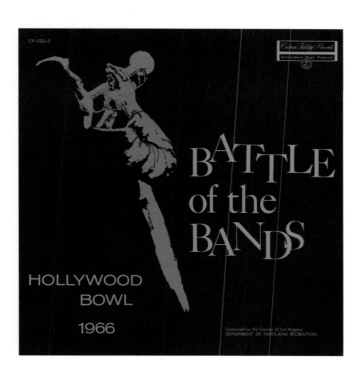

Page 24: The Richard Carpenter Trio rehearsing at home, Downey, CA, 1966

Right: Scorecard for the Hollywood Bowl Battle of the Bands, 1966

Below: Album of performances from the 1966 Hollywood Bowl Battle of the Bands

ANNUAL
BATTLE OF THE BANDS
HOLLYWOOD BOWL

COUNTY OF LOS ANGELES—DEPARTMENT OF PARKS AND RECREATION / 155 W. WASHINGTON BLVD. L.A. 90015 / RICHMOND 9-6911

HOLLYWOOD BOWL FINALS

NAME OF CONTESTANT __RICHARD CARPENTER TRIO__

DIVISION OF ENTRY __III COMBO__

POSSIBLE SCORE __350__ POINTS   YOUR SCORE __322__ POINTS

POINT SYSTEM: SUPERIOR - 5 PTS.   ABOVE AVERAGE - 4 PTS.
                AVERAGE - 3 PTS.   BELOW AVERAGE - 2 PTS.   POOR - 1 PT.

		JUDGE 1	2	3	4	5	TOTAL
ENSEMBLE PERFORMANCE	TONE QUALITY	3	5	4	5	5	22
	ACCURACY	4	5	4	5	5	23
	INTONATION	4	5	4	5	5	23
	EXPRESSION & PHRASING	4	5	4	5	5	23
	CONSISTENCY OF TEMPO	5	5	4	5	5	24
SOLO PERFORMANCE (S)	TONE QUALITY	3	5	4	5	5	22
	ACCURACY	4	5	4	5	5	23
	INTONATION	2	5	4	5	5	21
	EXPRESSION & PHRASING	4	5	4	5	5	23
	IMPROVISATION	4	4	4	5	5	22
ARRANGEMENTS	SUITABILITY FOR STYLE & ABILITY OF GROUP	5	5	4	5	5	24
	INTERPRETATION & EXECUTION	5	5	4	5	5	24
	ORIGINALITY	5	5	4	5	5	24
	QUALITY	5	5	4	5	5	24

GRAND TOTAL __322__

COMMENTS:

This group displayed exceptional talent and originality. Each player showed great restraint and respect for the other. All three can stand alone on talent. Group has great future.

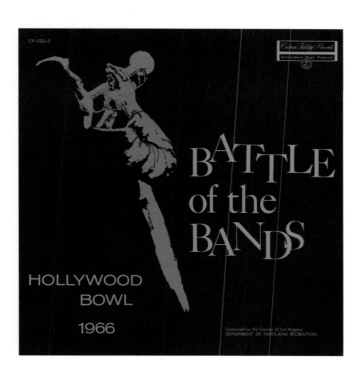

CF-1553-2
Custom Fidelity Records

BATTLE of the BANDS

HOLLYWOOD BOWL 1966

Sponsored by the County of Los Angeles
DEPARTMENT OF PARKS AND RECREATION

1.
1. "STRIKE UP THE BAND" Bellflower Chorus/Production Band
2. "GEE, OFFICER KRUPKE" Production Band
3. "BLAST OFF"
4. "BLUES FOR SITA" The Ambassadors (1st Place: School Dance Band Division)
5. "COMIN' HOME BABY" The Gentlemen, Combo
6. "TRY TO REMEMBER" Both of Us, Vocal Group
7. "A SHOT IN THE DARK" The Esquires, School Dance Band
8. "I CAN'T GIVE YOU ANYTHING BUT LOVE" Trombones Inc., Combo

2.
1. "ALL MY TOMORROWS" Fat Hodges, Vocal Soloist
2. "DEAR HEART" Tempos, School Dance Band
3. "GIRL FROM IPANEMA"
4. "ICED TEA" The Richard Carpenter Trio (1st Place: Combo Division)
5. "76 TROMBONES" Mayfair Chorus/Production Band
6. "DOLLY MEDLEY" Pioneer Chorus/Production Band

3.
1. "CORONET MAN"
2. "NO MORE SONGS FOR ME" Karen Philipp (1st Place: Vocal Soloist Division)
3. "BAG'S NEW GROOVE"
4. "THE KID FROM RED BANK" Pico Rivera Stage Band (1st Place: Dance Band Division)
5. "COME AND GO WITH ME"
6. "THIS LAND" The Happy Rock Society (1st Place: Vocal Group Division)
7. "EXODUS" Playboys, Dance Band
8. "HE TOUCHED ME" Pam Weber, Vocal Soloist

4.
1. "ROMP STOMPER" Sentimentalities, Dance Band
2. "YOU WERE ON MY MIND" The Modellas, Vocal Group
3. "GOTHAM CITY MUNICIPAL SWING BAND"
   "GIRL TALK"
   "WALTZ FOR JEANNIE"
   "BLUES FOR JEAN"
   "BATMAN" Production Band/Santa Fe Chorus

ROBERT MACDONALD / Production Band Director
NEAL HEFTI / Composer
JOHN RODBY / Accompanist

BATTLE of the BANDS

Coordinated By
The Los Angeles County
Department Of Parks And Recreation

Judges:
CALVIN JACKSON
LEONARD FEATHER
JERRY GOLDSMITH
GERALD WILSON
BILL HOLMAN

GORDON JENKINS, JR. / Hollywood Bowl Stage Manager

JERRY DEXTER / Master of Ceremonies   . . . and BONNIE JENKINS / Production Director

CUSTOM FIDELITY RECORDS are a non-commercially distributed product of the Custom Fidelity Company, 222 East Glenarm Street, Pasadena, California.
For longest record life, handle this recording by its center and outer edges only, and store it vertically in this protective cover away from extreme heat. Use RIAA curve.

The Custom Fidelity Company

and into the garage studio. A few minutes later, in walked the copartner, who turned out to be Joe Osborn—in my opinion, studio bassist nonpareil. As I always read album credits, I was familiar with the name. The meeting was as late as it was because his last recording session had wrapped at midnight. Osborn has been described as "taciturn," and quiet he was. And no doubt tired. But he wanted to hear this girl singer. Karen was sixteen, I was nineteen, and we were taken aback by all of this.

But I accompanied Karen as she sang "Ebb Tide," I believe—and nervously. The great voice was just beginning to show itself. It was a bit twangy, but I could hear where it was going, and Joe and Don were impressed. With our parents' signatures, Karen was signed to Magic Lamp Records, spring of '66, a bit before the Hollywood Bowl event.

Did it feel like things were falling into place at this point?

Yeah. Right around this time, a Poli Sci major named John Bettis became a member of the [Long Beach State] University choir. Frank Pooler, the director, introduced us, and I discovered John could write pretty decent lyrics. I *knew* my melodies had promise, but not my lyrics. So we started writing together.

But, getting back to the Bowl, at the end of the evening, June 25, as I was walking to the car holding some of our trophies, this well-dressed, distinguished-looking fellow approached me. He was impressed with our group and, in so many words, asked me if we'd be interested in recording. And, full of myself, I replied, thinking of Magic Lamp, "Oh, we already have a recording contract," or words to that effect. Handing me his card, he said, "If things change…" The card read: "Neely Plumb, head of A&R, West Coast, RCA Victor."

I knew this name, as I owned a few records he had produced. So I said, trying to get my foot out of my mouth, "Oh, well, actually it's Karen. Karen's the one who's signed. I'm available." Of course, he hadn't heard Karen sing, as our Bowl appearance consisted of two instrumentals. And, as it turned out, that's what he was interested in—the trio, but featuring the tuba: "rock tuba" to be precise. Maybe it could become something. So, later that year, '66, Wes, Karen, and I signed with RCA Victor.

Page 26: Parental
consent form and
Karen's Magic Lamp
recording contract,
1966

Right: RCA Victor
acetate reference
discs for the Richard
Carpenter Trio, 1966

RCA VICTOR RECORD DIVISION
RADIO CORPORATION OF AMERICA

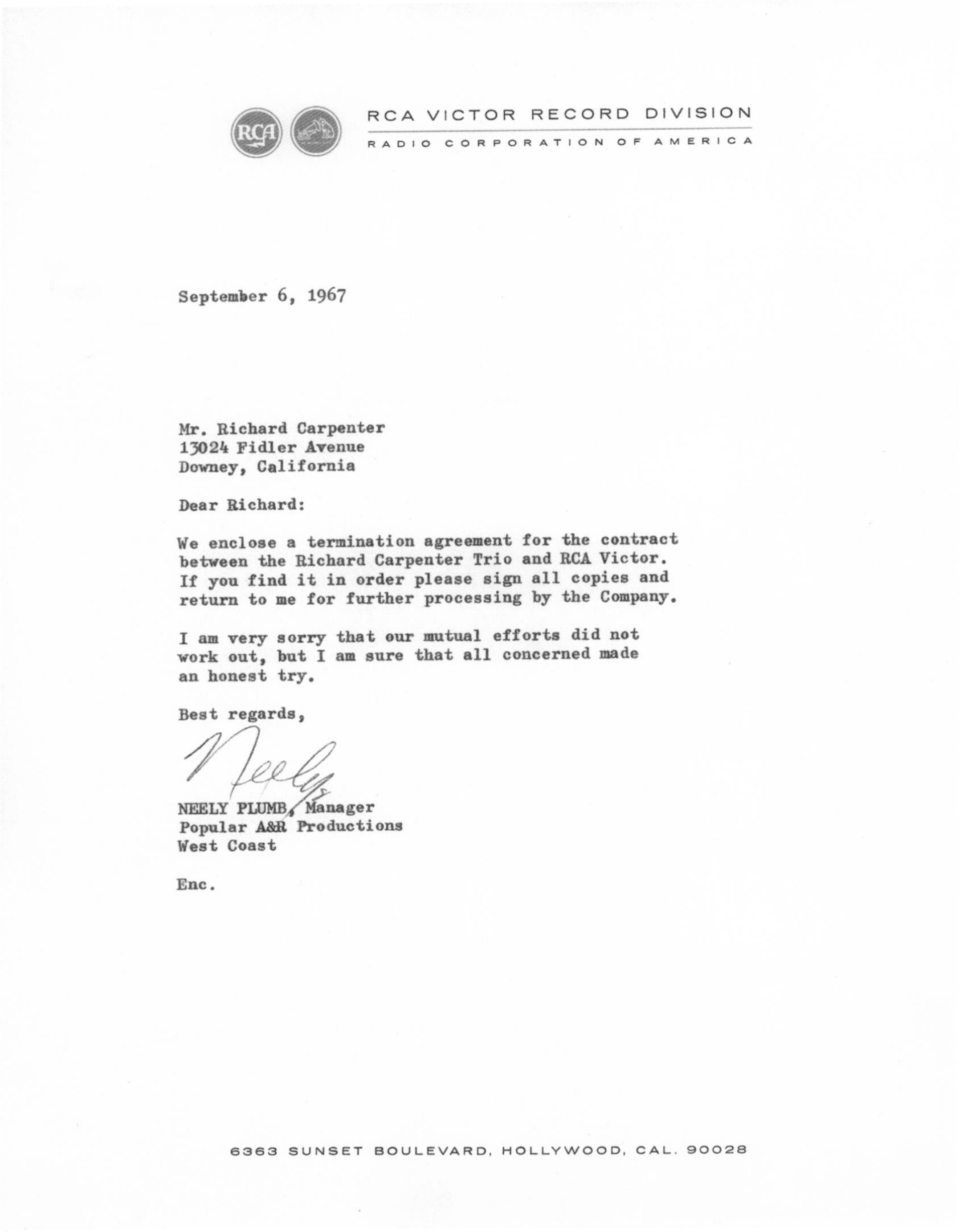

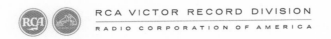

September 6, 1967

Mr. Richard Carpenter
13024 Fidler Avenue
Downey, California

Dear Richard:

We enclose a termination agreement for the contract between the Richard Carpenter Trio and RCA Victor. If you find it in order please sign all copies and return to me for further processing by the Company.

I am very sorry that our mutual efforts did not work out, but I am sure that all concerned made an honest try.

Best regards,

Neely

NEELY PLUMB, Manager
Popular A&R Productions
West Coast

Enc.

6363 SUNSET BOULEVARD, HOLLYWOOD, CAL. 90028

Left: RCA Victor termination letter to the Richard Carpenter Trio, 1967

Page 29: A- and B-sides of Karen's first solo single, "Looking for Love"

A young chap named Rick Jarrard was assigned as our A&R man. New to the job, good guy. The other new group Rick would produce was Jefferson Airplane. Jefferson Airplane and the R. C. Trio. Wow! What a combination. Now, I was a born A&R man, which is a rare gift, and in my case a talent that would show itself in the next few years. I knew that rock tuba wasn't going anywhere, and so did Rick. But I dutifully put together four different charts: The Beatles' "Every Little Thing," Bert Kaempfert's "Strangers in the Night," and my "I Never Had a Love Before," and, of course, the tuba-driven "Iced Tea." I asked for a harpsichord for "Every Little Thing," which was ready and waiting, and we recorded these four and several others. This was at the RCA Studios on Ivar and Sunset, and all very exciting, but it went nowhere.

Some time goes by, and we are asked to meet with Neely Plumb. I knew we were getting the ax.

But he was a nice man and was very polite about it all. He gave Karen a little stuffed Nipper—the Victor terrier and long-time corporate mascot. This was early '67.

Several months earlier, you cut "Looking for Love" and "I'll Be Yours," which was released as a Karen Carpenter single for Magic Lamp.

Well, "released" for lack of a better term. Magic Lamp was one of countless new ventures that was well intentioned but lacking a really strong record, and in particular, a promo team and nationwide distribution. Unlike most start-ups, Magic Lamp had a classy, colorful label, and the records were pressed using quality vinyl. But it folded. However, this wasn't the last we'd see of Joe Osborn.

Approaching the summer of '67, you and Karen were recording, you and Bettis were playing at Coke Corner at Disneyland as a banjo/piano act, and you all were in a vocal group called Summerchimes. Great name.

Better than the group. While we were playing at Disneyland, Bettis sometimes stayed with me at my parents' home. His parents' home was in San Pedro, which was a ways out. He slept a lot in the back of his '57 Ford station wagon, which was a little short on facilities. He was a real bohemian.

From our place in Downey, it took maybe twelve minutes to get to Disneyland. This was before traffic got so crazy. So, before nodding off, John and I would discuss possible group names. So, Summerchimes. It still has a nice ring to it.

Literally.

Literally. And then it got changed to Spectrum, which is still…that's a damn good name.

Who was in Spectrum?

Summerchimes. Oh, it ended up being Karen, another girl named named Leslie Johnston, Gary Sims, Danny Woodhams, John, and me. All from choir.

You played the Whisky a Go Go one night.

Yes, we did. We opened for a group named Evergreen Blueshoes.

How'd it go?

All right. We weren't booed off the stage.

Spectrum played on the same bill as Steppenwolf?

It was at a big warehouse-cum-rock-venue like the Fillmore. A huge pile in Torrance called the Blue Law. Ed Sulzer found these gigs for us, all in his spare time. He really believed.

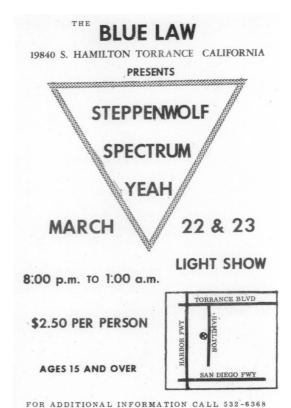

THE **BLUE LAW**
19840 S. HAMILTON TORRANCE CALIFORNIA
PRESENTS

STEPPENWOLF

SPECTRUM

YEAH

MARCH 22 & 23

LIGHT SHOW

8:00 p.m. TO 1:00 a.m.

$2.50 PER PERSON

AGES 15 AND OVER

TORRANCE BLVD
HAMILTON
HARBOR FWY
SAN DIEGO FWY

FOR ADDITIONAL INFORMATION CALL 532-6368

Did you eventually get into a proper studio with Spectrum?

Early '68. We all saved up and paid for a demo at Sunset Sound in Hollywood. Awful. I mean the demo. We so wanted this group to work, because they were all good friends and really tried. But I finally thought, "You know, they're my arrangements, vocals and all. And Karen and I can sing all the parts ourselves." So that was that.

Magic Lamp folded in late '67. But the studio was usable. And with Spectrum disbanded in mid-'68, Joe urged you and Karen to come back and do more recording.

Well, something like that, but that's where the whole Carpenters thing came together—the stacked, overdubbed vocals. It was new for Joe as an engineer, and new to Karen and me. To actually hear for real what I was hearing in my head was something I'll never forget.

Was this when you recorded the four songs for the demo tape?

Yes, the stuff Herb [Alpert] ultimately heard. It's a helluva demo. The songs sound like masters. "Invocation" is on there. And "All I Can Do," "Don't Be Afraid," "Your Wonderful Parade."

So you and Karen are now a duo, and you decide on a name: "Carpenters," not "The Carpenters"— and pretty much everyone will get it wrong till the end of time.

Of course. It was a silly idea. It should have just been "Carpenters" for the album and singles, not to be announced for when you appeared on Johnny Carson, you know.

What was the reasoning?

Because, I thought it sounded hipper without the "The." The best thing that came out of it was that logo, where I believe if we were called "The Carpenters," it may not have happened.

We know you had a lot of other irons in the fire at this time.

Some very promising things that almost happened, *almost* happened. But didn't. We knew damned well we had it. But even with our youthful exuberance, we were bummed out. Yet Eddie kept going. And I'll be damned, if not very long afterward, he came through: "Herb Alpert likes you and you're going to sign to A&M Records."

How'd Eddie pull that off?

I never got the exact story. But Ed was not about to give up. He had a day job at Autonetics, a division of North American Aviation. Ed gave the tape to a coworker, Jack Kennedy, who then took it to another coworker. The tape eventually made it to a Jack Daugherty, an executive with the firm. At one time Jack had played trumpet with some name big bands, and although he'd transitioned to the business world, Daugherty kept his music-industry contacts. From Jack, the demo made it to Ron Gorow, who was quite impressed and gave it to a friend, John Pisano, who happened to be the guitarist for Herb Alpert's Tijuana Brass. From John, the demo went to Herb.

So, a lot of time goes by, and Sulzer is telling us, in so many words, "This one's going to give it to that one, who's going to give it to another one, and *that* one's going to get it to Herb Alpert."

And damned if it didn't happen.

Page 30, left: John Bettis and Richard at Disneyland's Coke Corner, 1967

Page 30, right: Richard and Karen's pre-Carpenters band Spectrum shared the bill with Steppenwolf, 1968

Right (left to right): A&M Records cofounder Jerry Moss, staff producer Jack Daugherty, and personal manager Ed Sulzer at Richard and Karen's signing to the label, 1969

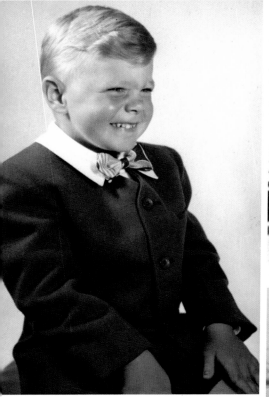

55 HALL ST.

New Haven, CT (clockwise from upper left): Richard, Karen, and cousin Joanie, 1953; Karen and Richard, 1954; Richard going through his father's collection, late 1950s; 55 Hall Street goes up for sale as the Carpenter family heads west; Richard, 1950

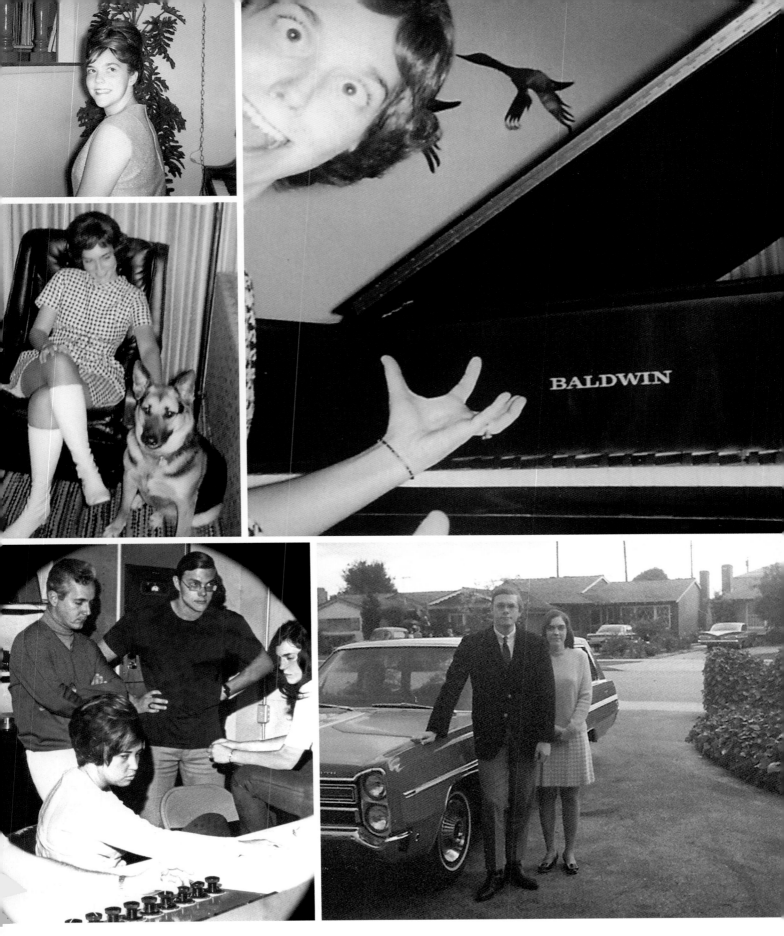

Downey, CA (clockwise from upper left): Karen, 1967; Karen mugging for the camera, 1968; Richard with the Plymouth Fury that got them to gigs, 1968; Richard and Karen with manager Ed Sulzer and Spectrum bandmate Leslie Johnston at Sunset Sound, Los Angeles, 1968—and not happy; Karen and Lady, 1968

Chapter 2

Let's Hope We Have Some Hits

1969–1970

Album
Offering

—

US release date
10/9/69

—

*Offering failed to make
any of the Billboard charts*

Page 34: Lake
Tahoe, 1970

Left: With
the *Offering*
cover and promo
items for deejays—
a hammer for
the jocks and
a makeup kit for
their wives

Album
Offering /
Ticket to Ride

**"This was an album of its time.
And the time was 1967."**

April 29, 1969. Exactly one week after signing with A&M, Richard and Karen were in the label's Studio B to begin recording the first Carpenters album, *Offering*.

"It's not like we were in a hurry to meet a deadline," Richard recalls. "We weren't famous. It's not like, 'The world is waiting for this album.'"

The pressure to get going was self-imposed. Richard and Karen were excited and ready to work. Richard had mapped out much of *Offering* in his head for more than a year.

"This was an album of its time," he says. "And the time was 1967." Of *Offering*'s thirteen songs, the album's ten originals were composed between 1967 and 1968. And the remaining three tunes, gleaned from other songwriters, were written in the mid-1960s: John Lennon and Paul McCartney's "Ticket to Ride," Chet Powers's brotherhood anthem "Get Together," and Neil Young's angry, autobiographical "Nowadays Clancy Can't Even Sing."

The album's title should be taken at face value, as per Richard. "It *is* an offering."

Plain as day. But by no means simple.

The Carpenters Sound

Perhaps most importantly, *Offering* served as the springboard for what would quickly be dubbed "the Carpenters sound." Its many elements would be refined over time. But development of the harmonic-vocal aspect of the Carpenters' brand was well underway in this debut.

Richard cites the sound's key influences. These include Les Paul and Mary Ford, the married singer-guitarists who pioneered multitrack recordings in the 1950s. Richard also credits Jud Conlon, whose vocal arrangements stylized the soundtracks of the Disney classics *Alice in Wonderland* (1951) and *Peter Pan* (1953). "He was the founder of the close harmony or tight harmony, getting away from more of a barbershop sound," Richard says.

The vocal facet of the Carpenters sound had one more key ingredient: what Richard calls "familial harmony," referring to the virtually insepara-ble vocal blend created when members of the same family sing together.

On many of *Offering*'s tracks, it sounds like a wall of singing Carpenters. But it's only Richard and Karen.

"Karen and I sang the parts two at a time, and then listened. And once we thought they were the way they should be, then we doubled.

"And then we tripled them, so we had to do a lot of bouncing," he continues, referring to the process where vocals would be recorded onto a track, then combined and transferred or "bounced" to another track to free up room on the tape for additional vocals. The process would be repeated until the two voices could be made to sound as large as a choir or chorus.

On the Album

Offering opens with the a cappella choral piece "Invocation." The tune, composed by Richard and cowriter John Bettis, was a vehicle for the Carpenters to have some fun in the studio with vocal overdubbing. The version on *Offering* is merely a remix of the original recording done a year earlier in mentor Joe Osborn's garage studio.

Offering's other notable tracks include "Your Wonderful Parade," which is a deceptively cheery piece of up-tempo pop. It serves as a medium for Richard to deliver partner Bettis's searing castigation of the financially and politically powerful "establishment":

Stand in line try to climb
Meet your wife at cocktail time
You're sure to lose so try and choose the better way to fall

"It's a pretty damn good song, actually," observes Richard, who then returns to being his own worst critic. "In retrospect, I counted it off too fast. Way too fast. You can hardly understand the lyrics."

The Carpenters never intended to cover Powers's "Get Together." Richard first heard The Youngbloods' record of the song in late summer 1967. "When the tune was released the first time, it didn't happen. Their

Right: *Offering* master-tape box

Page 39: Trade ad for "Ticket to Ride," 1970

**THE CARPENTERS
HAVE MADE A THING
OF BEAUTY**

And the people you sell records to like beautiful things.

They like "**Ticket To Ride**" by **the Carpenters** (A & M 1142).

So they're buying it. And more radio stations are playing it.

And that's good. Because it's a beautiful record.

From their first album, "**Offering**"

(SP 4205). Which is also beautiful. Very.

Music by Richard and Karen Carpenter.

Produced by Jack Daugherty.

Single
"Ticket to Ride"

—

US release date
11/5/69

—

Billboard Hot 100

Chart entry date (position)
2/14/70 (No. 92)

Peak date, position (weeks at peak)
5/9/70, No. 54

Total weeks on chart
12*

Year-end chart rank
n/a

*The single fell off the charts
for two weeks, 4/4/70 and 4/11/70*

—

**Billboard Top 40
Easy Listening**

Chart entry date (position)
12/27/69 (No. 35)

Peak date, position (weeks at peak)
1/31/70, No. 19 (1)

Total weeks on chart
8
Year-end chart rank
n/a

version stalled on the *Billboard* Hot 100 at No. 62. This puzzled me, as I thought it would become a major hit."

So the Carpenters gave it a shot. "Unfortunately, by the time we got around to recording it, The Youngbloods' record had been re-released." September 6, 1969, just a month after the Carpenters completed *Offering*, The Youngbloods' "Get Together" reached its Hot 100 peak of No. 5.

With its weird vocal effects, the Carpenters' version is pretty out there. "Let's not forget that this was the late '60s. I had this idiotic idea of singing the lead through a keyboard amplifier with the tremolo activated," Richard remembers, shaking his head. "The result was an eerie, haunting, ultimately bizarre sound that made perfect sense at the time."

During the recording of "Get Together," Richard says A&M cofounder Herb Alpert "came in to hear how things were coming along." He adds that Alpert, who rarely offered input, *offered input*. "So, after the first chorus leading into the second verse, he suggested trombones to give it a bit more punch. That was Herb's idea."

"All of My Life" is a lilting yet mournful ballad that Richard calls "a pretty song." It's one of the few original Carpenters vocal tracks that Richard wrote without a collaborator. "It sounds like one of my lyrics—corny," he comments, laughing.

It took a while for "All of My Life" to get from start to finish. It was first recorded in 1967 by Spectrum. "Karen, Gary, Bettis, Leslie, Danny, and I did it at our home in Downey, the Fidler house," Richard says. We did the track in the living room, then took the recorder into the bathroom and sang in the shower stall to try to give it a little bit more reverb."

Once Richard and Karen had access to a full studio in Osborn's garage, they rerecorded the song. And then they recorded it again at A&M, allowing Richard to flesh out the arrangement with strings and woodwinds. That's the version on the album.

Richard came up with the gloomy ballad "Eve" after seeing a 1968 episode of the short-lived British sci-fi anthology series *Journey to the Unknown*. The story follows a young man (portrayed by Dennis Waterman) who falls for a mannequin (Carol Lynley) that periodically comes to life. Things do not end well for them.

"And so I went from the Zenith [TV] to the Baldwin [piano] and…" Richard sings the song's first word: "*Eve …*"

"That's where my lyrics ran out," he says, laughing. "Bettis completed them."

Karen wasn't happy with her lead vocal on the recording, Richard says. "A lot of her leads from '69 were just too husky for her. And there was one note that's a little out of tune. It's one of the ones that Karen and I were going to redo, you know."

The album closes with "Benediction," which, like "Invocation," is a choral piece meant to showcase the Carpenters sound. "I wanted to bookend the album. So, I wrote, and then John put the lyric to it. And that's all. No deeper meaning."

The Single

See "Ticket to Ride" sidebar, below.

Richard's Take

Offering was an ambitious debut album by the young Karen and Richard. They didn't waste the freedom and resources given by A&M. Richard chose a wide array of material and delivered first-class arrangements and production. It was an indication of what would come.

"It saddens me greatly that, for the short time Karen was with us, we didn't make a far better album for our debut," Richard says. "It has lovely vocals and all of that, but Karen was only nineteen at the time."

Richard regrets not taking the time he was given to seek out stronger material. "Certainly other than 'Invocation,' 'Benediction,' 'Your Wonderful Parade,' and, of course, 'Ticket'—nothing else should be on that album.

"And we should have used a studio drummer, letting Karen focus on singing, handing off duties to a veteran with chops, such as Hal Blaine."

But all in all, "For a debut album by a young act, *Offering* is not too shabby," Richard says.

Single

Ticket to Ride

"Perfect for Karen, me, and the whole Carpenters sound."

Richard Carpenter had always been a Beatles fan. But the Fab Four's 1965 chart topper "Ticket to Ride" was never one of his favorites. Then, one day in early 1969, the tune popped up on the radio, and it was as though Richard were hearing it for the first time.

"It never hit me until then that it could be turned into a ballad, perfect for Karen and the whole Carpenters sound."

To transform the original, Richard didn't simply slow the tempo down and place it in Karen's key. Taking a bit of artistic license, he reshaped some of the melody, changed a few chords, and created a four-part, twelve-voice tag:

Think I'm gonna be sad
Think I'm gonna be sad

Those voices, combined with a solo horn obbligato, made for a splendidly somber outro.

Richard chose "Ticket to Ride" as *Offering*'s first single. The album was released October 9, 1969, and was serviced to radio stations a few days earlier. A handful of Los Angeles–area program directors and disc jockeys quickly began playing a variety of *Offering* tracks, including "Invocation," "Your Wonderful Parade," "All of My Life," and, especially, "Ticket to Ride."

Richard says the record's high-profile fans included Bill Gavin, whose tip sheet, the *Gavin Report*, was among the most influential guides for broadcasters across North America. "He loved *Offering* and was really behind us," Richard says.

The Carpenters were starting to pick up support at a national level just as the "Ticket to Ride" single arrived November 5. In the music-trade magazine *Record World* dated November 29, KCBQ in San Diego reported "Ticket" was "in rotation," meaning it was added to the station's playlist. All three music trades—*Record World*, *Cash Box*, and the music-biz granddaddy *Billboard*—reported numerous stations across the country adding the single throughout December.

Finally, in the issue dated December 27, 1969—the last week of the last month of the last year of the 1960s—the Carpenters made a promising *Billboard* chart debut, with "Ticket to Ride" entering the Top 40 Easy Listening survey at No. 35.

February 14, 1970, more than three months after its release, "Ticket" entered the *Billboard* Hot 100 at No. 92. And after three months on and off (mainly on) the survey, "Ticket to Ride" peaked at No. 54 on May 9—just a week before the release of "(They Long to Be) Close to You."

Richard says he's grateful for the Carpenters' first single paving the way for their *next* one. But he adds neither he nor Karen were pleased with that first "Ticket to Ride" release.

"We never got the mix to where any of us was happy with 'Ticket to Ride,'" he says. "I knew darn well we could do it better. And Karen was never happy with her lead. We were just maturing, especially noticeable if you listen to Karen's voice. It's very husky. She was still growing into it."

And that's why Richard and Karen would, eventually, "ride" again.

The Response

A deep dig comes up with only a handful of *Offering* reviews.

The album was chosen as a *Billboard* "pick"—one of the trade magazine's most promising releases of the week. *Billboard*'s three-sentence critique praised Richard's songs and arrangements, especially the "overdubbing of his and Karen's voices," and made specific mention of only one track: "Get Together"! "Carpenters," the review concluded, "should have a big hit on their hands."

In agreement: Johnny Magnus, a popular personality at Los Angeles, 50,000-watt powerhouse KMPC. "Every now and again, Magnus would drop in at what he called 'Herbie Alpert's A&M Records' and check and see what was new," Richard says. "He got *Offering* and he was crazy about it. He let us know, and he let the label know."

Magnus would soon let his listeners know. "In those days, a handful of DJs still had the power to play what they wanted," Richard notes. Richard recalls that he, Karen, and their parents were paying a visit to the Carpenters' secretary, Evelyn Wallace, the night Magnus planned to debut *Offering*. The duo excused themselves, went out to Richard's '69 Imperial, turned on the radio, and there was Magnus.

"He talked about how special we were. And to prove this point that we were different—the vocals, and all that—he played, of all things, 'Invocation,'" Richard recalls, with a chuckle.

The Carpenters were hearing their record on the radio for the very first time. "We no doubt looked at ourselves and just kept listening." Magnus kept playing tracks from *Offering*, also including "All of My Life" and, most importantly, "Ticket to Ride." KMPC played a major role in the song becoming the Carpenters' first chart hit.

About seven months after Magnus gave Karen and Richard their maiden voyage on the airwaves, the duo personally met the DJ at the entrance of KMPC. They came bearing the demo for the first single for their next album. It was "(They Long to Be) Close to You."

"He went right on it," Richard says. "I remember he just bought a Dodge Challenger." Within weeks, the Carpenters had their breakthrough hit and "Close to You" would be blaring from car speakers all over the country.

Offering never appeared on any of the major trades' album-sales charts.

Richard says the album's budget was "pretty big" and that it was a "net loss" for A&M in 1969—not such a big deal in a year when the label had numerous "net loss" releases.

Fast-forward thirteen months after *Offering*'s release, following the successes of "(They Long to Be) Close to You" and "We've Only Just Begun," and with the Carpenters *Close to You* album racing up the US charts, A&M gives *Offering* a second chance. It repackaged and retitled the album *Ticket to Ride* and released it on November 10, 1970.

The rechristened album entered the *Billboard* Top LPs chart on March 6, 1971, and stayed there for sixteen weeks, peaking at No. 150. The *Ticket* album also charted in Australia (peaking at No. 19 in 1971), the United Kingdom (No. 20 in 1972), and Zimbabwe (No. 18 in 1976).

"Ticket to Ride" reaches its Hot 100 peak, 1970

Billboard HOT 100

FOR WEEK ENDING MAY 9, 1970

★ STAR PERFORMER—Sides registering greatest proportionate sales progress this week. Ⓡ Record Industry Association of America seal of certification as million selling single.

THIS WEEK	Wks. Ago	2 Wks. Ago	3 Wks. Ago	TITLE, Artist (Producer), Label & Number	Weeks On Chart
1	4	5	8	AMERICAN WOMAN/ NO SUGAR TONIGHT — Guess Who (Jack Richardson), RCA 74-0325	8
2	1	1	2	ABC — Jackson 5 (Corporation), Motown 1163	9
3	2	2	1	LET IT BE — Beatles (George Martin), Apple 2764	8
4	9	19	32	VEHICLE — Ides of March (Lee Prod.), Warner Bros. 7378	7
5	3	8	13	SPIRIT IN THE SKY — Norman Greenbaum (Erik Jacobsen), Reprise 0885	11
6	6	8	8	LOVE OR LET ME BE LONELY — Friends of Distinction (Ray Cork, Jr.), RCA 74-0319	10
7	16	21	37	EVERYTHING IS BEAUTIFUL — Ray Stevens (Ray Stevens), Barnaby 2011	6
8	5	4	4	INSTANT KARMA (We All Shine On) — John Ono Lennon (Phil Spector), Apple 1818	11
9	10	10	14	TURN BACK THE HANDS OF TIME — Tyrone Davis (Willie Henderson), Dakar 616	8
10	13	14	18	REFLECTIONS OF MY LIFE — Marmalade (Marmalade), London 20058	9
11	15	16	17	WOODSTOCK — Crosby, Stills, Nash & Young (Crosby, Stills, Nash & Young), Atlantic 2723	7
12	11	12	15	SOMETHING'S BURNING — Kenny Rogers and the First Edition (Jimmy Bowen-Kenny Rogers), Reprise 0888	13
13	30	48	—	UP AROUND THE BEND/ RUN THROUGH THE JUNGLE — Creedence Clearwater Revival (John Fogerty), Fantasy 641	3
14	19	27	38	CECELIA — Simon & Garfunkel (Paul Simon, Arthur Garfunkel & Roy Halee), Columbia 4-45133	7
15	17	18	28	FOR THE LOVE OF HIM — Bobbi Martin (Henry Jerome), United Artists 50602	9
16	20	33	40	LOVE ON A TWO WAY STREET — Moments (Sylvia), Stang 5102	8
17	12	11	10	UP THE LADDER TO THE ROOF — Supremes (Frank Wilson), Motown 1162	10
18	8	7	7	COME AND GET IT — Badfinger (Paul McCartney), Apple 1815	14
19	24	32	33	GET READY — Rare Earth (Rare Earth), Rare Earth 5012	9
20	28	31	46	WHAT IS TRUTH — Johnny Cash (Bob Johnston), Columbia 4-45134	5
21	14	9	6	BRIDGE OVER TROUBLED WATER — Simon & Garfunkel (Simon, Garfunkel & Halee), Columbia 4-45079	14
22	7	6	5	LOVE GROWS (Where My Rosemary Goes) — Edison Lighthouse (Tony Macaulay), Bell 858	12
23	32	38	48	WHICH WAY YOU GOIN' BILLY? — Poppy Family (T. Jacks), London 129	8
24	18	13	11	EASY COME, EASY GO — Bobby Sherman (Jackie Mills), Metromedia 177	9
25	35	40	41	MAKE ME SMILE — Chicago (James William Guercio), Columbia 4-45127	5
26	41	46	72	THE LETTER — Joe Cocker (Denny Cordell-Leon Russell), A&M 1174	4
27	29	34	35	LITTLE GREEN BAG — George Baker Selection (Negram), Colossus 112	11
28	23	23	24	TENNESSEE BIRDWALK — Jack Blanchard & Misty Morgan (Little Richie Johnson), Wayside 010	11
29	26	25	34	EVERYBODY'S OUT OF TOWN — B. J. Thomas (Burt Bacharach-Hal David), Scepter 12277	7
30	37	49	—	REACH OUT AND TOUCH (Somebody's Hand) — Diana Ross (N. Ashford & V. Simpson), Motown 1165	4
31	49	—	—	DAUGHTER OF DARKNESS — Tom Jones (Peter Sullivan), Parrot 40048	3
32	34	35	44	AIRPORT THEME — Vincent Bell (Tom Morgan), Decca 32627	7
33	31	20	20	LONG LONESOME HIGHWAY — Michael Parks (James Hendricks), MGM 14104	11
34	38	56	86	PUPPET MAN — 5th Dimension (Bones Howe), Bell 880	4
35	36	54	74	VIVA TIRADO, Part 1 — El Chicano (Billy Watson & Eddie Davis), Kapp 2085	5
36	40	41	61	COME SATURDAY MORNING — Sandpipers (Allen Stanton), A&M 1185	13
37	33	24	25	SHILO — Neil Diamond (Jeff Barry-Ellie Greenwich), Bang 575	14
38	43	52	65	HEY LAWDY MAMA — Steppenwolf (Gabriel Mekler), Dunhill 4234	5
39	48	58	88	LET ME GO TO HIM — Dionne Warwick (Burt Bacharach-Hal David), Scepter 12276	4
40	42	43	52	OH HAPPY DAY — Glen Campbell (Al De Lory), Capitol 2787	5
41	21	17	12	THE BELLS — Originals (Marvin Gaye), Soul 35069	14
42	46	53	77	HITCHIN' A RIDE — Vanity Fare (Roger Easterby & Des Champ), Page One 21029	8
43	44	44	47	THE GIRLS' SONG — Fifth Dimension (Bones Howe), Soul City 781	7
44	45	47	64	MISS AMERICA — Mark Lindsay (Jerry Fuller), Columbia 4-45125	5
45	25	28	30	YOU NEED LOVE LIKE I DO (Don't You) — Gladys Knight & the Pips (Norman Whitfield), Soul 50071	8
46	22	22	23	YOU'RE THE ONE — Little Sister (Sly Stone), Stone Flower 9000	11
47	63	78	90	THE SEEKER — The Who (Kit Lambert), Decca 32670	4
48	53	59	80	DON'T STOP NOW/ SINCE I DON'T HAVE YOU — Eddie Holman (Peter De Angelis), ABC 11261	6
49	39	39	43	COME RUNNING — Van Morrison (Morrison-Merenstein), Warner Bros. 7383	6
50	51	60	67	CHICKEN STRUT — Meters (Marshall E. Sehorn-Allen Toussaint), Josie 1018	6
51	60	79	93	UNITED WE STAND — Brotherhood of Man (Tony Hiller), Deram 85059	4
52	52	68	79	MY WIFE THE DANCER — Eddie & Dutch (Eddie Mascari), Ivanhoe 502	6
53	56	63	63	LOVE LAND — Charles Wright & the Watts 103rd Street Rhythm Band (Charles Wright), Warner Bros.-Seven Arts 7365	5
54	55	76	81	TICKET TO RIDE — Carpenters (Jack Daugherty), A&M 1142	11
55	59	74	—	HUM A SONG (From Your Heart) — Lulu with the Dixie Flyers (Jerry Wexler-Tom Dowd-Arif Mardin), Atco 6749	3
56	50	55	75	YOU MAKE ME REAL/ ROADHOUSE BLUES — Doors (Paul A. Rothchild), Elektra 45685	5
57	68	—	—	SOOLAIMON (African Trilogy II) — Neil Diamond (Tom Catalano), UNI 55224	2
58	62	87	91	MY BABY LOVES LOVIN' — White Plains (Roger Greenaway/Roger Cook), Deram 85058	4
59	71	94	96	CALIFORNIA SOUL/THE ONION SONG — Marvin Gaye & Tammi Terrell (Ashford-Simpson), Tamla 54192	3
60	77	—	—	BROTHER RAPP (Part I) — James Brown (J. Brown), King 6310	2
61	54	64	73	SO EXCITED — B. B. King (Bill Szymczyk), BluesWay 61035	4
62	67	89	—	LAY DOWN (Candles in the Rain) — Melanie with the Edwin Hawkins Singers (Peter Schekeryk), Buddah 167	3
63	47	45	45	CALIFORNIA GIRL — Eddie Floyd (Booker T. Jones), Stax 0060	12
64	69	77	98	CINNAMON GIRL — Gentrys (Knox Phillips), Sun 1114	4
65	88	—	—	MISSISSIPPI QUEEN — Mountain (Felix Pappalardi), Windfall 532	2
66	74	93	—	BAND OF GOLD — Freda Payne (Holland-Dozier), Invictus 9075	3
67	76	91	92	SUGAR SUGAR — Wilson Pickett (Jerry Wexler-Tom Dowd), Atlantic 2722	6
68	66	66	66	O-O-H CHILD/ DEAR PRUDENCE — 5 Stairsteps (Stan Vincent), Buddah 165	8
69	64	67	70	DEEPER (In Love With You) — O'Jays (Gamble & Huff), Neptune 22	6
70	61	61	68	CRYIN' IN THE STREETS (Part 1) — George Perkins & the Silver Stars (Ebb-Tide-Jimmy Angel-Ron Shaab), Silver Fox 18	6
71	72	72	74	HE MADE A WOMAN OUT OF ME — Bobbie Gentry (Rick Hall), Capitol 2798	5
72	73	83	95	OPEN UP MY HEART/NADINE — Dells (Bobby Miller), Cadet 5667	4
73	80	—	—	GROVER HENSON FEELS FORGOTTEN — Bill Cosby (Christian Wilde), UNI 55223	2
74	75	85	89	FARTHER ON DOWN THE ROAD — Joe Simon (J.R. Ent. Inc.), Sound Stage 7 2656	4
75	78	81	82	CAN YOU FEEL IT — Bobby Goldsboro (Bob Montgomery & Bobby Goldsboro), United Artists 50650	4
76	81	99	—	IT'S ALL IN THE GAME — Four Tops (Frank Wilson), Motown 1164	3
77	79	80	—	WELFARE CADILLAC — Guy Drake (Don Hosea for Trip Universal), Royal American 1	12
78	94	—	—	QUESTION — Moody Blues (Tony Clarke), Threshold 67004	3
79	—	—	—	BABY HOLD ON — Grass Roots (Steve Barri), Dunhill 4237	1
80	86	—	—	YOU GOT ME DANGLING ON A STRING — Chairmen of the Board (Holland/Dozier/Holland), Invictus 9078	3
81	84	84	97	MY WAY — Brook Benton (Arif Mardin), Cotillion 44072	4
82	83	90	—	FIRE & RAIN — R.B. Greaves (Ahmet Ertegun), Atco 6745	3
83	85	88	99	I CAN'T LEAVE YOUR LOVE ALONE — Clarence Carter (Rick Hall), Atlantic 2726	4
84	91	—	—	LUCIFER — Bob Seger System (Hideout Prod.), Capitol 2748	3
85	—	—	—	RIDE CAPTAIN RIDE — Blues Image (Richard Podolor), Atco 6746	1
86	—	—	—	GO BACK — Crabby Appleton (Don Gallucci), Elektra 43687	1
87	87	—	—	THEM CHANGES — Buddy Miles & the Freedom Express (Robin McBride), Mercury 73008	2
88	89	100	—	GET DOWN PEOPLE — Fabulous Counts (Ollie McLaughlin & the Fabulous Counts), Moira 108	3
89	93	—	—	DARKNESS DARKNESS — Youngbloods (Charles E. Daniels), RCA 74-0342	2
90	—	—	—	INTO THE MYSTIC — Johnny Rivers (Lou Adler), Imperial 66448	1
91	—	—	—	BABY I LOVE YOU — Little Milton (Calvin Carter), Checker 1227	1
92	—	—	—	I CALL MY BABY CANDY — Jaggerz (Sixuvus Prod.), Kama Sutra 509	1
93	—	—	—	TOBACCO ROAD — Jamul (Gabriel Mekler), Lizard 21001	1
94	—	—	—	PATCH OF BLUE — Frankie Valli & the Four Seasons (Bob Gaudio & Bob Crewe), Philips 40662	1
95	—	—	—	IF YOU DO BELIEVE IN LOVE — Tee Set (T.S.R. Prod.), Colossus 114	1
96	—	—	—	SWEET FEELING — Candi Staton (Rick Hall), Fame 1466	1
97	99	—	—	CHECK YOURSELF — Italian Asphalt & Pavement Co. (Jerry Ross), Colossus 110	2
98	98	—	—	LOVE LIKE A MAN — Ten Years After (Chrysalis), Deram 7329	2
99	—	—	—	SHE DIDN'T KNOW (She Kept on Talking) — Dee Dee Warwick with the Dixie Flyers (Dave Crawford), Atco 6754	1
100	—	—	—	AND MY HEART SANG (Tra La La) — Brenda & the Tabulations (Van McCoy & Gilda Woods), Top & Bottom 403	1

HOT 100—A TO Z—(Publisher-Licensee)

BUBBLING UNDER THE HOT 100

The Tale of Two Covers

"The DJ said, 'Really talented.' But then he said, 'The album cover! You ought to see the album cover!'"

Offering introduced the public to Richard and Karen in what is arguably one of their all-time worst cover photos, foreshadowing a discography with a number of worst-cover contenders.

After The Beatles' success, it seemed like every male pop musician had to grow his hair long," he says. "And the longer it got, the worse it looked. This really became obvious after we saw the *Offering* photos." For the shoot, A&M staff photographer Jim McCrary took Richard and Karen to a vacant lot at the intersection of Highland and Franklin Avenues in Hollywood.

"So, Karen looked fine," Richard recalls. "Of course, I had the dummy oily hair, which embarrasses me to this day. But a later visit to Sebring's salon, and his trademark cut, would rectify that. And there were these sunflowers. They picked them up. And this, again, was the late '60s. So, it's all understandable, the flower thing. Gives them to Karen. And, you know, 'Scowl for the camera!' Plus, I never had hay fever or any allergies, but it looks like I do. Of course, you'd never shoot up into a person's nose." But McCrary did.

Richard says it was A&M Records' cofounder Herb Alpert who unwittingly put the kibosh on any effort to avert the inevitable *Offering* cover calamity. While Richard and Karen knew they'd hate whatever was to come from that photo session, the new kids on the lot felt that they were in no position to question the boss.

Richard remembers, "They were showing us slides, and Herb was there, and he said, 'I think that one!' Of course Karen and I said, 'Certainly, we agree.'"

Right: Richard recalls, "Dummy oily hair" on the front, pimples on the back— "no touchup"

44

Music is simple magic. A rhythm, a melody, a dash of word...presto. It's medicine for the soul, food for love, the essence of divinity, a reason for being. It can soar through an infinite range of ups and downs, strike a million discordant chords, and topple the strongest resistance.

But for all its travels, however wide, however deep, it never forgets to make its simple offering.

Enclosed, neatly tucked between the confines of this cardboard jacket, is one of the most beautiful gifts two people can offer.

The vocal sound is a product of Richard and Karen Carpenter.

In addition to the vocals Karen (age 19) plays drums on all the selections and on two of the offerings she plays electric bass...

Her brother, Richard, sings, plays the keyboard instruments, composed ten of the songs, and arranged all of them.

It is with pleasure A&M Presents:
CARPENTERS — Herb Alpert

CARPENTERS TICKET TO RIDE

SIDE ONE:
1. INVOCATION 1:00
   (Carpenter/Bettis) Irving Music, Inc. BMI
2. YOUR WONDERFUL PARADE 2:57
   (Carpenter/Bettis) Irving Music, Inc. BMI
3. SOMEDAY 5:13
   (Carpenter/Bettis) Irving Music, Inc. BMI
4. GET TOGETHER 2:32
   (Chet Powers) Irving Music, Inc. BMI
5. ALL OF MY LIFE 3:00
   (Richard Carpenter) Irving Music, Inc. BMI
6. TURN AWAY 3:09
   (Carpenter/Bettis) Irving Music, Inc. BMI

SIDE TWO:
1. TICKET TO RIDE 4:10
   (Lennon/McCartney) Maclen Music, Inc. BMI
2. DON'T BE AFRAID 2:05
   (Richard Carpenter) Irving Music, Inc. BMI
3. WHAT'S THE USE 2:43
   (Carpenter/Bettis) Irving Music, Inc. BMI
4. ALL I CAN DO 1:42
   (Carpenter/Bettis) Irving Music, Inc. BMI
5. EVE 2:51
   (Carpenter/Bettis) Irving Music, Inc. BMI
6. NOWADAYS CLANCY CAN'T
   EVEN SING 4:15
   (Neil Young) Ten-East/Springalo-Cotillion Music BMI
7. BENEDICTION .... :40
   (Carpenter/Bettis) Irving Music, Inc. BMI

Produced by Jack Daugherty / Engineer: Ray Gerhardt / Special Credits: Bass: Joe Osborn and Bob Messenger / Guitar: Gary Sims / Shaker: H. Alpert / Art Director: Tom Wilkes / Photography: Jim McCrary / This album is also available on stereo tapes / A&M Records, 1416 North La Brea, Hollywood, California 90028.

"This album was previously released under the title of 'Offering.' It has been re-designed and re-titled 'Ticket To Ride'; however, the tunes remain the same." CARPENTERS/TICKET TO RIDE/SP 4205

Offering's black-and-white back-cover portrait was taken at the graphics studio at A&M, and it appears just as little effort went into that photo, as well.

"I had my pimples still," Richard grumbles. "They didn't bother...no touch up."

Richard and Karen weren't alone in their disappointment with the cover of their first album. Richard remembers "Ticket to Ride" being played on top-rated Los Angeles station KMPC, and the DJ noting, "'Really talented,' but then he said, 'The album cover! You ought to see the album cover!'"

When it was clear that "(They Long to Be) Close to You" was becoming a hit, executives at A&M decided *Offering* would be reissued and retitled *Ticket to Ride*. Richard says he and Karen weren't consulted on the rerelease. "We got the message, and it was fine by me." It was even finer when A&M informed Richard and Karen that the original cover photos would be replaced with new images.

These were taken on June 12, 1970, while the Carpenters were in the midst of a gig, playing King's Castle Casino near Lake Tahoe. A&M rented a sailboat for the shoot, apparently unaware Richard was a landlubber. "I get motion sickness, big time," he explains. "I said, 'I can't go on it.' I was not happy."

Little matter. "It's one of the best pictures of us ever taken," Richard notes. He adds that he and Karen liked it so much, they lobbied A&M to use it for the cover of *Close to You*. But that's another cover for another album in another chapter.

Left: A new, retitled, and greatly improved *Offering*, Lake Tahoe, June 1970

The Itinerary:
A Year in the Life

From "(They Long to Be) Close to You" to *Carpenters* [The Tan Album]

The 364 days starting with the release of "(They Long to Be) Close to You" and ending with the arrival of *Carpenters* [The Tan Album] were arguably the most significant in the Carpenters' career. These were when Karen and Richard went from virtual unknowns to the top of the music world. Of course, details about major events—release dates, chart positions, awards, national TV appearances—in the duo's breakthrough year are readily available.

But it's a mystery as to why so much of the Carpenters' activity during that time is undocumented—"a mystery to the few who find this kind of arcana interesting," jokes Richard. Nevertheless, he accepts that the elusive data will result in more than a mere timeline. It will tell the essence of the Carpenters' story.

Soon enough, he is down to his archives and back with itineraries that, for the first time, allow for the compilation of a detailed schedule for the Carpenters' first big year. It's when they skyrocketed to success but weren't prepared for what would follow. "It was all too much, too soon," Richard says.

Perhaps most significantly, there were too many concert bookings. Initially, the enthusiastic young Carpenters (in May 1970, Karen was twenty and Richard was twenty-three) were having too much fun to notice.

And yet it wasn't long before Richard began to see the drawback of all the touring. In mid-October 1970, as "We've Only Just Begun" was peaking on the charts, he was already worried about coming up with the next hit. Richard had been too busy touring to prepare for the next album, and the next, and the next.

The work overload took its toll on the Carpenters' recordings and, ultimately, the Carpenters themselves. That said, going through the timeline, is anything but a downer. As you're about to see, May 15, 1970–May 14, 1971, was a generally happy period for Richard, Karen, and "the guys," their road band.

More than once, Richard looks down at an itinerary, remembers an event or experience or a moment, and says, "We had the time of our lives."

Promo shot for summer replacement series, *Make Your Own Kind of Music*, Burbank, CA, 1971 Richard: "'Carpenters.' Get it?"

1970

May 16 ♫
Share benefit for special-needs children, Century Plaza Hotel, Los Angeles, California. "My Plymouth Barracuda is brand new and we're driving home," Richard recalls. "The gas gauge wasn't working correctly, and we ran out of gas on the Long Beach Freeway."

Along comes a California Highway Patrol officer.

"Now, we were all dressed like cowboys, because of the theme of the benefit," Richard says. "So the first thing he says is, 'Where's the rodeo, partner?' And then he shines his flashlight in my eyes, and I tell him, 'The car is new and we're out of gas.' And he leaves us there. Just takes off."

May 20 ⊘
"Rehearsal at A&M soundstage," Richard says, reading from an itinerary from the period.

May 26 ⊘
Richard: "Tape another *Groovy*," referring to a local pop-music TV show in Los Angeles.

May 27 ✈
Los Angeles to New York City

May 29–30 ♫
Open for Burt Bacharach, Westbury Music Fair, Westbury, New York

June 6 ✈
Baltimore, Maryland, to Los Angeles

June 9 🚗
Drive eight hours from Los Angeles to Lake Tahoe, Nevada

June 10 📊
"(They Long to Be) Close to You" enters the *Cash Box* Top 100 at No. 80 and the *Record World* 100 Top Pops at No. 93.

June 10–22 ♫
King's Castle Hotel and Casino, Lake Tahoe. "The time of our lives," Richard recalls.

June 12 ⊘
"Meet Tom and Jim for pictures," Richard notes, referring to A&M's art director Tom Wilkes and photographer Jim McCrary.

Between shows in Tahoe, Karen and landlubber Richard board a sailboat to pose for photos for the repackaging of the Carpenters' debut album *Offering* as *Ticket to Ride*. In spite of Richard's queasiness, the duo looks great in the shots.

The Carpenters are so happy with the results that they want A&M to use the photos for the *Close to You* cover. But no.

June 17 📊
"(They Long to Be) Close to You" enters the *Billboard* Hot 100 at No. 56. It moves to No. 70 on *Cash Box* and No. 76 on *Record World*.

June 24 ⊘📊
Richard: "Tape *The Dating Game*."

"(They Long to Be) Close to You" No. 37 *Billboard*, No. 56 *Cash Box*, and No. 53 *Record World*

June 25 ⊘
Richard: "Tape *The Virginia Graham Show* and then go to A&M."

"It was the A&M picnic," he explains, noting it was an annual event for the record label's artists and staff held at a private location in Malibu Canyon, California.

June 29 ✈
Los Angeles to St. Louis, Missouri

July 1 📊
"(They Long to Be) Close to You" No. 14 *Billboard*, No. 18 *Cash Box*, and No. 25 *Record World*

July 1–2 ♫✈
Open for Burt Bacharach, the Muny, St. Louis. "It was an outdoor theater," Richard remembers, "hot and humid as hell, with the lighting, but not quite prestigious or very exciting for Karen and me."

St. Louis to Los Angeles

July 7 ⊘📺
Richard: "Set up and rehearse to open for Burt Bacharach at the Greek Theatre."

Tape appearance on *Groovy*

July 8 📊
"(They Long to Be) Close to You" No. 7 *Billboard*, No. 11 *Cash Box*, No. 11 *Record World*

July 8–12 ♫
Open for Burt Bacharach, the Greek Theatre, Los Angeles

July 13–17 ⊘
Richard: "Record promo film for '(They Long to Be) Close to You,' A&M Studio B."

July 15 📊
"(They Long to Be) Close to You" No. 3 *Billboard*, No. 3 *Cash Box*, No. 6 *Record World*

July 17 ⊘🎧
Richard: "'(They Long to Be) Close to You' hits a million."

Recording session for the *Close to You* album

July 18 🎧
Richard and Ron Gorow work on orchestrations for *Close to You* album.

July 20 🎧
Record strings for *Close to You* album

July 21 ⊘
Richard: "Tape *The Don Knotts Show*."

July 22 ⊘📊
Richard: "'(They Long to Be) Close to You' No. 1 *Billboard*."

"That's 'Weeeeeeeeeeee We're No. 1'" he continues, referring to the celebratory note written by A&M Records' cofounder Herb Alpert."

"(They Long to Be) Close to You" No. 2 *Cash Box*, No. 2 *Record World*

July 24 🎧
Recording session for *Close to You*

July 25 ⊘
Richard: "Oh, clothes."

"That was the meeting about the damned clothes for the *Close to You* cover," he explains.

To prepare for the cover shoot, Richard is taken to Mr. Guy, an upscale men's clothing store in Beverly Hills. He goes home with a handsome cashmere jacket straight off the rack, which won't do for his broad-shouldered, slim-waisted physique.

That evening, the Carpenters' mom, an accomplished seamstress, has no time to make proper alterations. But she works miracles taking in Richard's coat. It looks professionally altered on the *Close to You* photo.

July 26 📷
The *Close to You* cover shoot takes place on the beach at Rancho Palos Verdes, California.

How'd it go? Following her thoughtful critique of *Close to You* in *High Fidelity* magazine, critic Morgan Ames notes, "Whoever took the picture of the Carpenters on the album cover ought to be shot."

Arriving at Westbury Music Fair, Westbury, NY, 1970

July 27–28 🎧

Mix *Close to You* album

July 29 ⊘ ✈

Richard: "This week '(They Long to Be) Close to You' was No. 1 on all three [*Billboard*, *Cash Box*, and *Record World*]." "Number one, number one, number one," he adds, smiling.

Los Angeles to Seattle, Washington

July 29–August 1 ⊘

Richard: "Seattle, the Impact Tavern."
   "Oh, that was great!" Richard recalls, laughing. "A thrown-together 'discotheque.' It was a barn [a large and cavernous space]. Management had yellow stickers reading, 'Impact Tavern.' I should have kept one. [Band member] Doug Strawn got a hold of a bunch of them and he would stick them on unknowing people. Like, some guy would get on the airplane and Doug would stick it on the back of his coat."

August 2 ✈

Seattle to Los Angeles

August 3 🎧

Mix *Close to You* album

August 5 📈 🚗

"(They Long to Be) Close to You" remains No. 1 on *Billboard*, *Cash Box*, and *Record World*.

Eight-hour drive from Los Angeles to Reno, Nevada

August 6–8 🎵 📞

Open for Paul Anka, Harrah's Reno Hotel and Casino, Reno

News from the Carpenters' management: Two more shows. Richard recalls, "One-nighters: Twin Falls, Iowa; Boise, Idaho."

August 11 ⊘

Richard: "Petula Clark comes to the dinner show."

August 12 ◎ 📈

"(They Long to Be) Close to You" is certified Gold.

"(They Long to Be) Close to You" spends one last week at the top in *Billboard*, making it summer 1970's longest-running No. 1 single on the Hot 100.

August 19 ◎

Close to You album released in US

August 20 🚗

Drive six and a half hours from Reno to Twin Falls

August 21 ◎ 🎵

"We've Only Just Begun" released in US

Fine Arts Center, College of Southern Idaho, Twin Falls

August 22 🚗 🎵

Drive two hours from Twin Falls to Boise

Capital High gymnasium, Boise

August 23 🚗

Drive thirteen hours from Boise to Los Angeles. "After three weeks in Reno, and these two one-nighters, we all wanted to get home," Richard says. "So, we all drove from Boise straight home. It was a longer drive than it appeared on the map. Doug had his girlfriend, Carol, with him in his '68 Barracuda Formula S, road manager Jerry Luby and Karen were together in his '69 Camaro SS, and I drove my new Plymouith 'cuda—playing the radio and having a good old time. We stopped in the middle of the night for some petrol, food, and a short rest, and Doug said he was hallucinating. He was so tired."
   Richard continues, "I remember hearing 'We've Only Just Begun' for the first time on the radio as we were getting into the L.A. city limits."

September 5 ◎

"(They Long to Be) Close to You" single debuts on the Official UK Top 40 chart, peaks at No. 6 for two nonconsecutive weeks, and stays on the survey for eighteen weeks.

September 6 ✈ 🚗 🎵

Los Angeles to Chicago

Drive four hours to Marshfield, Wisconsin

Central Wisconsin State Fair, Marshfield

September 7 ✈

Return to Los Angeles

September 9 📈

"We've Only Just Begun" enters *Billboard* Hot 100 at No. 84.

September 11 🚗 ⊘ 🚗

Three-hour drive to Fresno, California

Richard: "We opened for Bread in Fresno. I wasn't happy about it—nothing against Bread."
   Richard grumbled to management that he felt Bread should have been the opener, given the Carpenters were coming off the biggest single of the summer while Bread had just scored its first *Billboard* Hot No. 1 ("Make it With You").

Three-hour drive from Fresno to Los Angeles

September 12 📹 ✈

Tape appearances on Los Angeles pop-music TV shows *Groovy* and *Boss City*

Los Angeles to Twin Falls, Idaho

September 14 🎥

The Carpenters rehearse and film performance of "Help!" for TV special *Peggy Fleming in Sun Valley* at the Boiler Room nightclub, Sun Valley, Idaho

September 16 📈 ✈

Close to You debuts at No. 60 on *Billboard* Top LP's chart.

Boise to New York City

September 18 🎥

Debut on *The Tonight Show Starring Johnny Carson*, New York City

September 23 ✓ ✈

Richard: "*The David Frost Show* in New York."
     The Carpenters perform "(They Long to Be) Close to You."
     "They didn't want us to do 'We've Only Just Begun,'" Richard remembers. "I said, 'This is becoming a hit.' And they said no. It had to be '(They Long to Be) Close to You.' No imagination."

New York City to Miami, Florida

September 25– October 8 🎵

Hump Room, Eden Roc Hotel, Miami

October 10 📈 🎵

US version of *Close to You* enters Japan's Oricon album chart, peaks at No. 88, stays four weeks on survey.

Open for Henry Mancini, Kent State University, Kent, Ohio

October 13 ✈

Fly to Washington, D.C.

October 14 ✓ 🎥

Richard: "Go to Walter Reed Hospital, rehearse, tape at Walter Reed Hospital."

Perform the "Bacharach/David Medley" for Vietnam War soldiers recovering at the Walter Reed Army Medical Center in Washington, D.C. The performance is recorded and airs on a special *Ed Sullivan Show* episode November 8. "Big coincidence," Richard notes, [his father] "Harold Carpenter's 62nd birthday."
     "It was very moving," Richard says of the experience at Walter Reed. "The soldiers were very appreciative, something you never forget. I also found it unusual that they knew us, better for 'Ticket to Ride' than 'Close to You.' Armed Forces Radio must have played 'Ticket' quite a bit in Vietnam."

October 15 ✈

Washington, D.C., to New York City

October 18 🎥

Perform "We've Only Just Begun" and "(They Long to Be) Close to You" on their first *Ed Sullivan Show* appearance, New York City

October 19 ✈ 🎵 🎬

New York City to Toronto, Ontario, Canada

Set up and sound check for shows with Engelbert Humperdinck, O'Keefe Centre, Toronto

After an afternoon sound check, Richard and Karen see the movie *Lovers and Other Strangers* and hear "For All We Know" for the first time. Richard calls the record company the following day about having a demo of the song ready upon his return.

October 20–31 🎵

First international dates, opening for Engelbert Humperdinck in sold-out run, O'Keefe Centre, Toronto

October 22–23 🥔

Between shows in Toronto, the Carpenters record a jingle and tape a promotional video for Morton's Potato Chips.

October 25 💿

"We've Only Just Begun" debuts on Japan's Oricon singles chart, peaks at No. 71, and has a thirteen-week run.

October 28 💿 📈

Close to You and "We've Only Just Begun" surpass the million-sales mark.

"We've Only Just Begun" peaks at No. 2 on *Billboard* Hot 100 and stays there for four weeks, kept from the top spot by the Jackson 5's "I'll Be There."

November 1 ✈ 🎵

Toronto to Ottawa, Ontario, Canada

Ottawa Civic Center, open for Engelbert Humperdinck, Ottawa

November 2 ✈

Ottawa to Chicago, Illinois

November 2–8 🎵

Mill Run Playhouse. "Still with 'Engie,'" Richard notes, explaining that the Carpenters were opening for Engelbert Humperdinck, Chicago, Illinois

November 10 🎵 💿

University of Dayton, Dayton, Ohio

Debut album *Offering* reissued, repackaged, and retitled *Ticket to Ride*.

November 11–17 🎧

Recording sessions for "Merry Christmas, Darling"

November 13 💿 🎥 ✈

Close to You and "We've Only Just Begun" are certified Gold.

Return to *The Tonight Show*, New York City

New York City to Los Angeles

November 18 ✈

Los Angeles to Tokyo, Japan

November 20 💿

"Merry Christmas, Darling" released in the US

November 20–22 🎵 ✈

Carpenters perform a twenty-minute set at the World Popular Song Festival, Tokyo.
     For the remainder of their time in Tokyo, Karen and Richard sit for interviews and appear on numerous pop-music TV shows.

Tokyo to Honolulu, Hawai'i

November 23–25 🎵

Cinerama Reef Towers Hotel's Polynesian Palace, Honolulu
     Richard: "Two shows nightly. Opening night was actually the same day we left Tokyo."

November 26 Thanksgiving ✓

Richard: "Honolulu to Los Angeles, Los Angeles to Montgomery, Alabama."
     He recalls, "Here's where the tailor making our tuxedos meets us for fittings—during the layover at LAX. That's how tight the schedule was. Sherwin [Bash, the Carpenters' manager] hard at work."

November 27 🎵

Alabama State Coliseum, Montgomery

November 28 🎵

Birmingham, Alabama

November 29 🎵

Murray, Kentucky

November 29 ⊘

Richard: "Drive [fifteen hours] from Murray to Aberdeen, South Dakota."
Why drive?
"A plane had gone down with a college team on it," he replies. "We were nervous about flying. So, we drove from Murray all the way to South Dakota, without stopping, without sleeping. No time."

December 1 ♬

Aberdeen, South Dakota

December 2 ♬ ✈ ◎

Minot, South Dakota

Fly to San Francisco, California

Close to You peaks at No. 2 on *Billboard* Top LPs chart for one week, kept from the top spot by Santana's *Abraxas*. *Close to You* would log eighty-seven weeks on *Billboard* and be ranked No. 3 on the magazine's year-end album chart for 1971.

December 4 ♬

Coheadline with the 5th Dimension, San Francisco Civic Auditorium

December 5 🎥

Tape appearance on *American Bandstand*

December 10 ⊘

Richard: "Take delivery of new '71 Continental Mark III, drive from Beverly Hills Lincoln to A&M soundstage for rehearsal."

December 11 🎤

Rehearsal for benefit concert, Long Beach, California

December 12 ♬

Benefit concert for the Cal State Long Beach choir, Cal State Long Beach State gym, Long Beach

Mid–Late December 🎧

Recording sessions for "For All We Know"

December 16 📊

"Merry Christmas, Darling" debuts on *Billboard* Best Bets for Christmas chart at No. 2, climbs to No. 1 the following week.

December 22 🎧

At his own request, José Feliciano contributes an instrumental opening for "For All We Know." His manager soon phones Richard demanding, "Take him off the record!" Richard keeps Feliciano's melody but replaces his guitar with Jim Horn's oboe.

December 23 ⊘ 📊 📺

Richard: "Taping of *This Is Your Life*. We couldn't believe it. We had been famous for only seven months. We thought they were doing it for Herb or someone who'd actually *had* a career. But this is just one example of how famous we had become, so fast."

Carpenters are all over *Billboard* year-end surveys, with "(They Long to Be) Close to You" the No. 2 Hot 100 single of 1970, behind Simon & Garfunkel's "Bridge over Troubled Water."

December 31 🚗

Drive eight hours from Los Angeles to Reno

Richard remembers listening to the radio with Karen on the road trip. "We heard KHJ counting down the year-end hits," he says, "and '(They Long to Be) Close to You' was No. 2 in L.A. In San Francisco, it was KFRC, and 'Bridge' was No. 2 and 'Close to You' was No. 1, which we thought was pretty nifty. It was a very important record."

1971

January 1– January 8 ♬ 📊

Open for Joey Heatherton, Harrah's Reno Hotel and Casino, Reno

January 9 📊

"We've Only Just Begun" debuts on the Official UK Top 40 chart, peaks at No. 28, and stays on the survey for seven weeks.

January 11 📺

Richard catches Bette Midler's performance of "Superstar" on *The Tonight Show* and stumbles into another future hit for the Carpenters.

January 15 ♬ 📷 ◎

Headline Pasadena Civic Auditorium, with Seals and Crofts their opening act, Pasadena, California.

Before showtime, the Carpenters race out to Richard's car to hear "For All We Know" on the radio for the first time.

"For All We Know" released in the US

January 16 ♬

Santa Monica Civic Center, Santa Monica, California

January 22 ⊘

Richard: "Tape *The Andy Williams Show*."

January 23 ♬

San Diego Civic Theatre, San Diego, California

January 30 ♬

Civic Auditorium, Bakersfield, California

February 2 ♬

RKO Orpheum, Davenport, Iowa

February 3 ◎ ♬

"For All We Know" enters *Billboard* Hot 100 at No. 87.

KRNT Theatre, Des Moines, Iowa

February 4 ☆ ♬

Grammy nominations: Album of the Year (*Close to You*), Record of the Year and Best Performance by a Duo or Group "(They Long to Be) Close to You," and Best New Artist.

Men's Gymnasium of State College, Cedar Falls, Iowa

February 5 ♬

Mayo Civic Center, Rochester, Minnesota

February 6 📊 ♬

Japanese edition of *Close to You* enters the Oricon album chart, peaks at No. 53, and stays on survey thirteen weeks.

Mason City High School Gymnasium, Mason City, Iowa

February 7 ♬

University of South Dakota, Vermillion, South Dakota

February 8 ⊘

Richard comments, as he makes note of all the concert bookings, "So, keep in mind that, all this time, *an album* was supposed to be being made."

February 9 ♬

Kearney State College, Kearney, Nebraska

February 10 ♬

Coe College, Cedar Rapids, Iowa

February 11 ♬

Hara Arena, Dayton, Ohio

February 13 ♬

Syria Mosque, Pittsburgh, Pennsylvania

Promo shot for summer replacement series *Make Your Own Kind of Music*, Burbank, CA, April 1971

February 14 ♫
Academy of Music, Philadelphia, Pennsylvania

February 20 ♫
University Auditorium, Bloomington, Indiana

February 21 ♫
Merrimac University, St. Louis
    Richard: "We spent the night here," due to a wicked winter storm hammering the Southern Plains and stranding travelers.
    Richard chuckles, recalling that the Carpenters' manager, Sherwin Bash, had chosen the night's previous stop—blizzard-paralyzed Bloomington, of all times and places—to make a rare drop in to check on his clients' welfare.

February 22 ✈ ♫
Depart St. Louis 10:10 a.m., arrive Oklahoma City 12:22 p.m., American flight 125

Southwestern Oklahoma State University Auditorium, Weatherford, Oklahoma

February 23 ♫
Tulsa, Oklahoma

February 24 ♫
Dallas, Texas

February 25 ♫
University of Arkansas, Robinson Memorial Auditorium, Little Rock, Arkansas

February 26 ♫
University of Georgia Stegeman Coliseum, Athens, Georgia

February 27 ♫ ✈
East Tennessee State University, Johnson City, Tennessee

Return to Los Angeles

February 28 ♫
Coheadline with Diana Ross at benefit performance at NARM (National Association of Recording Merchandisers) Scholarship Foundation Dinner, Century Plaza Hotel, Los Angeles

February 28 ☆
"For All We Know" is nominated for Best Original Song by the Academy of Motion Picture Arts and Sciences.

March 2 ⊘
Richard: "And on Karen's birthday, it says, 'Go to A&M.'"

March 3 ⩗
Ticket to Ride, the repackaged reissue of debut album *Offering*, enters *Billboard* Top LPs chart at No. 191.

March 9 ⊘
Richard: "Wolfman Jack interview."

What was he really like? "Oh, fine," Richard replies, with a smile. "A pleasant fellow. You know. Normal. He went into character when he was on the air."

March 9–14 ∩
"Record, record, record," Richard says, as he reviews the entries.

The Carpenters were only a week or so away from their deadline for *Carpenters* (The Tan Album).

March 10 📈

"For All We Know" peaks at No. 3 on *Billboard* Hot 100 for two weeks, logs thirteen weeks on survey.

March 15 🎤

Rehearsal for the Grammy Awards at the Hollywood Palladium, Los Angeles

March 16 ☆

Grammy Awards: in the ceremony's first live telecast, the Carpenters take statuettes for Best Performance by a Duo or Group for "(They Long to Be) Close to You" and Best New Artist. They lip-synch their performance of "We've Only Just Begun."

March 17 🎧

Recording session for *Carpenters* (The Tan Album)

March 19 ✈

Los Angeles to Honolulu

March 20–21 🎵✈

Honolulu International Center, Honolulu
    "Another barn," says Richard. "Sold out, but lousy acoustics."

March 22 ✈🚗

Honolulu to Los Angeles

Drive from Los Angeles to Las Vegas

March 23–April 4 🎵

The Carpenters' final performances as an opening act, for Don Adams at the Sands Copa Room on the Las Vegas Strip. Between performances, Richard sequences the tracks for *Carpenters* [The Tan Album].

April 6 🎥

Record promotional films for "Rainy Days and Mondays" and "Superstar," Desert Inn Hotel, Las Vegas

April 7 📈

Ticket to Ride peaks for the first of two times at No. 150 on the *Billboard* Top LPs chart.

April 12 💿

"For All We Know" is certified Gold in the US.

April 15 ☆

"For All We Know" wins Best Original Song at the 43rd Academy Awards. In spite of the Carpenters having the hit, Petula Clark performs at the ceremony. Accepting his Oscar, cowriter Fred Karlin thanks his "new friends" Karen and Richard Carpenter.

April 16 📷

Publicity-photo shoot for summer replacement TV series *Make Your Own Kind of Music*.

April 16–20 🎧

Record "Bless the Beasts and Children" in just a week
    "We cooked through that," Richard notes.

April 21 🎵

Baylor University, Waco, Texas

April 22 🎵

East Texas State University, Commerce, Texas

April 23 🎵💿

Texas State Technical College, Lubbock, Texas

"Rainy Days and Mondays" released in the US

April 24 🎵

Taylor County Coliseum, Abilene, Texas

April 25 🎵

Houston Music Hall, Houston, Texas

April 27 🎵

Loyola University, New Orleans, Louisiana

April 28 🎵

Northwestern State University, Natchitoches, Louisiana
    "This is where I got another bug and was barfing again," Richard recalls. "And that's when I decided that was it for all of the Big Macs and Pepsi Colas. And I lost a good twenty pounds, which I needed to lose, because I stopped eating at midnight."

April 29 🎵

Civic Center, Monroe, Louisiana

April 30–May 1 🎵

Mississippi State Fair, Jackson, Mississippi

May 2 🎵

Stokely Athletic Center, University of Tennessee, Knoxville, Tennessee

May 4 🎵

Memorial Auditorium, Greenville, South Carolina

May 5 🎵

Municipal Auditorium, Atlanta, Georgia

May 6 🎵

Carolina Coliseum, Columbia, South Carolina
    "Right around here, I wanted to call home," Richard remembers, "and back then you had to get an operator to do so. I said, 'I'd like to place a call to Los Angeles.' And the girl says, 'You're Richard Carpenter.' Wow! You know you've arrived."

May 7 🎵

Civic Center, Roanoke, Virginia

May 8 🎵

Appalachian State University, Boone, North Carolina

May 9 🎵

Coliseum, Charlotte, North Carolina

May 11 🎵

Boston Music Hall, Boston, Massachusetts

May 12 🎵📈

Loews Theatre, Providence, Rhode Island

"Rainy Days and Mondays" enters the *Billboard* Hot 100 at No. 46. Richard recalls, "As the preorder totaled 800,000 units, it 'shipped Gold,' a relatively new phenomenon in the record industry."

May 14 🎵💿

Carpenters perform to a sell-out crowd at Carnegie Hall in New York City. The opening act is Mark Lindsay ("Arizona"), whose backup band includes lead guitarist Tony Peluso.
    Richard and Karen hire Peluso to perform the fuzz-guitar solo on "Goodbye to Love," and the Carpenters deliver what is arguably the first power-pop ballad. Peluso joins the Carpenters.

The duo's eponymously titled third studio album, *Carpenters* (The Tan Album), is released in the US.

Taping "(They Long to
Be) Close to You" for
The Johnny Cash Show,
Nashville, 1971

A Year in the Life of the Carpenters

Presenting an
award to engineer
Ray Gerhardt
for his work on
"(They Long to Be)
Close to You," A&M
Studios, Los Angeles,
November 11, 1970

Karen and
Richard in A&M
Studio B, Los
Angeles, 1970

Billboard HOT 100

For Week Ending August 1, 1970

STAR PERFORMER — Records showing greatest increase in retail sales activity over the previous week, based on accrual market reports.

Record Industry Association Of America seal of certification as "million seller." ●

THIS WEEK	LAST WEEK	TITLE, Artist (Producer) Label, Number (Distributing Label)
1 ★	1	(They Long to Be) CLOSE TO YOU — Carpenters (Jack Daugherty), A&M 1183
2 ★	5	MAKE IT WITH YOU — Bread (David Gates), Elektra 45686
3	2	MAMA TOLD ME (Not to Come) ● — Three Dog Night (Richard Podolor), Dunhill 4239 (Capitol)
4	3	BAND OF GOLD ● — Freda Payne (Holland-Dozier) Invictus 9075
5 ★	9	SIGNED, SEALED, DELIVERED (I'm Yours) — Stevie Wonder (Stevie Wonder), Tamla 54196 (Motown)
6	4	THE LOVE YOU SAVE/I FOUND THAT GIRL — Jackson 5 (Corporation), Motown 1166
7 ★	14	SPILL THE WINE — Eric Burdon & War (Jerry Goldstein), MGM 14118
8	6	BALL OF CONFUSION (That's What the World Is Today) — Temptations (Norman Whitfield), Gordy 7099 (Motown)
9	11	TIGHTER, TIGHTER — Alive & Kicking (Tommy James-Bob King), Roulette 7078
10	8	O-O-H CHILD — 5 Stairsteps (Stan Vincent), Buddah 165
11	7	RIDE CAPTAIN RIDE — Blues Image (Richard Podolor), Atco 6746
12 ★	25	WAR — Edwin Starr (Norman Whitfield) Gordy 7101 (Motown)
13	12	HITCHIN' A RIDE ● — Vanity Fare (Roger Easterby & Des Champ) Page One 21029 (Bell)
14	15	ARE YOU READY? — Pacific Gas & Electric (John Hill), Columbia 4-45158
15	10	LAY DOWN (Candles in the Rain) — Melanie with the Edwin Hawkins Singers (Peter Schekeryk) Buddah 167
16	16	TEACH YOUR CHILDREN — Crosby, Stills, Nash & Young (D. Crosby, S. Stills, G. Nash & N. Young), Atlantic 2735
17	18	OHIO — Crosby, Stills, Nash & Young (D. Crosby, S. Stills, G. Nash & N. Young), Atlantic 2740
18 ★	20	I JUST CAN'T HELP BELIEVING — B.J. Thomas (Chips Moman), Scepter 12283
19 ★	24	LAY A LITTLE LOVIN' ON ME — Robin McNamara (Jeff Barry), Steed 724 (Paramount)
20	19	A SONG OF JOY — Miguel Rios (Hispavox), A&M 1193
21 ★	26	(If You Let Me Make Love to You Then) WHY CAN'T I TOUCH YOU? — Ronnie Dyson (Billy Jackson) Columbia 4-45110
22 ★	32	IN THE SUMMERTIME — Mungo Jerry (Barry Murray), Janus 125
23	13	GIMME DAT DING — Pipkins (John Burgess), Capitol 2819
24	17	THE WONDER OF YOU/MAMA LIKED THE ROSES — Elvis Presley, RCA Victor 47-9835
25	28	SILVER BIRD — Mark Lindsay (Jerry Fuller), Columbia 4-45180
26	30	WESTBOUND #9 — Flaming Ember (Stagecoach Prod.), Hot Wax 7003 (Buddah)
27 ★	39	TELL IT ALL BROTHER — Kenny Rogers & the First Edition (Jimmy Bowen & Kenny Rogers), Reprise 0911
28 ★	41	OVERTURE FROM TOMMY — Assembled Multitude (Bill Buster), Atlantic 2737
29 ★	60	PATCHES — Clarence Carter (Rick Hall), Atlantic 2748
30 ★	57	GET UP I FELL LIKE BEING A SEX MACHINE (Part I & Part II) — James Brown (James Brown), King 6318
31	29	MISSISSIPPI QUEEN — Mountain (Felix Pappalardi), Windfall 532 (Bell)
32	31	LOVE LAND — Charles Wright & the Watts 103rd Street Rhythm Band (Charles Wright), Warner Bros. 7365
33 ★	47	SUMMERTIME BLUES — Who (Kit Lambert-Chris Stamp), Decca 32708
34 ★	44	THE SLY, THE SLICK AND THE WICKED — Lost Generation (Eugene Record), Brunswick 55436 (Decca)
35 ★	38	MAYBE — Three Degrees (Richard Barrett), Roulette 7079
36	35	MISSISSIPPI — John Phillips (Lou Adler), Dunhill 4236
37 ★	43	EVERYBODY'S GOT THE RIGHT TO LOVE — Supremes (Frank Wilson), Motown 1167
38 ★	50	25 OR 6 TO 4 — Chicago (James William Guercio), Columbia 4-45194
39 ★	56	DO YOU SEE MY LOVE (For You Growing) — Jr. Walker & the All Stars (Jimmy Bristol), Soul 35073 (Motown)
40	34	CHECK OUT YOUR MIND — Impressions (Curtis Mayfield), Curtom 1951 (Buddah)
41	27	SAVE THE COUNTRY — 5th Dimension (Bones Howe), Bell 895
42 ★	51	BIG YELLOW TAXI — Neighborhood (Jimmy Bryant), Big Tree 102
43	46	MY MARIE — Engelbert Humperdinck (Peter Sullivan), Parrot 40049 (London)
44	36	GO BACK — Crabby Appleton (Don Gallucci), Elektra 45687
45	49	PAPER MACHE — Dionne Warwick (Burt Bacharach-Hal David), Scepter 12285
46	37	STEAL AWAY — Johnnie Taylor (Don Davis), Stax 0063
47 ★	52	I WANT TO TAKE YOU HIGHER — Ike & Tina Turner & the Ikettes (Ike Turner), Liberty 56177
48	48	HOW ABOUT A LITTLE HAND (For the Boys in the Band) — Boys In the Band (Bob Feldman-Herman Griffin) Spring 103 (Polydor)
49 ★	69	HAND ME DOWN WORLD — Guess Who (Jack Richardson & Nimbus 9), RCA 74-0367
50	53	PEARL — Tommy Roe (Steve Barri), ABC 11266
51 ★	71	AMERICA, COMMUNICATE WITH ME — Ray Stevens (Ray Stevens), Barnaby 2016 (Columbia)
52	45	WHEN WE GET MARRIED — Intruders (Gamble-Huff Productions), Gamble 4004
53	54	I'LL BE RIGHT HERE — Tyrone Davis (Willie Henderson), Dakar 618 (Atlantic)
54 ★	61	EVERYTHING A MAN COULD EVER NEED — Glen Campbell (Al DeLory), Capitol 2843
55	55	CINNAMON GIRL — Neil Young & Crazy Horse (David Briggs & Neil Young), Reprise 0911
56	59	COTTAGE CHEESE — Crow (B. Monaco), Amaret 119
57 ★	62	SUNSHINE — Archies (Jeff Barry), Kirshner 63-1009 (RCA)
58	40	TRYING TO MAKE A FOOL OF ME — Delfonics (Stan & Bell Prod.), Philly Groove (Bell) 162
59 ★	74	WIGWAM — Bob Dylan (Bob Johnston), Columbia 4-45199
60 ★	64	SOLITARY MAN — Neil Diamond (Jeff Barry-Ellie Greenwich), Bang 578
61 ★	—	(I Know) I'M LOSING YOU — Rare Earth (Norman Whitfield), Rare Earth 5017 (Motown)
62	65	GROOVY SITUATION — Gene Chandler (Gene Chandler), Mercury 73083
63	63	STEALING IN THE NAME OF THE LORD — Paul Kelly (Buddy Killen), Happy Tiger 541
64	67	YOU'VE BEEN MY INSPIRATION — Main Ingredient (Silverstein-Simmons-McPherson), RCA 74-0340
65	72	HELLO DARLIN' — Conway Twitty (Owen Bradley), Decca 32661
66 ★	77	GLORY GLORY — Rascals with the Sweet Inspirations (Rascals & Arif Mardin), Atlantic 2743
67 ★	90	SING A SONG FOR FREEDOM — Frijid Pink (Pink Unlimited), Parrot 349 (London)
68	68	THAT SAME OLD FEELING — Pickettywitch (John MacLeod), Janus 118
69 ★	80	SNOWBIRD — Anne Murray (Brian Ahern), Capitol 2738
70	70	SONG FROM M*A*S*H — Al DeLory (Phil Wright), Capitol 2811
71 ★	—	JULIE, DO YA LOVE ME — Bobby Sherman (Jackie Mills), Metromedia 194
72 ★	—	HI-DE-HO — Blood, Sweat & Tears (Roy Halee & Bobby Colomby), Columbia 4-45204
73	73	SUPERMAN — Ides of March (Frank Rand & Bob Destocki), Warner Bros. 7403
74	75	LONG LONELY NIGHTS — Dells (Bobby Miller), Cadet 5672 (Chess)
75	76	GIRLS WILL BE GIRLS, BOYS WILL BE BOYS — Isley Brothers (R. Isley, O. Isley, R. Isley), T-Neck 921 (Buddah)
76 ★	99	IT'S A SHAME — Spinners (Stevie Wonder), V.I.P. 25057 (Motown)
77	86	QUE SERA, SERA (Whatever Will Be, Will Be) — Mary Hopkin (Paul McCartney), Apple 1823 (Capitol)
78	85	HUMPHREY THE CAMEL — Jack Blanchard & Misty Morgan (Little Richie Johnson), Wayside 013 (Mercury)
79 ★	88	HUMMINGBIRD — B.B. King (Bill Szymczyk), ABC 11268
80	83	DOWN BY THE RIVER — Buddy Miles & the Freedom Express (Robin McBride & Buddy Miles), Mercury 73086
81	81	APARTMENT #21 — Bobbie Gentry (Rick Hall), Capitol 2849
82	82	DROP BY MY PLACE — Little Carl Carlton (Mike Terry), Back Beat 613
83	84	BLACK FOX — Freddy Robinson (Higgins & Ervin), Pacific Jazz 88155 (Liberty/United Artists)
84	78	LET THE MUSIC TAKE YOUR MIND — Kool & the Gang (Gene Redd), De-Lite 529
85 ★	—	I'VE LOST YOU/THE NEXT STEP IS LOVE — Elvis Presley, RCA Victor 47-9873
86	87	SOMETHING — Booker T. & the MG's (Booker T. & the MG's), Stax 0073
87	96	YELLOW RIVER — Christie (Mike Smith), Epic 5-10626 (Columbia)
88	97	CANDIDA — Dawn (Tokens & Dave Appell), Bell 903
89	98	MORNING MUCH BETTER — Ten Wheel Drive with Genya Ravan (Guy Draper), Polydor 14037
90	92	IT'S YOUR LIFE — Andy Kim (Jeff Barry), Steed 727 (Paramount)
91	100	BIG YELLOW TAXI — Joni Mitchell (Joni Mitchell), Reprise 0906
92	—	MILL VALLEY — Miss Abrams & the Strawberry Point School Third Grade Class (Erik Jacobsen & Rita Abrams), Reprise 0928
93	94	NO ARMS CAN EVER HOLD YOU — Bobby Vinton (Billy Sherrill), Epic 5-10629 (Columbia)
94	—	BLACK HANDS WHITE COTTON — Caboose (Larry Rogers), Enterprise 9015 (Stax/Volt)
95	—	ONLY YOU KNOW AND I KNOW — Dave Mason (Tommy LiPuma & Dave Mason), Blue Thumb 114
96	—	EVERYTHING'S TUESDAY — Chairmen of the Board (Holland-Dozier-Holland), Invictus 9079 (Capitol)
97	—	YOURS LOVE — Joe Simon (John R.), Sound Stage 7 2664 (Monument)
98	—	BALL AND CHAIN — Tommy James (Tommy James & Bob King), Roulette 7084
99	—	A SONG THAT NEVER COMES — Mama Cass Elliot (Steve Barri), Dunhill 4244
100	—	BRING IT ON HOME — Lou Rawls (Rick Hall & David Axelrod), Capitol 2856

HOT 100 A TO Z—(Publisher-Licensee)

America, Communicate With Me (Ahab, BMI) 51
Apartment 21 (Wits End, BMI) 81
Are You Ready? (PG & E, BMI) 14
Ball and Chain (Big Seven, BMI) 98
Ball of Confusion (That's What the World Is Today) (Jobete, BMI) 8
Band of Gold (Gold Forever, BMI) 4
Big Yellow Taxi (Joni Mitchell) (Siquomb, BMI) 91
Big Yellow Taxi (Neighborhood) (Siquomb, BMI) 42
Black Fox (Special Agent, BMI) 83
Black Hands White Cotton (Wren, BMI) 94
Bring It On Home (Kags, BMI) 100
Candida (Jillbern/Pocketfull of Tunes, BMI) 88
Check Out Your Mind (Camad, BMI) 40
Cinnamon Girl (Cotillion/Broken Arrow, BMI) 55
Close to You (Blue Seas/Jac/U.S. Songs, ASCAP) 1
Cottage Cheese (Yuggoth/Forty Tunes, BMI) 56
Do You See My Love (For You Growing) (Jobete, BMI) 39
Down By the River (Cotillion/Broken Arrow, BMI) 80
Drop By My Place (Toini Don, BMI) 82
Everybody's Got the Right to Love (Think Stallman, BMI) 37
Everything a Man Could Ever Need (Ensign, BMI) 54
Everything's Tuesday (Gold Forever, BMI) 96
Get Up I Feel Like Being a Sex Machine (Part 1 and Part 2) (Dynatone, BMI) 30
Gimme Dat Ding (Duchess, BMI) 23
Girls Will Be Girls, Boys Will Be Boys (Triple Three, BMI) 75
Glory Glory (Slacsar, ASCAP) 66
Go Back (Meemoo, BMI) 44
Groovy Situation (Cachand/Patcheal, BMI) 62
Hand Me Down World (Expressions, BMI) 49
Hello Darlin' (Twitty Bird, BMI) 65
Hi-De-Ho (Screen Gems-Columbia, BMI) 72
Hitchin' a Ride (Intune, BMI) 13
How About a Little Hand (For the Boys in the Band) (Yellow Dog, ASCAP) 48
Hummingbird (Skyhill, BMI) 79
Humphrey the Camel (Little Richie Johnson) 78
I Just Can't Help Believing (Screen Gems, BMI) 18
I Want to Take You Higher (Ike & Tina Turner) (Daly City, BMI) 47
(If You Let Me Make Love to You Then) Why Can't I Touch You? (Chappell, ASCAP) 21
I'll Be Right Here (Julio Brian/Jadan, BMI) 53
(I Know) I'm Losing You (Jobete, BMI) 61
In the Summertime (Our Music/Kirshner, BMI) 22
It's a Shame (Jobete, BMI) 76
It's Your Life (Unart/Joachim, BMI) 90
I've Lost You/The Next Step Is Love (Gladys, ASCAP/Gladys, ASCAP) 85
Julie, Do Ya Love Me (Lucon/Sequel, BMI) 71
Lay a Little Lovin' On Me (Unart, BMI) 19
Lay Down (Candles in the Rain) (Kama Rippa/Amelanie, ASCAP) 15
Let the Music Take Your Mind (Stephanye, BMI) 84
Long Lonely Nights (Arc/G & H, BMI) 74
Love Land (Wright/Gerstl/Tamerlane, BMI) 32
Love You Save, The (Jobete, BMI) 6
Make It With You (Screen Gems-Columbia, BMI) 2
Mama Liked the Roses (Press, BMI) 24
Mama Told Me (Not to Come) (January, BMI) 3
Maybe (Nom, BMI) 35
Mill Valley (Great Honesty, BMI) 92
Mississippi (Alchemy, ASCAP) 36
Mississippi Queen (Upfall, ASCAP) 31
Morning Much Better (Schefrin-Zager/Noma, BMI) 89
My Marie (January, BMI) 43
No Arms Can Ever Hold You (Gil, BMI) 93
Ohio (Cotillion/Broken Arrow, BMI) 17
Only You Know and I Know (Irving, BMI) 95
O-O-H Child (Duckstun/Kama Sutra, BMI) 10
Overture From Tommy (Track, BMI) 28
Paper Mache (Blue Seas/Jac, ASCAP) 45
Patches (Gold Forever, BMI) 29
Pearl (Low-Twi, BMI) 50
Que Sera, Sera (Whatever Will Be, Will Be) (Artist, ASCAP) 77
Ride Captain Ride (ATM, ASCAP) 11
Save the Country (Tuna Fish, BMI) 41
Signed, Sealed, Delivered (I'm Yours) (Jobete, BMI) 5
Silver Bird (Kangaroo, BMI) 25
Sing a Song for Freedom (Knip Unlimited, BMI) 67
Sly, the Slick and the Wicked, The (Julio-Brian, BMI) 34
Snowbird (Beechwood, BMI) 69
Solitary Man (Tallyrand, BMI) 60
Something (Harrisongs, BMI) 86
Song From M*A*S*H (20th Century, ASCAP) 70
Song of Joy (Barnegat, BMI) 20
A Song That Never Comes (Ampco, ASCAP) 99
Spill the Wine (Far Out, BMI) 7
Steal Away (Fame, BMI) 46
Stealing in the Name of the Lord (Tree, BMI) 63
Sunshine (Kirshner, BMI) 57
Summertime Blues (Rumbalero/Presley, BMI) 33
Superman (Ides, BMI) 73
Teach Your Children (Giving Room, BMI) 16
Tell It All Brother (Sunbeam, BMI) 27
That Same Old Feeling (January, BMI) 68
Tighter, Tighter (Big Seven, BMI) 9
Trying to Make a Fool of Me (Nickel Shoe, BMI) 58
25 or 6 to 4 (Aurelius, BMI) 38
War (Jobete, BMI) 12
Westbound =9 (Gold Forever, BMI) 26
When We Get Married (Frost, BMI) 52
Wigwam (Big Sky, ASCAP) 59
Wonder of You, The (Duchess, BMI) 24
Yellow River (Noma, BMI) 87
Yours Love (Wilderness, BMI) 97
You've Been My Inspiration (Multimood, BMI) 64

Chapter 3

We're No.1...

1970–1974

Album

Close to You

"People were saying, 'I've never heard anything like this.'"

Album
Close to You

—

US release date
8/19/70

—

Billboard Top LPs

Chart entry date (position)
9/19/70 (No. 60)

Peak date, position (weeks at peak)
12/24/70, No. 2 (1)

Total weeks on chart
87

Year-end rank
No. 3

Left: 1970

Page 56: "(They Long to be) Close to you" has the longest No. 1 run of any single in the US

The commercial failure of *Offering* came at the worst time for the Carpenters' record label, which failed to score even one *Billboard* Top 10 pop single or album in 1969. Yet there was a bright side to that bad news. As Richard explains it, because *everyone* was having a lousy year at A&M, no artist was assigned blame. And that's one reason why he and Karen weren't terribly concerned about their job security following the disappointing debut.

Still, Richard recalls, "I sensed that most of the people on the lot wanted to see the back of us." The label wanted to go in a new, "hipper" direction, signing such blues- and psychedelic-rock bands as Blodwyn Pig and Tarantula. "We were the last thing they wanted: some brother-sister act from the suburbs."

A&M cofounder Herb Alpert recalls, "The word I was getting from my own company was, 'Why did you sign these two kids?'"

His reply? "Her voice. She didn't even know what she had. He's a genius at picking, arranging, and producing songs—and he knew just what to do with her voice. And, in the end, talent wins out."

By November 21, 1969, six weeks after *Offering*'s release, the duo was back in the studio working on four tracks. These included Burt Bacharach and Hal David's show tune "I'll Never Fall in Love Again." Richard secularized Ralph Carmichael's contemporary Christian folk song, "Love Is Surrender," by making one change to the lyrics, from "You must surrender to His will" to "You must surrender if you care." And there were two works that Richard and John Bettis had cowritten a couple of years earlier: "Mr. Guder" and "Another Song."

As work in the studio progressed, it was becoming apparent that the Carpenters might achieve tenure at A&M after all. "There was too much going on, too much interest in us," Richard explains. "We were on the *Virginia Graham Show*, followed by a beautifully filmed performance of 'Ticket to Ride' in Squaw Valley for John Byner's nationally syndicated TV show, *Something Else*, on Karen's twentieth birthday [March 2, 1970], the Della Reese show [*Della*], and a number of local pop-music TV shows. And this was over a number of months."

It also didn't hurt that *Offering*'s single, "Ticket to Ride," was slowly taking off. By February 14, 1970, it broke into *Billboard* magazine's pop-singles chart, the Hot 100, at No. 92. "So we never got the idea that our days were numbered," Richard says.

And the Carpenters' momentum kept building. They received news that Burt Bacharach wanted them as his opening act at a benefit performance, and for Richard to arrange a medley of his tunes for the Reiss-Davis Child Study Center, set for late February. Richard says Bacharach heard "Ticket" on L.A. powerhouse station KMPC and, in a conversation with A&M cofounder Jerry Moss, mentioned how much he admired the record. "Jerry said, 'Oh, that's our act,' which led to the whole thing."

For the benefit performance, Richard pored over the catalog of Burt Bacharach and Hal David and Mack David (Hal's brother) tunes to compile the medley. "That's when Herb came to me with a lead sheet to '(They Long to Be) Close to You,'" Richard notes. "I thought he originally meant it to be part of the medley. He didn't."

Alpert wanted Richard to arrange it, but also the Carpenters to record the song for their new album. "At first I wasn't crazy about it, and Karen wasn't either," Richard admits.

"(They Long to Be) Close to You" had been kicking around since 1963. Actor Richard Chamberlain first released it as a single; it failed to chart. Dionne Warwick took on the tune in 1963 and Dusty Springfield in 1964, but neither recording was released as the A-side of a single.

Richard recalls Alpert saying that he possessed a recording of the song but that he didn't want Richard to hear it, didn't want it to be any influence. Alpert's only request was to keep one element of Bacharach's original arrangement: the piano quintuplets, the pair of five notes that come at the end of the first bridge following the lyrics, "So they sprinkled moondust in your hair of gold and starlight in your eyes of blue" [quintuplet, quintuplet].

As Alpert expected, Richard found the song's long-elusive sweet spot. He created a dynamic new arrangement that not only showcased Karen's lead and the multiharmony Carpenters sound but also proved that Alpert's instinct in putting Richard, Karen, and the song together would result in a smash hit record.

Billboard for *Close to You* album, outside A&M Studios, Los Angeles, 1970

Page 61: Performing for injured Vietnam soldiers at Walter Reed Army Medical Center in Washington, D.C., November, 1970

Single
"(They Long to Be) Close to You"

—

US release date
May 15, 1970

—

Billboard Hot 100

Chart entry date (position)
6/20/70 (No. 56)

Peak date, position (weeks at peak)
7/25/70, No. 1 (4)

Total weeks on chart
17

Year-end chart rank
No. 2

—

**Billboard Adult
Contemporary Chart**

Chart entry date (position)
6/13/70 (No. 33)

Peak date, position (weeks at peak)
7/11/70, No. 1 (6)

Total weeks on chart
16

Year-end chart rank
No. 1

It took a number of passes to create the masterpiece. Richard recalls that for the first take, "The harmonies were there and all, but Herb wasn't pleased [with them], nor with Karen's original approach to her lead."

Karen, with Richard's encouragement, adopted the whimsical style of "Everybody's Talkin'" singer Harry Nilsson. "It wasn't just the lead vocal that [Herb] wanted redone, but the rhythm tracks—using studio pros, to add some punch."

For take two, Richard stepped away from the piano bench to make room for keyboard man Larry Knechtel. Richard says, "I wrote the whole damned piano chart out for Larry, who was great at what he did with the gospel-like honky-tonk stuff, [Simon & Garfunkel's] 'Bridge over Troubled Water,' [Johnny Rivers's] 'Rockin' Pneumonia and the Boogie Woogie Flu,' and The Mamas & the Papas. But not for '(They Long to Be) Close to You,' as Knechtel was too heavy handed."

Soon, Richard was back on keyboards.

Up to this point, all of the Carpenters' tracks featured Karen on drums. "Karen was a fine drummer with great time, like a metronome," Richard says. "She had great 'wrists,' as they called it in the business. So, for things like 'Flat Baroque' and 'This Masquerade' [tracks requiring more precision than power], she was great."

However, drummer Hal Blaine had what Karen did not: the studio chops, the originality, and the sheer weight to give the drums a more muscular sound. "The difference between Hal Blaine and Karen, on '(They Long to Be) Close to You,' was night and day," Richard says.

As "(They Long to Be) Close to You" was coming together, buzz about the record was building around the studio. Richard remembers A&M employees breaking protocol, interrupting recording by opening the doors to get into the studio to hear, while the red light was on. "People were saying, 'I've never heard anything like this.'" Such comments had to boost the Carpenters' confidence in the potential chart success of the song. But Richard still had his doubts.

After all, "(They Long to Be) Close to You" wasn't typical fodder for Top 40 radio. It was an extremely sophisticated song, performance, and production.

Furthermore, it was an unapologetically romantic love song coming out less than eight months after the Woodstock music festival had propelled antiestablishment sensibility into the mainstream and helped rock firmly plant its flag aside pop and soul at the upper reaches of the singles charts.

A&M released "(They Long to Be) Close to You" on May 20, 1970. The single blasted onto the *Billboard* Hot 100 dated June 20 at No. 56—an incredibly strong debut. "It went through the roof," says Richard, "and immediately [A&M cofounder] Jerry Moss called [producer] Jack [Daugherty] who called me and said, 'We need an album, like, now.'"

This would be the story of the Carpenters' lives as recording artists for the next three years.

On the Album

Richard says The Beatles' "Help!" served as an effective opener for the Carpenters' live act. "We used it a lot early on."

As with "Ticket to Ride," Richard approached the Lennon-McCartney tune, a 1965 chart topper, from a new angle—turning the up-tempo original into a driving ballad, featuring plenty of the Carpenters' harmonies.

(For the record: the Carpenters' version was listed as "Help." Richard, a major Beatles fan, says he had nothing to do with the removal of John Lennon and Paul McCartney's exclamation point from the original title, "Help!")

The Burt Bacharach/Mack David (Hal's brother)/Luther Dixon (aka Barney Williams) collaboration, "Baby It's You," enjoyed two successful runs on the US pop-singles charts before the Carpenters recorded it for the *Close to You* album. The original doo-wop, ballad version by The Shirelles reached No. 8 on the *Billboard* Hot 100 in early 1962, and the blues-rock band Smith, with an entirely fresh approach, drove it back up the survey to No. 5 in 1969.

"It's such a great song," Richard observes. "It can be a hit with several disparate arrangements where, say, 'Close to You' cannot."

For the Carpenters' version, Richard gave the tune his "Ticket to Ride" treatment, slowing down the tempo and adding strings, English horn, a melodic tenor sax solo by Bob Messenger, a pinch of plaintive melancholy, and, of course, those trademark Carpenters multilayered vocals. "Mostly they're me, on this track" Richard notes—"in fact *all* of them."

The thumbnail version of the "Mr. Guder" backstory goes like this: Richard and John Bettis were hired to portray turn-of-the-century musicians at Disneyland's Coke Corner on Main Street, U.S.A. The duo—Richard on piano and John on six-string banjo—was directed to play the greatest hits of 1900. But they couldn't resist fulfilling requests from park guests wanting to hear more contemporary tunes—"particularly 'Somewhere, My Love,'" Richard recalls, referring to the popular song based on a leitmotif from the recent box-office blockbuster *Doctor Zhivago*.

The frequent anachronisms proved problematic for their supervisor, Vic Guder, who himself had to play by the theme park's strict rules. "Mr. Guder" is Richard and John's response to their boss's reprimands:

LAX to JFK, 1970

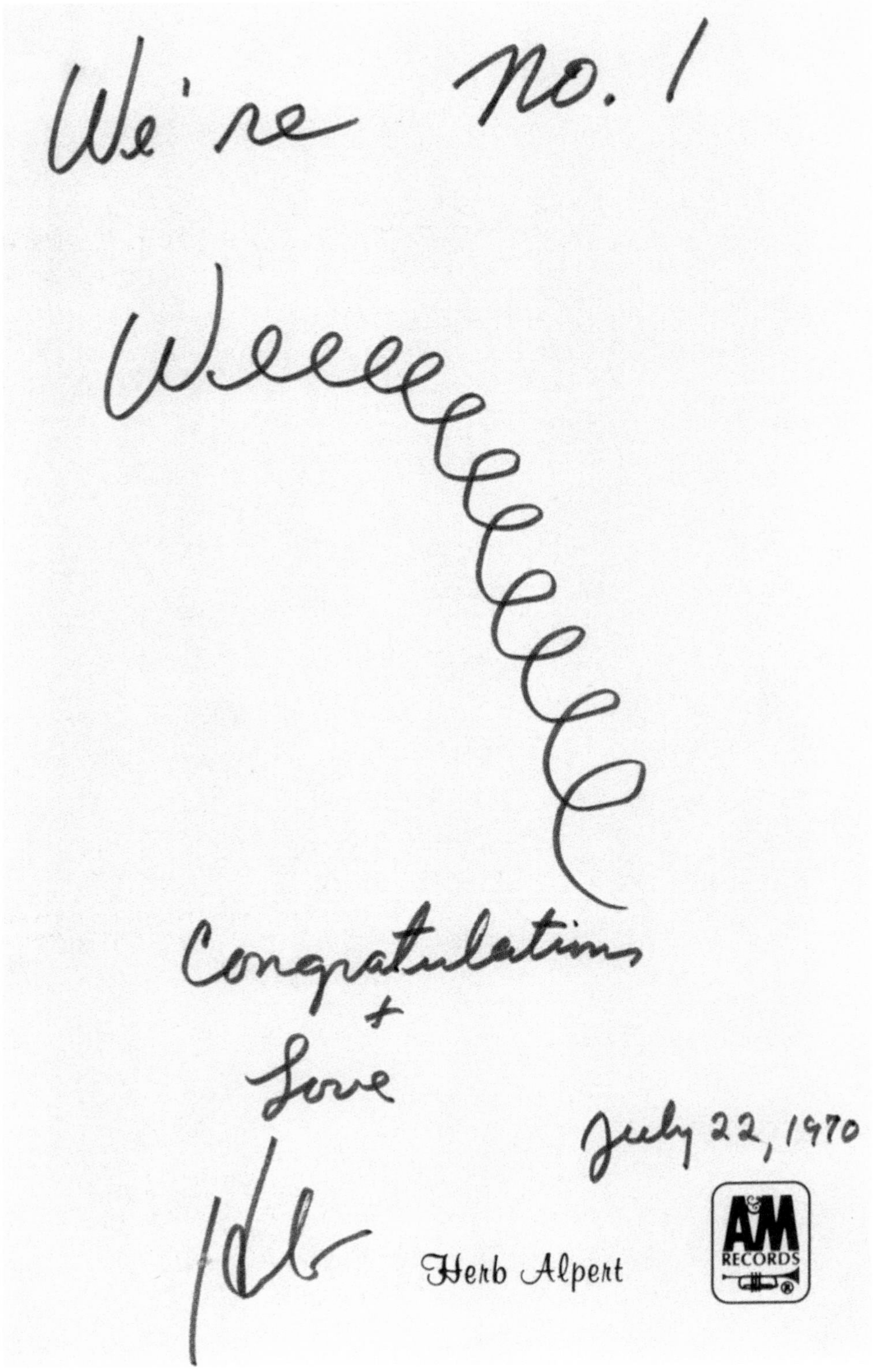

We're No. 1

Weeeeeeeeeeeee

Congratulations
+
Love

July 22, 1970

Herb Alpert

A&M RECORDS

Left: A&M cofounder Herb Alpert's note to Karen and Richard on the day news broke that "(They Long to Be) Close to You" reached the top of the *Billboard* Hot 100

Page 65: "(They Long to Be) Close to You" reaches No. 1 on the *Billboard* Hot 100 chart for the week ending on July 25, 1970

STAR PERFORMER — Records showing greatest increase in retail sales activity over the previous week, based on accrual market reports.

RED ARROW — Records most likely to show sharp rise in chart position next week, as predicted by computer.

BLACK ARROW — Records most likely to show moderate rise in chart position next week, as predicted by computer.

Record Industry Association Of America seal of certification as "million seller."

Billboard HOT 100

THIS WEEK / LAST WEEK / TITLE, Artist, Producer, Label, Number (Distributing Label)

This	Last	Title / Artist / Producer / Label / Number
1	3	(They Long to Be) CLOSE TO YOU — Carpenters (Jack Daugherty), A&M 1183
2	1	MAMA TOLD ME (Not to Come) — Three Dog Night (Richard Podolor), Dunhill 4239 (Capitol)
3	4	BAND OF GOLD — Freda Payne (Holland-Dozier), Invictus 9075
4	2	THE LOVE YOU SAVE — Jackson 5 (Corporation), Motown 1166
5	10	MAKE IT WITH YOU — Bread (David Gates), Elektra 45686
6	5	BALL OF CONFUSION (That's What the World Is Today) — Temptations (Norman Whitfield), Gordy 7099 (Motown)
7	6	RIDE CAPTAIN RIDE — Blues Image (Richard Podolor), Atco 6746
8	8	O-O-H CHILD — 5 Stairsteps (Stan Vincent), Buddah 165
9	18	SIGNED, SEALED, DELIVERED (I'm Yours) — Stevie Wonder (Stevie Wonder), Tamla 54196 (Motown)
10	7	LAY DOWN (Candles in the Rain) — Melanie with the Edwin Hawkins Singers (Peter Schekeryk) Buddah 167
11	12	TIGHTER, TIGHTER — Alive & Kicking (Tommy James-Bob King), Roulette 7078
12	11	HITCHIN' A RIDE — Vanity Fare (Roger Easterby & Des Champ), Page One 21029 (Bell)
13	9	GIMME DAT DING — Pipkins (John Burgess), Capitol 2819
14	24	SPILL THE WINE — Eric Burdon & War (Jerry Goldstein), MGM 14118
15	15	ARE YOU READY? — Pacific Gas & Electric (John Hill), Columbia 4-45158
16	22	TEACH YOUR CHILDREN — Crosby, Stills, Nash & Young (D. Crosby, S. Stills, G. Nash & N. Young), Atlantic 2735
17	13	THE WONDER OF YOU/MAMA LIKED THE ROSES — Elvis Presley, RCA Victor 47-9835
18	26	OHIO — Crosby, Stills, Nash & Young (D. Crosby, S. Stills, G. Nash & N. Young), Atlantic 2740
19	14	A SONG OF JOY — Miguel Rios (Hispavox), A&M 1193
20	30	I JUST CAN'T HELP BELIEVING — B.J. Thomas (Chips Moman), Scepter 12283
21	20	THE LONG AND WINDING ROAD/FOR YOU BLUE — Beatles (Phil Spector), Apple 2832 (Capitol)
22	19	MY BABY LOVES LOVIN' — White Plains (Roger Greenaway/Roger Cook), Deram 85058 (London)
23	17	GET READY — Rare Earth (Rare Earth) Rare Earth 5012 (Motown)
24	37	LAY A LITTLE LOVIN' ON ME — Robin McNamara (Jeff Barry), Steed 724 (Paramount)
25	44	WAR — Edwin Starr (Norman Whitfield), Gordy 7101
26	41	(If You Let Me Make Love to You Then) WHY CAN'T I TOUCH YOU? — Ronnie Dyson (Billy Jackson) Columbia 4-45110
27	27	SAVE THE COUNTRY — 5th Dimension (Bones Howe), Bell 895
28	29	SILVER BIRD — Mark Lindsay (Jerry Fuller), Columbia 4-45180
29	25	MISSISSIPPI QUEEN — Mountain (Felix Pappalardi), Windfall 532 (Bell)
30	31	WESTBOUND #9 — Flaming Ember (Stagecoach Prod.), Hot Wax 7003 (Buddah)
31	16	LOVE LAND — Charles Wright & the Watts 103rd Street Rhythm Band (Charles Wright), Warner Bros. 7365
32	68	IN THE SUMMERTIME — Mungo Jerry (Barry Murray), Janus 125
33	21	UNITED WE STAND — Brotherhood of Man (Tony Hiller), Deram 85059 (London)

This	Last	Title / Artist / Producer / Label / Number
34	28	CHECK OUT YOUR MIND — Impressions (Curtis Mayfield), Curtom 1951 (Buddah)
35	32	MISSISSIPPI — John Phillips (Lou Adler), Dunhill 4236
36	36	GO BACK — Crabby Appleton (Don Gallucci), Elektra 45687
37	38	STEAL AWAY — Johnnie Taylor (Don Davis), Stax 0068
38	43	MAYBE — Three Degrees (Richard Barrett), Roulette 7079
39	59	TELL IT ALL BROTHER — Kenny Rogers & the First Edition (Jimmy Bowen & Kenny Rogers), Reprise 0911
40	42	TRYING TO MAKE A FOOL OF ME — Delfonics (Stan & Bell Prod.), Philly Groove (Bell) 162
41	61	OVERTURE FROM TOMMY — Assembled Multitude (Bill Buster), Atlantic 2737
42	40	END OF OUR ROAD — Marvin Gaye (Norman Whitfield), Tamla 54195 (Motown)
43	74	EVERYBODY'S GOT THE RIGHT TO LOVE — Supremes (Frank Wilson), Motown 1167
44	45	THE SLY, THE SLICK AND THE WICKED — Lost Generation (Eugene Record), Brunswick 5543E (Decca)
45	46	WHEN WE GET MARRIED — Intruders (Gamble-Huff Productions), Gamble 4004
46	47	MY MARIE — Engelbert Humperdinck (Peter Sullivan), Parrot 40049 (London)
47	69	SUMMERTIME BLUES — Who (Kit Lambert-Chris Stamp), Decca 32708
48	48	HOW ABOUT A LITTLE HAND (For the Boys in the Band) — Boys in the Band (Bob Feldman-Herman Griffin) Spring 103 (Polydor)
49	65	PAPER MACHE — Dionne Warwick (Burt Bacharach-Hal David), Scepter 12285
50	—	25 OR 6 TO 4 — Chicago (James William Guercio), Columbia 4-45194
51	56	BIG YELLOW TAXI — Neighborhood (Jimmy Bryant), Big Tree 102
52	53	I WANT TO TAKE YOU HIGHER — Ike & Tina Turner & the Ikettes (Ike Turner), Liberty 56177
53	58	PEARL — Tommy Roe (Steve Barri), ABC 11266
54	54	I'LL BE RIGHT HERE — Tyrone Davis (Willie Henderson), Dakar 618 (Atlantic)
55	57	CINNAMON GIRL — Neil Young & Crazy Horse (David Briggs & Neil Young), Reprise 0911
56	66	DO YOU SEE MY LOVE (For You Growing) — Jr. Walker & the All Stars (Jimmy Bristol), Soul 35073 (Motown)
57	72	GET UP I FEEL LIKE BEING A SEX MACHINE (Part I & Part II) — James Brown (James Brown), King 6318
58	51	SO MUCH LOVE — Faith, Hope & Charity (Van McCoy-Joe Cobb), Maxwell 805 (Crewe)
59	62	COTTAGE CHEESE — Crow (B. Monaco), Amaret 119
60	90	PATCHES — Clarence Carter (Rick Hall), Atlantic 2748
61	70	EVERYTHING A MAN COULD EVER NEED — Glen Campbell (Al DeLory), Capitol 2843
62	63	SUNSHINE — Archies (Jeff Barry), Kirshner 63-1009 (RCA)
63	76	STEALING IN THE NAME OF THE LORD — Paul Kelly (Buddy Killen), Happy Tiger 541
64	80	SOLITARY MAN — Neil Diamond (Jeff Barry-Ellie Greenwich), Bang 578
65	77	GROOVY SITUATION — Gene Chandler (Gene Chandler), Mercury 73083
66	52	A LITTLE BIT OF SOAP — Paul Davis (Illene Berns & Paul Davis), Bang 576
67	75	YOU'VE BEEN MY INSPIRATION — Main Ingredient (Silverstein-Simmons-McPherson), RCA 74-0340

This	Last	Title / Artist / Producer / Label / Number
68	67	THAT SAME OLD FEELING — Pickettywitch (John MacLeod), Janus 118
69	89	HAND ME DOWN WORLD — Guess Who (Jack Richardson & Nimbus 9), RCA 74-0367
70	71	SONG FROM M*A*S*H — Al DeLory (Phil Wright), Capitol 2811
71	—	AMERICA, COMMUNICATE WITH ME — Ray Stevens (Ray Stevens), Barnaby 2016 (Columbia)
72	78	HELLO DARLIN' — Conway Twitty (Owen Bradley), Decca 32661
73	64	SUPERMAN — Ides of March (Frank Rand & Bob Destocki), Warner Bros. 7403
74	—	WIGWAM — Bob Dylan (Bob Johnston), Columbia 4-45199
75	100	LONG LONELY NIGHTS — Dells (Bobby Miller), Cadet 5672 (Chess)
76	—	GIRLS WILL BE GIRLS, BOYS WILL BE BOYS — Isley Brothers (R. Isley, O. Isley, R. Isley), T-Neck 921 (Buddah)
77	—	GLORY GLORY — Rascals with the Sweet Inspirations (Rascals & Arif Mardin), Atlantic 2743
78	79	LET THE MUSIC TAKE YOUR MIND — Koni & the Gang (Gene Redd), De-Lite 529
79	81	THE WITCH — Rattles (H. Hildebrandt), Probe 480 (ABC/Dunhill)
80	86	SNOWBIRD — Anne Murray (Brian Ahern), Capitol 2738
81	83	APARTMENT #21 — Bobbie Gentry (Rick Hall), Capitol 2849
82	82	DROP BY MY PLACE — Little Carl Carlton (Mike Terry), Back Beat 613
83	94	DOWN BY THE RIVER — Buddy Miles & the Freedom Express (Robin McBride & Buddy Miles), Mercury 73086
84	—	BLACK FOX — Freddy Robinson (Higgins & Ervin), Pacific Jazz 88155 (Liberty/United Artists)
85	85	HUMPHREY THE CAMEL — Jack Blanchard & Misty Morgan (Little Richie Johnson), Wayside 013 (Mercury)
86	95	QUE SERA, SERA (Whatever Will Be, Will Be) — Mary Hopkin (Paul McCartney), Apple 1823 (Capitol)
87	—	SOMETHING — Booker T. & the MG's (Booker T. & the MG's), Stax 0073
88	—	HUMMINGBIRD — B.B. King (Bill Szymczyk), ABC 11268
89	92	HAND CLAPPING SONG — Meters (Allen R. Toussaint & Marshall E. Sehorn), Josie 1021 (Jay-Gee)
90	—	SING A SONG FOR FREEDOM — Frijid Pink (Pink Unlimited) Parrot 349 (London)
91	93	BABY IS THERE SOMETHING ON YOUR MIND — McKinley Travis (Bobby Sander), Pride 2
92	—	IT'S YOUR LIFE — Andy Kim (Jeff Barry), Steed 727 (Paramount)
93	97	THE LIGHTS OF TUCSON — Jim Campbell (Laurie), Laurie 3546
94	96	NO ARMS CAN EVER HOLD YOU — Bobby Vinton (Billy Sherrill), Epic 5-10629 (Columbia)
95	99	I CAN'T BE YOU (You Can't Be Me) — Glass House (Holland-Dozier-Holland), Invictus 9076 (Capitol)
96	98	YELLOW RIVER — Christie (Mike Smith), Epic 5-10626 (Columbia)
97	—	CANDIDA — Dawn (Tokens & Dave Appell), Bell 903
98	—	MORNING MUCH BETTER — Ten Wheel Drive with Genya Ravan (Guy Draper), Polydor 14037
99	—	IT'S A SHAME — Spinners (Stevie Wonder), V.I.P. 25057 (Motown)
100	—	BIG YELLOW TAXI — Joni Mitchell (Joni Mitchell), Reprise 0906

Close to You

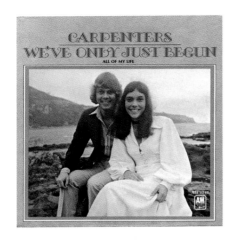

Single

"We've Only Just Begun"

—

US release date
8/21/70

—

***Billboard* Hot 100**

Chart entry date (position)
9/12/70 (No. 84)

Peak date, position (weeks at peak)
10/31/70, No. 2 (4)

Total weeks on chart
17

Year-end chart rank
No. 65

—

***Billboard* Top 40 Easy Listening**

Chart entry date (position)
9/19/70 (29)

Peak date, position (weeks at peak)
10/10/70, No. 1 (7)

Total weeks on chart
16

Year-end chart rank
No. 3

You reflect the company image
You're everything a robot lives for
Walk in at nine and roll out the door at five

Richard says he quickly regretted recording the song.

"Vic was a really good guy. I really feel bad. I do, really do. Oh, boy. Yet, changing it to 'Mr. Cooper' or anything else, it wouldn't have been the same."

The track closes with something new on a Carpenters recording: a scat. Richard says it was inspired by popular French vocal group the Swingle Singers. "The track has big choral things," he says, "great vocals."

The Response

Richard was ready for the Carpenters to have a smash hit. "I was trying to picture it," he says, "because when KHJ was playing a ballad, they went from [Richard sings jingle] '93 K-H-J' to [he sings an alternate, slower version] '93 Kayyy-H-Jayyyy.' And I always imagined hearing 'Ticket' on there, which I never did.

Richard says the first time he heard "(They Long to Be) Close to You" on the radio was, indeed, on the station he'd imagined: KHJ—one of the most powerful and influential Top 40 outlets in the US. "We were so excited. So we called home and Mom answered. And Karen and I pretty much yelled, 'KHJ's on the record!'"

In fact, KHJ was the first radio station to report that it was playing "(They Long to Be) Close to You" to the trade magazine *Cash Box*. And with the Top 40 trailblazer's endorsement, stations were all over the record within a week, and A&M was reporting sales of nearly 100,000 by mid-June.

When the single reached the summit of the *Billboard* Hot 100, on the chart dated July 25, 1970, Richard and Karen received a handwritten message from Alpert: *"We're No. 1 Weeeeeeeeeee…"* it read, the *e*'s spilling down the page from Alpert's personalized A&M notepad. And that would be just the start of it. The following week, the song climbed to No. 1 on the pop-singles charts of the other two music trades, *Cash Box* and *Record World*.

By then, the record couldn't be avoided. It seemed to be everywhere. "The height of doing what you do, as far as making pop singles," Richard says, "is to have two stations playing it at the same time." Richard recalls bandmate Doug Strawn was in one car, he and Karen were in another, both vehicles moving side by side near Cal State Long Beach. "We had our windows down, and Karen and I bopped from either KRLA or KHJ to KMPC."

One car radio was tuned to one station. The other was tuned to another. And both stations were playing "(They Long to Be) Close to You." Richard and Karen looked across at Strawn in disbelief.

"Just being played so much that your record is on two 50,000-watt stations at the same time, you know you have a hit on your hands."

"(They Long to Be) Close to You" spent a total of four weeks atop the Hot 100, the longest No. 1 run for any single that summer. By September, it sold two million copies, making it the best-selling single in A&M's history.

Close to You
photo-shoot
outtake, Palos
Verdes, CA, 1970
(Jim McCrary
photo, A&M/UMe)

Another Cover Story: "Learn to Live with It"

Richard Carpenter recounts how the *Close to You* album cover came together— or fell apart, depending on your perspective. "The schedule's already jammed," he says, "and we were told, 'Report [to an address] in Palos Verdes' [for the photo shoot]. Then [A&M executive] Gil Friesen decides I need a sports jacket. He was right about that. He takes me to Mr. Guy," a tony Beverly Hills haberdashery.

Richard, whose broad, lean build required off-the-rack items to be tailored, was given an unaltered cashmere jacket. "It's lovely," he recalls. But when Richard and Karen got their cover wardrobes home to Mom, an accomplished seamstress, out came the sewing kit. "Because she didn't have time to get to the tailor to pull [the jacket] in, she pinned it, so at least it tapered at

the waist." Karen's outfit was no better. A&M gave her "this horrid thing," Richard says, referring to her full-length, white, eyelet dress.

The ill-conceived wardrobe choices should have prepared them, but Richard and Karen were nonetheless shocked by the shoddy photo shoot. "We had to climb over rocks," says Richard. "Gloomy day. Spray's coming off from the ocean, hitting the rocks and showering us. I said, 'What kind of creativity is this?' It was a snapshot. Twenty feet away from us was a couple taking the same fucking picture. And another couple after them. If you look at it, my hair is frizzed out, but at least the jacket comes in at the waist. But Karen's hair, from the salt-water spray, is all flattened

out—makes her face look long. And then her hose was falling a bit.

"I was furious," Richard continues. "I told them, 'This can't be good. Just *look* at the photo! There's no way this can be good. There's no creativity to it whatsoever, and we look like hell.'"

The Carpenters were back in Studio B finishing up the album when, Richard says, "Friesen comes in with that goddamned cover and says, 'What do you think of it?' We said, 'We think it's terrible.' He said, 'Learn to live with it.' I'll never forget it. I've never learned to live with it, especially after [the album] sold five million copies in its first go-round; eighty-seven weeks it was on the charts." "And where the hell is the big-time manager we just hired?"

The Other Single

Richard was at home when he first saw a TV commercial for the Crocker Bank. It was a soft-sell ad: a montage of moments in a young couple's life, underscored by a pop ballad starting with this lyric: "We've only just begun to live."

Richard says he immediately recognized the singer as Paul Williams. "I knew it had to be a [Roger] Nichols/Williams song. But I didn't know whether it was a whole song, as the commercial only featured a verse or two."

Richard saw Williams on the A&M lot and asked him if there was more than a mere minute to "We've Only Just Begun," which was published by one of A&M's divisions, Irving Music. "Paul said, 'Yes,'" Richard continues. "So I went over to publishing and played the demo of the complete song and knew right off the bat it needed a smoother transition to get into the bridge."

The Carpenters' recording came together with relative ease. "I thought, it's going to go [Richard sings] 'to-ge-ther, to-*GE*-ther' at the close of the second bridge. It was one of those where the whole arrangement just popped up finished in my head, and all we had to do was record it. Karen and I knew it was going to be a hit."

Not everyone agreed that they should record the tune. "A couple of people tried to talk me out of it," Richard remembers. "Somebody said, 'You know, Mark Lindsay's done it. It's on his album—the latest one, *Silverbird*.' So I gave it a listen, and I said, 'It's all right. But it's not the right arrangement.' An arrangement can make or break a record. So we went ahead with it."

On the US Charts

Close to You entered the Top LPs chart dated September 19, 1970, at No. 60. On December 5, the album reached its peak of No. 2, where it remained for one week—kept from the top spot by Santana's *Abraxas*. *Close to You* spent a total of 87 weeks on the survey. No other Carpenters album has enjoyed a longer *Billboard* album-chart run.

Below: A&M family picnic, Malibu Canyon, CA, June 1970

Pages 69–71: Pulp fiction: A&M press release issued shortly after "(They Long to Be) Close to You" topped the charts

The press release, at right, celebrates the Carpenters' first chart topper in the summer of 1970. But it's riddled with so many inaccuracies, it's downright hilarious. (See The Richard Carpenter Interview earlier in this book for the real story.)

What's not so funny is that it shows how A&M's publicity and marketing machines mishandled –and, as per Richard, downright loathed– what would soon be their most valuable commodities. The label's first No. 1 in nearly two years? Grammy awards? Sales in the millions? Global superstars? Groovy.

But, God forbid, they were two happy siblings from the 'burbs who made some of the greatest pop records ever. "They just didn't know what to do with us," Richard says.

NEWS FROM A&M RECORDS

1416 NORTH LA BREA AVENUE, HOLLYWOOD, CALIFORNIA 90028 · TELEPHONE 461-9931

CARPENTERS ZOOM TO PROMINENCE
WITH NUMBER ONE SINGLE IN NATION

     Carpenters are the Number One group in America today with the
Number One record in the country today -- "CLOSE TO YOU," written
by Burt Bacharach.
     But it seems that very few people even know who the group is.
Sure they had a top single almost a half a year ago with the
Beatles' "Ticket to Ride," but even then they were a relatively
unknown Southern California group.
     So here's the real story of how and when and why Carpenters
came to be.
     The rise of the Carpenters to popular music stardom has
followed a relatively linear path from Richard Carpenter's accordion
lessons in New Haven, Conn. to a fine summer day in Hollywood when
A&M Records received word that the group's second single, "Close to
You" had sold its one-millionth copy and risen to number one in the
nation. Between those two points, the very youthful Karen and
Richard Carpenter have crammed in a lot of musical experience.
     Richard Carpenter didn't like playing accordion and soon found
the piano more to his liking. He was a smash hit in his high school
orchestra and soon made it big on the New Haven party circuit.
Before his family finally moved from New Haven to California, Rich
had gained a wealth of experience playing sedate cocktail music in
parties, small clubs and dumpy bars.

                                            more ....

Close to You   69

Karen Carpenter purports to be three years younger than her elder brother. As a typically finicky female little sister, Karen wanted to tag along with big brother Richard on his musical forays. To do that, she not so uneventfully decided to learn to play an instrument. She settled on drums.

Rich and Karen, whose collective family ego overwhelmed the classically-trained tuba player they persuaded to play bass for them, formed the Carpenter Trio and started playing jazz on a more sophisticated level. Sophisticated enough, anyway, to win a Hollywood Bowl Battle of the Bands in 1966 when the bass player switched over to tuba for the last song and literally blew the judges' minds.

The Carpenter Trio was signed to a Los Angeles company where they recorded two singles, neither of which were released. With fame so fleeting, the Trio soon became the Duo.

Next stop was a group called Spectrum, fronted by the vocals of R. and K.. The Carpenters played their respective instruments and four friends filled in the holes ably enough so that after a year, Spectrum was being noticed by record companies, audiences and (horrors) maybe even nubile young groupies. The five guys in the group finally came to blows over the latter problem and the group broke up and went to college.

It is near this point that A&M Records bought the services of Rich and Karen. With a contract to wave at everyone's collective nose, two former Spectrum people were lured back into the fold, thus forming a new group which was to be called Carpenters. A couple more musicians were added and it was indeed called Carpenters.

A first album for A&M was recorded in the spring and summer of 1969, released under the title Offering. Out of this came a hit single rendition of the Beatles' "Ticket to Ride." The clever approach to the time-honored Liverpool standard was masterminded by Richard, who laid and lays claim to the group's arranging chores.

more ....

The next step for the budding young group was to get ready to perform again. As is quite common, by studying too much music in college, the members of the group had lost the ability to play their instruments on a stage. The entire band, from Karen on up (or down, as she would have it) could name and identify by date of composition all of Bach's works, but they could not keep a steady beat. It took a couple of months to overcome this hurdle, and by the dawn of the seventies, the Carpenters and their entourage were ready to hit the beloved road.

The Big Day came on February 27, 1970, when the group debuted in a large Southern California club. They then joined Burt Bacharach as second act on many of his concerts, and he finally gave them one of his songs to get them off his tail and onto their own path to glory. The song was called "Close to You." Karen sang a bang-up version of it and it hopped its way up the charts to Number One in about six weeks.

Not so strangely, the second Carpenter album has subsequently been entitled, Close to You. It is, like Offering, produced by Jack Daugherty, with arrangements by Richard and the group, some pretty vocals and zesty drumming by Karen (who swears she will give up breathing before she gives up drumming to be a torch singer).

Carpenters also includes Dan Woodhams, Doug Strawn and Bob Messenger. Dan is one of the holdovers from Spectrum and bops away on bass guitar for the group. Doug plays reeds, once sang in barbershop quartets and wants to be rich and famous when he grows up. Bob Messenger plays several instruments and has been around. When not playing good music for Carpenters, his job is to keep the kids out of trouble — he's the oldest member of the band. Another former Spectrum member, guitarist Gary Sims, is away in military service.

The Critics vs. The Carpenters

"We got nasty stuff."

It's no secret that, for quite some time, there was a chasm between many of the Carpenters' critics and the duo's millions of devoted fans. But a random selection of nearly two hundred reviews of Carpenters albums and concerts from 1969 to 1981 reveals something surprising: about a third are positive, another third mixed.

The problem is that the reviews in the final third are so hostile, so hateful, that they overwhelm the others. Here's how Barry Cain opens his review of the duo's 1977 album *Passage*: "Karen Carpenter: the dummy in the shop window. Devoid of emotion, each song a rerun of the last. Flat monotones whether she's singing about pain or love, depression or joy."

For all of the love the Carpenters got in the United Kingdom, a solid chunk of their haters in the media were there. Andrew Tyler's *New Musical Express* review of a 1974 concert in Frankfurt, Germany, says the Carpenters' singing is "Four Freshman[sic]-slanted, and instead of rolling around inside the head, the voices bludgeon indiscreetly against the skull."

Much of this Carpenters bashing had to do with timing. The duo's breakthrough in 1970 came just as the counterculture was becoming popular culture. Karen and Richard delivered classic pop with roots dating back to the 1940s and 1950s.

The Carpenters just weren't hip. And hip was *everything* for many young critics, meaning an assignment to cover the Carpenters probably felt like punishment.

Veteran musician and music critic Morgan Ames says the Carpenters' friendly persona also likely fueled the critical bonfire. In the early 1970s, Ames critiqued a number of Carpenters albums for *High Fidelity* magazine. She recalls, "Music reviewers, mostly young and nervous, saw cynicism as important, much of art as boring, and snideness as meaningful and cool. Poor wages added bitterness."

So, between the hipsters and the cynics, the Carpenters didn't stand a chance. Many of these writers, instead of giving the duo a serious listen and analysis, took the low road—making snide remarks about their suburban roots, their audiences, their clothes, their hair, their bodies. The reviewers got personal.

Critical Condition: A *Stereo Review* Sampler

American readers in the 1970s didn't need to go far to find harsh criticism of the Carpenters. The decade's two go-to magazines for pop-album reviews, *Stereo Review* and *Rolling Stone*, could be found at most newsstands in the country—and their critics were rarely kind to Karen and Richard. A sampling from *Stereo Review*:

Close to You
"So, even as many prefer these tours of marshmallow factories, I remain content in my cynical conviction that Shirley Temple was a midget, Deanna Durbin a forty-five-year-old castrato, the New Christy Minstrels the Stern Gang, June Allyson a notorious Mexican gun moll, John Davidson a Haitian vice king—and Debbie Reynolds wears Army shoes. I should have the lowdown on the Carpenters for you any day now."
Performance: Cloying. Recording: Expert.
—Peter Reilly, September 1971

Carpenters [The Tan Album]
"The emotional connection between the Carpenters and their songs is about as strong as my last resolution to quit smoking. I say it's either spinach or Doris Day, and I say the hell with it."
Performance: Bloodless. Recording: Good.
—Noel Coppage, October 1971

The Singles 1969–1973
"They still strike me, depressingly, as the fictive offspring of a screen marriage between Robert Young and Doris Day."
Performance: Golly! Recording: Superb.
—Peter Reilly, June 1974

As Richard discusses the worst of them, you can tell he still hasn't gotten over how cruelly the Carpenters were treated. "We got nasty stuff," he acknowledges.

Back to the pile of two hundred critiques. The good stuff, the positive reviews, most frequently appeared in local newspapers. This means the Carpenters probably never saw most of them, as they were already en route to the next concert date before those papers were delivered.

The US's two go-to magazines for pop-music reviews in the 1970s were *Rolling Stone* and *Stereo Review*. (The latter's audiophile-oriented cousin, *High Fidelity*, ranked a distant third.) Few expected *Stone*, Jann Wenner's rock bible, to be kind to the Carpenters, and, for the most part, it wasn't. Yet Stephen Holden (who later wrote for the *New York Times*) no doubt infuriated his Carpenters-bashing boss with high praise for the track "A Song for You" and a near rave for the entire *Horizon* album.

You'd think *Stereo Review*, which served an older demographic who owned mid- to high-level audio gear, would be more Carpenters friendly. But no. The magazine was known for its one-word summations of each album's artistic and technical merits, and Richard has memorized the pithy teardown of *Close to You*: "Performance: Cloying," he recalls, with a laugh. The magazine's thumbnail review of *Carpenters* [The Tan Album]: "Performance: Bloodless. Recording: Good."

Criticism of the Carpenters wasn't reserved for *Stereo Review*'s reviewers alone. In a May 1972 editorial, William Anderson lets a reader take aim at Karen and Richard—calling their recordings "effortless, superficial, inconsequential fluff," as he bemoans the duo's brisk commercial success while long-established blues musicians struggle to sell records. The reader compares the Carpenters to the Partridge Family. That may be the nastiest review of them all.

Unearthing a Rarity

Richard Carpenter had not seen the review, right, of the Carpenters' 1970 *Close to You* album until working on this book. It was first published in the December 1970 issue of *High Fidelity* magazine. Richard was interested not only because it was a positive review. "This could be the only review written by someone who really got us," he says.

It turns out that Richard and the critic, musician Morgan Ames, had a mutual friend, Carpenters' amanuensus (musical secretary) Ron Gorow, and that Richard and Ames had worked together when Richard had a project in Japan. Richard requested that the review be reprinted in its entirety here, much to Ames's delight. "It's an honor," she says, noting her high regard for the Carpenters and Richard himself. "And I must say," she adds, "I kind of like this review."

the lighter side

reviewed by

MORGAN AMES

R. D. DARRELL

JOHN GABREE

JOHN S. WILSON

✱ symbol denotes an exceptional recording

✱

CARPENTERS: Close to You. Karen Carpenter, vocals and drums; Richard Carpenter, vocals, piano, and arr. (Help; Mr. Guder; Baby It's You; nine more.) A & M SP 4271, $4.98. Tape ⊞ 8T 4271, $6.98; ⊞ CS 4271, $6.98.

The Carpenters (brother and sister) recently had the kind of hit that everyone in music lusts for. It went across the boards, from rock radio stations to easy listening and back. The tune, *Close to You*, was early Bacharach-David (Dionne Warwick included it in an album years ago and nothing happened). The Carpenters' first album also contained a hit number—Lennon-McCartney's *Ticket to Ride*. I remember the record well because this was one of the few discs about which I have made an accurate prediction of success. But *Ticket to Ride* was not nearly the monster that *Close to You* turned out to be.

The combined talents of the Carpenters are irresistible. Richard is the axis; from the sound of things he works ferociously—hundreds of hours must have gone into this album. With lyricist John Bettis he wrote four of the songs. While the lyrics do not strike me as particularly noteworthy, Richard's melodies are just that, and his piano playing is not only skilled but beautifully placed within the orchestral texture. His twelve arrangements produce music that is smooth, melodious, and natural, both orchestrally and vocally. The real achievement is in the concept—each tune is meticulously planned and worked out and emerges with its own personality. Considering his youth (he's about twenty), Richard Carpenter has an alarming number of bases covered.

The other part of this winning combination is Karen Carpenter's voice, warmly innocent, full and dark and deep. She never has to reach for a note because Richard knows exactly how to write for her. Rumor has it that Karen's first love is drums, which is too bad. For while she is competent and interesting in live performances, her drumming on recordings is not of a high enough quality (especially for this album). Her singing, however, is superb in any setting. As a matter of fact, she has several distinct voices—one is the now familiar solo voice, the others are used to create layers of vocal chorus. Richard is also a fine group singer himself. Sparked by his gorgeous vocal arrangements, together the two create a texture of pure velvet.

There are few albums that are easier to listen to than this one. If you liked *Close to You*, this follow-up disc won't disappoint you.

Whoever took the picture of the Carpenters on the album cover ought to be shot.   M.A.

Single
"Merry Christmas, Darling"

"It's one of my all-time favorites of ours, and the vocals in particular. We just love it."

Single
"Merry Christmas, Darling"

—

US release date
11/22/70

—

***Billboard* Best Bets for Christmas**

Chart year, positions (chart dates)
1970, No. 2 (12/19),
No. 1 (12/26)

1971, No. 2 (12/18),
No. 1 (12/25)

1972, No. 7 (12/9), No. 12 (12/16),
No. 4 (12/23)

1973, No. 1 (12/8), No. 2 (12/15),
No. 12 (12/22)

—

***Billboard* 1983 Christmas Hits**

Peak date, position (weeks at peak)
12/24/83, No. 10 (1)

—

***Billboard* Holiday Streaming Songs**

Peak date, position (weeks at peak)
12/24/16, No. 19 (13)

Chart debut–latest appearance
12/10/16–1/01/20*

—

The Carpenters' first holiday recording, "Merry Christmas, Darling," was released in 1970, but its backstory begins some thirty-five years earlier. It was the mid-1940s in Onalaska, Wisconsin, and young songwriter Frank Pooler was inspired by the huge holiday hits of the wartime era. Tunes such as "White Christmas" and "I'll Be Home for Christmas" told of those longing to be with loved ones oceans away, if only in their dreams. Pooler was out of town with his parents, and he was longing for a girl back home. He decided the best way to convey his romantic feelings would be to give her a Christmas gift of song:

Merry Christmas, darling
We're apart that's true
But I can dream and in my dreams
I'm Christmasing with you

(Clockwise from left rear) Harold, cousin Joan, Agnes, Richard, Joan's daughter Suzie, and Karen, Downey, CA, Christmas 1970

Billboard Holiday 100

Peak date, position (weeks at peak)
12/08/12, No. 24 (1)

Chart debut–latest appearance:
12/10/11–01/04/20*

—

Billboard Holiday Airplay

Peak date, position (weeks at peak)
12/20/03, No. 1 (78)

Chart debut–latest appearance
12/15/01–01/03/15*

*as of 3/15/21

Before Pooler was able to get the song to her, he learned that their romantic relationship was over.

Twenty years later, in 1966, Pooler was director of the university choir at California State University, Long Beach. Unhappy with the melody he'd written for "Merry Christmas, Darling," Pooler brought the song's lyrics to his nineteen-year-old student, Richard Carpenter. Pooler was hoping his words from yesterday would finally get some worthy music. "He asked me to take a crack at it," Richard says.

By lunchtime, Richard was at work on the tune in one of the music department's practice rooms. The lyrics made musical sense to Richard, and it turned out to be an easy assignment. "That one just kind of wrote itself—maybe ten minutes, if that."

A holiday classic was born, but it took some time to gain that status. Richard says he and Karen occasionally performed the song in their pre-Carpenters days, "when we were able to play a casual—a gig where it wasn't a club and Karen would be allowed to get in."

Four years passed between the time Richard completed the tune and the Carpenters recorded the song. "It was my idea," Richard says. "We were on the road and it was getting to be close to Christmas— driving from one gig to the next. Somehow, it just came into my mind that we should record 'Merry Christmas, Darling,' which we did as soon as we were able to get the time in the studio."

Richard and Karen laid the music and vocal tracks down in less than one week in mid-November. Then Richard made a call to Pooler. "We have something to play for you," he said. "Can you come up to the studio?"

With anticipation, Pooler drove to Hollywood and got his first listen of "Merry Christmas, Darling" in A&M's Studio B. "Of course, it knocked him just about flat. Frank said, 'This may be the greatest day of my life.' And that's pretty much the story of it. It's one of my all-time favorites of ours, and the vocals in particular. We just love it."

"Merry Christmas, Darling" hit record stores on November 22, 1970, and it was an instant smash, topping the *Billboard* holiday singles chart in the issue dated December 26. Timing might have had a little something to do with its success. As with those enduring 1940s classics, this new/old holiday tune struck a chord with listeners longing for loved ones in another war zone: this time, in Vietnam.

The song also reached No. 1 on the holiday singles charts in 1971 and 1973. A reissue of the single containing the 1978 rerecording of Karen's vocal reached No. 10 on the holiday charts the year of Karen's death, 1983.

"Merry Christmas, Darling" has enjoyed one of the longest chart runs of any Carpenters release. The single debuted at No. 2 on the Best Bets for Christmas chart December 19, 1970, and its most recent appearance, as of this writing, was at No. 40 on the *Billboard* Holiday 100 on January 4, 2020. Start to finish, that's forty-nine years and seventeen days. Talk about gifts that keep on giving.

At the Movies

"It's like I'm the only person in the record business who noticed 'For All We Know.'"

Single
"For All We Know"

—

US release date
1/15/71

—

***Billboard* Hot 100**

Chart entry date (position)
2/6/71 (No. 87)

Peak date, position (weeks at peak)
3/13/71, No. 3 (2)

Total weeks on chart
13

Year-end chart rank
No. 35

—

***Billboard* Top 40 Easy Listening**

Chart entry date (position)
2/13/71 (No. 13)

Peak date, position (weeks at peak)
2/27/72, No. 1 (4)

Total weeks on chart
11
Year-end chart rank
No. 8

Richard and Karen spent so much time on the A&M Records lot that Hollywood was pretty much their home away from home. So, it's a bit curious that the Carpenters' road to the Oscars began 2,500 miles northeast of L.A.

The siblings were riding high when they arrived in Toronto to begin a two-week gig on October 19, 1970. They were opening for singer Engelbert Humperdinck at the O'Keefe Centre. "We've Only Just Begun" was reaching its height of popularity back home, marking the duo's second smash hit since "(They Long to Be) Close to You" was released as a single in May.

Now, the bad news. A&M wanted a new Carpenters single straight away, but not something pulled from the *Close to You* album, which had shipped more than a million copies. A third single would have been old news to all those record buyers. Richard was stressed. "I thought, 'We don't have anything to follow this with.'"

The Carpenters had the night off before starting the string of concerts with Humperdinck. Manager Sherwin Bash suggested Richard and Karen go out, relax, and see a movie. He recommended *Lovers and Other Strangers*, a well-reviewed romantic comedy about a young couple negotiating the mayhem in the days leading up to their wedding.

Wedding scene from *Lovers and Other Strangers*, where Richard discovered "For All We Know" (ABC Pictures Corp./ 20th Century Fox)

Above: "For All
We Know" trade
ad, 1971

Below: José
Feliciano, 1970

Richard says an instrumental for the film's bittersweet ballad, "For All We Know," caught his attention when it appeared in a sequence preceding the wedding ceremony. But it wasn't until a vocal version of the song played during the wedding that "It just said 'hit' to me."

While being interviewed for this book, Richard was surprised to learn that the movie had been in theaters more than two months and was already a modest box-office hit before he and Karen saw it. Its ballad had just been sitting there for the taking by any recording artist. "But it's like I'm the only person in the record business who noticed 'For All We Know,'" Richard says.

Fortunately, once he found the song, Richard hustled. And by the time he and Karen returned to the States, Richard had transformed the film version's delicate acoustic string arrangement into a lean but luscious orchestral showcase for Karen's salted-caramel vocal and Joe Osborn's fluid bass line. Richard says the Carpenters knocked out the recording in four or five sessions in mid-November.

"For All We Know" was released as a single January 15, 1971. Radio started playing the record the minute it arrived. "We happened to be performing at Pasadena Civic Center on the 15th, and we were told KHJ would be playing it," Richard recalls. "I remember us going to hear it on the radio in my new Continental Mark III." After all their success the previous year, hearing their latest record on the radio was still a big deal for the Carpenters.

"Are you kidding?" Richard replies, beaming.

Anyone listening carefully to "For All We Know" could hear the Carpenters were maturing quickly.

Just five months after "We've Only Just Begun" celebrated a bride and groom's idealism, white lace, and promises, "For All We Know" was the Carpenters' cautiously optimistic bookend. This song was about a couple who consummated their wedding vows before reaching the altar and who didn't have a clue whether the relationship stood a chance:

No Way, José

For the most part, the recording of "For All We Know" was smooth sailing, but there was one unexpected day of rough waters.

Richard remembers, "We ate a lot at Martoni," an Italian restaurant and bar just a few blocks away from the A&M lot in Hollywood, frequented by entertainment-industry heavyweights. One of them was singer-guitarist José Feliciano, who was still riding high following his smash 1968 cover version of The Doors' "Light My Fire." And his holiday classic "Feliz Navidad" had just been released.

"José said, 'I want to play on one of your records.' So, I thought, 'For All We Know.' On December 22, Feliciano was in the studio with the Carpenters. "And it was actually José who came up with the melody for the song's instrumental intro. And that was that."

Or so everyone thought.

"We get a call not all that long afterward from this really smarmy manager of José's—I mean, just rude as can be. 'Take him off the record! Take him off the record!' When I tried to explain it was José's idea, he said, 'I don't care. Take him off the record!' And so I did."

Feliciano's guitar intro was replaced by Jim Horn's oboe. "Of course, José didn't have that manager for long," Richard says.

Single
"Bless the Beasts and Children"

—

US release date
8/12/71 (B-side of "Superstar")

—

***Billboard* Hot 100**

Chart entry date (position)
12/4/71 (No. 89)

Peak date, position (weeks at peak)
1/15/71, No. 67 (1)

Total weeks on chart
8, as an A-side,
following 13 weeks listed
as the B-side of "Superstar"

Year-end chart rank
n/a

—

***Billboard* Top 40 Easy Listening**

Chart entry date (position)
12/11/71 (No. 39)

Peak date, position (weeks at peak)
1/8/71, No. 26 (2)

Total weeks on chart
6

Year-end chart rank
n/a

Let's take a lifetime to say
I knew you well
For only time will tell us so
And love may grow for all we know

Coincidentally, the release date and success of "For All We Know" perfectly coincided with the timeline for 1971's Academy Awards. The music branch was selecting its five best original song nominees from January 28 to February 12, just as the single was sprinting up the charts.

Lovers and Other Strangers received Oscar nominations for original song as well as supporting actor (Richard S. Castellano) and adapted screenplay. "For All We Know" reached its peak at No. 3 on the *Billboard* Hot 100 on March 6, meaning Motion Picture Academy members were likely familiar with the tune as they voted just two and a half weeks later. The record was certified Gold three days before the ceremony.

And yet the Carpenters were nowhere to be seen on the Oscar telecast April 15. Audiences heard singer and actress Petula Clark sing "For All We Know." "It was a great disappointment not to be invited to perform at the Oscars," Richard admits. An Academy of Motion Picture Arts and Sciences spokesperson explains there is no official rule about who performs original song nominees at the Oscars. But, she adds, there was a tradition of having movie stars perform instead of the actors or singers who introduced the songs on-screen or recording artists who made them popular.

A review of Oscar-song performers reveals that by the end of the 1970s, show producers finally broke from that tradition. And by 1980, it appears producers' first choices were the performers who introduced the nominated songs in the films. Show producers only looked elsewhere if the original performer was unavailable.

At the end of the day, "It's a good thing we didn't do it," Richard says, holding back a laugh. "I had…both ends. What's it called? Gastroenteritis!"

In fact, Richard was so sick, he missed the segment of the telecast where "For All We Know" won the Oscar and the Carpenters got a shoutout. At the end of cowriter Fred Karlin's acceptance speech, he thanked the film's director "and two other friends, Richard and Karen Carpenter, for their very moving interpretation of 'For All We Know.'"

At Last, Their Oscar Moment

In early 1971, the Carpenters were busy blasting out *Carpenters* [The Tan Album] before a long, hot summer of concert dates. The last thing they needed was an interruption. "Stanley Kramer wants to talk to you, Richard," recording engineer Ray Gerhardt announced over the talkback at A&M Records' Studio B.

Carpenter was intrigued. He knew of producer and director Kramer, a Hollywood legend, with credits as wide-ranging as *High Noon* (1952), *It's a Mad, Mad, Mad, Mad World* (1963), and *Guess Who's Coming to Dinner* (1967). "I said, 'Oh sure,'" Richard recalls. "But I went in, and damned if it wasn't.'"

Kramer explained his next film would be based on the novel *Bless the Beasts and Children*, about troubled kids who break out of a dude ranch to save a buffalo herd. "He said, 'There's a song in it, and I'd really like the Carpenters to do it.'" Richard was honored that Kramer himself called. But the Carpenters still had to hear the song.

Zip ahead a few weeks to the Sands Hotel, where Richard and Karen were performing. The Carpenters were grabbing a bite, and along came Kramer and the song's cowriter Barry De Vorzon with a demo of the tune in hand. Richard couldn't believe someone of Kramer's stature would go to such lengths.

"I mean, he was really doing it personally. And I'm thinking, 'Good God, I hope this doesn't suck,' because the odds were that it would," Richard says. "But you know what? Nice song. Good for my type of arranging, and good for Karen."

In August, just as the film debuted in the United States, the Carpenters' recording of "Bless the Beasts and Children" was released on the B-side of "Superstar." It received enough of its own airplay that *Billboard* listed the single "Superstar"/"Bless the Beasts and Children" for the record's first thirteen weeks on the Hot 100.

Then "Bless the Beasts" began its own Hot 100 run, thanks to the song publisher's campaign to get radio programmers to flip "Superstar" over and play the tune, with the hope that it would get the attention of Academy Awards voters.

"Bless the Beasts and Children" went on to earn an Oscar nomination for best original song for composers Perry Botkin Jr. and Barry De Vorzon. This time, the Carpenters received an invitation to perform at the Academy Awards ceremony.

Performing "Bless the Beasts and Children" at Academy Awards, Los Angeles, 1972

Richard and Karen attended, but they missed out on much of the Oscar glitz and glamour because they had to catch a midnight flight to Georgia. They had a concert the following night in Savannah.

"The whole thing was a rush job. We went down for rehearsal in the afternoon and we saw that all we were getting was a piano for me and a mic for Karen. They didn't even make me up."

Richard seemed to have the most fun before the ceremony, including a memorable conversation with nominee James Caan about his legendary "death by a thousand bullets" tollbooth scene in *The Godfather*. "I said, 'Tell me that the Lincoln Continental that they shot up was not a real one.' And he said, 'It was a real one.' It really killed me."

Richard and Karen had no delusions of Oscar grandeur. "We were up against 'Theme from *Shaft*,' which was a phenomenon. I knew it was going to win." And "Shaft" did win, which was an academy choice Richard respected. In fact, Richard owns a copy of composer Isaac Hayes's *Shaft* soundtrack. But, like some Oscar watchers, he questioned the placement of "Theme from *Shaft*" in the original song category.

"I mean, it wasn't really a *song*, it was a production—a good production," Richard observes. For four minutes and thirty-nine seconds, Hayes and his backup singers sing or speak for only thirty-five seconds.

On the subject of movie music, Richard says he and Karen turned down offers to record love themes from both *Love Story* and *The Godfather*. He notes that neither was right for Karen or the Carpenters, "especially because the lyrics for both were dreadfully corny." Andy Williams recorded both, climbing the Hot 100 to No. 9 with "(Where Do I Begin?) Love Story" and to No. 34 with "Speak Softly Love (Love Theme from *The Godfather*)."

After "Bless the Beasts and Children," the Carpenters never recorded another song for a feature film, and they never returned to the Oscars. "Don't know why," Richard says. "It's just that the right song never came along."

Movie poster, 1971

Page 81: Attendee program for 1972 Oscars

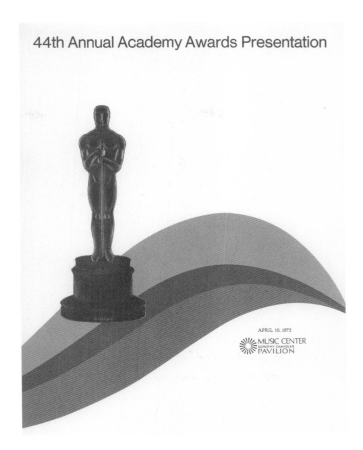

44th Annual Academy Awards Presentation

APRIL 10, 1972

MUSIC CENTER
DOROTHY CHANDLER
PAVILION

"LIGHTS, CAMERA, ACTION"

Starring JOEL GREY

Written by BILLY BARNES

Choreography by RON FIELD

* * *

The Performers

JOHNNY MATHIS — "Life Is What You Make It"

DEBBIE REYNOLDS — "The Age Of Not Believing"

CHARLEY PRIDE
HENRY MANCINI
and
THE MITCHELL BOYS CHOIR —
"All His Children"

ISAAC HAYES — "Theme From Shaft"
Choreography by RON FIELD

CARPENTERS — "Bless The Beasts & Children"

Best Scoring [Adaptation and Original Song Score]

(For which the composer, lyricist and the adapter shall be eligible if the song score was written for or first used in an eligible motion picture, but only the adapter shall be eligible if the material, song score or otherwise, is an adaptation from another medium or has been previously used)

BEDKNOBS AND BROOMSTICKS, Walt Disney Productions, Buena Vista Distribution Company.
Song Score by Richard M. Sherman and Robert B. Sherman.
Adapted by Irwin Kostal.

THE BOY FRIEND, A Russflix, Ltd. Production, Metro-Goldwyn-Mayer.
Adapted by Peter Maxwell Davies and Peter Greenwell.

FIDDLER ON THE ROOF, Mirisch-Cartier Productions, United Artists.
Adapted by John Williams.

TCHAIKOVSKY, A Dimitri Tiomkin-Mosfilm Studios Production.
Adapted by Dimitri Tiomkin.

WILLY WONKA AND THE CHOCOLATE FACTORY, A Wolper Pictures, Ltd. Production, Paramount.
Song Score by Leslie Bricusse and Anthony Newley.
Adapted by Walter Scharf.

Best Achievement in Film Editing

THE ANDROMEDA STRAIN, A Universal-Robert Wise Production, Universal.
Stuart Gilmore and John W. Holmes.

A CLOCKWORK ORANGE, A Hawks Films, Ltd. Production, Warner Bros.
Bill Butler.

THE FRENCH CONNECTION, D'Antoni Productions, 20th Century-Fox.
Jerry Greenberg.

KOTCH, A Kotch Company Production, ABC Pictures Presentation, Cinerama.
Ralph E. Winters.

SUMMER OF '42, A Robert Mulligan-Richard Alan Roth Production, Warner Bros.
Folmar Blangsted.

Best Song [Original for the Picture]

THE AGE OF NOT BELIEVING from "Bedknobs And Broomsticks", Walt Disney Productions, Buena Vista Distribution Company.
Music and lyrics by Richard M. Sherman and Robert B. Sherman.

ALL HIS CHILDREN from "Sometimes A Great Notion", A Universal-Newman-Foreman Company Production, Universal.
Music by Henry Mancini.
Lyrics by Alan and Marilyn Bergman.

BLESS THE BEASTS & CHILDREN from "Bless The Beasts & Children", Columbia.
Music and lyrics by Barry DeVorzon and Perry Botkin, Jr.

LIFE IS WHAT YOU MAKE IT from "Kotch", A Kotch Company Production, ABC Pictures Presentation, Cinerama.
Music by Marvin Hamlisch.
Lyrics by Johnny Mercer.

THEME FROM SHAFT from "Shaft", Shaft Productions, Ltd., Metro-Goldwyn-Mayer.
Music and lyrics by Isaac Hayes.

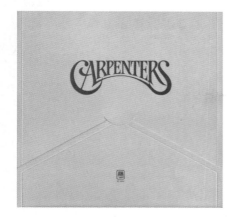

Album
Carpenters
[The Tan Album]
"There wasn't nearly enough time."

Album
Carpenters

—

US release date
5/14/73

—

Billboard **Top LPs**

Chart entry date (position)
6/5/71 (No. 15)

Peak date, position (weeks at peak)
7/3/71, No. 2 (2)

Total weeks on chart
59

Year-end chart ranking
No. 3 (1971), No. 43 (1972)

After all that went into recording and supporting two albums and six singles between April 1969 and January 1971, the Carpenters needed a break. But no luck. The duo was under pressure to deliver a third album. This would become the self-titled *Carpenters*—soon dubbed The Tan Album for its simple cover design: the Carpenters logo against a tan backdrop.

"There wasn't nearly enough time to do my job," Richard says, explaining management had underestimated the importance of recording to the Carpenters' career. The Carpenters' producer understandably delegated his song-selection duties to Richard, whose track record at picking hits was impressive. In just seven months, between May 1970 and January 1971, the Carpenters had struck gold four times in a row, with "(They Long to Be) Close to You," the *Close to You* album, "We've Only Just Begun," and "For All We Know."

The problem was that the Carpenters were already overwhelmed with touring and TV appearances. As Richard thumbs through the Carpenters' two itineraries, it's exhausting just listening to him run down their concert-tour and TV-appearance schedule from mid-October through the end of November.

Start with twenty days of back-to-back gigs without a break: eleven days opening for Engelbert Humperdinck in Toronto, then a show in Ottawa, a week playing Chicago, and a stop in Sioux Falls, South Dakota. During a brief return home to Los Angeles, they recorded "Merry Christmas, Darling." Next stop, Tokyo, with a schedule including a twenty-minute performance at a music festival, press interviews, and appearances on a number of pop-music TV shows.

To return to L.A. they had to make a connection in Hawai'i, so management seized the opportunity to book the Carpenters for three nights in Honolulu. They spent the Thanksgiving holiday traveling across the country. November wrapped with shows in Montgomery and Birmingham, Alabama, and, finally, Murray, Kentucky. "And *then* I'm supposed to come up with an album—hopefully one with hits."

On the Album

Richard says he had to scramble to find most of the songs for The Tan Album. "I was running out of luck"—no more unexpected finds such as "We've Only Just Begun" in a bank commercial and "For All We Know" in a movie. Fortunately, there were a couple of new gems awaiting the Carpenters in the stack of demos at A&M, both from "We've Only Just Begun" composers Paul Williams and Roger Nichols. Richard also dug

Left: Portrait inside the packaging of *Carpenters* [The Tan Album], 1971

up one of the last remaining jewels he had co-written back in the day with John Bettis. "Candy" was inspired by a waitress at Disneyland's Coke Corner. She had caught the eye of both Richard and John when they worked together at Disneyland in 1967. For The Tan Album, the lyrics were rewritten and the song retitled "One Love." The song was reworked into a sweet piece of ear candy, replete with dulcet strings, sweeping harp, and sumptuous vocal harmonies.

Richard took the lead on two other Carpenter-Bettis collaborations, the sprightly, slickly produced "Saturday," also written in 1967, as well as their newly composed "Druscilla Penny." (See sidebar: "From Pokey to 'Penny,'" page 88.)

The only Tan Album track that really—and, he stresses, "*really*"—rankles Richard is the "Bacharach/David Medley." The medley's classic songs, by composers Burt Bacharach and Hal David, aren't the issue for Richard. His problem is that the medley is played too fast. He explains that after countless times performing the piece on TV and being told by show producers, "It needs to be tighter," the Carpenters instinctively picked up the pace during recording. "And we zoomed through it."

The album concludes with the ballad "Sometimes." It was the result of famed composer Henry Mancini ("Moon River") putting music to a touching Christmas-card message from his daughter Felice, who was unable to be home for the holiday. Richard and Karen were impressed when the legendary Grammy-, Emmy-, and Oscar-winning Mancini personally came to see them on the A&M lot and played the demo for them. "I thought it would be the perfect way to close the album," Richard recalls.

When all was said and done, *Carpenters* logged in at just thirty-one minutes, making it the duo's shortest studio album. There would have been more on it, but Richard and Karen had to call it a wrap. They were scheduled to begin a three-week gig opening for comic Don Adams in Las Vegas on March 18. And the album still wasn't completed.

Between shows at the Sands, Richard was sequencing the album's tracks when manager Sherwin Bash dropped by with a major-label record executive. "Sherwin happened to be there for a little bit," says Richard, "and I was going back and forth between 'Rainy Days and Mondays' and 'Superstar,' which I thought were both singles. 'Which would come first?' And Sherwin says, 'Here's this big label guy, play 'em for him,' which we did. And the guy says, 'Well, to be honest, I don't think either one of them is a single.'"

Both "Rainy Days" and "Superstar" ended up peaking at No. 2 on the *Billboard* Hot 100 and were certified Gold. Reflecting on the encounter with the exec from the other label, Richard says, "I'm sure glad Karen and I were with A&M."

Richard's Take

In terms of chart performance, sales, number of Gold singles, and awards, The Tan Album is one of the Carpenters' most successful albums. Artistically, "I think it's the best we could have done given the time we had to make it," Richard says.

He's no doubt proud of the album's hits, all Carpenters classics: "For All We Know," "Rainy Days and Mondays," and "Superstar." And he speaks fondly of a few of the album tracks, notably "Let Me Be the One," "One Love," and "Saturday."

"We got the Grammy for best vocal performance and were nominated for album of the year. (Richard himself was nominated for his

**Single
"Rainy Days and Mondays"**

—

US release date
4/23/71

—

Billboard Hot 100

Chart entry date (position)
5/15/71 (No. 46)

Peak date, position (weeks at peak)
6/19/71, No. 2 (3)

Total weeks on chart
12

Year-end chart rank
No. 38

—

Billboard Top 40 Easy Listening

Peak date, position (weeks at peak)
5/29/71, No. 1 (4)

Total weeks on chart
12

Year-end chart rank
No. 4

Trade ad for
"Rainy Days and
Mondays"

arrangement of "Superstar" and Ray Gerhardt and Dick Bogert for engineering.) So, I think, for most people, most Carpenters fans, they liked it just fine. The whole album served its purpose: for us, for the label, for fans. But I knew it could have been better."

On the US Charts

The Tan Album entered the Top LPs *Billboard* chart dated June 5, 1971, at No. 15. On July 3, the album reached its peak of No. 2, where it remained for two consecutive weeks—kept from the top spot by Carole King's *Tapestry*. The Tan Album spent a total of 59 weeks on the survey. Only the Carpenters' *Close to You* (87 weeks) and *Christmas Portrait* (55 weeks) have had longer *Billboard* album-chart runs.

Carpenters: Rainy Days And Mondays.

Relax. And let your mind play-back all of the Carpenters great hits: "Close to You," "We've Only Just Begun," "For All We Know"... Select the best ingredients from their past performances, add a dynamic dash of something new, roll them all into one, and you'll have some idea of the fluid grace that is "Rainy Days and Mondays." That's the name of Karen and Richard's new single-it's warm, introspective, essential. It's Carpenters. Haunting lyric, flowing musical arrangement, and the intangible spirit that makes their songs Music for All Seasons. "Rainy Days and Mondays" is a song you're going to remember for a long time. **And that's the truth. AM 1260**

Produced by Jack Daugherty
A&M Records and Tapes

Single
"Superstar"

—

US release date
8/12/71

—

Billboard Hot 100

Chart entry date (position)
9/4/71 (No. 49)

Peak date, position (weeks at peak)
10/16/71, No. 2 (2)

Total weeks on chart
13

Year-end chart rank
No. 30

—

Billboard Top 40 Easy Listening

Peak date, position (weeks at peak)
10/9/71, No. 1 (2)

Total weeks on chart
13

Year-end chart rank
No. 7

Page 87: Trade ad
for "Superstar"

The Singles

Arriving three weeks before the album, "Rainy Days and Mondays" set the stage for the release of The Tan Album on May 14, 1971.

Like "We've Only Just Begun," it was a ballad from songwriters Roger Nichols and Paul Williams. But this time, Richard didn't need to glean it from a bank commercial. He got this old-fashioned love song the old-fashioned way.

"It was a demo of Roger and Paul's, and was on a ten-inch acetate," Richard recalls. "I listened and it didn't grab me at first. But I liked the hook. So I played it one more time and I thought, 'This will work for us.' So that's one of those things where I pictured the finished record immediately."

The ballad sounds tailor-made for the Carpenters, but Richard acknowledges, "That was not written for us, by the way. A lot of people, including Karen and me, thought it was, but it wasn't. It was written for somebody else who didn't do it. The one that was written for us was 'An Old Fashioned Love Song,' which I didn't care for."

No doubt, "Rainy Days" was a better fit for the Carpenters. Karen was just about to turn twenty-one when she recorded the vocal:

Talkin' to myself and feeling old
Sometimes I'd like to quit
Nothing ever seems to fit

"Karen sounds like a singer who's actually lived a long life," Richard says. "She interprets it like she was born to do it, which, in a way, she was. We were both old souls. But, you know, there's something with Karen. It's not just the pitch and everything else being right. But to pull off a song like that, sing it like she really experienced it—when Mondays didn't get her down at all—it's phenomenal."

Richard first heard "Superstar" in early 1971. At the time, he and Karen were still living with their parents in Downey, California—in the Newville Avenue house that was featured on the *Now & Then* album cover.

"For whatever reason, we were home early—relatively early, studio-wise—to see the *Tonight Show*," Richard says, adding one of the night's musical guests was Bette Midler. "She was discovered by host Johnny Carson, and he was a big fan. So, it wasn't the first time I'd seen her."

"Bette introduced the song, something like, 'It's a modern-day torch song,'" Richard continues. "She must've said 'Superstar,' because the title is nowhere in the song. I think she just sang it with a pianist. And I heard it and I thought that, with the right arrangement, this song was a hit."

"Superstar" had been kicking around for a while. Co-written by Leon Russell and Bonnie Bramlett, the ballad portrays a woman who has an encounter with a touring rock guitarist, then awaits his return. Bramlett recorded the song with her duo Delaney & Bonnie. They released it with the title "Groupie (Superstar)" as the B-side of the single "Comin' Home" in December 1969.

Richard quickly came up with an arrangement that is lavish and complex, yet kept the intimacy of Midler's acoustic "torch song" treatment. His arrangement earned a Grammy nomination.

"It just kind of arranged itself," he humbly notes.

While the song was never sexually explicit, its subject matter was as close as any Carpenters tune had come to sexual content. As per

Superstar
AM-1289

A&M Records and Tapes
Produced by Jack Daugherty

Richard, "Karen was indeed a bit tentative about 'Superstar' but agreed to give it a go at my urging. She quickly changed her mind, of course."

Still, Richard felt the need to slightly revise Bramlett's original lyrics from "and I can hardly wait to 'sleep' with you again" to "and I can hardly wait to 'be' with you again."

"It's not like Herb [Alpert] or Jerry [Moss] or anybody said anything," Richard explains. "I just thought this may cause a little too much stink, given our image and all."

"I think it's a great song, one of my best arrangements, nominated for a Grammy, and a perfect song for the two of us," he continues, "not only Karen's lead, but our background vocals, the 'Ooh babies.' It was just a glorious sound and gave me chills."

"Superstar" later went on to be revered by a new generation of rock artists. Richard says that during the production of the 1994 album *If I Were a Carpenter*, in which fifteen alt-rock stars paid homage to their favorite Carpenters songs, "everyone wanted to do 'Superstar,' which didn't surprise me in the least." (The track was ultimately recorded by Sonic Youth.)

Page 89: Karen during filming of the "Superstar" promo at the Desert Inn, Las Vegas, NV, April 6, 1971

From the Pokey to "Penny"

The Tan Album track "Druscilla Penny," a cheeky two-minute ditty about a groupie and her life of "instant love," was originally a song about a real-life cop who arrested Richard following a gig in Miami.

"I'd met a girl, and we headed out to wherever we were heading," Richard recalls. "I was driving an Impala convertible with the top down. I hang a right on a red. You didn't do that in Florida. I didn't know that."

But that apparently wasn't Richard's only offense.

"I had the long hair, and he didn't like that. So he arrested me and threw me in a cell–*threw me in a cell!*"

Unfortunately, Richard wouldn't be lodging alone that night.

"They arrested some other guy who was a real thug. I mean, a strong, nasty guy. Then they pitched him in the cell and he proceeded to beat the shit out of me—with the other cops watching."

When Richard asked for his one phone call, he was told, "Later." Then the officer asked to see Richard's AAA card. "It's phony," the cop said.

The harassment continued until the sun came up, when Richard was finally released, his date still sitting in the waiting room.

Richard and lyricist John Bettis wrote a snarky song about a redneck cop as an ode to his captor.

Bettis had named the officer in the original title and lyrics. Richard says manager Sherwin Bash didn't think a song about contempt for a cop was such a smart idea at the time. This was in the wake of a recent rash of violent police–protester clashes, including the Kent State shootings.

So, the lyrics were rewritten as a tongue-in-cheek teardown of a groupie inspired, in name only, by an acquaintance of Bettis. Now, instead of the protagonist being a rogue cop, it's a roguish girl with a penchant for musicians.

Druscilla Penny what a girl
Where's the purpose to the crazy
life you lead
It doesn't matter after all you're so sure
that instant love is all you need

The real Druscilla Penny's reaction to the honor?

"From what Bettis told me," Richard says, "I don't think it was good."

The Logo

"Karen and I were just blown away."

The Carpenters' logo has represented the duo's brand since it debuted on May 14, 1971. That's the day it appeared on the cover of *Carpenters*, known by fans and Richard and Karen alike as *The Tan Album*. The cover could not have been more spot-on. Its only image is the logo—a stylized treatment of the name "Carpenters"—printed in brown on a cream-colored board stock.

Richard says he and Karen were not consulted on the design. "But when they first showed us the Carpenters logo, Karen and I were just blown away," he says. "And then we wanted to put it on everything we did." Since then, that logo has appeared on hundreds of Carpenters-branded items. And, of course, it has served as the nameplate for nearly all of the duo's authorized albums and singles.

In truth, the logo was never intended to be a logo. It was merely The Tan Album's title treatment, the work of Grammy-winning media-design legend Craig Braun and his team.

Braun recalls getting a sneak preview of the upcoming Carpenters album before starting work on the cover, and he liked what he heard. "It made an immediate impact," he says. "Richard and Karen brought back melody and romance, and the feeling that goes with it."

The music inspired Braun to reach back to the past—to the early part of the twentieth century, when family photos were commonly presented in cardboard folder folding frames and placed on pianos or mantles. He applied that concept to The Tan Album package and designed top and bottom panels that folded apart to reveal a portrait of Richard and Karen. (That soft-focus portrait is no favorite of Richard; it's among many shots with Karen he has called "awkward.") The panels could be folded back and attached together at the bottom, creating a freestanding frame for the picture.

For the title-treatment-turned-logo, "I was aiming for vintage typefaces that would be appropriate for the jacket concept," Braun says. "Therefore, the type should have serifs, which are more classical in style."

Illustrator Walter Velez reworked the typeface, taking a number of attempts to nail Braun's vision. "It's symmetrical," Braun explains. "It evokes two people, two sides. And it's kind of a bridge, one to the other."

For all of the eventual logo love, the treatment was initially destined for buyers' trash bins—literally. Braun first planned to print the title on a transparent sticker attached to the shrink-wrap protecting the album. The shrink-wrap would have to be torn apart to get to the record inside—likely destroying the sticker as well.

Fortunately, A&M's art department was so impressed with the logo that they convinced Braun to move it to a permanent location—on the album cover itself. The logo was also upgraded by printing it in embossed (raised) type on The Tan Album's initial pressings.

Braun's costly photo-album cover design with the embossed version of the logo was used only for releases of The Tan Album in the United States and Canada. In most other countries, the logo and inside portrait of the Carpenters were placed together on the front of a conventional album cover.

Page 91, top: Patch, key chain, and belt buckle with Carpenters logo

One Designer, Two Logo Legacies

At the time Craig Braun was working on The Tan Album, his company had another assignment for a major album: The Rolling Stones' *Sticky Fingers*. The package featured a closeup photo of a man's crotch and a working zipper that could be opened to reveal cotton briefs.

Sticky Fingers' inner sleeve marked the debut of the Stones' iconic "tongue and lips" logo, which was commissioned from British art designer John Pasche. Braun says that Pasche missed his deadline for the image to make the album's US release. So Braun and illustrator Walter Velez were left scrambling to come up with their own version of "tongue and lips" based on a blurry fax of a Pasche pencil sketch. Braun's version is the one the Stones continue to use today.

Which brings Braun back to the Carpenters. He says, "I think it's extraordinary that these two acts, completely different from each other, have this tie that binds them, this same trajectory."

Left, above: Craig Braun, whose design firm worked on packages for both The Tan Album and The Rolling Stones' *Sticky Fingers* at the same time

**Keychain and watch
featuring the
Carpenters logo**

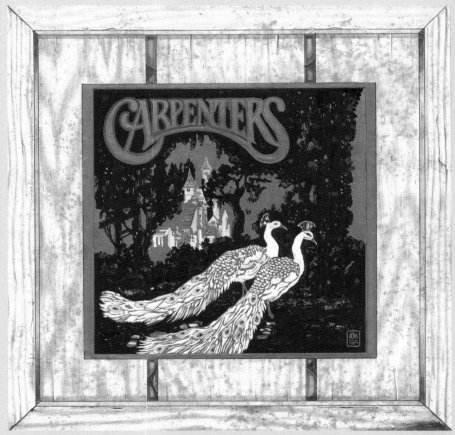

Craig Braun's team designed these prototypes for "shelf talkers"—crates to display The Tan Album at record store cash registers. A&M passed on the idea.

A SONG FOR YOU

Album
A Song for You

—

US release date
6/13/72

—

***Billboard* Top LPs and Tape**

Chart entry date (position)
7/8/72 (No. 31)

Peak date, position (weeks at peak)
8/12/72, No. 4 (3)

Total weeks on chart
41

Year-end chart rank
No. 78

Album
A Song for You

"The best."

After the mad dash of producing *Carpenters* [The Tan Album], Richard was determined to make A&M management understand that he wanted less time on the road and more in the studio to write and find songs and to record with Karen. In fact, Richard says the Carpenters didn't even *need* to tour by this point for promotion, as the records were already selling. And touring surely wasn't for the money, because getting the Carpenters' show on the road was a big-budget affair. Richard cites costs including the highly trained and versatile musicians that backed the duo, a road manager, roadies, a lighting director, as well as equipment rentals. "By 1974, we were told by our financial manager we needed to play 142 shows a year just to break even."

Conversely, the Carpenters' studio recordings were far better investments. The early albums were making money right off the bat. They, not concerts, were more important in the big picture, as they laid the foundation for the Carpenters' long-term career and their musical legacy.

Richard recalls that as the duo prepared to dive into their fourth studio album, *A Song for You*, he requested that the upcoming tour be trimmed to devote more time to the album. "I made the point as much as I could without a confrontation."

Left: Inner-sleeve portrait for *A Song for You*, 1971

Right: In A&M Studio B, Los Angeles, 1972

Single
"Hurting Each Other"

—

US Release Date
12/23/71

—

***Billboard* Hot 100**

Chart entry date (position)
1/15/72 (No. 76)

Peak date, position (weeks at peak)
2/26/72, No. 2 (2)

Total weeks on chart
12

Year-end chart rank
No. 65

—

***Billboard* Top 40 Easy Listening**

Chart entry date (position)
1/15/72 (31)

Peak date, position (weeks at peak)
2/5/72, No. 1 (2)

Total weeks on chart
13

Year-end chart rank
No. 12

Richard wasted his breath. With their agency and management getting a cut off the top of each booking, it was little surprise that the Carpenters' 1972 concert schedule had even more dates than 1971. And yet Richard and Karen still pulled off *A Song for You*, which Richard ranks as "the best" of the Carpenters' albums.

And no wonder, as it's a beautifully conceived album, with a start-to-finish arc, crammed with hits and some of the Carpenters' all-time favorite album tracks.

There are many reasons why Richard and Karen were able to make it happen. In this case, time was on their side—a bit. In hindsight, it appears that even a little more time seemed to make a big difference.

The thirteen months between the release of *A Song for You* and its predecessor were the Carpenters' longest gap yet. So was their seven-month start-to-finish stretch in the studio (which doesn't include a week in April 1971 when they banged out "Bless the Beasts and Children").

Now, to be perfectly clear, during this period—which should have been devoted to making the new record—the Carpenters still had to live up to concert commitments. So they were on a crazy stop-and-go cycle. They'd record, then they'd stop to get the show on the road, then return to Los Angeles and the studio, only to have to stop to return to the road again.

July 1972

Karen on stage
at the Ohio State
Fair. Richard says
one of their two nights
(August 26–27, 1971)
attracted more than
50,000 attendees,
the duo's largest
concert audience ever.

On the Album

"A Song for You" first appeared on Leon Russell's 1970 debut album, but Richard didn't hear the tune until a 1971 recording by singer/game-show panelist Jaye P. Morgan. Adopting Russell's rough-and-rugged bluesy style, Morgan's version of the lover's lament was released as a single and bubbled under the *Billboard* Hot 100, peaking at No. 105. "She did a good job with it," Richard says, "and I thought, 'This will work for Karen, for us.'"

Actually, "A Song for You" did more than that. It built on the sublime suburban soul revealed in "Superstar" and proved the Carpenters could handle themselves downtown too. While keeping the production firmly rooted in pop, Richard augmented Karen's soulful vocal with an elegant four-part choral-jazz break and a minimalistic accompaniment—giving Bob Messenger a show-stopping tenor sax solo.

Even the Carpenters' haters at *Rolling Stone* loved the track. Its review called "A Song for You" "the album's best" and "perhaps their finest record to date."

Richard continues, "[Carpenters guitarist] Tony Peluso once said, 'You could wake her in the middle of the night and say, 'Sing 'Superstar!' And she would. But she had something on her larynx for that whole damned album. So, 'A Song for You,' I want to remember, goes to a low D, below middle C, and she does it acceptably. But she doesn't lay it out the way she would have any other time."

In their spare time on tour, Carpenters bandmates Danny Woodhams and Gary Sims composed "Road Ode," which became the Carpenters' version of such tour-weary classics as Bob Seger's "Turn the Page" and Journey's "Faithfully." But for all his talk of concert overload, Richard says Woodhams and Sims weren't speaking for the duo.

"I guess Danny and Gary were getting tired," Richard comments, smiling. "Everybody always thinks everything's autobiographical, that there's some hidden meaning in every single thing you do. But not at this point. We were still having fun out there."

Left: With their director's chairs from *The Carol Burnett Show*, 1972

Page 99: Trade ad for "It's Going to Take Some Time"

Carpenters' last seven singles in a row sold over ten million.

Announcing:

A new single from their forthcoming album, "A Song For You."
On A&M Records
(SP 35111)

On the US Charts

A Song for You entered the *Billboard* Top LPs and Tape chart dated July 8, 1972, at No. 31. On August 12, it reached its peak of No. 4, where it remained for four consecutive weeks. *A Song for You* spent a total 41 weeks on the *Billboard* chart, a run that would be matched by the upcoming *Now & Then*. The Carpenters' *Close to You* (87 weeks), *Carpenters* [The Tan Album] (59 weeks), *Christmas Portrait* (55 weeks), and *The Singles 1969–1973* (49 weeks) had longer *Billboard* chart runs.

The Singles

Ruby & the Romantics seemed poised for a comeback. The group topped the charts in 1963 with "Our Day Will Come." But they hadn't seen the Top 40 in six years when they released "Hurting Each Other" in March 1969.

Richard recalls the record getting some airplay on one of the big Los Angeles radio stations. "I heard it driving home from school and I thought, 'This is going to be a hit.'" On this rare occasion, Richard, who could pick 'em, was wrong about the single—but not about the song.

With US President Richard Nixon at the White House, Washington, D.C., 1972

It's Going To Take Some Time

Single
"It's Going to Take Some Time"

—

US release date
4/13/72

—

***Billboard* Hot 100**

Chart entry date (position)
4/29/72 (No. 79)

Peak date, position (weeks at peak)
6/10/72, No. 12 (2)

Total weeks on chart
10

Year-end chart rank
n/a

—

***Billboard* Top 40 Easy Listening**

Chart entry date (position)
4/29/72 (No. 79)

Peak date, position (weeks at peak)
6/3/72, No. 2 (4)

Total weeks on chart
12

Year-end chart rank
No. 29

"A couple of years later, we were setting up a sound check," he recalls. "I was just playing some chord progressions on the Wurlitzer, and they reminded me of 'Hurting Each Other.' Should have been a hit. So I did my arrangement."

For the Carpenters' version, Richard kept Ruby & the Romantics' Wall of Sound production for the chorus, but he removed their subtle samba beat from the verses. Add those Karen-and-Richard overdubs, and the result was a fresh, new variation on the Carpenters sound—and, at last, massive chart success for the song.

Richard says "Hurting Each Other" is among his favorite of the duo's recordings, with one exception. The problem that plagued Karen's throat throughout *A Song for You* showed itself while they were recording this track.

"It was only one note, G sharp above middle C, and one she normally would have knocked off without any trouble," Richard says, explaining that this bothered Karen enough to see a specialist. "It took several passes to get it right. The song was a bitch anyway—to overdub, as far as the lead [vocal]."

Richard and Karen got a sneak preview of "It's Going to Take Some Time" when Carole King was on the A&M lot recording her *Music* album. And yes, Richard confirms, when King heard the Carpenters' recording she said, "You've made mine sound like a demo!"

"There's not much of a story to it," Richard says. "I did my arrangement." He feels it's a solid album track, and on the album it should have stayed. "I made the mistake of thinking it was a single." The song reached only No. 12 on the *Billboard* Hot 100 and so broke the Carpenters' string of six straight Top 10 Gold-certified hit singles.*

Richard Carpenter shakes his head when given credit for creating the power-pop ballad. He says "Goodbye to Love," which he co-wrote with John Bettis, featured "the first melodic fuzz guitar solo," and that helped solidify the power ballad as a pop-music staple. Then he thinks for a moment and comes up with an example to dispute the claim of being first. He cites Paul McCartney's "Maybe I'm Amazed," which, released on McCartney's solo debut album in February 1970, predates "Goodbye to Love" by more than two years.

Richard's inspiration for the amped-up lament was a 1940 comedy called *Rhythm on the River*. It starred Bing Crosby and Mary Martin as ghost songwriters for a famous composer, played by Basil Rathbone, going through a dry patch. The characters reference Rathbone's greatest hit, called "Goodbye to Love," which is never performed in the movie.

Richard says that the song's title provided inspiration for his opening melody and lyric. "In my mind, I heard just the opening line, 'I'll say goodbye to love. No one ever cared if I should live or die,'" he recalls. "And that's where my lyrics stopped—a little more than usual, but the melody kept going." Collaborator Bettis wrote the remainder of the lyrics, while Richard finished up the music, what he calls "the big choral thing at the end."

In 1971, singer Mark Lindsay was opening for the Carpenters backed by a band called Instant Joy. That group's leader and lead guitarist was Tony Peluso.

Richard remembers, "We'd play a lot of college gymnasiums. Our dressing rooms were the locker facilities downstairs, and I'd come up just to listen to him play the solo in this one song. Each night, it was a little bit different because he improvised, but everything he played was melodic. So, when the idea of the melodic fuzz guitar came along for 'Goodbye to Love,' I wanted to use Tony.

A Song for You

Single
"Goodbye to Love"

—

US release date
6/19/72

—

***Billboard* Hot 100**

Chart entry date (position)
7/15/72 (No. 68)

Peak date, position (weeks at peak)
8/26/72, No. 7 (2)

Total weeks on chart
10

Year-end chart rank
n/a

—

***Billboard* Top 40 Easy Listening**

Chart entry date (position)
7/22/72 (No. 33)

Peak date, position (weeks at peak)
9/9/72, No. 2 (1)

Total weeks on chart
11

Year-end chart rank
No. 44

"We came into Studio B," Richard continues. "He was already out in the studio with this Big Muff [fuzz box] and this little amplifier. We'd forgotten just how thin Tony was, and how long his hair was. We called him, 'The Bone.' 'Tony the Bone.' And he said, 'Now, I don't read music.' I said, 'You don't have to read music. We're the Carpenters!'"

Richard says he played Peluso the track and told him, "'I'll sing you the melody until you're comfortable with it. And then I'll show you where I want you to improvise.' So he did it, he played the melody. He went into the improvisation and knocked most of it off in the first take." But Richard felt Tony could do better near the end of the song, just before the fade-out. "So we did one more take," he recalls. "That did it."

The two takes were spliced together. Tony's fuzz guitar provided an unexpected counterpoint to the glorious chorus of "ahs" sung by a slightly inebriated Karen and Richard, who had been to dinner and knocked back a few glasses of wine in preparation for the big chore ahead.

The result was the first Carpenters original to become a global smash. The single performed solidly in the United States, reaching No. 7 on the Top 40 charts in *Cash Box* and *Billboard*, and No. 6 in *Record World*. Good, but not certified Gold, which was a disappointment. However, the single was a smash in Canada (No. 4) and New Zealand (No. 2), and most importantly, it got the Carpenters back in the Top 10 in the United Kingdom (No. 9) for the first time in two years since their debut with "(They Long to Be) Close to You."

"All I knew is the hunch worked," Richard says. "I felt Tony, rather than an established studio musician, was the guy for this solo, and he was. And then, of course, we asked him to join the group."

Richard says that reports of a fan backlash to Peluso's guitar break have been greatly exaggerated. "A few Carpenters fans felt we had sold out and gone hard rock," he says. "But a majority of folks loved it."

Left: 1972

Page 103: Trade ad for "Goodbye to Love"

CARPENTERS

GOODBYE TO LOVE

And hello to Carpenters' ninth single. AM 1367.
(Their last eight in a row have now sold over eleven million.)
From "A Song For You" (SP 3511). Produced by Jack Daugherty.

Album
Now & Then

The oldies medley "wasn't just about the music and the records. It was the love of Top 40 radio."

Album
Now & Then

—

US release date
5/1/73

—

***Billboard* Top LPs**

Chart entry date (position)
6/22/73 (No. 81)

Peak date, position (weeks at peak)
7/21/73, No. 2 (1)

Total weeks on chart
41

Year-end chart rank
No. 51

Left: A&M's art department hides its best-selling act behind the closed windows of Richard's 1972 Ferrari "Daytona." Outtake from the cover shoot for *Now & Then*, Downey, CA, March 1973

Pages 106-107: Karen laughs at a frustrated Richard in this outtake from the cover shoot for *Now & Then*, Downey, CA, 1973

When it came time for the Carpenters to deliver 1973's new album, it was yesterday once more, one last time. Just as in 1971 with *Carpenters* [The Tan Album] and 1972 with *A Song for You*, in 1973 the Carpenters were scheduled for too many concerts, and there was not enough time for Richard to compose and compile material for the next album.

But Karen and Richard appeared to be managing the work overload just fine.

With approximately three million sales in the US alone, *A Song for You* had fallen about a million short of its predecessor. But the album earned the Carpenters some of their best reviews, and the set proved to be a hit machine that kept on delivering singles longer than anyone had dreamed.

The Carpenters' 1972 concert schedule was crammed: 174 shows. But Richard says he and Karen were still enjoying performing live. And a look at a video recorded during a rehearsal for the summer 1972 tour bears this out. Richard, in particular, appears to be having fun collaborating with the band on an extended medley of rock-era classics that would serve as the updated concert's cornerstone.

Revisiting rock-era classics was a relatively new thing. Oldies-revival group Sha Na Na was formed in 1969, and the first performance of *Grease* was in February 1971. Later that year, KOOL-FM in Phoenix, Arizona, became the first so-called oldies radio station in the US, programming Top 40 hits from the mid-1950s through the 1960s. Following its ratings success, dozens of other stations across North America adopted the format.

Like those stations, the Carpenters' oldies sets included favorites from the 1960s. But Richard was unafraid to dig farther back to rock's roots. The duo's stage show included covers of such early rock-era favorites as The Crew Cuts' "Sh-Boom" (1954), The Monotones' "The Book of Love" (1958), and Chuck Berry's "Johnny B. Goode" (1958).

All those hours that Richard and Karen listened to 45s in their New Haven basement seemed to have led to this period. For the Carpenters, these would prove to be brighter days of years gone by.

The days were so good, in fact, that not even Richard's nasty early 1973 motorcycle crash could keep him down for long. With his left wrist in a cast, he forged ahead. The Carpenters fulfilled management's continuing demands to perform a calendar-filling number of live shows, promotional appearances, and television programs.

In between all those commitments, they were supposed to squeeze out a new album. This one would be titled *Now & Then*.

On the Album

"This Masquerade" marked the Carpenters' third dip into the well of tunes by singer-songwriter Leon Russell. Russell had debuted the song on his highest-charting album, 1972's experimental *Carny*. And it was no surprise that Richard jumped at the opportunity. Russell's "Superstar" and "A Song for You" had provided what numerous critics praised as the highlights of the Carpenters' previous two albums.

"This Masquerade" followed suit. "I had heard that it was *written* for us," Richard recalls. "That could be a lot of baloney. But it actually *sounds* like it was. I mean, that's a perfect song for the two of us."

Indeed, Russell's dark, smooth saga of romantic gamesters sounds tailor-made for Karen's cool contralto. But Richard is even more impressed with his sister's creative drumming on the track.

"This Masquerade" also provides a platform for some of Richard's finest piano work. It teases the listener in the intro, then delivers big time during an improvised-jazz break so smooth, nimble, and artful that Richard's contemporaries still wonder how he did it. That solo continues with Karen and Richard's trademark four-part harmonies cushioning a clever flute solo courtesy of Bob Messenger.

"I knew the damned song was hit material," Richard says, adding the only reason the track was never released as a single was its length: over four minutes, verboten in the world of Top 40 radio. And Richard just didn't have the heart to chop the recording down.

(Three years later, George Benson scored hugely with his 1976 single of "This Masquerade," winning the Grammy for Record of the Year and

Below: Reflecting on the cover shoot for *Now & Then*, Richard says, "It was as if A&M completely forgot we were even releasing an album."

In a pinch, the most creative concept the art department could muster was shooting Richard and Karen in front of their own home. (!) All that's missing is Karen holding a "sold" sign. Enough said, this pic didn't make the cut.

Using his 1972 Ferrari "Daytona" as a prop was Richard's idea. And although Richard still isn't keen on the resulting photos, the shot that ended up on the outside of the tri-fold album package is a favorite of many album-art critics and Carpenters fans.

As for the so-called "overpainted" photos of the duo inside the album? (See the "Yesterday Once More" picture sleeve, page 111.) Well, in this case, two pictures say two-thousand words—none of them suitable for family audiences.

Page 109: Karen rehearses at home, 1973

reaching No. 10 on the US *Billboard* Hot 100. But Benson had to take a hatchet to his brilliant eight-minute-plus album version to get pop-radio play. His single ran just 3:17.)

In addition to "Masquerade," Richard had a few other things in his back pocket to fill *Now & Then*. "Sing," detailed later in the singles section of this story, had been released as a 45 in January 1973. It was a top-five, Gold-certified smash and needed a studio-album home. Also in the can were the fixings for the Carpenters' cover the 1950s country and pop smash "Jambalaya (On the Bayou)," which Karen and Richard would need to complete. They'd recorded a rhythm track—piano, bass guitar, drums—for the song in 1972, but everything else was still needed.

Otherwise, however, Richard had nothing for the new album. "I was in big trouble," he says, "because we were scheduled to be back on the road." So, just as he padded The Tan Album's second side with a concert favorite, the "Bacharach/David Medley," Richard brought the Carpenters' *latest* road-show highlight—the oldies medley—into the studio.

However, he gave this stage-to-studio adaptation far greater thought. Richard wanted the album version of the medley to recreate the experience he and Karen had listening to those oldies when they were first released.

"It wasn't just about the music and the records," he says. "It was the love of Top 40 radio and fast-talking jocks and the contests." It happened that the Carpenters' guitarist Tony Peluso could do a big-bopping deejay voice and was more than game to play the role with the band. The hilarious laugh-filled outtakes (especially Peluso's numerous goof ups during the radio contest) prove what a ball everyone had as he recorded the medley's interstitials.

While some of the tunes from the concerts were included on *Now & Then*, Richard deconstructed the live version for the album, seizing opportunities provided by the studio that weren't available on the stage. Richard cut favorites from the concerts and replaced them with other oldies to give the album an artistic flow and arc. Then he and Karen went to town with the vocal multitracking: the heavenly choir of Karen's opening for "Johnny Angel" is a prime example.

Well-planned as the medley was, one of its highlights was a last-minute addition: a rollicking adaption of The Chiffons' 1963 hit "One Fine Day." "It turned out that the medley wasn't quite long enough, and it needed an ending, Richard says. "And it turned out to be something. Karen did all those *shoobie-doobie-doobie-doobie-doo-wop-wop*s, we overdubbed them, and it turned out to be in the same key as 'Yesterday Once More,'" a reprise of which concludes the album.

On the US Charts

Now & Then entered the *Billboard* Top LPs chart on June 22, 1973 at No. 81 and reached its chart peak of No. 2 on July 21 for one week, held out of the top spot by George Harrison's *Living in the Material World*. *Now & Then* enjoyed a total 41 weeks on *Billboard*, matching the run of *A Song for You*.

Single
"Yesterday Once More"

—

US release date
5/16/73

—

***Billboard* Hot 100**

Chart entry date (position)
6/2/73 (No. 79)

Peak date, position (weeks at peak)
7/28/73, No. 2 (1)

Total weeks on chart
14

Year-end chart rank
No. 70

—

***Billboard* Top 50 Easy Listening**

Chart entry date (position)
6/23/73 (No. 79)

Peak date, position (weeks at peak)
7/7/73, No. 1 (3)

Total weeks on chart
16

Year-end chart rank
No. 10

1973

The Singles

Only one Richard Carpenter–John Bettis original appears on *Now & Then*, but this one—"Yesterday Once More"—was enough. Richard felt the oldies medley "couldn't start with an oldie," he says. "It had to be a new song that set it up."

Richard recalls that he was driving to the studio and "heard" the melody for the song's *Every Sha-la-la-la* chorus in his head. "I pictured the hook first, of course, and then was worried I wasn't going to get a verse as strong. But it all came pretty easily."

By the time he pulled into the A&M lot, Richard also came up with the song's opening lines:

> *When I was young*
> *I'd listen to the radio*
> *Waiting for my favorite songs*
> *When they played I'd sing along*
> *It made me smile*

Single
"Sing"

—

Billboard Hot 100

Chart entry date (position)
2/24/73 (No. 61)

Peak date, position (weeks at peak)
4/21/73, No. 3 (2)

Total weeks on chart
14

Year-end chart rank
No. 59

—

Billboard Top 40 Easy Listening

Chart entry date (position)
2/24/73 (37)

Peak date, position (weeks at peak)
3/31/73, No. 1 (2)

Weeks on chart
12

Year-end chart rank
No. 6

Page 113:
Promoting *Now
& Then* at the
Sahara Tahoe,
Lake Tahoe, 1973

Richard's writing partner Bettis then ran with it. Just as he did with the opening and closing tracks for *A Song for You*, Richard decided to wrap the oldies medley with a brief atmospheric reprise of "Yesterday Once More." This was a nod to the fleeting nature of time and how this new song would, itself, soon be an oldie and be part of the soundtrack of these good old days.

The new song and the old favorites were perfect, and perfectly timed.

Just two weeks after "Yesterday Once More" reached its American-chart peak in July 1973, Universal Pictures released *American Graffiti*, director George Lucas's 1962 period drama about high school friends spending one last summer together. The film became a phenomenon, grossing a then-strapping $100 million worldwide and earning an Academy Award nomination for best picture.

Richard says he was unaware that the film was released so close to *his* rock 'n' roll period piece, and he didn't know whether it boosted *Now & Then*'s sales. But, clearly, the Carpenters had tapped into the pop-culture zeitgeist. In fact, given both "Yesterday Once More" and *American Graffiti* offered bittersweet takes on nostalgia, the song could have easily served as the main-title tune for Lucas's movie.

"Yesterday Once More" became the Carpenters' second-biggest hit worldwide and their biggest hit in Japan. Richard says the Carpenters' Japanese concert promoter Tatsuji "Tats" Nagashima dubbed the tune, "The 'Stardust' of Japan," referring to Hoagy Carmichael's 1927 ballad, which became one of the most-covered songs of the twentieth century.

The Joe Raposo tune "Sing" was introduced on the children's television program *Sesame Street* in 1971 and was frequently performed by the show's cast and characters. Barbra Streisand sensed it was a hit and released her version as a single in 1972, but it reached only No. 92 on the *Billboard* Hot 100.

Richard says he and Karen never heard the song until it was performed on an early 1973 television special "Robert Young with the Young," where they were guests.

"Sing" reminded Richard of a song from Rodgers and Hammerstein's musical *The King and I*, which he had seen with his parents when the film was released in 1956. "The teacher-student singalong 'Getting to Know You' just had an effect on me," he says. "So I'd heard of The Jimmy Joyce Children's Choir and got them into Studio B. It was all written out, but they weren't that good. We went over it a few times and realized it wasn't going to work. We overdubbed, thanked them and Jimmy, and then sent Karen out. She sang in her upper voice, like a kid, and we doubled it."

For an artist so concerned about a too-wholesome image, releasing "Sing" as a single on the heels of the rocking "Goodbye to Love" seemed a curious move at the time. But Richard says he doesn't feel it made any difference, and he doesn't at all regret his decision.

"A&M, of course, was having a fit about our releasing 'Sing,' but I knew it would be a hit, and that it was one of my stronger arrangements."

The label eventually gave in, and Richard was proved right. The single was a chart smash, certified Gold, and the recording earned two Grammy nominations.

Single
Jambalaya (On the Bayou)

International release date: Fall 1973

The Carpenters were thinking "album track" when recording "Jambalaya (On the Bayou)" for *Now & Then*. A country chart topper for composer Hank Williams and a pop smash for singer Jo Stafford in 1952, the tune turned out to be a favorite of the Carpenters' concert audiences, and A&M, fulfilling radio-programmer demand, agreed to release the track as a single internationally in 1973. It did well in Japan, reaching No. 28 on the charts, but scored even higher in Belgium and New Zealand (No. 13), Ireland and the United Kingdom (No. 12), and Austria (No. 8), and it became the Carpenters' biggest hit in the Netherlands (No. 3). "Jambalaya" was never released as a single in the United States.

Album
The Singles
1969–1973

—

US release date
11/9/73

—

Billboard Top LPs

Chart entry date (position)
12/1/73 (No. 95)

Peak date, position
(weeks at peak)
1/5/74, No. 1 (1)

Total weeks on chart
49

Year-end chart rank
No. 23

*Left: Outtake
during the shoot
for The Singles
1969–1973*

Album
The Singles
1969–1973

"I didn't want it to be just another greatest-hits album."

Between the release of "Ticket to Ride" in November 1969 and the chart peak of "Yesterday Once More" in July 1973, Karen and Richard racked up twelve *Billboard* Hot 100 singles, with nine reaching the Top 10. Eight were certified Gold. It was time for a greatest-hits album.

"But I didn't want it to be just another greatest-hits album," Richard says, "as I've long believed the term 'greatest hits' to be one of the most abused and misleading terms in the record business."

The title, *The Singles 1969–1973*, distinguished the set from other compilations of artists' greatest hits. And from the first track, the new Carpenters album was something different: it opened with Karen singing the first two lines of "(They Long to Be) Close to You." She then stepped out of the spotlight, making way for Richard and the orchestra to perform a segue into the introduction of "We've Only Just Begun."

On the Album

The majority of *The Singles*' tracks offered at least a little something new to those who already owned every one of the Carpenters' previous releases.

Perhaps the most renovated recording was, ironically, the Carpenters' least-successful chart performer, "Ticket to Ride." It peaked at No. 54 on the *Billboard* Hot 100 and, up to that time, was the duo's only single that failed to make the pop Top 15. But "Ticket" deserved a place on the album, if only because it was the duo's first single and one of their favorite recordings.

Still, neither Richard nor Karen were happy with the original take, aware it had far greater potential—and they were proved right after the revisions made for *The Singles*. They recorded new piano, drum, and guitar tracks. But most significant was Karen's fresh vocal. Her voice and technique at twenty-three were now fully mature, compared with at nineteen when she first recorded the song. Karen and Richard could finally take rerecording the tune off their to-do list.

Another item off the list was the sequencing of "Superstar" and "Rainy Days and Mondays." Richard had originally planned for the tunes to be placed back-to-back and linked together when they debuted on *Carpenters* [The Tan Album]. But he was talked out of it by A&M Records' cofounder Herb Alpert, who felt that the recordings were so strong they should be separated and positioned as the tracks to kick off each of the album's sides. Though Richard was unhappy about this, he realized Alpert was right.

On *The Singles*, the two tracks appeared in the order Richard always intended: "Superstar" into "Rainy Days," and with the addition of

Single
"Top of the World"

—

US release date
9/17/73

*See the following section,
"Top of the World"*

"Goodbye to Love," along came a trilogy that would serve as a mainstay of Carpenters concerts for years to come.

Richard's Take

When asked about the album itself, Richard brings up a problem. "Of course, if I had more time, it would've been a little more produced."

Otherwise, Richard speaks highly of *The Singles*, noting that he was happily surprised by one response: "We got a lot of airplay on the segue leading into 'We've Only Just Begun.' I remember hearing that quite a bit on the radio."

The Singles represents Richard's original visions fulfilled. With his remixes and rerecordings, Richard was finally able to deliver the recordings as he heard them in his head. History wasn't rewritten with *The Singles*. It was simply corrected, as much as time limitations and the technology of the era would allow.

Overall, the Carpenters had good reason to be pleased with the album. But Richard shares a second concern: in hindsight, he says the title *The Singles* probably wasn't such a great idea.

"Maybe we should have gone with 'Greatest Hits,' after all," Richard notes. "'The Singles' just doesn't pop. It should have been, 'Carpenters: Greatest Hits' with a great photograph of Karen and me *on the cover*—not smiling necessarily, but bright and attractive, to catch the consumer's eye."

"The inside of the existing package," he continues, "is done in sepia tones to carry over the brown-and-gold cover theme, but features a two-panel, soft-focus picture of the two of us that doesn't pop either: a shadowy mishmash."

On the US Charts

The Singles 1969–1973 entered at No. 95 on the Top *Billboard* LPs chart dated December 1, 1973. It reached the top spot on January 5, 1974, and remained at No. 1 for just a week. It spent a total of 49 weeks on the survey. Only *Carpenters* [The Tan Album] (59 weeks), *Christmas Portrait* (55 weeks), and *Close to You* (87 weeks) had longer *Billboard* album-chart runs.

While it was the only Carpenters album to reach the *Billboard* summit, Richard admits disappointment. "It was number one, but it should've just been a monster," he explains. "It crept its way to number one without a bullet, only to remain there for one week. Maybe it was the packaging," he continues, shaking his head. "Or maybe the whole 'hip' thing was catching up with the trades."

Page 117: *The Singles 1969–1973* reaches No. 1 on the *Billboard* Top LP's and Tape chart for the week ending on January 5, 1974

Pages 118–19: Outtake from photo shoot for *The Singles 1969–1973*

Billboard TOP LP's & TAPE

Compiled from National Retail Stores by the Music Popularity Chart Department and the Record Market Research Department of Billboard.

STAR PERFORMER—LP's registering greatest proportionate upward progress this week.

Awarded RIAA seal for sales of 1 Million dollars at manufacturers level. RIAA seal audit available and optional to all manufacturers. (Seal indicated by colored dot.)

SUGGESTED LIST PRICE

This Week	Last Week	Weeks on Chart	Artist / Title / Label, Number (Dist. Label)	Album	4-Channel	8-Track	Q-8 Tape	Cassette	Reel to Reel
1	2	6	CARPENTERS — The Singles, 1969-1973 — A&M SP 3601	6.98		7.98		7.98	
2	1	12	ELTON JOHN — Goodbye Yellow Brick Road — MCA 210003	11.98		12.98		12.98	
★ 3	5	46	JIM CROCE — You Don't Mess Around With Jim — ABC ABCX 756	5.98		6.95	6.95	6.95	
4	3	12	STEVE MILLER BAND — The Joker — Capitol 11235	5.98		6.98		6.98	
5	4	10	NEIL DIAMOND — Jonathan Livingston Seagull — Columbia KC 32550	6.98		6.98		6.98	
★ 6	12	4	JIM CROCE — I Got A Name — ABC ABCX 797	5.98		6.98		6.98	
7	7	9	THE WHO — Quadrophenia — MCA 2-10004	11.98		12.98		12.98	
8	6	8	RINGO STARR — Ringo — Apple SWAL 3413 (Capitol)	6.98		6.98		6.98	
★ 9	16	5	BETTE MIDLER — Atlantic SD 7270	5.98		6.97		6.97	
10	11	9	LOGGINS & MESSINA — Full Sail — Columbia KC 32540	5.98		6.98		6.98	
★ 11	15	5	ALICE COOPER — Muscle Of Love — Warner Bros. BS 2748	5.98		6.97		6.97	
12	8	47	JIM CROCE — Life & Times — ABC ABCX 769	5.98		6.98		6.98	
13	13	34	CHARLIE RICH — Behind Closed Doors — Epic KE 32247 (Columbia)	5.98		6.98		6.98	
★ 14	21	3	PAUL McCARTNEY & WINGS — Band On The Run — Apple SO 3415 (Capitol)	6.98		7.98		7.98	
15	9	11	GLADYS KNIGHT & THE PIPS — Imagination — Buddah BDS 5141	5.98		6.98		6.98	
★ 16	23	5	JOHN DENVER — Greatest Hits — RCA CPL1-0374	6.98		7.95		7.95	
17	19	7	GREG ALLMAN — Laid Back — Capricorn CP 116 (Warner Bros.)	5.98		6.98		6.98	
18	10	7	JOHN LENNON — Mind Games — Apple SD 3415 (Capitol)	5.98		7.98		7.98	
★ 19	27	4	EMERSON, LAKE & PALMER — Brain Salad Surgery — Manticore MC 66669 (Atlantic)	5.98		6.98		6.98	
20	14	18	CHEECH & CHONG — Los Cochinos — Ode SP 77019 (A&M)	5.98		6.98		6.98	
21	18	21	FRANK SINATRA — Ol' Blue Eyes Is Back — Reprise FS 2155	5.98		6.98		6.98	8.95
22	17	21	STEVIE WONDER — Innervisions — Tamla T 326 L (Motown)	5.98		6.98		6.98	
23	20	19	AMERICAN GRAFITTI — Soundtrack — MCA 2-8001	9.98		10.98		10.98	11.95
24	26	18	LOVE UNLIMITED — Under the Influence Of — 20th Century T 414	5.98		6.98		6.98	
25	22	9	BARRY WHITE — Stone Gon' — 20th Century TC-423	5.98		6.98		6.98	
26	25	6	SANTANA — Welcome — Columbia PC 32445	6.98		7.98		7.98	
27	24	15	ROLLING STONES — Goats Head Soup — Rolling Stones COC 59101 (Atlantic)	5.98		6.98		6.98	
28	29	8	THE BAND — Moondog Matinee — Capitol ST 11214	5.98		6.98		6.98	
29	30	30	TODD RUNDGREN — Something/Anything? — Bearsville 2BX 2066 (Warner Bros.)	6.98		7.97		7.97	
★ 30	45	3	BOB DYLAN — Dylan — Columbia PC 32747	6.98		7.98		7.98	
31	28	9	DAVID BOWIE — Pin Ups — RCA APL1-0291	5.98		6.98		6.98	7.95
32	32	43	PINK FLOYD — The Dark Side Of The Moon — Harvest SMAS 11163 (Capitol)	5.98		6.98		6.98	
33	31	11	ISAAC HAYES — Joy — Enterprise ENS 5007 (Columbia)	5.98		6.98		6.98	
34	34	20	ALLMAN BROTHERS BAND — Brothers & Sisters — Capricorn CP 0111 (Warner Brothers)	5.98		6.97		6.97	7.95
35	33	18	RICHARD HARRIS — Jonathan Livingston Seagull — Dunhill DSD 50160	6.98		7.95		7.95	
36	35	17	MARVIN GAYE — Let's Get It On — Tamla T329V (Motown)	5.98		6.98		6.98	
37	36	8	DIANA & MARVIN — Together At Last — Motown 803	5.98		6.98		6.98	
38	41	26	CHICAGO — VI — Columbia KC 32400	5.98		6.98		6.98	
★ 39	52	5	BEACH BOYS — In Concert — Reprise 2RS 6484	9.98		11.97		11.97	
40	39	9	GEORGE CARLIN — Occupation: Foole — Little David 1005 (Atlantic)	5.98		6.97		6.97	
41	42	8	BILLY COBHAM — Spectrum — Atlantic SD 7268	5.98		6.97		6.97	
42	43	9	O'JAYS — Ship Ahoy — Philadelphia International KZ 32408 (Columbia)	5.98		6.98		6.98	
43	46	22	HELEN REDDY — Long Hard Climb — Capitol SMAS 11213	5.98		6.98		6.98	
44	37	29	JOE WALSH — The Smoker You Drink The Player You Get — Dunhill DSX 50140	5.98		6.95		6.95	
45	44	9	JACKSON BROWNE — For Everyman — Asylum SD 5067	5.98		6.98		6.98	
46	47	39	LED ZEPPELIN — Houses of the Holy — Atlantic SD 7255	5.98		6.97		6.97	
47	40	8	AMERICA — Hat Trick — Warner Brothers BS 2728	5.98		6.97		6.97	
48	38	15	GARFUNKEL — Angel Clare — Columbia KC 31474	5.98		6.98		6.98	
49	54	6	SUNSHINE — Original Television Soundtrack — MCA 387	5.98		6.98		6.98	
50	51	7	ELVIS PRESLEY — Raised On Rock — RCA APL1-0388	5.98		6.98		6.98	
51	53	6	J. GEILS BAND — Ladies Invited — Atlantic SD 7286	5.98		6.97		6.97	
52	55	19	WAR — Deliver the Word — United Artists UA LA128-F	5.98		6.98		6.98	7.95
53	50	18	ISLEY BROTHERS — 3+3 — T-Neck KZ 32453 (Columbia)	5.98		6.98		6.98	
★ 54	64	9	MIKE OLDFIELD — Tubular Bells — Virgin VR 13-105 (Atlantic)	5.98		6.97		6.97	
55	56	12	LINDA RONSTADT — Don't Cry Now — Asylum SD 5064	5.98		6.98		6.98	
56	48	10	TRAFFIC — On The Road — Island SMAS 9336 (Capitol)	5.98		6.98		6.98	
57	65	80	CHEECH & CHONG — Big Bambu — Ode SP 77014 (A&M)	5.98		6.98		6.98	
58	58	21	DOOBIE BROTHERS — The Captain & Me — Warner Brothers BS 2694	5.98	6.97	6.97	7.97	6.97	8.95
59	63	38	SEALS & CROFTS — Diamond Girl — Warner Brothers BS 2699	5.98	6.97	6.97	7.97	6.97	8.95
60	61	9	HAROLD MELVIN & THE BLUENOTES — Black & Blue — Philadelphia International KZ 32407 (Columbia)	5.98		6.98		6.98	
61	62	110	LED ZEPPELIN — Atlantic SD 7208	5.98		6.98		6.98	
★ 62	90	3	MAHAVISHNU ORCHESTRA — Between Nothingness And Eternity — Columbia KC 32766	5.98		6.98		6.98	
63	60	23	Z.Z. TOP — Tres Hombres — London XPS 631	5.98		6.95		6.95	
64	57	21	GRAND FUNK — We're An American Band — Capitol SMAS 11207	5.98		6.98		6.98	
★ 65	77	3	PINK FLOYD — A Nice Pair — Harvest SABB 11257 (Capitol)	7.98		9.98		9.98	
66	66	14	THE MOTHERS — Over-Nite Sensation — Disc Reet MS 2149 (Warner Brothers)	5.98		6.97		6.97	7.95
67	68	16	LYNYRD SKYNYRD — MCA Sounds of the South 363	5.98		6.98		6.98	
68	71	24	CAT STEVENS — Foreigner — A&M SP 4391	5.98		6.98		6.98	
69	70	79	ROBERTA FLACK — Killing Me Softly — Atlantic SD 7271	5.98		6.98		6.98	
70	73	7	STYLISTICS — Rockin' Roll Baby — Avco AV 11010	5.98		6.98		6.98	
★ 71	89	5	DONNY OSMOND — A Time For Us — MGM SE 4930	5.98					
72	78	12	TONY ORLANDO & DAWN — New Ragtime Follies — Bell 1130	5.98		6.98		6.98	
73	74	6	RICK DERRINGER — All-American Boy — Blue Sky KZ 32481 (Columbia)	5.98		6.98		6.98	
74	49	11	GRATEFUL DEAD — Wake Of The Flood — Grateful Dead GD01	5.98		6.98		6.98	
75	67	7	BARBRA STREISAND — And Other Musical Instruments — Columbia KC 32655	5.98		6.98		6.98	
76	69	8	FLEETWOOD MAC — Mystery To Me — Reprise MS 2158	5.98		6.97		6.97	7.56
77	59	9	DAVE MASON — It's Like You Never Left — Columbia KC 31721	5.98		6.98		6.98	
78	75	31	EARTH, WIND & FIRE — Head to the Sky — Columbia KC 32194	5.98		6.98		6.98	
79	79	11	BILLY PRESTON — Everybody Likes Some Kind Of Music — A&M SP 3526	5.98		6.98		6.98	
80	80	57	BETTE MIDLER — The Divine Miss M — Atlantic SD 7238	5.98	6.97	6.97	7.97	6.97	
81	85	39	BEATLES — 1967-1970 — Apple SKBO 3404 (Capitol)	9.98		11.98		11.98	
82	72	12	THREE DOG NIGHT — Cyan — Dunhill DSX 50158	5.98		6.95		6.95	
83	81	29	THE POINTER SISTERS — Blue Thumb BTS 48	5.98		6.95		6.95	
84	82	6	WISHBONE ASH — Live Dates — MCA 2-8006	9.98		10.98		10.98	
85	86	32	CARPENTERS — Now & Then — A&M SP 3519	5.98		6.98		6.98	
86	76	14	URIAH HEEP — Sweet Freedom — Warner Brothers BS 2724	5.98		6.97		6.97	7.95
87	83	16	KRIS KRISTOFFERSON & RITA COOLIDGE — Full Moon — A&M SP 4403	5.98		6.98		6.98	
88	84	11	NEIL YOUNG — Time Fades Away — Reprise MS 2151	5.98		6.97		6.97	7.95
89	87	23	BOB DYLAN/SOUNDTRACK — Pat Garrett & Billy the Kid — Columbia KC 32460	5.98		6.98		6.98	
90	88	44	KRIS KRISTOFFERSON — Jesus Was A Capricorn — Monument KZ 31909 (Columbia)	5.98		6.98		6.98	
91	92	41	BREAD — The Best Of — Elektra EKS 75056	5.98	6.97	6.97	7.97	6.97	7.95
★ 92	103	4	SHAWN PHILLIPS — Bright White — A&M SP 4402	5.98		6.98		6.98	
93	93	84	DEEP PURPLE — Machine Head — Warner Bros. BS 2607	5.98		6.97		6.97	6.95
★ 94	108	31	PINK FLOYD — Meddle — Harvest SMAS 832 (Capitol)	5.98		6.98		6.98	
95	100	144	CAROLE KING — Tapestry — Ode SP 77009 (A&M)	5.98	6.98	6.98	7.98	6.98	
96	95	14	JESSE COLIN YOUNG — Song For Juli — Warner Brothers BS 2734	5.98		6.97		6.97	
97	96	57	EDGAR WINTER GROUP — They Only Come Out at Night — Epic KE 31584 (Columbia)	5.98	6.98	6.98	7.98	6.98	
98	94	16	MARIA MULDAUR — Reprise MS 2148	5.98		6.97			7.35
99	91	27	MARSHALL TUCKER BAND — Capricorn CP 0112 (Warner Brothers)	5.98		6.97		6.97	
★ 100	139	2	AL GREEN — Livin' For You — Hi ASHL-32082 (London)	6.98		6.98		6.98	
★ 101	111	10	QUEEN — Elektra EKS 75064	5.98		6.98	6.98	6.98	
102	102	60	STEVIE WONDER — Talking Book — Tamla T 319 L (Motown)	5.98		6.98		6.98	
103	101	33	PAUL SIMON — There Goes Rhymin' Simon — Columbia KC 32280	5.98		6.98		6.98	
★ 104	136	2	TEMPTATIONS — 1990 — Gordy G-966V1 (Motown)	5.98		6.98		6.98	
105	98	13	KOOL & THE GANG — Wild & Peaceful — De-Lite DEP 2013 (P.I.P.)	5.95		6.95		6.95	
106	109	48	ELTON JOHN — Don't Shoot Me I'm Only the Piano Player — MCA 2100	5.98		6.98		6.98	7.95

The Singles 1969–1973

Single
Top of the World

"Well, it gets the job done. It's a nice album cut."

Single
"Top of the World"

—

US release date
9/17/73

—

Billboard Hot 100

Chart entry date (position)
10/6/73 (No. 80)

Peak date, position (weeks at peak)
12/1/73, No. 1 (2)

Total weeks on chart
20

Year-end chart rank
No. 39

—

Billboard Top 40 Easy Listening

Chart peak (weeks at peak)
No. 2 (2)

Peak date, position (weeks at peak)
11/17/73, No. 2 (2)

Total weeks on chart
18

Year-end chart rank
n/a

One of the most popular songs about being on cloud nine has an origin story that couldn't be more earthbound. Richard Carpenter recalls being in the publishing department of the Carpenters' record label, A&M, and spotting a demo for a song titled "Top of the World."

"I never heard it," Richard notes. "I just saw that title and pictured the tune in my head. [Richard sings] 'I'm on the top of the world—*da da...*' That was it for my lyrics, but my melody kept going. And then that was it."

Well, not quite. The story of the nearly two-year journey of "Top of the World" to the summit of the *Billboard* Hot 100 has enough twists, turns, and players—including a US president, in a roundabout way— that it sounds like a tall tale. But it's all true.

The song was created out of necessity, as a track to round out the Carpenters' fourth album, *A Song for You*, which was released in June 1972. It might have been titled "Top of the World," but Richard did not have high hopes for what he had co-written with John Bettis. Upon completion of its recording, Richard and Karen thought, "Well, it gets the job done. It's a nice album cut."

Wrong. "One of the first reviews I saw said, in so many words, 'Great album. The strongest thing on it is "Top of the World."'"

That reviewer wasn't alone.

"The first night of the summer tour of '72 was in Houston," Richard says. "After we opened with a couple of songs, we acknowledged our new album, *A Song for You*. And Karen said, 'We'd like to do one of the new tracks, called 'Top of the World.' The crowd cheered! That had never happened before with a brand-new song. That right there should have told me."

There were more hints. "We were getting inundated with fan mail about the song," Richard recalls. "Singers were performing the tune on various TV variety shows. And, thanks to listener demand, radio programmers in several secondary markets in the United States placed it on their singles charts even though it wasn't yet a single."

By September, Richard at long last got the message. During the duo's engagement at the Riviera in Las Vegas, Karen announced "Top of the World" as the new Carpenters single.

Word moved quickly. Very quickly. The next thing the Carpenters knew, an A&M Record executive made a special trip from Los Angeles to talk to Karen and Richard between shows.

"You really shouldn't be putting out 'Top of the World,'" he counseled. "It would be too many singles from one album." They'd already released three. "So we didn't," Richard says.

Reflecting on the conversation, Richard says he believes that the exec simply wasn't convinced that "Top" was single material, just as Richard himself wasn't convinced for quite some time.

A month later, the Carpenters were what Richard calls "the token youth" at a star-studded reception. Ontario Airport, about thirty miles east of downtown Los Angeles, would be the last campaign stop for President Richard Nixon, who was running for reelection. Among the luminaries there were Jack Benny, Jimmy Stewart, George Murphy, Red Skelton, Ronald Reagan, and Danny Thomas—as well as singer Lynn Anderson, still hot from her 1970 country-crossover smash, "Rose Garden."

As the group waited for Air Force One to touch down and Nixon to arrive, Richard remembers, "We're all just having cocktails and talking, and Lynn Anderson comes up to me, introduces herself, and says, 'I'm doing "Top of the World" on my next album.' 'Oh, good,' I said. And, of course, they cloned my arrangement. But that's OK. Imitation is the sincerest form of flattery. And the darn thing went to No. 2 on Country and started crossing over to the pop charts." (It reached No. 74 on the *Billboard* Hot 100.)

Richard was not pleased. "I'm saying, 'Dummy, dummy, dummy! You should have released it yourself!'"

King Records, A&M's affiliate in Japan, released the original album version as a single in late 1972. It proved a smart move and resulted in the duo's second-biggest hit (behind "Superstar") up to that time in that country.

In early 1973, A&M's affiliates in Australia and New Zealand followed Japan's lead, and "Top of the World" went to the top of the charts in both countries. In Australia, the record spent four weeks at No. 1 and an impressive twenty-five weeks on the pop singles survey. But, by then, the Carpenters had moved on to recording a new album, soon striking gold again with *Now & Then* and its two smash hits, "Sing" and "Yesterday Once More."

And yet concert audiences kept screaming for "Top of the World." Finally, the Carpenters did what came naturally: giving the people what they wanted.

"Top of the World" would be the single for their upcoming hits compilation. But before its release, the Carpenters made some changes to the original recording. Karen, never happy with her original lead, rerecorded it.

With the road crew, 1976

"We recorded it in [A&M Records'] Studio C, which was the best sounding as far as the vocal," Richard explains.

Notable additions to the recording include a new pedal-steel guitar intro and part, played by renowned session player Buddy Emmons; electric guitar fills by Tony Peluso; and Richard's complete rerecord of his Wurlitzer electric piano.

"It was just a far better record, and it sounded better on radio," Richard says. "The original would have been a hit, but I'm happy it all turned out as it did."

On September 17, 1973, "Top of the World" was released as a single in the US and proved to be a dream kickoff for the new album, *The Singles 1969–1973*, which arrived November 9. The song was No. 1 on *Billboard*'s Hot 100 for the first two weeks of December, at the height of the Christmas shopping season, helping boost *The Singles* into the No. 1 spot on the album chart the first week of 1974.

In fact, *The Singles 1969–1973* would become the Carpenters' first and only No. 1 album in the US. By contrast, the 1972 album *A Song for You*—which contained the original version of "Top of the World"—peaked at No. 4, selling an impressive three million units in the US alone by the end of its first run.

But Richard says "Top of the World" could have done better "if we'd released it as a single right away, and the *Song for* You album would have sold two million more copies more than it did," he explains. "It would've gone to No. 1, not No. 4. "One of the great mistakes I made was to underestimate 'Top of the World.'"

It's clear that there's a special place in Richard's heart for "Top of the World." As the song's cowriter and performer, he's heard rapturous responses to it from live audiences of all ages, and he's watched it endure in extraordinary ways.

"Top of the World" was introduced to new listeners when it (as well as "I Need to Be in Love") was used in the miniseries *Miseinen* (Minors). It has since won over new generations in Japan—becoming one of the Carpenters' biggest streaming-era successes in that country, where it was certified Platinum for digital sales.

Richard seems particularly happy with the song's use in the 2010 animated feature *Shrek Forever After*, a global box-office blockbuster that employs the tune lovingly. *Shrek Forever After* has become a family film classic, introducing "Top of the World" to a new generation of children.

Other notable authorized uses of "Top of the World" include director Tim Burton's 2012 thriller *Dark Shadows* starring Johnny Depp, an international box-office hit, and Ricky Gervais's critically acclaimed Netflix dramedy *After Life*, where the song is played in its entirety during the opening scene of the second season premiere. The recording was recently featured in the promos for the fall 2020 premiere of American television network ABC's high profiled whodunit series, *Big Sky*.

As for the magic of "Top of the World"? "Oh, I figured it out years ago," Richard says, with a laugh. "It's very catchy. It's catchy, and it has a very special lyric."

I'm on the top of the world lookin' down on creation
And the only explanation I can find
Is the love that I've found ever since you've been around
Your love's put me at the top of the world

Page 123:
"Top of the World" reaches No. 1 on the *Billboard* Hot 100 chart for the week ending on December 1, 1973

The Herb Alpert Interview

"I grew to love those two kids."

For Herb Alpert, hearing the Carpenters was a case of love at first listen. It is Alpert, the Grammy-winning leader of the Tijuana Brass and cofounder of A&M Records, who brought Richard and Karen close to us.

The duo signed to the label in April 1969, and they surely lived up to expectations. They delivered more hits for A&M than any other artists in the 1970s.

For Alpert, this wasn't just a business relationship. "I grew to love those two kids," he says.

Richard and Karen's four-song demo tape got to Alpert in early 1969, as counterculture tastes were making their way into the mainstream. Alpert and label cofounder Jerry Moss took notice and realized that forging ahead in the 1970s meant moving away from A&M's middle-of-the-road roots and into rock's fast lane.

To many at the company, taking on a brother-and-sister pop act seemed to be a step backward. But, in Richard and Karen, Alpert saw and heard A&M's future. Alpert's mantra: "Talent always wins out." From the four songs on their demo, he had no doubt the Carpenters were winners.

Mike Cidoni Lennox and Chris May: Tell us about the first time you heard the Carpenters.

Herb Alpert: Out of curiosity, I put on the tape in my office at A&M. I always listen with my eyes closed and try to get into exactly what I'm hearing. And I heard something that was kind of unique with those four songs. There was something that intrigued me about what I heard.

What was it about their sound that struck you?

They were making music that was authentic to them: American pop. I'm basically a jazz musician. That's where my heart lies. When I heard their music, it felt like it was real. I didn't know they were going to end up being renowned around the world. There was something about their music that touched me.

On signing day, Richard was just twenty-two and Karen nineteen—really young. But, from the start, you let them do their thing in the studio.

It was obvious that Richard knew what he was doing: a terrific producer and arranger who knew how to record Karen's amazing pipes. And that's the reason they were so successful.

1969 was a tough year for A&M Records. The label didn't have one domestic top 10 album or single during that time. What about reports that there was pressure to drop the Carpenters after their debut album flopped?

The word I was getting from my own company was, "Where did you find these two kids? I mean, they're kind of soft and easy-listening. And that's not what radio is playing at the moment." The rumor was that it wasn't such a good signing.

When "(They Long to Be) Close to You" was released on May 15, 1970, the No. 1 single on the *Billboard* Hot 100 was "American Woman" by The Guess Who. The majority of the other top 10 songs that week were either rock or up-tempo pop and soul. What made you think the Carpenters' sweet love song could compete in that climate?

You've got to deal with a good melody. You have to have a good song to start with. I don't care how much technique you have, and how wonderful a singer or instrumentalist you might be. You have to deal with a good song, a song that has substance. "Close to You" was a beautiful tune by Burt Bacharach and Hal David that obviously met that bar.

With A&M
cofounder Herb
Alpert after their
show, Anaheim,
CA, January 22,
1972

As hands-off as A&M was with its artists, there were rare occasions when you stepped in to guide the Carpenters. After the initial attempt at "Close to You," you told them to bring in studio musicians. What wasn't working?

The first take was a nice little recording. Karen was playing drums, and it was obvious they needed a little more meat, a little more depth on the recording. And I guess that was a big aha moment for both of them, and it produced the monster record. I played it over the phone for Burt, and he just couldn't have been happier. He almost passed out when he heard it.

Many people thought you were playing the trumpet solo on "Close to You," but that wasn't you. It was veteran studio musician Chuck Findley.

I guess he was playing off my style. [Laughs.)] I don't really remember it, but obviously, I wasn't there.

***Billboard* Hot 100?**

I can't say much other than it was a good feeling. I don't wallow in that stuff. I expected it to be a big record. It would have surprised me if it wasn't No. 1. It was a great record. I was delighted, obviously, and proud of them.

And the hits just kept on comin'.

You need momentum, and you need to have timing. Once timing was on their side, once they broke through with "Close to You," the door just opened wide. And they kept picking really good songs to record. Richard was brilliant at that.

It didn't happen with all of your artists, but your professional relationship evolved into a personal one with Richard and Karen.

I spent a lot of time weeding out people that I didn't like being around, and these were artists

that I enjoyed. And they were smart! They were smart with what they were doing, and they were 100% involved. They wanted to know how many records were being sold in various areas, as well as the chart positions. They were in it more than I was! I mean, I was just doing my thing, and happy for them. The minutiae of what they were doing was beautiful.

Richard says that one of the best times of Karen's life was when she was recording the *Made in America* album in 1981. Did you find she was happiest working in the studio?

She was happiest in the studio. One of the saddest memories I have of Karen was when she bounced into my office. I think it was [late 1982], two weeks or so after she got out of the facility in New York. She was so excited about wanting to record and do concerts again. Karen was somebody you couldn't help but like. When I asked her, "What do you really love to do?" She'd say—I'm not joking— "I love to play drums!" She couldn't accept the fact that she was a world-class singer. And then the worst happened. I just get teary-eyed when I think about it. Maybe, in another era, it would have been possible to deal differently with her problem.

You've stayed close to Richard all these years later.

We don't communicate daily, but, whenever we do, we're right back to being square and honest with each other. He calls me, or I call him. He's a solid guy who's a solid friend. So if I needed somebody to help me, he would definitely be on my list.

If you had passed on the Carpenters, did not sign them to A&M, do you think they would have made it anyway?

When they started happening around the world, it was like, "Wow, it's certainly a feather in my cap for signing them." But, darn it, they had the goods! Would they have happened at other labels? Probably. You know, talent always wins out.

**With Herb
Alpert, 1977**

Chapter 4

All Over the World: Global Success

All Over the World

Tripping through the Carpenters' International Success

Almost from the beginning, the Carpenters' music inspired a kind of hush. Since "(They Long to Be) Close to You" hit the airwaves in the United States in May 1970, listeners pricked up their ears and quieted down.

Two months after the release of "(They Long to Be) Close to You," the Carpenters reached the *Billboard* Hot 100's summit on the chart dated July 25, and they stayed there a month—longer than any other act that summer.

"(They Long to Be) Close to You" quickly crossed the US border and invaded Canada. On the *RPM* magazine survey dated August 8, the duo scored their first international No. 1. The single bumped A&M labelmate Miguel Rios's "A Song of Joy" out of the top spot and spent two weeks at the top of the Canadian chart. Success down under followed, when "(They Long to Be) Close to You" spent three weeks at the chart summit in Australia.

This trio of territories stayed true to the Carpenters for the next eight years. Each of the Carpenters' globally released singles made the Top 100 of the pop surveys in these countries during the duo's most productive period, spanning from "(They Long to Be) Close to You" (1970) to "Sweet, Sweet Smile" (1978).

Listeners elsewhere would get close to the Carpenters quickly. In autumn 1970, the "(They Long to Be) Close to You" single reached the Top 10 in Ireland and the United Kingdom (peaking at No. 6 in both places) and New Zealand (No. 9). And in early 1971 the single reached the Top 10 in Spain and Zimbabwe (both No. 8).

But while Richard and Karen's run of releases flew high and struck Gold in the States and in Canada, global success was hit and miss until three key releases solidified their international stardom.

Page 128:
England, 1974

Left and pages
132–33: Royal Albert
Hall, London, 1971

- "Superstar" (1972)—a No. 2 smash in the US, No. 4 in Canada, and Top 10 in New Zealand and one of the Carpenters' most revered recordings—inexplicably fizzled almost everywhere else. It stalled at No. 18 in the UK and the Netherlands. It was even a dud with their usually devoted following in Australia (No. 35). But the release was a game changer in Japan, selling six times as many singles as "(They Long to Be) Close to You," "We've Only Just Begun," and "Rainy Days and Mondays" combined. While it didn't yet seal the deal, guaranteeing future generations of fans in Japan, it blazed a trail for the kind of success no one would have believed.

- "Goodbye to Love" (1972) was not quite a block-buster in the US, hitting only No. 7 and not certified Gold—making it an underachiever during the Carpenters' chart heyday. But it did better in Canada (No. 4) and New Zealand (No. 2). And it became their second Top 10 hit in the UK—two years and five releases after they'd reached No. 6 with "(They Long to Be) Close to You" in 1970.

- "Yesterday Once More" (1973) put the Carpenters on top of the world-*music* scene (although "Top of the World" *was* one of their biggest international successes). This Richard Carpenter/John Bettis original celebrated how songs from years gone by have the unique ability to make our gloomy todays suddenly shine…just like before. Richard says that for years "Yesterday Once More" was the duo's most-popular single released worldwide, but it finally had to settle for No. 2 (see below). It's no exaggeration to say that "Yesterday Once More" was a monster smash: a pop Top 10 in almost every country the authors were able to monitor for this book, the sole holdout being Germany, where it stalled at No. 21. The single was the Carpenters' biggest hit in Japan, selling nearly 600,000 copies in its original run. This would be a solid amount in the States, but it's a crazy number for a country with a third of the US population and less than ten percent English fluency.

And Japan was just the start of it. Though it's impossible to acquire reliable chart information for most countries in Asia, the song continues to be hugely popular in (especially) China, Vietnam, and the Philippines. Richard recalls hearing "Yesterday Once More" countless times in public places in Asia. He says he usually heard the Carpenters' recording of it, but the tune has also been covered among other international successes:

· "Jambalaya (On the Bayou)" (1973)—the Hank Williams classic popularized by singer Jo Stafford in the 1950s—was never intended to be released as a single off the Carpenters' *Now & Then* album. But A&M's Japanese affiliate felt that it would be a hit and was proved right. The single landed on Japan's charts in November 1973, went to No. 28, stayed on the charts for 33 weeks, and was certified Gold. By early 1974, numerous other countries followed suit, and the track enjoyed success in the Netherlands (No. 3), Austria (No. 8), UK and Ireland (No. 12), and New Zealand and Belgium (No. 13).

· "Please Mr. Postman" (1974), the Carpenters' remake of The Marvelettes' 1961 chart topper, surely isn't the duo's highest-brow musical moment. But it's a

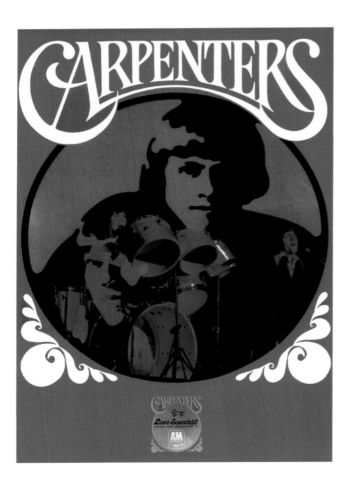

hell of a record, with Richard's tower of power-pop production surrounding a vocal from Karen that has all the complexities of Christmas—so joyous, so sparkling, and, oh yes, so in *tune*. (Go ahead, purists. Give the Motown original a serious listen. Ouch!) You just never want the thing to end. The Carpenters' "Postman" was their first single to be celebrated for selling more than one million copies outside the US, and the timing couldn't have been better, as things were cooling a bit for the duo in North America.

· *Horizon* (1975) was the Carpenters' first album since 1969 that failed to reach the *Billboard* Top 10 in the US, peaking at No. 13, although it was instantly certified Gold and, eventually, Platinum stateside. But it was a sensation in the UK, debuting at No. 1 and staying there for five weeks, while *The Singles 1969–1973* was still selling in the UK like crazy, following a seventeen-week (nonconsecutive) stay at No. 1.

· "Calling Occupants of Interplanetary Craft (The Recognized Anthem of World Contact Day)" (1978), the Carpenters' epic remake of the sci-fi themed power ballad by Canadian rock group Klaatu, was never intended to be released as a single, Richard says. But as *Star Wars* emerged as a box-office phenomenon in summer 1977, A&M saw a marketing opportunity and suggested that the tune could click with listeners. For a rare change, the label was right—to a degree. Richard reluctantly trimmed the seven-minute album version to just four minutes for radio (and the single itself), and it was the week's highest-charting new release on the *Billboard* Hot 100 October 7, 1978. While it climbed to only No. 32 in the US, it did return the duo to the pop Top 40, and brought them back to the Top 10 in Canada, the United Kingdom, and Ireland, as well as the Top 20 in Australia and New Zealand.

· *Only Yesterday: Richard & Karen Carpenter's Greatest Hits* (1990) came on the heels of a highly rated UK airing of the telefilm *The Karen Carpenter Story*. The duo's record label, A&M, was caught by surprise when consumers demanded a new Carpenters-career compilation. A&M's UK office gave Richard an emergency call, he sequenced the album, and the label had it in stores within three months. Little could they have imagined what was to come. The album spent 7 weeks at No. 1, went five-times Platinum, and charted for a strapping 107 weeks in the UK. And its success wasn't limited to Great Britain. *Only Yesterday* spent 7 weeks at No. 1 in New Zealand and 3 weeks at No.3 in the Netherlands. It was also a success in Norway (No. 8), Australia (No. 13), and Spain (No. 34).

Above: June
1974, Japan

Page 134: A
Japanese concert
program, 1974

- Nearly twenty years after "I Need to Be in Love" failed to woo record buyers, it got a second chance at romance in 1995. Superstar TV writer-producer Shinji Nojima (think the Shonda Rhimes, Aaron Sorkin, or Ryan Murphy of Japan) asked Richard for permission to use the long-forgotten ballad as the main-title theme for *Miseinen* (Minors), his lavish 1995 miniseries spinning around a group of young friends. The show was more than a ratings smash, but a Japanese pop-culture phenomenon. And Nojima was such a big Carpenters fan, he licensed both "I Need to Be in Love" and "Top of the World" for the soundtrack. A single including both songs soared up the Japanese pop charts and ended up selling more than half a million copies.

- But that was nothing compared to what was next. A new compilation, *Twenty-Two Hits of the Carpenters*, was assembled and sold some three million units in Japan. While this would indicate a huge success anywhere, consider Japan has about one-third the population of the US. To this day, the Carpenters are among the top international recording artists in Japan, and Richard receives rock-star treatment each time he visits.

Two Lives, One Connection:
The Carpenters Are the Tie That Binds

Denise Quan
Contributing Writer

Name
Simon Worsley

Location
Liverpool, England

Age
20

Occupation
university student

On the Carpenters
"If you compare them with musicians nowadays, their melodies are so much stronger."

Simon Worsley is a Carpenters historian who lives just outside Liverpool, England—a city with a rich musical heritage. With his rosy cheeks and flawless complexion, he looks all of seventeen.

"I'm twenty," he corrects. "I was born in 2000." That's thirty years after Karen and Richard scored their first No. 1 hit, "(They Long to Be) Close to You."

Welcome to the next era of Carpenters fans: Generation Z.

He's a fan of Adele, Lana Del Rey, and Shawn Mendes, but also old-school music legends such as Dolly Parton, Bobbie Gentry, and Frank Sinatra and his daughter Nancy.

"People like to say, 'It was the music of my life,'" Worsley says. "And it really is, because you go through life and it's always there. I always have music playing."

Worsley was fourteen when he decided to explore the Carpenters' discography. His interest was piqued when he heard the duo's "(They Long to Be) Close to You" on the soundtrack of *The Simpsons Movie*.

"Karen's voice really connected with me personally," he says. "It's just one of those voices that gets to you. And the Carpenters were new—to me, at least. They were refreshing and, really, the first of their kind. If you compare them with musicians nowadays, their melodies are so much stronger."

Worsley was so enamored with the duo's recordings that he was inspired to write Richard a letter. In it, he expressed his admiration for the Carpenters' production and arrangements as well as for Karen's singing.

Just after Worsley's sixteenth birthday, along came a text from his mum as he was returning from school. "There's a letter," it read. "I think it's from America."

"So I came home, and it was on the sideboard in the hallway—this big, padded brown envelope with American stamps on it," Worsley remembers.

"I rushed upstairs and opened it. And it was a double-sided letter from Richard, with a signed photo of him and Karen, which was really nice."

The handwritten note was from Richard's personalized notepad. "Hi, Simon," it read. "Thanks so much for your kind words. They mean a great deal to me. You are quite an articulate young lad, who also possesses good taste in music." It was signed, "R."

The letter affected Worsley greatly, and he's since shared his love of the Carpenters with others. "Last summer, I got one of my oldest friends into the Carpenters," Worsley notes, adding that he's observed many others in his generation who also highly regard Richard and Karen.

Many of the Carpenters' classics were originally recorded nearly fifty years ago, yet Worsley says the music speaks to him as if it were released only yesterday.

"Right now, the Official Charts are a mixture of current and legacy artists," he says, adding that he's not surprised the duo's releases continue to hit the UK Top 40 today. "The music truly does deserve to be called 'timeless.'"

On any given day, the Carpenters' music is sure to be found on the charts all around the world. Here is a snapshot of how the duo's album *Gold: Greatest Hits* did on the iTunes/Apple Music survey on March 9, 2021 at 21:00 GMT.

Source: www.kworb.net

No. 3 in Mongolia
No. 23 in Australia
No. 35 in the Philippines
No. 39 in the United Kingdom
No. 77 in Canada
No. 90 in the United States
No. 95 in Hong Kong
No. 107 in El Salvador
No. 110 in Sri Lanka
No. 110 in Singapore
No. 111 in Barbados
No. 113 in Oman
No. 126 in Paraguay

No. 121 in Thailand
No. 135 in Vietnam
No. 146 in Malaysia
No. 159 in New Zealand
No. 160 in Honduras
No. 167 in India
No. 179 in Bolivia
No. 183 in Costa Rica
No. 197 in Qatar
No. 209 in Ireland
No. 321 in Indonesia
No. 471 in Norway
No. 499 in Spain

Name
Akira Tsukahara

Location
Tokyo, Japan

Age
59

Occupation
music publisher

On the Carpenters
"The Carpenters sound
is truly timeless."

Akira Tsukahara was nine years old in 1971, the year "Superstar" became a breakout hit for the Carpenters in his native Japan. Although American audiences couldn't get enough of "(They Long to Be) Close to You" and "We've Only Just Begun," also released in 1971, they didn't gain much traction in Japan. But the Carpenters' fate in the Land of the Rising

Sun changed when "Superstar" became a sensation on the airwaves.

In hindsight, Tsukahara says the song's success could almost be predicted. "It's a sentimental ballad with minor chords, which Japanese audiences particularly love," he explains. "Japanese people tend to react more positively to melodic sensibilities, rather than beats or rhythm. So 'Superstar' was an ideal product for the Japanese market." At the time, he couldn't understand the song's lyrics, but that would eventually change. "I learned English from the Carpenters' music," he says.

So it is somewhat prophetic that Tsukahara would grow up to become a top music executive in Tokyo, working with the Carpenters on both sides of the Pacific. "I first met Richard in the summer of 1987," he recalls. "I was working as a young, aspiring A&R rep at Fujipacific Music, the Japanese subpublisher for Rondor Music, which Richard was signed to as a writer."

As part of Tsukahara's extended duties, he was responsible for pitching entertainment stories to *Sankei Shimbun*, the daily newspaper owned by Fujipacific's parent company. "When I learned that Richard was making his first solo album, *Time*, I twisted their arms and forced them to agree that I would go and have an exclusive interview with him," he recounts with amusement. "I flew to LA and met him in the office of A&M Records. It was the moment I had been dreaming of all my life."

In 1973, the Carpenters released yet another single that worked perfectly in the Japanese market. "You can say that 'Superstar' put Richard and Karen on the map of the Japanese music market," Tsukahara notes, "but it was 'Yesterday Once More' that made them superstars." "Yesterday Once More" sold nearly 600,000 copies in Japan, and it remains the Carpenters' biggest hit single there.

Historically, the Japanese music market had been dominated by homegrown acts singing in their native tongue. "That ratio back in the '70s was 65% local and 35% international," Tsukahara explains. "The Carpenters were rare international artists who made it to the bigger side of the market." When the Carpenters arrived at Tokyo Airport to kick off their triumphant 1974 Japanese tour, they were met by five thousand screaming fans.

A look at recent Spotify and iTunes streaming sales show that Japan remains one of the Carpenters' strongest markets. "The Carpenters sound is truly timeless," Tsukahara says. "Japanese audiences have never stopped embracing their music, as we appreciate the value of melodic, sentimental, warm, honest, sincere, clean sound."

CARPENTERS

on Friday
24th September 1971
at 7.30 p.m

at the Royal Albert Hall
General Manager : F. J. Mundy

with Labi Siffre   compere David Symonds

Presented by.. ....
PAUL ROWE in association with
Arthur Howes Ltd. and M.A.M. Ltd.

Proceeds in aid of   **Royal National Institute for the Deaf**   RNID
PATRON HIS ROYAL HIGHNESS THE DUKE OF EDINBURGH K.G

Page 138: Concert program, 1971

Right: Setting up at Royal Albert Hall, London, 1971

Pages 140–41: Taping an appearance on French singer-composer Gilbert Becaud's series *Becaud*, Paris, 1971

Right: Taping an appearance on French singer Gilbert Becaud's series *Becaud*, Paris, 1971

Page 142, top: 1971

Page 142, bottom: Receiving a gift in Amsterdam, 1971

On a chartered
plane, European
tour, 1974

Right: At a press
conference in
Tokyo, 1974

Japan, 1974

Right:
Fresno, 1976

146

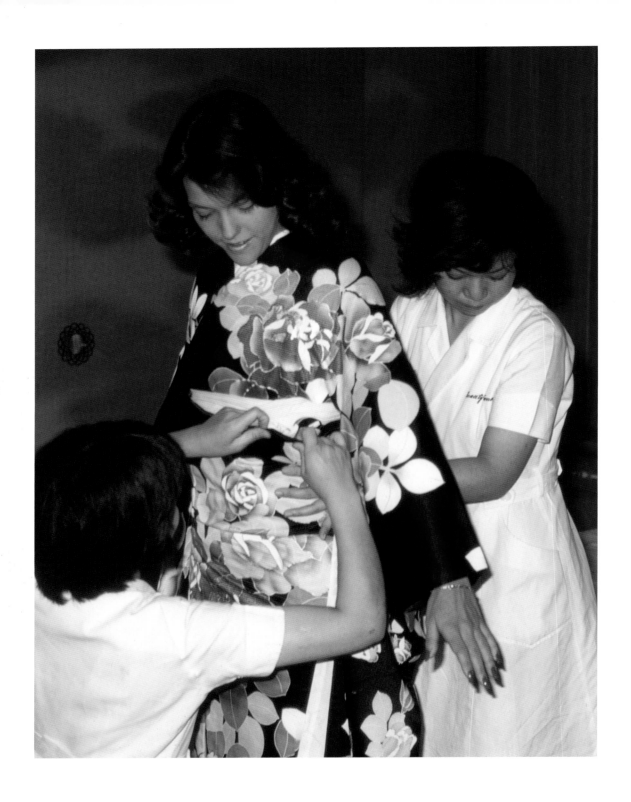

Tokyo, 1974

Right:
Globetrotting,
1976

Chapter 5

New Horizons

1975–1977

Album
Horizon

—

US release date
6/6/75

—

Billboard Top LPs

Chart entry date (position)
6/28/75 (No. 38)

Peak date, position (weeks at peak)
7/26/75, No. 13 (3)

Total weeks on chart
18

Year-end chart ranking
n/a

Page 150:
At Selland Arena,
Fresno, CA, 1976

Left: Filming the
"Only Yesterday"
promo at Huntington
Botanical Gardens,
San Marino, CA, 1975

Album
Horizon

**"Karen, who was always in peak form,
somehow seemed to be more so."**

Coming off their second *Billboard* Hot 100 chart-topping single and their first No. 1 on the magazine's Top LPs survey, the Carpenters should have been on top of the world at the start of 1974. But no. Richard recalls, "It was not a good time for me for any number of reasons."

One good reason: the Carpenters' personal management had topped themselves again, booking Karen and Richard to play more concerts in 1974 than in any other year.

They would perform some two hundred shows in the United States and abroad, including Germany, the Netherlands, Belgium, the United Kingdom, and Japan.

Add time for travel, promotional interviews, a Grammy Awards appearance, and TV performances on *Evening at Pops* and *The Perry Como Christmas Show*—no wonder this would be the first year without a new Carpenters studio album. *Horizon*, the subject of this chapter, would not be released until late spring 1975.

But, in the interim, the Carpenters would not leave fans and radio programmers empty-handed in 1974—releasing three singles: covers of "Please Mr. Postman" and "Santa Claus Is Comin' to Town" (the latter detailed in the "The Carpenters and Christmas"), as well as "I Won't Last a Day without You."

This was pretty much the "Top of the World" story all over again. "I Won't Last a Day," co-written by Paul Williams and Roger Nichols, was originally intended to be an album track for *A Song for You*, released in June 1972. There was an early indicator that the track had hit potential. A&M's UK branch released the song as a single in September 1972 and saw it debut on the UK chart at No. 40. A week later, the record disappeared. It appears there was an error, as "Goodbye to Love" was on the flip. The sides were switched, and "Goodbye to Love" became the Carpenters' second Top 10 single in the UK.

Both lyrically and musically, "I Won't Last a Day" was never a favorite of Richard's. Furthermore, this was yet another *A Song for You* selection on which Karen was vocally challenged, thanks to a node on her larynx. So, between troubles with the tune and its performance, the Carpenters never considered it single worthy.

Two albums and some twenty months after the release of *A Song for You*, there came a call. "It was Paul Drew, who had succeeded Bill Drake as vice president of programming for the RKO General chain," Richard remembers. Drew wanted A&M to release "Won't Last a Day" as a single. "He said, 'If you put that out, I'll put it on all the big stations in the RKO chain.'"

Instead of simply releasing the album version of the song on a 45, Richard brought Tony Peluso back into the studio. It helped. Peluso's

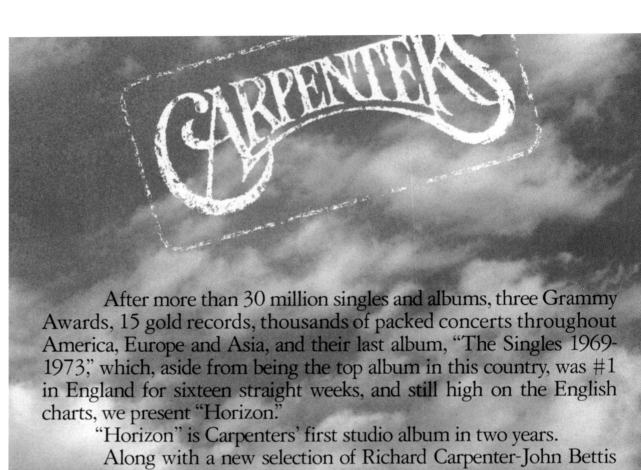

After more than 30 million singles and albums, three Grammy Awards, 15 gold records, thousands of packed concerts throughout America, Europe and Asia, and their last album, "The Singles 1969-1973," which, aside from being the top album in this country, was #1 in England for sixteen straight weeks, and still high on the English charts, we present "Horizon."

"Horizon" is Carpenters' first studio album in two years.

Along with a new selection of Richard Carpenter-John Bettis songs, it features the two latest Carpenters hits, "Please Mr. Postman" and "Only Yesterday." And Carpenters versions of Neil Sedaka's "Solitaire" and Eagles' "Desperado."

Karen's vocals are filled with new emotion and Richard's talent for arrangement and orchestration is dazzling.

By any standard, a new "Horizon."

Produced by Richard Carpenter Associate Producer Karen Carpenter (SP 4530)

Trade ad for
Horizon

Pages 156–57:
Recording
Horizon, A&M
Records, Los
Angeles, 1975

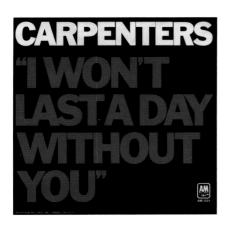

Single
"I Won't Last a Day without You"

—

US release date
3/25/74

—

Billboard Hot 100

Chart entry date (position)
4/13/74 (No. 70)

Peak date, position (weeks at peak)
5/25/74, No. 11 (1)

Total weeks on chart
12

Year-end chart rank
n/a

—

Billboard Top 40 Easy Listening

Chart entry date (position)
4/13/74 (35)

Peak date, position (weeks at peak)
6/1/74, No. 1 (1)

Total weeks on chart
12

Year-end chart rank
No. 27

smooth, melodious electric-guitar fills were interwoven throughout the arrangement, breathing new life into the old track.

Although the single never quite satisfied Richard and Karen, and millions already owned the original recording on *A Song for You*, "Won't Last a Day" became a hit anyway, verifying Paul Drew's instincts. It reached No. 11 on the *Billboard* Hot 100, and hit No. 1 on the magazine's Easy Listening chart.

The Carpenters' nonstop touring continued throughout 1974, but somehow Richard and Karen found a slot in July to record again. This time, it was a remake of The Marvelettes' 1961 chart-topping "Please Mr. Postman." Richard says he felt, on a whim, that it could be a hit again.

As for Richard's new arrangement of the song? "Everything just fell into place: the background vocals, Bob Messenger's sax solo, Tony Peluso's guitar, and especially Karen's lead. She was able to make this lyric of longing sound like she was singing an ode to joy."

"It was a great radio record," Richard continues. "It was the perfect single. And it was, like, 2:40, 2:35. It was such a big hit that [Chicago's No. 1 Top 40 radio station] WLS and a number of other stations were playing it twice an hour—because it was so short and so popular."

It was so big that the Carpenters received news from A&M International that "Postman" had sold over a million copies, excluding its massive sales in the United States.

While Richard says he never doubted the hit potential of "Postman," he admits that he never felt recording the song was such a good idea. "Here we are bitching about our image and all of this," he says, "and then we go and remake 'Please Mr. Postman.'"

US picture sleeve for "Please Mr. Postman"

Single
"Please Mr. Postman"

—

US release date
11/8/74

—

Billboard Hot 100

Chart entry date (position)
11/23/74 (No. 77)

Peak date, position (weeks at peak)
1/25/75, No. 1 (1)

Total weeks on chart
17

Year-end chart rank
No. 3

—

Billboard Top 50 Easy Listening

Chart entry date (position)
11/23/74 (No. 77)

Peak date, position (weeks at peak)
1/25/75, No. 1 (1)

Total weeks on chart
17

Year-end chart rank
No. 16

Richard explains, "The Carpenters needed a new single, and I felt it would be a hit—but never the worldwide success it became."

He continues, "When they did *The Nation's Favourite Carpenters Songs* in the UK in 2016, 'Postman' came in number one, and that's not good. You want your number one to be 'Yesterday Once More' or 'Superstar.' But God forbid."

On the Album

Horizon was the Carpenters' first album to be recorded in A&M's state-of-the-art Studio D, the so-called studio the Carpenters built. *Horizon* has a sonic sparkle that Richard believes makes it seem a better album than it actually is. "The material wasn't there," he says. "But Karen, who was always in peak form, somehow seemed to be more so. And engineer Roger Young was, as well."

Trade ad,
January 1975

Horizon

159

Billboard HOT 100®

©Copyright 1975, Billboard Publications, Inc. No part of this publication may be reproduced, stored in a retrieval system, or transmitted, in any form or by any means, electronic, mechanical, photocopying, recording, or otherwise, without the prior written permission of the publisher.

*Chart Bound

EMOTION—Helen Reddy (Capitol 4021)
I'VE BEEN THIS WAY BEFORE—Neil Diamond (Columbia 3-10084)
SEE TOP SINGLE PICKS REVIEWS, page 58

THIS WEEK	LAST WEEK	WKS. ON CHART	TITLE—Artist (Producer) Writer, Label & Number (Distributing Label)	
★1	2	10	PLEASE MR. POSTMAN—Carpenters (Richard & Karen Carpenter), B. Holland, F. Gorman, R. Bateman, A&M 1646	SGC
2	3	15	LAUGHTER IN THE RAIN—Neil Sedaka (Neil Sedaka, Robert Appere), N. Sedaka, Cody, MCA 40313	WBM
3	1	11●	MANDY—Barry Manilow (Barry Manilow, Ron Dante, Clive Davis), S. English, R. Keer, Bell 45613 (Arista)	SGC/HAN
★4	11	7	FIRE—Ohio Players (Ohio Players), J. Williams, C. Satchel, I. Bonner, M. Jones, R. Middlebrooks, M. Pierce, W. Beck, Mercury 73643 (Phonogram)	
5	6	11	BOOGIE ON REGGAE WOMAN—Stevie Wonder (Stevie Wonder), S. Wonder, Tamla 54254 (Motown)	SGC
★6	21	8	YOU'RE NO GOOD—Linda Ronstadt (Peter Asher), C. Ballard Jr., Capitol 3990	HAN
7	8	12	ONE MAN WOMAN/ONE WOMAN MAN—Paul Anka with Odia Coates (Denny Diante, Spencer Proffer), P. Anka, United Artists 569	MCA
8	9	11	MORNING SIDE OF THE MOUNTAIN—Donny & Marie Osmond (Mike Curb), Manning, Stock, MGM 14765	WBM
9	10	13	NEVER CAN SAY GOODBYE—Gloria Gaynor (Meco Mondardo), Tony Bongiovi, Jay Ellis), C. Davis, MGM 14748	SGC
★10	14	8	PICK UP THE PIECES—Average White Band (Arif Mardin), R. Ball, H. Stuart, Average White Band, Atlantic 45-3229	
11	5	9	LUCY IN THE SKY WITH DIAMONDS—Elton John (Gus Dudgeon), J. Lennon, P. McCartney, MCA 40344	WBM
★12	15	7	SOME KIND OF WONDERFUL—Grand Funk (Jimmy Ienner), J. Ellison, Capitol 4002	SGC
13	13	9	DOCTOR'S ORDERS—Carol Douglas (Ed O'Loughlin—DCA Prod.), G. Stephens, Greeaway, Cook, Midland International 10113 (RCA)	SGC
★14	17	10	GET DANCIN'—Disco Tex & The Sex-O-Lettes (Bob Crewe), B. Crewe, K. Nolan, Chelsea 3004	B-3
★15	19	9	BEST OF MY LOVE—Eagles (Glyn Johns), Henley, Frye, J.D. Souther, Asylum 45218	WBM
16	16	8	ROCK 'N ROLL (I Gave You The Best Years Of My Life)—Mac Davis (Rick Hall), K. Johnson, Columbia 3-10070	SGC
17	7	12	SALLY G/JUNIOR'S FARM—Paul McCartney & Wings (Paul McCartney), P. McCartney, Apple 1875 (Capitol)	HAN
18	4	13	YOU'RE THE FIRST, THE LAST, MY EVERYTHING—Barry White ● (Barry White), B. White, T. Sepe, P.S. Radcliffe, 20th Century 2133	CPI
★19	25	10	FREE BIRD—Lynyrd Skynyrd (Al Kooper), A. Collins, R. Van Zandt, MCA 40328	MCA
★20	24	6	BLACK WATER—Doobie Brothers (Ted Templeman), P. Simmons, Warner Bros. 8062	WBM
★21	29	6	#9 DREAM—John Lennon (John Lennon), J. Lennon, Apple 1878 (Capitol)	B-3
★22	26	7	STRUTTIN'—Billy Preston (Billy Preston), B. Preston, G. Johnson, L. Johnson, A&M 1644	TMK
★23	27	6	LOOK IN MY EYES PRETTY WOMAN—Tony Orlando & Dawn (Hank Medress, Dave Appell), D. Lambert, B. Potter, Bell 45620 (Arista)	B-3
24	18	13	BUNGLE IN THE JUNGLE—Jethro Tull (Ian Anderson), I. Anderson, Chrysalis 2101 (Warner Bros.)	WBM
★25	30	5	SWEET SURRENDER—John Denver (Milton Okun), J. Denver, RCA 10148	HAN
★26	32	8	READY—Cat Stevens (Paul Samwell-Smith, Cat Stevens), C. Stevens, A&M 1645	SGC
27	12	11	ONLY YOU—Ringo (Richard Perry), B. Ram, A. Rand, Apple 1876 (Capitol)	PLY
★28	36	4	NIGHTINGALE—Carole King (Lou Adler), C. King, D. Palmer, Ode 66106 (A&M)	SGC
★29	37	5	LONELY PEOPLE—America (George Martin), Peek & Peek, Warner Bros. 8048	WBM
★30	38	6	YOUR BULLDOG DRINKS CHAMPAGNE—Jim Stafford (Phil Gernhard & Lobo), J. Stafford, D. Bellamy, MGM 14775	HAN
★31	39	7	LADY—Styx (John Ryan For Chicago Kid Prod.), D. De Young, Wooden Nickel 10102 (RCA)	WBM
★32	40	10	MY EYES ADORED YOU—Frankie Valli (Bob Crewe), B. Crewe, K. Nolan, Private Stock 45003	SGC
★33	41	6	CAN'T GET IT OUT OF MY HEAD—Electric Light Orchestra (Jeff Lynne), J. Lynne, United Artists 573	HAN
34	31	9	I BELONG TO YOU—Love Unlimited (Barry White), B. White, 20th Century 2141	
35	34	9	THE ENTERTAINER—Billy Joel (Michael Stewart), B. Joel, Columbia 3-10064	BB
36	22	15	ANGIE BABY—Helen Reddy ● (Joe Wissert), A. O'Day, Capitol 3972	WBM
37	23	16	RIDE 'EM COWBOY—Paul Davis (Paul Davis), P. Davis, Bang 712 (Web IV)	SGC
38	20	16	KUNG FU FIGHTING—Carl Douglas ● (Biddu), C. Douglas, 20th Century 2140	CHA
★39	55	5	I'M A WOMAN—Maria Muldaur (Joe Boyd, Lenny Waronker), J. Leiber, M. Stoller, Reprise 1319	HAN
★40	51	5	BIG YELLOW TAXI—Joni Mitchell (Joni Mitchell), J. Mitchell, Asylum 45221	WBM
41	43	6	HAPPY PEOPLE—Temptations (Jeffrey Bowen, Berry Gordy), J. Bowen, D. Baldwin, L. Richie, Gordy 7138 (Motown)	SGC
42	28	9	FROM HIS WOMAN TO YOU—Barbara Mason (B. Crutcher, L. Snell, J. Smith), B. Crutcher, L. Snell, Buddah 441	SGC
43	45	8	CHANGES—David Bowie (Ken Scott), D. Bowie, RCA 74-0605	
44	35	17	CAT'S IN THE CRADLE—Harry Chapin ● (Paul Leka), H Chapin, S. Chapin, Elektra 45203	WBM
45	47	16	I FEEL A SONG (In My Heart)/Don't Burn The Bridges—Gladys Knight & The Pips (Tony Camillo), T. Camillo, M. Sawyer, Buddah 433	SGC
★46	59	3	DING DONG, DING DONG—George Harrison (George Harrison), G. Harrison, Apple 1879 (Capitol)	
★47	58	8	DON'T CALL US, WE'LL CALL YOU—Sugarloaf/Jerry Corbetta (Frank Slay), J. Corbetta, J. Carter, Claridge 402	B-3
48	42	16	YOU GOT THE LOVE—Rufus Featuring Chaka Khan (Bob Monaco, Rufus), C. Khan, R. Parker, ABC 12032	HAN
49	33	10	DARK HORSE—George Harrison (George Harrison), G. Harrison, Apple 1877 (Capitol)	HAN
50	50	8	BABY, HANG UP THE PHONE—Carl Graves (John Florez), P. McManus, L. Pedroski, A&M 1620	SGC
51	52	5	AS LONG AS HE TAKES CARE OF HOME—Candi Staton (Rick Hall), P. Mitchell, Warner Bros. 8038	
52	56	10	DANCIN' FOOL—Guess Who (Jack Richardson), B. Cummings, D. Troiano, RCA 10075	CHA
53	60	7	WHEN A CHILD IS BORN—Michael Holm (Rainer Pietsch, Michael Holm), Zacar, F. Jay, Mercury 73642 (Phonogram)	B-3
54	62	13	WOMAN TO WOMAN—Shirley Brown (Al Jackson, Jim Stewart), J. Banks, E. Marion, H. Tigpen, Truth 3206	SGC
★55	67	2	ROLL ON DOWN THE HIGHWAY—Bachman-Turner Overdrive (Randy Bachman), C.F. Turner, R. Bachman, Mercury 73656 (Phonogram)	SGC
56	65	7	I AM, I AM—Smokey Robinson (Smokey Robinson), W. Robinson, Tamla 54251 (Motown)	SGC
★57	69	6	TO THE DOOR OF THE SUN (Alle Porte Del Sole)—Al Martino (Peter De Angelis), Pace, Panzeri, Dilat, Conti, Newell, Capitol 3987	BB
★58	70	2	MOVIN' ON—Bad Company (Bad Company), M. Ralphs, Swan Song 70101 (Atlantic)	CHA
59	63	6	DAY TRIPPER—Anne Murray (Brian Ahern), J. Lennon, P. McCartney, Capitol 4000	WBM
★60	72	4	POETRY MAN—Phoebe Snow (Dino Airali), P. Snow, Shelter 40353 (MCA)	SGC
★61	84	4	LADY MARMALADE—LaBelle (Allen Toussaint, B. Crewe, K. Nolan), Epic 8-50048 (Columbia)	SGC
★62	86	4	UP IN A PUFF OF SMOKE—Polly Brown (Philip Swern, Gerry Shury), G. Shury, P. Swern, GTO 1002 (ABC)	
★63	NEW ENTRY		HAVE YOU NEVER BEEN MELLOW—Olivia Newton-John (John Farrar), J. Farrar, MCA 40349	
★64	74	3	YOU ARE SO BEAUTIFUL/IT'S A SIN WHEN YOU LOVE SOMEBODY—Joe Cocker (Jim Price), B. Preston, B. Fisher, J. Webb, a&M 1641	TMK
★65	75	3	AIN'T THAT PECULIAR—Diamond Reo (David Shaffer), W. Robinson, W. Moore, M Tarplin, R. Rogers, Big Tree 16030 (Atlantic)	SGC
66	68	6	HOPPY, GENE AND ME—Roy Rogers (Snuff Garrett), Garrett, Dorff, Brown, 20th Century 2154	HAN
67	76	4	DON'T TAKE YOUR LOVE FROM ME—Manhattans (Bobby Martin and Manhattan Prods.), A. Felder, B. Sigler, R. Kensey. Columbia 3-10045	
★68	78	3	SAD SWEET DREAMER—Sweet Sensation (Tony Hatch, Des Farton), D. Parton, Pye 71002 (ATV)	MCA
69	57	18	DO IT ('Til You're Satisfied)—B.T. Express ● (J. Lane For Doo Prods.), Nichols, Scepter 12395	SGC
★70	80	2	LOVIN' YOU—Minnie Riperton (Scorbu Prod.), M. Riperton, R. Rudolph, Epic 8-50057 (Columbia)	SGC
71	46	18	SHA-LA-LA (Makes Me Happy)—Al Green (Willie Mitchell), A. Green, Hi 2274 (London)	SGC
72	66	20	I'VE GOT THE MUSIC IN ME—The Kiki Dee Band (Gus Dudgeon), B. Boshell, MCA 40293	HAN
73	77	4	MIDNIGHT SKY PART 1—Isley Bros. (Isley Bros.), R. Isley, O. Isley, R. Isley, M. Isley, C. Jasper, E. Isley, T-Neck 8-2255 (Columbia)	
★74	87	2	I AM LOVE Part 1 & 2—Jackson 5 (Jerry Marcellino, Mel Larson), M. Larson, J. Mane, D. Fencetone, R. Rancifer, Motown 1310	SGC
75	79	4	RHYME TYME PEOPLE—Kool & The Gang (K&G Prods.), D. Thomas, P. Saunders, Kool & The Gang, De-Lite 1563 (PIP)	SGC
★76	88	3	SHAME, SHAME, SHAME—Shirley & Company (Sylvia), S. Robinson, Vibration 532 (All Platinum)	
77	82	7	COSTAFINE TOWN—Splinter (George Harrison), R.J. Purvis, W. Elliott, Dark Horse 10002 (A&M)	SGC
★78	89	2	STAR ON A TV SHOW—Stylistics (Hugo & Luigi), Hugo & Luigi, G.D. Weiss, Avco 4549	
79	54	18	WHEN WILL I SEE YOU AGAIN—Three Degrees ● (Kenny Gamble, Leon Huff), K. Gamble, L. Huff, Philadelphia International 8-3550 (Columbia)	BB
★80	90	2	HOT DAWGIT—Ramsey Lewis & Earth, Wind & Fire (Maurice White), M. White, C. Stepney, Columbia 3-10056	SGC
★81	94	2	NEVER LET HER GO—David Gates (David Gates), D. Gates, Elektra 45223	SGC
★82	NEW ENTRY		MY BOY—Elvis Presley (Not Listed), B. Martin, RCA 10191	SGC
83	83	2	FUTURE SHOCK—Hello People (Todd Rundgren), G. Geddes, R. Sedita, N.D. Smart II, L. Tasse, ABC/Dunhill 15023	SGC
84	61	18	I CAN HELP—Billy Swan ● (Chip Young, Billy Swan), B. Swan, Monument 8-8621 (Columbia)	B-3
★85	NEW ENTRY		EXPRESS—B. T. Express (Jeff Lane), B.T. Express, Roadshow 7001 (Scepter)	SGC
★86	97	2	THANKS FOR THE SMILES—Charlie Ross (Amigo Prod.), K. O'Dell, Big Tree 16025 (Atlantic)	SGC
87	91	4	LET ME START TONITE—Lamont Dozier (McKinley Jackson), L. Dozier, ABC 12044	SGC
★88	100	2	IT'S ALL RIGHT—Jim Capaldi (Jim Capaldi), J. Capaldi, Island 003	SGC
★89	NEW ENTRY		IF LOVING YOU IS WRONG I DON'T WANT TO BE RIGHT—Millie Jackson (Brad Shapiro, Millie Jackson), H. Bunks, R. Jackson, C. Hampton, Spring 155 (Polydor)	SGC
★90	NEW ENTRY		I GET LIFTED—George McCrae (H.W. Casey, R. Finch), H.W. Casey, R. Finch TK 1007	SGC
91	85	8	ONE TEAR—Eddie Kendricks (Frank Wilson, Leonard Caston), L. Caston, Tamla 54255 (Motown)	SGC
92	71	15	WISHING YOU WERE HERE—Chicago (James William Guercio), P. Cetera, Columbia 3-10049	HAN
93	96	3	I WON'T LAST A DAY WITHOUT YOU/LET MET BE THE ONE—Al Wilson (Jerry Fuller), P. Williams, R. Nichols, Rocky Road 30202 (Arista)	TMK
94	NEW ENTRY		WE MAY NEVER LOVE LIKE THIS AGAIN—Maureen McGovern (Carl Maduki), A. Kasha, J. Hirshorn, 20th Century 2158	WBM
95	NEW ENTRY		DEVIL IN THE BOTTLE—T. G. Shepard (Jack Gilmer, Bill Browden, Don Crus), B. David, Melodyland 6002 (Motown)	
96	81	6	GEE BABY—Peter Shelley (Peter Shelley), P. Shelley, Bell 45614 (Arista)	SGC
97	NEW ENTRY		CHICO AND THE MAN—Jose Feliciano (Jose & Janna M. Feliciano), J. Feliciano, RCA 10145	
98	98	5	CRAZY TALK—Chilliwack (Terry Jacks), Henderson, Sire 716 (ABC)	
99	NEW ENTRY		ISN'T IT LONELY TOGETHER—Stark & McBrien (David Spinozza), R. McBrien, E. Levitt, RCA PB-10109	
100	NEW ENTRY		I'LL STILL LOVE YOU—Jim Weatherly (Jimmy Bowen), Jim Weatherly, Buddah 444	WBM

★ STAR PERFORMER: Stars are awarded on the Hot 100 chart based on the following upward movement. 1-10 Strong increase in sales / 11-20 Upward movement of 4 positions / 21-30 Upward movement of 6 positions / 31-40 Upward movement of 8 positions / 41-100 Upward movement of 10 positions. Recording Industry Association Of America seal of certification as "million seller" (Seal indicated by bullet.)

Sheet music suppliers are confined to piano/vocal sheet music copies and do not purport to represent mixed publications distribution. ALF = Alfred Publishing Co.; B-M = Belwin Mills; BB = Big Bells; B-3 = Big Three Pub.; CHA = Chappell Music; CPI = Cimino Pub.; CRIT = Criterion Music Corp.; FMC = Frank Music Corp.; HAN = Hansen Pub.; IMM = Ivan Mogull Music; MCA = MCA MUSIC; PSP = Peer Southern Pub.; PLY = Plymouth Music; PSI = Publishers Sales Inc.; SGC = Screen Gems/Columbia; TMK = Triangle Music/Kane. WBM = Warner Bros. Music.

HOT 100 A-Z-(Publisher-Licensee)

A reflection of National Sales and programming activity by selected dealers, one-stops and radio stations as compiled by the Charts Department of Billboard.

May 5, 1975

Mr. Sherwin Bash
BNB Associates
9454 Wilshire Boulevard
Beverly Hills, California 90212

Dear Sherwin:

Just thought you'd like to know that to
date the Carpenters' single "Please Mr. Postman"
has gone over the one million mark internationally
with a total of 1,082,116 as of March 31, 1975.
This figure <u>does not</u> include the United States,
but does include Canada, England and Japan.

Also, wanted you to be aware that we sent
out a total of thirty-six requested "Please Mr.
Postman" film clips, which is the most we have
sent to date for any A&M artist.

Best regards,

Jack Losmann
International Operations Manager

JL:dpw

cc: Ed Sulzer

A&M Records, Inc. 1416 North La Brea Avenue, Hollywood, California 90028   (213)469-2411

Page 160: "Please Mr. Postman" reaches No. 1 on the *Billboard* Hot 100 chart for the week ending on January 25, 1975

Page 161: A letter from A&M's International Operations Manager Jack Lossman regarding the success of "Please Mr. Postman," June 1975

Right: Karen's 25th birthday, Downey, CA, 1975

Single
"Only Yesterday"

—

US release date
3/14/75

—

***Billboard* Hot 100**

Chart entry date (position)
3/29/75 (No. 74)

Peak date, position (weeks at peak)
5/24/75, No. 4 (2)

Total weeks on chart
13

Year-end chart rank
No. 94

—

***Billboard* Top 50 Easy Listening**

Chart entry date (position)
4/5/75 (No. 33)

Peak date, position (weeks at peak)
5/3/75, No. 1 (1)

Total weeks on chart
12

Year-end chart rank
No. 21

Richard calls *Horizon* a "sleepy" album. And, indeed, seven of its ten tracks are either total downers or at least low key. If we overlook the set's brief bookends, "Aurora" and "Eventide," the album contains just two Carpenter/Bettis originals. Among them is the breakup song "(I'm Caught Between) Goodbye and I Love You," which was Bettis's portrait of the kind of relationships he, Richard, and Karen were having at the time. In a word: fuzzy. It's tough to keep yourself, no less a romance, healthy when you spend more time on the road and in the studio than you do at home. Nevertheless, Bettis and Karen are in supreme form here. And Tony Peluso's ethereal electric-guitar work and Buddy Emmons's pedal-steel guitar are showstoppers.

Inspired by Harry Nilsson's 1973 album *A Little Touch of Schmilsson in the Night*, Richard added a standard to *Horizon*. He selected the 1937 Sammy Fain/Irving Kahal ballad "I Can Dream, Can't I?" and brought in veteran Billy May for the period-appropriate arrangement. Richard was in heaven, working with one of his heroes (they'd work together again a few years later on the Christmas recordings).

But this experience had a downside. "He was taking it too slow tempo-wise," Richard notes. "I'd say, 'Billy, let's take this up a little bit.' It didn't make any difference. That's my only regret about that."

Surprise, surprise, even *Rolling Stone* raved. Critic Stephen Holden: "Beautifully orchestrated and co-arranged by Billy May, one of the finest studio band leaders and arrangers of the ['40s and '50s], 'Dream' is such a gem of updated schmaltz it makes me wish that veteran masters of the studio like Gordon Jenkins, Ray Ellis, Nelson Riddle, and Percy Faith would have been encouraged to collaborate with other best-selling MOR acts of the Seventies."

At right and opposite page: Fresno, 1976

June 6, 1975

Mr. Richard Carpenter
9828 Newville Avenue
Downey, California

Dear Richard,

I've just been listening to your new "Horizon" album.
I just wanted to let you know that it's one of the
finest recordings I've ever had the pride and pleasure
to be associated with.

Karen's singing is better than ever. And, that's
saying something..... But this album is more than
great songs sung better than anyone else could hope
to sing them. It's a brilliant example of the
recording art at its very highest level. The extraordinary blend of material, arrangements and orchestrations, all complemented with that unique Carpenters'
sound, I believe, could be approached by perhaps
just a handful of producers in the industry today.

I guess what I'm trying to say is "Congratulations
Richard". You made one hell of an album!

Warm regards,

Jerry Moss
JM:k

A&M Records, Inc. 1416 North La Brea Avenue, Hollywood, California 90028   (213)469-2411

Single
"Solitaire"

—

US release date
7/18/75

—

***Billboard* Hot 100**

Chart entry date (position)
8/2/75 (No. 76)

Peak date, position (weeks at peak)
9/20/75, No. 17 (1)

Total weeks on chart
10

Year-end chart rank
n/a

—

***Billboard* Top 50 Easy Listening**

Chart entry date (position)
8/9/75 (No. 43)

Peak date, position (weeks at peak)
9/6/75, No. 1 (1)

Total weeks on chart
11

Year-end chart rank
No. 40

Right: Picture sleeve
for "Solitaire"

Page 166:
Letter from A&M
cofounder Jerry Moss,
regarding success of
Horizon, 1975

On the US Charts

Horizon entered the *Billboard* Top LPs chart dated June 28, 1975, at No. 38. On July 36, it reached its peak of No. 13, where it remained for three consecutive weeks, logging eighteen weeks on the charts. It marked the first Carpenters album that failed to reach the Top 10 of the survey since *Offering/Ticket to Ride*.

The Other Singles

"*Another* 'Yesterday' song," Richard begins, with a roll of the eyes. He explains Carpenters' listeners would forever be confused whether the title was referring to the classic "Yesterday Once More" or this later—and, in his mind, lesser—release, "Only Yesterday."

"The point was to come up with another hit," he says. "It's a better record than it is a song." There's so much going on in the recording that a kitchen sink literally *could* be one of the instruments. You can listen to "Only Yesterday" a thousand times and hear something new in it.

"It's definitely contrived," Richard says, "but, for an arranger, it laid itself wide open for all sorts of things. It's brilliantly engineered [by Roger Young]. And Karen: low E flat right off of the bat. And, so, it's a marvelously made record."

The Neil Sedaka/Phil Cody dirge "Solitaire" boasted what may just be Karen's strongest vocals and one of Richard's most imaginative arrangements. But, when the single was released, it was wrong for Top 40 radio, which had started a serious love affair with up-tempo soul and dance music. Disco was coming. The Bee Gees' "Jive Talkin'" was No. 3 the week "Solitaire" debuted on the US *Billboard* Hot 100, and KC and the Sunshine Band's "Get Down Tonight" was just about to enter the chart.

Imagine "Solitaire" played back-to-back against either of those records.

"It's too slow, and it goes on too long," Richard says. "I could have cut one chorus near the end, and it would've made it better. But it was slow. It's like that whole album: all so slow. But Karen sings the hell out of it."

And yet she didn't like the song. She never wanted to perform it in concert. Why? "She just didn't like it," Richard replies.

Album
A Kind of Hush

"Hush was, really, a nothing album."

Album
A Kind of Hush

—

US release date
6/11/76

—

***Billboard* Top LPs**

Chart entry date (position)
7/10/76 (No. 33)

Peak date, position (weeks at peak)
8/14/76, No. 33 (2)

Total weeks on chart
16

Year-end chart rank
n/a

At the start of recording *Horizon* in autumn 1974, Karen Carpenter was receiving compliments on her newly svelte figure. But by the following summer, she was down to just eighty pounds.

Between touring, recording, an *American Music Awards* appearance, and other responsibilities, Richard and Karen were working nonstop from the start of 1975 through to a late-summer booking in Las Vegas.

Karen was exhausted. Richard says, "It had gotten so bad that she had had to lie down on the sofa in her dressing room between shows."

That meant canceling tours and disappointing thousands of fans in Japan and the United Kingdom. Richard boarded a plane to Tokyo for a September 22 press conference to apologize for canceling a twenty-five-date tour there. Promoter Tatsuji "Tats" Nagashima said the box office would have broken records in Japan, and the loss was $1.2 million.

Then Richard was off to London to express regrets. According to a report in the British music magazine *Record Mirror*, the Carpenters canceled thirty-eight sold-out concerts in the United Kingdom, which included the Royal Variety Performance, where Queen Elizabeth II was to be in attendance.

Karen was finally back in the recording studio at the end of 1975 to work on the Carpenters' seventh studio album, *A Kind of Hush*.

"*Hush* was, really, a nothing album," Richard comments. "It was, of course, well performed, well produced, all of that." And Richard is fond of a few of the album's tracks: "We had a singer-songwriter, Lewis Anderson, open for us for a while, and he wrote 'One More Time.' We heard him sing it on the road, and I thought, "That's a nice song for Karen." Richard and partner John Bettis co-wrote the breezy "Sandy," with Bettis offering a sweet tribute to Karen's hairdresser Sandy Holland. And then there's the other Carpenter/Bettis original, "I Need to Be in Love."

"But the album is not one of my favorites," Richard says. He recalls A&M cofounder Herb Alpert making a rare visit to the studio and talking about the album. "He asked, 'Are you happy with this?' This was Herb's way of saying, 'I'm *not* happy with this.' I wasn't either. But what was I supposed to say? So, I just said, 'Yes.'"

Left: *A Kind of Hush* inner-sleeve portrait, 1976

Single
"There's a Kind of Hush (All Over the World)"

—

US release date
2/12/76

—

***Billboard* Hot 100**

Chart entry date (position)
2/28/76 (No. 75)

Peak date, position (weeks at peak)
4/24/76, No. 12 (1)

Total weeks on chart
13

Year-end chart rank
n/a

—

***Billboard* Top 50 Easy Listening**

Chart entry date (position)
3/6/76 (No. 33)

Peak date, position (weeks at peak)
4/3/76, No. 1 (1)

Total weeks on chart
11

Year-end chart rank
n/a

page 171:
Trade ad for
A Kind of Hush

On the US Charts

A Kind of Hush entered the *Billboard* Top LPs chart dated July 10, 1976, at No. 68. On August 14, 1976, the album reached its peak of No. 33, where it remained for one week. *Hush* spent a sixteen weeks on the survey, the shortest *Billboard* album-chart run for any Carpenters studio album since *Ticket to Ride* in 1971.

The Singles

"There's a Kind of Hush (All Over the World)" is yet another Carpenters cover, a remake of Herman's Hermits' cheery Top 5 pop smash from 1967.

Richard said he was reminded of the tune while thumbing through *The Miles Chart Display of Popular Music*, which documents the chart performances of records released since 1955. "I was just going through it to see, and said, 'Ah! I always liked that record and the song.'"

Richard reflects: "Bad idea. I think we'd done enough oldies by then."

The single actually did fairly well, reaching No. 12 on the *Billboard* Hot 100 and No. 1 on the Easy Listening charts. While the Carpenters delivered yet again, this surely was no "Please Mr. Postman." "It was fun to do the oldies." Richard says, "But enough was enough."

With "I Need to Be in Love," Richard's co-writer John Bettis again got autobiographical. This time, he reflected on the ties that bound him to Karen when it came to romance:

So here I am with pockets full of good intentions
But none of them will comfort me tonight
I'm wide awake at 4 a.m. without a friend in sight
hanging on a hope, but I'm alright

With that powerful lyric, one of Richard's most sophisticated compositions and arrangements, and Karen singing as if her life depended on it, no wonder the duo had high hopes for the single. But, by this point in the 1970s, even the best of the Carpenters just wasn't what pop-radio programmers were looking for. Richard says, "The image thing was catching up to us."

It was the duo's first nonholiday A-side since 1969's "Ticket to Ride" that failed to reach the Top 20 on the *Billboard* Hot 100. Go ahead and blame the image. But the ballad's lackluster chart success also had something to do with changing pop-music trends. The Carpenters had been on top for five years, an eternity in pop music. And while ballads were still the stuff of chart hits, increasingly they would be coming from artists who had established fan bases in other genres: most notably soul, rock, and country—bases that Karen and Richard didn't have.

And then there was the disco factor. Consider that the week "I Need to Be in Love" debuted on the Hot 100, June 12, 1976, Wings' "Silly Love Songs," Silver Convention's "Get Up and Boogie," and Dorothy Moore's "Misty Blue" were the three top singles in the US.

Another problem is that "I Need to Be in Love" didn't scream "classic Carpenters." The song's melodic and lyrical structures were among the most sophisticated of any Carpenters single since "(They Long to Be) Close to You." With this single, it was clear that the Carpenters weren't just getting older, they were getting better. But relatively few took notice.

THE NEW CARPENTERS ALBUM IS HERE.
NOW.

CARPENTERS "A KIND OF HUSH" ON A&M RECORDS AND TAPES
(SP 4581)
JERRY WEINTRAUB/⊛MANAGEMENT THREE/400 South Beverly Drive/Beverly Hills, Calif. 90212 (213) 277-9633

Produced by Richard Carpenter   Associate producer: Karen Carpenter

Single
"I Need to Be in Love"

—

US release date
5/21/76

—

Billboard Hot 100

Chart entry date (position)
6/12/76 (No. 55)

Peak date, position (weeks at peak)
7/24/76, No. 25 (2)

Total weeks on chart
11

Year-end chart rank
n/a

—

Billboard Top 50 Easy Listening

Chart entry date (position)
6/19/76 (20)

Peak date, position (weeks at peak)
7/24/76, No. 1 (1)

Total weeks on chart
11

Year-end chart rank
No. 43

Above: From
A Kind of Hush
cover shoot, 1976

Some radio programmers got the record immediately. It flew onto the *Billboard* Hot 100 chart at No. 55, a notch *higher* than "(They Long to Be) Close to You" six years earlier. But unlike most of the duo's singles, which grabbed listeners by the first chorus, *I Need to Be in Love*'s complex design required some fans to listen a few times before they'd start calling in a request or race out to buy the record. "It escaped a lot of people," Richard notes.

Like Richard and John themselves, the Carpenter/Bettis songwriting team was evolving. This happened with The Beatles' John Lennon and Paul McCartney and ABBA's Benny Andersson and Björn Ulvaeus, whose fans matured with them, stuck around, and bought the groups' albums without even caring if there was a new hit.

Contrary to their reputation as "a singles act," the Carpenters had millions of fans worldwide who bought their albums on release day. The problem in this case, as Richard points out above, is that *A Kind of Hush* "just wasn't worth buying." And "I Need to Be in Love" wasn't enough to make a difference.

After crashing onto the Hot 100 at 55, the single climbed just 30 points, where it stalled at No. 25. It did better on *Billboard*'s Easy Listening survey, scoring the Carpenters yet another No. 1 there.

Overall, "I Need to Be in Love" wasn't a disaster. But, by the Carpenters' standards, it was a big disappointment—especially so, given the tune was Karen's favorite of all the Carpenter originals, according to Richard.

Single
"Goofus"

—

US release date
6/11/76

—

Billboard Hot 100

Chart entry date (position)
9/4/76 (No. 89)

Peak date, position (weeks at peak)
9/25/76, No. 56 (2)

Total weeks on chart
5

Year-end chart rank
n/a

—

Billboard Top 50 Easy Listening

Chart entry date (position)
8/28/76 (No. 46)

Peak date, position (weeks at peak)
10/9/76, No. 4 (2)

Total weeks on chart
11

Year-end chart rank
n/a

However, this isn't the end of the song's success story. Zip ahead some twenty years, and the Japanese would give "I Need to Be in Love" a happy ending. It's detailed in this book's chapter "All Over the World."

What to say? "Goofus"—written by Wayne King, William Harold, and Gus Kahn—was written and popularized in 1930. But it wasn't a chart hit until 1950, when Les Paul—whose use of multitrack recording strongly influenced the Carpenters sound—took the song to No. 21 on the *Billboard* pop charts.

"I've always liked it, going back to it," Richard says. "But, of course, we never meant it to be a single, just an album cut."

For decades, fans have been baffled as to why the Carpenters ever thought their cover of old-timey novelty stood a chance of becoming a hit. "Karen wanted it to be a single," Richard replies. "I wasn't in any shape to argue."

"Goofus" continued the Carpenters' decline on the US pop charts, becoming their first A-side single since "Ticket to Ride" in 1970 to fail to make the Top 40 portion of the *Billboard* Hot 100 or to reach either No. 1 or No. 2 on the Easy Listening chart.

From *A Kind of Hush* cover shoot, 1976

Pages 174–75:
Richard and
concertmaster
Jimmy Getzoff,
A&M Records,
Los Angeles, 1976

Left and right:
Recording the
A Kind of Hush
album, A&M
Studio D, Los
Angeles, 1976

Pages 178–79:
Karen trying
to make the
musicians laugh
by balancing
a stack of music
charts on her
head during a
string session for
A Kind of Hush,
A&M Records,
Los Angeles, 1976

Love, John

John Bettis

"They, in their best moments, have crafted the musical equivalent of the original Fabergé eggs."

John Bettis

A gold chain hangs from the arm of a simple chrome desk lamp next to my computer screen. On it a gold chip, a small designer dog tag, sways with each keystroke. Engraved on one side of the tag: WORDS. On the reverse side: Love, KAREN & RICHARD.

It was a Christmas gift to me from Karen, a long time ago. If memory serves, Richard has a twin, engraved MUSIC. That tag, swaying within reach, is typical, even symbolic, of Karen's talent to bind the three of us together, permanently.

We were unlikely.

Richard is the type of pianist who already knew how to play before he tried. Lessons were just a finger exercise. Few people know how truly accomplished he is at his instrument.

Once, he did me a favor. I had co-written a musical. Richard consented to arrange and play an instrumental medley of the tunes for a recording. He ran late getting to the studio. Several of the dude players in L.A. were lounging, waiting, and grousing about how they would have to guide this pop star through the session. "He couldn't be that good."

I smiled. I knew. Richard rushed in, apologized, and went straight to the piano. He handed a thick score to each of the musicians, laid his own copy on the piano and went through it—playing his own part and theirs—simultaneously. Talking as his hands flew. No mistakes. With emotion. And, when they got lost, he corrected, with the kindly guidance of a great player who has nothing to prove. Now they knew. Killer. I think they had him sign the score afterward.

And yet, the magic of Richard is elsewhere.

Magic is irrational. It doesn't follow neat, Aristotelian lines of reason. Richard doesn't produce, arrange, or compose by linear thinking. He envisions music. To watch him listening to a song for the first time, eyes closed, enjoying, imagining, is somewhat like being a deaf and blind bystander on Sinai, standing right beside the burning bush. You're there. You can feel the heat, sense the inspiration—but you are not *in* the experience. You neither hear the voice nor see the light. Later, once he comes down to common ground and makes the record, you get it.

Where does that come from? Easy answer: I don't know. I do know that he has an interior universe. It is an infinite, musical, random-bozo place. In that place, his father's record collection plays on Frank Zappa's turntable: *The Beatles Perform* the *Perry Como Songbook* with the Sons of the Pioneers singing background vocals; Phil Spector produces The Beach Boys singing "The Look of Love" a cappella; Johann Sebastian Bach, Oscar Peterson, Liberace, and Spike Jones improvise "Bridge over Troubled Water" at Victor Borge's birthday party, and "Kitten on the Keys" is the national anthem. All of that and more were there when he envisioned the arrangement and recording of "Superstar." Imagine that. Magic.

Richard also has a religious faith in great players, songs, and music. Not good. Great. It is his coin of the realm. It doesn't matter where it comes from or, sometimes, even how well it is played. Great music comes from beneath technique. This has made him a very keen and egalitarian judge of talent. He picked all of us out of unlikely places. Bob Messenger, the amazing woodwind player, came from a casual gig in Downey, California, when Richard was still in college. A year later, Richard gave him a call. When you listen to Bob's solos—perfect, original, and so melodic— you wonder how Richard knew it would be so. But he did. The same is true of his picking Tony Peluso. How did Richard know that the guitar player in Mark Lindsay's backing band was capable of the guitar solo on "Goodbye to Love"? Good question. And me? How did he know? You would have to ask him.

But there was one of us who was right there all along.

Karen.

You and I, and hundreds of millions of others, have a personal relationship with Karen. That was her gift, and very few singers have it. Édith Piaf did, always. Bing Crosby, usually. But not many others. I am reluctant to intrude on that relationship. It is so intimate, so vulnerable, almost secretive. She sings as if she were speaking in whispers about heartbreaks to a trusted friend. In her absence, her voice has become almost oracular—someone or something one consults when life overwhelms. If humanity makes it as a species, she will be a source of solace for generations to come. She possessed a timeless voice. For me, she was a rollicking, mugging, funny, alluring, smart, drumming, smiling imp, zooming around. A tomboy kid sister, in a way. She didn't love music— she embodied it. She didn't think about it—she just waited for the count off and then *sang*. At once effortless and beyond her years. When she liked someone's playing, singing, or recording, she said it "cranked." She thought of herself as a drummer who could sing. She would have preferred Levon Helm's role to being the chanteuse. But the angels had other plans for her.

We—Richard and I—wrote for her from the beginning. Most of what you hear in our work is, to one degree or another, autobiographical. I am grateful that so many other writers were writing great songs at the same time. It took a load off our shoulders. She deserved the best.

However, she was always pushing us to get together. I remember a phone call: "Hi, John." "Hi, Karen." "Has Richard called you to get together to write?" "No, not yet." "He will. Bye." He did. We got together within the week, and in a two-day session we wrote "Top of the World" and "Goodbye to Love." Everyone should have a little sister like that.

Another scene comes to mind. On the day we wrote "Yesterday Once More," Richard and I struggled more than we normally did to finish it. The specific needs of its anthemic use on the record

made it tricky lyrically. We were just finishing when Karen flew in with shopping bags on her arms. "What did you write for me?" We barely knew the song ourselves, but Richard made his way through it as I watched and waited. Karen began to hum the chorus on the second iteration. After Richard finished, she gave me that smile and said, "Play it again." She craned her neck over Richard's shoulder and, unbelievably, read my illegible lyric sheet and sang it through, nearly perfectly. No questions. Just beauty.

That was the thing. Karen completely trusted us. If we wrote it, she sang it. A few times I would have to polish a line because it sang poorly, but she never, ever, changed the meaning or the message. We were alike, she and I, in the most contradictory of ways possible, inside. "I Need to Be in Love" is the best example of our singularity of soul. I miss that, a lot. But, at least, we were…

Successful.

On one hand, we were a cliché: three middle-class American kids forming a band with a couple of friends, Gary Sims and Dan Woodhams. On the other, we were unique: Spectrum's instruments were amplified, yet we weren't a rock 'n' roll band. The kind of band we were, in fact, was probably nameless. I don't remember worrying about that. Soon, it would become clear that other people would have a problem with categorizing us. We sang in five-part harmonies that only Richard could imagine. We wrote one song in 5/4 time. The rhythm was coming from a great jazz drummer, Karen. The arrangements were coming from a killer keyboard player, Richard, who had dived deeply into the vocal waters of Jud Conlon, Gene Puerling, and Brian Wilson. The bass player was a classically trained violinist, Danny. One guitarist was classically trained at acoustic guitar, Gary. And the other guy on guitar was an out-of-work folkie who was woefully undertrained, me. Together we were chasing originality and excellence. Perfection would have been nice, but we didn't get there. However, some days, some chords, and some performances were pretty good. I can still hear the echoes sometimes.

We tried. God knows, we tried. But the music world didn't want us. Well, they did want one thing. They wanted us to go away. In retrospect, the rejection itself was right and proper. Spectrum had no hits. Our original material, at that time, was very far away from anything anyone else was doing, and lyrically, it was very unfocused. Most importantly, the recordings we had made did not center on Karen as much as they should have. Strangely, the rejections we got did not address those aspects, and the force of them was stunningly aggressive.

Now, I am a veteran of many musical campaigns. I have been successful and defeated, applauded and ignored, awarded and passed over, and have even scratched my name on a summit or two. I have never known anything like what happened to me and Rich back then. They didn't say we weren't good, or even bad. They told us that we were loathsome noncon-formists. Infidels. Two twenty-one-year-old guys, me and Rich, had meetings across the desk from grown, and not so grown, men, who actually seemed to feel that their purpose in life was threatened by a love song. We were heretics to the popular-culture catechism of which they were disciples. We were desecrating the delivered wisdom and gospel of *Rolling Stone* magazine. In very clear language, they let us know that we had violated some community ethos of cool or had broken a societal rule about what kind of music was allowed. And they didn't like our wardrobe, either! Isn't that odd? Silly, really.

Anyway, we obliged the music world. In mid-'68, Spectrum broke up. Richard and Karen took it from there, thankfully. They focused themselves on what they had before them, a body of work. They got much closer to perfection than the band ever would have. They, in their best moments, have crafted the musical equivalent of the original Fabergé eggs, singular objects of high craft and elegant beauty, never to be duplicated. As you will see in the pages here, Richard is much more qualified than I to take you through the intricacies of the method and the depth of the dream. We can all agree, however, that these auditory objects are worth the herculean effort that it took to make them. Perhaps they are priceless. They are definitely enduring.

The gold chip is swaying more slowly on its chain. The memories are weighing more heavily, retarding the flow of the words. What remains to be said? Am I comfortable saying it? I am still strain-ing, reaching for the perfect ending, the thought that is within reach, and yet elusive. Maybe that's why the chip stays within my sight as I work, a reminder that creation is about seeing something that seems close enough to touch and yet having to reach out beyond comfort to touch it. The music that led you to hold this book is the product of that kind of effort. Good enough isn't. The cost of caring about origi-nality and excellence can be high, maybe too high. Timeless ain't cheap. It is, however, all there is that is worth the trouble.

PS I am pretty sure that Karen would not have engraved Richard's gold chip, the twin to mine, with my name. It would have seemed creepy to her, I think. And she would have been right. So, I'd like to correct that. On the reverse side of Richard's chip that says MUSIC, I would like to add:

Love,
John

Left: John and Richard in Studio D, 1976

Page 183: In England, 1974

182

Love, John

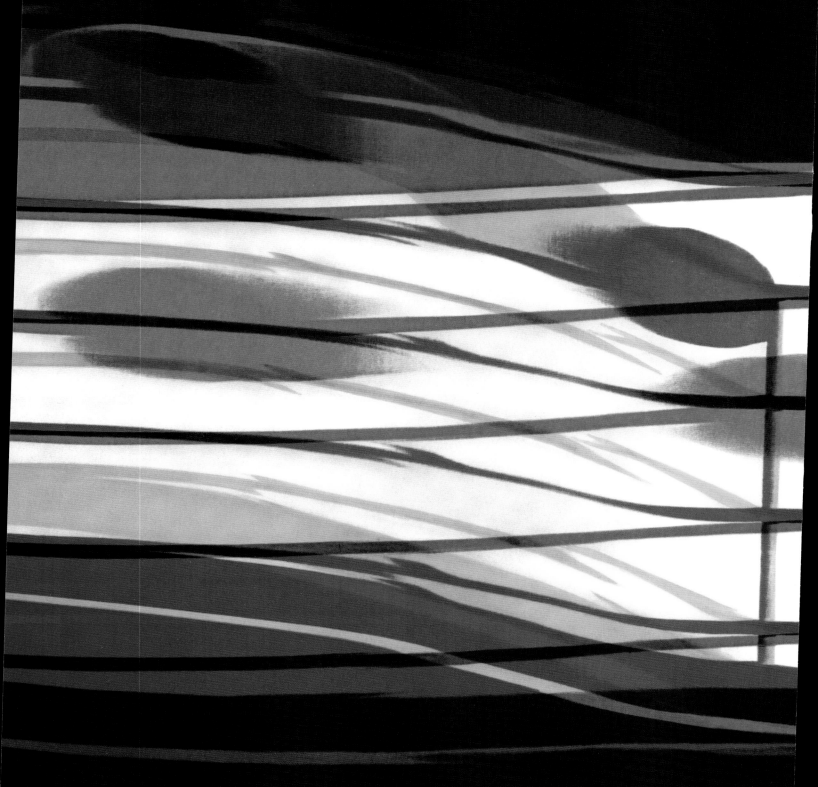

Passage

"Very well produced, but just a little out there—too much of a departure."

Album
Passage
—
US release date
9/23/77
—
***Billboard* Top LPs**

Chart entry date (position)
10/22/77 (No. 98)

Peak date, position (weeks at peak)
12/3/77, No. 49 (1)

Total weeks on chart
18

Year-end chart rank
n/a

Left: Detail of
***Passage* back cover**

For those not looking closely, the Carpenters were having a sparkling 1976. They had a new big-name manager, Jerry Weintraub; a reworked stage show; and a record-breaking European and Japanese concert tour that made 1975's costly cancelations seem to up and disappear.

The duo even ended the United States bicentennial year with cause to send up their *own* fireworks: airing December 8, *The Carpenters Very First Television Special* was a ratings smash, the sixth-most-watched show in the US for the week. It would be the first of five specials the duo made for the American television network ABC.

But those paying close attention to the Carpenters' narrative know that none of the above really mattered.

A Kind of Hush, released in June 1976, had no sell-through hit single. It was the first of the duo's albums to fail to reach the *Billboard* Top 30 since "(They Long to Be) Close to You" made them superstars six summers earlier. Something had to give.

Richard says that he believes it was A&M cofounder Jerry Moss who suggested he hand over the responsibility of producing the Carpenters' albums to someone else. Atop Richard's writing, arranging, and performing as well as touring and promotions, the job of producing—serving as an album's artistic leader—was just too much for one person.

"I thought, 'This is good. Let somebody else worry about it,'" Richard says. "But every producer we met with came up with some sort of an excuse why they couldn't do it."

Among them were Richard Perry (producer of Rod Stewart and Carly Simon) and Kyle Lehning (England Dan & John Ford Coley and Anne Murray). Joe Wissert, who was coming off his 1976 Grammy win for producing Boz Scaggs's *Silk Degrees*, agreed to sign on, but then had a change of heart. "We get a call," Richard says. "'Joe would like to meet you for lunch at Musso & Frank [a famous Hollywood grill].' We met him and he said, pretty much, 'I don't know that this is going to work.' And that was that."

Richard can only guess why no one would take on his producing role. He suspects one issue was that the new person would be producing the same old Carpenters. Even though Richard would not be producing, he'd still be in the studio—performing, arranging, and all the rest.

"Maybe they didn't like the idea of my possibly second-guessing them," Richard surmises. "Or maybe it was the image thing. But for whatever reason, they just didn't want to touch it." So Richard yet again forged ahead.

But this time was different. A&M wanted the Carpenters to pivot—to depart from…the Carpenters. "The label wanted a different

Single
"All You Get from Love Is a Love Song"

—

US release date
5/2/77

—

Billboard Hot 100

Chart entry date (position)
5/21/77 (No. 77)

Peak date, position (weeks at peak)
7/2/77, No. 35 (1)

Total weeks on chart
10

Year-end chart rank
n/a

—

Billboard Top 50 Easy Listening

Chart entry date (position)
5/21/77 (No. 37)

Peak date, position (weeks at peak)
6/25/77, No. 4 (3)

Total weeks on chart
15

Year-end chart rank
No. 29

Right: Trade ad for "Calling Occupants..." and *Passage*

Page 187: 1977

approach, stuff with more balls, which I understood and tried to accommodate."

The album was "very well produced," Richard continues, "but just a little out there—too much of a departure."

On the Album

"There's 'B'wana She No Home,' which was [smooth-jazz pioneer Michael Franks's] 'B'wana—*He* No Home,' but it's not my arrangement," Richard says. The 1930s calypso classic "Man Smart, Woman Smarter," popularized by Harry Belafonte in the 1950s, had recently been covered by Robert Palmer and was getting a little airplay overseas. "But we just copied that," Richard adds.

And then there's "Don't Cry for Me Argentina," from the new Andrew Lloyd Webber/Tim Rice musical *Evita*. "I foolishly thought, 'This will work for Karen,'" Richard says. "But with me, everything

Passage

CARPENTERS
Sweet, Sweet, Smile

From The
A&M Album
"PASSAGE" SP 4703
Produced
by Richard Carpenter
Associate Producer:
Karen Carpenter
Arranged by Richard Carpenter

© 1977 A&M RECORDS, Inc.
All Rights Reserved.
Printed in U.S.A.

AM 2008

Single
"Sweet, Sweet Smile"

—

US release date
1/20/78

—

Billboard Hot 100

Chart entry date (position)
2/4/78 (No. 89)

Peak date, position (weeks at peak)
4/15/78, No. 44 (1)

Total weeks on chart
13

Year-end chart rank
n/a

—

Billboard Top 50 Easy Listening

Chart entry date (position)
1/14/78 (No. 48)

Peak date, position (weeks at peak)
3/4/78, No. 7 (2)

Total weeks on chart
18

Year-end chart rank
No. 35

Page 188: Taping
*The Carpenters…
Space Encounters,*
Los Angeles, 1978

Right: 1977

turns into a production." So, rather than use his usual complement of strings, Richard decided to go all out, hiring some 150 musicians, including members of the Los Angeles Philharmonic, as well as the fifty-member Gregg Smith Singers to chant "Evita! Evita!" To accommodate this army, Richard put the A&M soundstage into service. Microphone cables connected from the soundstage to Studio D, where Karen sang her lead in the vocal booth.

"Don't Cry for Me Argentina" was recorded, and all seemed well to Richard. For a while. "Then, as the months went by, I realized this is *not* such a good song for Karen." He explains that most of its melody stays in a singer's upper range, not where Karen shined. "Taking it down a key would have been better for her, but if I'd given the whole idea more thought I wouldn't have recorded it at all."

Of all the *Passage* album tracks, Richard speaks most fondly of "I Just Fall in Love Again." Ironically, it is one of the most Carpenteresque tracks on an album attempting to *depart* from the Carpenters sound. A ballad from country composer Larry Herbstritt, it was a showcase for Karen's lead vocal and featured a soaring fuzz-guitar solo by Tony Peluso. The result seemed to scream, "Hit!" But Richard says the four-minute track was too long for radio and was impossible to trim

down. Dusty Springfield took a shot at the tune (and missed) in 1978, and Anne Murray ultimately scored a pop-chart success—and country and adult-contemporary smashes—in early 1979. The divine Murray, as always, sings her heart out on that record, but the sparse production makes it sound like a demo compared with the Carpenters' version.

On the US Charts

Passage entered the *Billboard* Top LPs chart dated October 22, 1977, at No. 98 and reached its chart peak on December 3 at No. 49—16 points lower than *A Kind of Hush*. *Passage* spent eighteen weeks on the charts, two weeks longer than *Hush*. However, *Passage* sold considerably fewer copies and was the Carpenters' first album in seven years, since *Ticket to Ride* (1970), that failed to be certified Gold.

The Singles

It's a rare moment when you drop the name of a Carpenters record and get *this* response from Richard Carpenter: "*That* is a great record," he says with a smile, adding that both he and Karen thought "All You Get from Love Is a Love Song" would be a bigger hit than it turned out to be.

And they weren't alone. "We were working a gig for Aksarben, a civic organization in Nebraska," says Richard. "It's 'Nebraska' spelled backward, we were informed. We played there for a week and 'All You Get' had just been released. I got a call from [A&M Records executive]

Below: 1977

Single

"Calling Occupants of Interplanetary Craft (The Recognized Anthem of World Contact Day)"

—

US release date
9/9/77

—

***Billboard* Hot 100**

Chart entry date (position)
10/8/77 (No. 71)

Peak date, position (weeks at peak)
11/26/77, No. 32 (1)

Total weeks on chart
13

Year-end chart rank
n/a

—

***Billboard* Top 50 Easy Listening**

Chart entry date (position)
10/17/77 (No. 47)

Peak date, position (weeks at peak)
11/12/77, No. 18 (2)

Total weeks on chart
13

Year-end chart rank
n/a

Bob Fead, and he said, 'I just want to let you know that I think that this is *the one*. This is the one that's going to bring you back.' At the time, I agreed. But you know, nothing happened with it, really."

So, what happened? "Some of it could just be that the lyrics are hard to remember, Richard says. "I don't know. To me, it's a radio record"—meaning a record that will get played on the radio, but listeners will not run out and buy.

"We were given a demo to 'Sweet, Sweet Smile,' a tune co-written by Otha Young and Juice Newton, who were unknown at that time," Richard recalls. "It had a bit of a country flavor, and I turned it into a combination ragtime piano, banjo-picking, fiddling, country-folk song. A&M had a tack piano, an old upright with the thumbtacks on the hammers. So, we got Tom Hensley, a great barrelhouse pianist, along with Larry McNealy on banjo, Bobby Bruce on fiddle, Ron Tutt on drums, and Tony Peluso on lead guitar."

Richard says he was happy with the result, both artistically and commercially. It marked the Carpenters' first and only time on the *Billboard* Hot Country Singles chart, reaching No. 8 for two weeks in spring 1978.

Buzz about a Carpenters country album followed that success, but Richard says there was nothing to it. However, "around 1975, we entertained the thought of doing an album in Nashville. But [A&M cofounder] Jerry [Moss] was dead set against that. I really don't know why, because Karen can interpret certain country songs beautifully. Country was somewhere in both of our souls. I always loved Western, cowboy music, Sons of the Pioneers, and all. So, writing a song like 'Top of the World' and doing the arrangement was just natural—and it was natural for Karen to sing this kind of thing."

Originally released in 1976, the science-fiction-themed power ballad "Calling Occupants of Interplanetary Craft" eventually became a cult hit for the Canadian rock group Klaatu. It even hit the lower reaches of the US *Billboard* Hot 100 in early 1977.

The cosmic song was perfect for the *Passage* concept. "The mantra then was, 'Anything that *doesn't* sound like the Carpenters,'" Richard comments.

The irony was that "Occupants" was perfect for Richard, who, as a sci-fi fan, says he just couldn't resist recording the song about sending out a telepathic message to outer space. Richard's epic Grammy-nominated arrangement ran for over seven minutes, and the Carpenters had no intention of releasing the track as a single. But when *Star Wars* emerged as a box-office phenomenon in summer 1977, it was suggested the tune could click with listeners.

Richard reluctantly trimmed the album version to 3:59 for radio (and the single itself), and it was the highest-charting release in its debut week on the *Billboard* Hot 100. While it climbed only to No. 32 in the US, it returned the Carpenters to the Top 10 in Canada, the United Kingdom, and Ireland, and the Top 20 in Australia and New Zealand. The album version has since emerged as an essential Carpenters track.

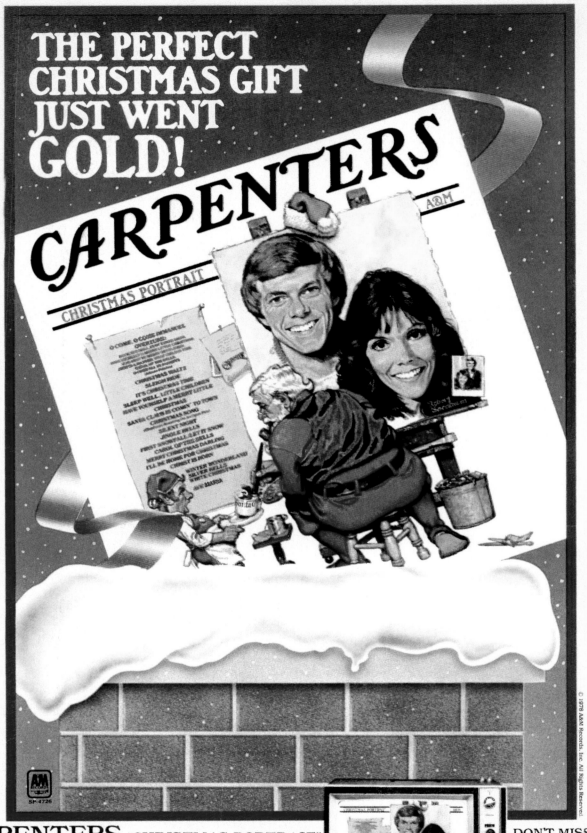

THE PERFECT CHRISTMAS GIFT JUST WENT GOLD!

CARPENTERS "CHRISTMAS PORTRAIT"
SP-4726
28 classic, popular songs of the Holiday Season
featuring a 50-piece orchestra and a 96-voice chorus.

ON A&M RECORDS & TAPES

Conceived and produced by Richard Carpenter. Associate Producer: Karen Carpenter.
"Merry Christmas Darling" produced by Jack Daugherty.
Personal Management: Jerry Weintraub/Management Three.

DON'T MISS THE CARPENTERS TV SPECIAL "A CHRISTMAS PORTRAIT" DEC. 19, ABC-TV, 9 P.M. (EST)

Chapter 6

The Carpenters and Christmas

1977–1978

The Carpenters and Christmas

"We felt we were born to perform Christmas music."

Album
Christmas Portrait

—

US release date
10/13/1978

Note: this entry includes chart activity for both the 1978 release and the 1984 *Christmas Portrait: Special Edition*

—

Billboard **Top LPs/** *Billboard* **200**

Chart entry date (position)
12/9/1978 (No. 178)

Peak date, position (weeks at peak)
1/9/2020, No. 56 (1)

Total weeks on chart
55

—

Billboard **Top Holiday Albums**

Chart entry date (position)
12/21/1985 (No. 8)

Peak date, position (weeks at peak)
12/21/1991, No. 5 (3)

Total weeks on chart
226

Page 192: Trade ad celebrating *Christmas Portrait* passing five-hundred-thousand sales mark, 1978

Left: The "Sleigh Ride" ensemble for *The Carpenters at Christmas*, Los Angeles, 1977

The Carpenters were ready to make a Christmas album even before they were the "Carpenters." In 1966, nineteen-year-old college student Richard Carpenter quickly composed a melody for choir director Frank Pooler's twenty-year-old lyrics to "Merry Christmas, Darling." On occasion, Karen would sing the song at Richard's gigs.

But, for the most part, it sat in a trunk until the Carpenters finally recorded the tune and released it as a single in November 1970. By year's end, the record was in the top spot on the *Billboard* Christmas chart, and it has remained part of the soundtrack of the season ever since.

"We were talking about a Christmas album, I think, in some of our earliest interviews," Richard recalls. "That's how long that Karen and I wanted to make one. We felt we were born to perform Christmas music."

However, after "Merry Christmas, Darling," it would be another four years before the duo released even another Christmas *single*. The Carpenters' version of "Santa Claus Is Comin' to Town" was virtually unrecognizable from the song's first recordings, including the 1934 fox-trot version by the American Novelty Orchestra that Richard and Karen knew and loved from Dad's record library.

For the Carpenters' update, Richard gave the tune a brassy big-band opening and then quickly brought it down to just bass, piano, drums, and vocals. He also transformed the upbeat original into an intimate ballad—perfect for Karen.

"As you know, certain melodies, like 'Ticket to Ride,' I like to make ballads," Richard says. "And I thought, 'I know this lyric doesn't necessarily suit a ballad, but the melody does.' I'd been playing around with it for years."

The basic track for "Santa Claus" was laid down in 1972, but the majority of the recording wasn't completed until 1974 for the Carpenters' appearance on *The Perry Como Christmas Show*, which aired in mid-December on CBS. Richard remembers Karen knocking "Santa Claus" out in just one take. "I mean, every now and again, we'd record a lead that was just about perfect, but Karen would say, 'I want to get *this* word.' Or 'I can do *that* better.' But on 'Santa Claus,' it was perfect."

Fall 1977: as the duo was doing prerecords for the ABC special *The Carpenters at Christmas*, the work also provided a foundation for their first Christmas album, which would be released the following year.

Richard says switching gears into the holiday mode came as a bit of a relief because he was having such trouble finding "regular songs" to record. His struggle was apparent on *A Kind of Hush* and *Passage*. They were well-produced and well-performed albums, but lacked the large number of strong songs on earlier Carpenters efforts. Christmas provided Richard with an embarrassment of riches.

Album

An Old-Fashioned Christmas

—

US release date
10/26/1984

—

Billboard **Top LPs**

Chart entry date (position)
1/5/1985 (No. 190)

Peak date, position (weeks at peak)
1/5/1985 No. 190 (1)

Year-end chart rank
n/a

With the huge responsibilities of recording material for both an album and a TV special, Richard brought in reinforcements. Veterans Peter Knight and Billy May would handle the vocal and orchestral arrangements, allowing Richard to focus on producing.

Among the first tracks completed was a cover of "The Christmas Song (Merry Christmas to You)," written by Robert Wells and Mel Tormé and introduced by the King Cole Trio in 1946. The song's melody lives primarily in the lower range, and its lyric is bittersweet, as if it were custom-made for Karen.

The Carpenters released "Christmas Song"—with its alternate subtitle ("Chestnuts Roasting on an Open Fire")—as a single in November 1978, and fans got another early Christmas present on the 45's B-side. There was a newly recorded lead vocal and remix of "Merry Christmas, Darling," which the Carpenters had originally recorded in 1970. As they did with "Ticket to Ride" in 1973, the duo replaced Karen's youthful, husky vocal with her now mature, now technically supreme lead. Again, it made a world of difference.

Other Christmas tracks the Carpenters recorded that fall include a medley straight from the 1956 album *Spike Jones Presents a Xmas Spectacular* ("It's Christmas Time"/"Sleep Well, Little Children") and lyricist Mitchell Parish's ingenious, tongue-twisting, (literally) breathtaking vocal adaptation of composer Leroy Anderson's orchestral standard "Sleigh Ride."

Richard says he is proud of *The Carpenters at Christmas*, particularly the "Sleigh Ride" opener. It begins with Karen in extreme closeup, looking healthy and gorgeous in a white fur coat and singing the opening verse with sparse accompaniment. She is joined by the orchestra and then by Richard at the electric piano. As the camera pans back, the

Right, above: "It's Christmas Time" piano chart written by Peter Knight for *Christmas Portrait*

Right, below: "Sleigh Ride" chart with arranger Billy May's cue for Karen, "Take it, Baby"

Page 196: On the set of *The Carpenters at Christmas*, Los Angeles, 1977

The Carpenters and Christmas

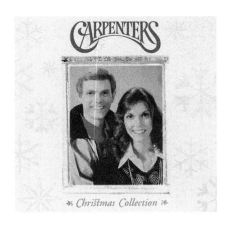

Album

Christmas Collection

—

US release date
11/1/1996

—

***Billboard* Holiday Albums**

Chart entry date (position)
10/10/2020 (No. 40)

Peak date, position (weeks at peak)
10/10/2020, No. 40 (1)

Total weeks on chart
1

audience sees Karen and company in a Victorian setting, everyone decked out in full period regalia.

The number, choreographed by Bob Thompson, morphs into something akin to a Vegas revue, complete with showgirls in full glam gear and guys in tuxedos. The Carpenters next appear in a gazebo, and a couple of longtime bandmates get opportunities to sing partial leads. This starts with saxman/bassist Bob Messenger, whose bashful reading is a charmer: *There's a Christmas party at the home of Farmer Gray.* Enter clarinetist/background vocalist Doug Strawn: *It'll be the perfect ending of a perfect day.* At last, Richard joins them: *We'll be singing the songs / We love to sing without a single stop.*

Then it's Karen in another closeup, looking confident: *These wonderful things are the things we remember all through our lives.* But her prerecord for this shot was a different story. "That one section of 'Sleigh Ride' is a tonal obstacle course," Richard notes. " Karen said, 'I don't know that I can do that.' And I'm thinking, '*Of course* you can.'"

Karen expressed her concern to arranger Billy May. Richard points to May's handwritten response on Karen's vocal chart for the song: "Billy wrote, when it comes to that part, 'TAKE IT, BABY.' He wrote that. And she nailed it. First take."

After the "Sleigh Ride" opener, *The Carpenters at Christmas* unfolds with a blend of typical variety-show fare. Writers Bill Larkin and Stephen Spears devised a plot about Karen hosting a Christmas party and Richard wondering whether he'll attend. Richard wanders around town and comes across special guests Harvey Korman, Kristy McNichol, and Burr Tillstrom's famed puppets Kukla and Ollie. Brief vignettes ensue.

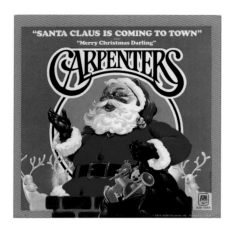

Single
"Santa Claus Is Coming to Town"

—

US release date
11/1974

Did not chart on any of the major music trade publications' surveys

Fortunately, the scales of this music-variety show are tipped in favor of the music, and of Karen. It's all but her own Christmas concert, definitely her show. And for her, Richard programmed the Carpenters' numbers to perfection—from the "Sleigh Ride" opener to the dramatic close. For this finale, the duo—joined by the choir from their alma mater, Long Beach State—performs the rarely heard Domenico Bartolucci/Ray Charles hymn "Christ Is Born."

"The special was all quite well done, and it did very well," Richard comments. *The Carpenters at Christmas* was the thirteenth most-watched Christmas special out of the thirty-three that aired in 1977.

Despite having all the songs prerecorded for the TV special and the 1974 "Santa Claus Is Coming to Town" and "Merry Christmas, Darling" recordings, the Carpenters were back in the studio in early 1978 to record even more to complete their first Christmas album, to be titled *Christmas Portrait*. It was a new year, but it didn't take much to get Karen back into the Christmas spirit.

"She was *always* in the Christmas spirit," Richard says. "And she was looking forward to this project probably more than anything else we did, because it was Christmas music."

The same could not be said for Richard. "I was pretty much waiting for it to become bedtime, so I could take my pills [Quaalude] and enjoy my few minutes of euphoria," he explains.

Richard had a long history with the prescription drug, which he first took in late 1971. "Mom, who also had trouble sleeping, had been prescribed them by our family doctor," he says. "And since the directions said, 'Take one or two at night for sleep,' I took two. Up until then, *no* sleeping pill or tranquilizer had any effect on me at all. So, I went downstairs and started watching an old sci-fi B movie, and thought, 'I don't *remember* it being this good.' Obviously, I was getting high. So, I bopped it down to one, and really took them for years with no problem—and only at bedtime."

However, Richard slowly built up a tolerance to the drug and began increasing his dosage, which came with side effects. To make them more effective, Richard stopped eating dinner and, before long, was noticeably dropping weight.

By the fall 1976 European tour, he says it was a challenge just holding glassware without his hands shaking, and that both he and Karen "looked like sticks" when they performed at the London Palladium in November. The six-foot Richard, whose typical weight was 175, was down to just 140 pounds.

Closing *The Carpenters at Christmas* with "Christ Is Born," Los Angeles, 1977

Single

**"Christmas Song
(Chestnuts Roasting
on an Open Fire)"**

—

US release date
11/11/1978

*Did not chart on any of the major music
trade publications' surveys*

Singing "White
Christmas" on
*The Carpenters
at Christmas,*
Los Angeles, 1977

"I still could work and get albums made," he said. "We still toured the world. Karen and I each were blessed with a remarkable constitution."

But that would serve them both for only so long. For Richard, work was becoming increasingly challenging by the start of recording sessions for *The Carpenters at Christmas* special and the *Christmas Portrait* album. Peter Knight and Billy May were hired as arrangers for more reasons than Richard let on at the time. "If I'd been healthy, of course, mentally healthy, in my prime," he explains, "*I'd* have done the arrangements."

"One of the biggest regrets of my life," he continues, "is that [*Christmas Portrait*] really isn't a *Carpenters* Christmas album. It's a *Karen Carpenter* Christmas album—which is dandy, but not the album we'd wanted to make for so long." With the exception of "Merry Christmas, Darling," the album didn't have a hint of the trademark Carpenters sound.

Nevertheless, there was a bright side. After the commercial disappointment of *Passage*, *Christmas Portrait* was another best seller for the Carpenters. A trade ad announcing the album was "Gold" appeared shortly before the airing of their fourth ABC special, *The Carpenters: A Christmas Portrait.*

Then again, make that a *not*-so-special special.

"Oh, I hate it," Richard quips. "I mean, again, I was rail thin and Karen didn't look much better," he continues. "And it was Kristy McNichol again. But she would only do it if we got [her brother] Jimmy McNichol—and Jimmy was no musical talent. Of course, Kristy didn't have much musical talent either. But she and Karen had great fun, great chemistry."

The special's other musical heavyweights included Georgia Engel (*The Mary Tyler Moore Show*), magician Peter Pit, and one guest with some *actual* musical cred: screen legend Gene Kelly.

Richard says Karen suggested Mom and Dad Carpenter make an appearance on the show. Richard and manager Jerry Weintraub were aghast, but Karen wanted it to happen. Which meant it happened. In the end, it resulted in happy moments and memories. "I'm really glad they did it," Richard says.

"Originally, it was meant to be a musical segment, which was good because it's the only time that Mom ever was dragged into a recording studio," Richard says. "She sang [the Irving Berlin standard], 'Play a Simple Melody,' and from the first note, she sounds like Karen."

The number was cut, but the parents stayed in the show, making a quick scene-stealing cameo. "Dad delivered whatever line it was," Richard says, "and, of course, the set cracked up because his delivery was so droll." And Gene Kelly gave Mom a peck on the cheek. "I can't wait to tell my friends that Gene Kelly kissed me," she tells Karen, with a smile.

While the duo's second Christmas special was nothing to write home about, it *was* worth the effort if only for giving us video records of the Carpenters performing "Merry Christmas, Darling," a divine treatment of the Frank Sinatra favorite "The Christmas Waltz," and Karen's heart-rending reading of the Johann Sebastian Bach/Charles Gounod "Ave Maria" (aka the *other* "Ave Maria").

In terms of ratings, *The Carpenters: A Christmas Portrait* performed nearly as well as *The Carpenters at Christmas*, ranking the fifteenth-highest of forty-six holiday specials in the 1978 season.

Nearly forty years after they first aired, those two specials finally saw the light of day again, when Richard not only authorized but

Single
"Little Altar Boy"
—

US release date
Fall 1984 (promo only)

*Did not chart on any of the major music
trade publications' surveys*

hosted a 2016 special of their highlights, titled Carpenters—*Christmas Memories*. The limited-edition out-of-print DVD of the presentation now ranks as among the most prized and pricey of the duo's rarities.

The Carpenters ended up recording considerably more tunes than could fit on the *Christmas Portrait* album. And Richard says he simply forgot to include the 1974 "Santa Claus Is Comin' to Town" single on the set. So in 1984 he gathered those *Portrait* session outtakes and the "Santa Claus" single and spent considerable time in London at Abbey Road Studios to complete unfinished tracks, as well as to record new material, to create a second Carpenters holiday album, *An Old-Fashioned Christmas*.

It became a commercial success, certified Gold. But Richard looks back on it as something of an old-fashioned blunder. "I was asked to do it, so I went to London. But I never should have done it. There isn't enough of Karen singing, so I wanted to give people their money's worth and ended including too much orchestral music."

On the upside, recording the album in London gave the *other* Carpenters, Richard and his wife, Mary, an overdue honeymoon. The recording sessions were in August 1984; Richard and Mary had been married the previous May.

All in all, when it comes down to *An Old-Fashioned Christmas*, Richard says he's not happy with any of it except two tracks. "In hindsight, only 'Home for the Holidays' and 'Little Altar Boy' were worth all the effort," he notes, adding that they're the only recordings that would make the transition to a new edition of *Christmas Portrait* should one ever come to pass.

The Carpenters:
A Christmas Portrait,
Los Angeles, 1978

The Carpenters and Christmas

Chapter 7

Made in America

1979–1981

Album

Made in America

—

US release date
6/16/81

—

Billboard Top LPs

Chart entry date (position)
7/4/81 (No. 99)

Peak date, position (weeks at peak)
8/15/81, No. 52 (1)

Total weeks on chart
15

Year-end chart ranking
n/a

Inner-sleeve photo
for *Made in America*,
1981

Album
Made in America

**"We were both quite happy with it,"
Richard says.
"All in all, it's a damn good album."**

By the time *Made in America* made it into record stores in June 1981, Carpenters fans had endured the longest gap ever between the duo's albums. More than two and a half years had gone by since the release of their previous set, *Christmas Portrait*.

Technically, Karen and Richard weren't back in the studio working on *Made in America* until June 1980. While the track "I Believe You"—completed in August 1978 and issued as a single that November—appeared on the album, it was merely a one-off, meant to fill the void between the Carpenters' previous single, "Sweet, Sweet Smile," released nine months earlier, and whatever would eventually follow it down the line.

After the release of "I Believe You," Richard was too ill to travel, so Karen was on her own for a mid-December tour of Europe to promote *Christmas Portrait* (and, to her surprise in the UK, *The Singles 1974–1978*). Wrapping the year was the *Christmas Portrait* TV special, which aired on ABC December 19.

Then, a Carpenters hiatus. For the first time since they became a duo, Karen and Richard went their own way. This by no means meant that they were splitting up the Carpenters. Rather, they were focusing on themselves as individuals.

On January 10, 1979, Richard finally dealt a deathblow to his Quaalude addiction. He boarded a plane for Topeka, Kansas, and checked into the rehab facility at the Menninger Clinic.

"It was six weeks in the facility," Richard says, "which, for the first several weeks, seemed like hell on Earth. Little by little, I found out I could sleep without any aid. Eventually, I was happy and healthy, and I gained my weight back—*overgained* my weight back—while I took the rest of the year off."

But Karen kept moving. On May 1, she was off to New York to work with producer Phil Ramone on the solo album she'd wanted to do for quite some time. While Karen loved working with Richard for all those years and often credited him for at least half of the Carpenters' success, she increasingly wanted her own identity, Richard explains—for at least one album.

There were high hopes for the endeavor. But even Karen's *biggest* fan, her brother, Richard, acknowledges that the album didn't come close to A&M's or his own expectations. "While it was beautifully produced and performed," he says, "the general feeling was that most of the material just wasn't right for Karen. Beyond that, there was not one track that had single potential."

This book doesn't dive deep into Karen's solo album for the same reason it doesn't touch upon Richard's individual efforts: *Karen*

Single
"I Believe You"

—

US release date
10/20/78

—

***Billboard* Hot 100**

Chart entry date (position)
12/9/78 (No. 83)

Peak date, position (weeks at peak)
12/23/78, No. 68 (2)

Total weeks on chart
5

Year-end chart ranking
n/a

—

***Billboard* Top 50 Easy Listening**

Chart entry date (position)
11/18/78 (No. 30)

Peak date, position (weeks at peak)
12/23/78, No. 9 (3)

Total weeks on chart
14

Year-end chart ranking
n/a

Right and
Page 209: 1981

Carpenter is *not* a Carpenters album. Yet at points it tried to be, which makes that aspect of it fair game for discussion here.

When Karen returned to Los Angeles with the album's final mixes in mid-March 1980, Richard admits that he was taken aback upon first listen. "I didn't know they were going to do all the multi-harmony overdubbed vocals," he says. "So, when I said, 'You've stolen our sound,' that's what I meant. Really, that hit me like a hammer. I wasn't expecting that. You would think if it was going to be different from a Carpenters album, it would be *different*."

Richard had no involvement in the decision to shelve the solo album. That came from A&M cofounders Herb Alpert and Jerry Moss, who had the tough task of giving their leading lady the bad news. Recalls Richard, "It was a great disappointment to all involved— particularly Karen, who had invested so much time and effort into the project."

As usual, she dealt with disappointment by diving back into work with Richard. After completing their fifth and final TV special, "Music Music Music," the duo began recording *Made in America* in early June.

Richard says that, following the departures that were *Passage* and *Christmas Portrait*, it had felt like forever since they'd made an actual "Carpenters" album.

Single
"Touch Me When We're Dancing"

—

US release date
6/19/81

—

Billboard Hot 100

Chart entry date (position)
6/20/81 (No. 76)

Peak date, position (weeks at peak)
8/1/81, No. 16 (4)

Total weeks on chart
14

Year-end chart ranking
n/a

—

Billboard Top 50 Adult
Contemporary

Chart entry date (position)
6/27/81 (No. 35)

Peak date, position (weeks at peak)
8/22/81, No. 1 (2)

Total weeks on chart
16

Year-end chart ranking
No. 15

---

*From the start, Karen's marriage to Tom Burris seemed doomed. She cut short their honeymoon on the tropical island paradise Bora Bora, and the two headed back to Los Angeles early. A day after their first anniversary, Karen had her will changed, leaving only household possessions to her husband—all else to her father, mother, and brother. A fight at a family gathering in November ended with Burris storming out of the house, announcing, "You can keep her."

"In hindsight, this had all happened too quickly," Richard notes. "If Karen had really thought this through, I believe she would have realized they simply weren't the right match."

Karen filed for divorce on October 28, 1982, but she died before it could be finalized.

Out of the gate, the duo was on a roll, recording Richard's ethereal pop adaptation of bluesman Randy Handley's country-flavored heartbreaker "When It's Gone (It's Just Gone)."

"It's a great track," Richard comments. "It's an interesting fusion of genres. The steel guitar and the two acoustic guitars, along with clever use of reverb and Karen's aching vocal, made for a really eerie effect. And the bass: Joe [Osborn] was playing his ass off on it—a perfect track for his fluid style of playing. All in all, one of our favorite tracks."

Just weeks after *Made in America* was up and running at full speed, Karen delivered news: she was getting married.

In April, Karen met and quickly began dating a real-estate developer, Tom Burris. The romance was whirlwind. There were only about four months between their meeting and marriage, which took place on August 31, 1980 in the Crystal Ballroom at the Beverly Hills Hotel.*

With the shower, the planning, the wedding, and the honeymoon, *Made in America* would just have to wait. The ceremony did, however, move the album forward at least a little. It resulted in the closing track, "Because We Are in Love (The Wedding Song)," on which Richard and cowriter John Bettis went big.

"It's like a song from a Broadway musical, beginning with a verse and leading to a chorus," Richard says. "We wanted to have it done

Single

"(Want You) Back in My Life Again"

—

US release date
8/28/1981

—

***Billboard* Hot 100**

Chart entry date (position)
9/12/81 (No. 88)

Peak date, position (weeks at peak)
10/17/81, No. 72 (2)

Total weeks on chart
8

—

***Billboard* Top 50 Adult Contemporary**

Chart entry date (position)
9/19/81 (No. 33)

Peak date, position (weeks at peak)
10/24/81, No. 14 (2)

Total weeks on chart
12

in time for the wedding, and Bettis and I worked into the night and I thought, 'Yeah, this is very good, with the Greek chorus and all.' But then, the next day…well…I wanted to send it to [arranger] Peter [Knight], and I played it out and I thought, 'Good grief! Its vocal range is almost two octaves.' So, I went back to the drawing board, and now it's maybe an octave and a sixth—no problem for Karen but, still, huge."

Not long after returning from her honeymoon, Karen was back in the studio. The *Made in America* sessions resumed in midfall, and the bulk of recording was completed in January and February 1981. The album was released in June.

"Looking back, there are certain songs we shouldn't have included," Richard says. He starts to cite flaws in particular tracks when he quickly but carefully reassesses with phrases such as, "But Karen really…" or "You know, that arrangement was…" or "That song wasn't so-and-so's best, but…" Richard's not hedging, just being who he is: every masterpiece has at least some flaw, and every disappointment has *something* worthwhile.

"There are a couple of lightweight things on there," he notes. "But it's loaded with vocals, very clever arrangements, really well recorded, and Karen sounds absolutely great. We were both quite happy with it. All in all, it's a damn good album."

On the US Charts

Made in America entered the *Billboard* Top LPs survey at No. 99 on June 6, 1981, and reached No. 52. Just seven weeks later, its run ended after only fifteen weeks. Up to that time, it was the duo's lowest-charting nonholiday album since *Ticket to Ride* reached No. 150, on the heels of the success of *Close to You*.

The Singles

Richard says that he received a copy of Dorothy Moore's 1977 Top 5 R&B hit "I Believe You" as a demo. While a soul-chart smash, Moore's single had only modest pop success. So, it made sense when the song's publisher got it to the Carpenters, hoping that the tune would enjoy a second ride up the *Billboard* Hot 100.

"I liked the tune, and I knew it would be very good for Karen," Richard recalls. To put a little different spin on it, Richard hired veteran Motown arranger Paul Riser to handle the rhythm and orchestra writing; Richard arranged the vocals. "Great chart by Riser," says Richard. "Great performance by Karen. Great record."

Both Carpenters predicted that "I Believe You" would be a hit. But not everyone at A&M was a believer. All these years later, Richard still gets fired up when he recalls presenting the recording to the label's latest national promotions director, Harold Childs. "He listens to it, with a studied look, and says, 'Well it's a work record.' And I'm thinking, 'Oh, fuck you, Harold! If we'd played you "(They Long to Be) Close to You," you would have said it was a "work record," you son of a bitch.'"

Richard explains that a "work record" is one that has to be worked by a record label's promotional department to become a hit. "'The Lady in Red' [by Chris de Burgh] is a rare example where this actually worked. *Very* rare."

No one can accuse A&M of working "I Believe You," which was given a nondescript trade ad, dumped into the marketplace in the

Single
"Those Good Old Dreams"

—

US release date
11/5/1981

—

***Billboard* Hot 100**

Chart entry date (position)
12/19/81 (No. 82)

Peak date, position (weeks at peak)
1/16/82, No. 63 (1)

Total weeks on chart
6

—

***Billboard* Top 50 Adult Contemporary**

Chart entry date (position)
12/12/81 (No. 37)

Peak date, position (weeks at peak)
1/23/82, No. 21 (2)

Total weeks on chart
13

Hype sticker for
Made in America

Made in America

midst of holiday madness, and ended up becoming the Carpenters' lowest-charting single up to that time. It reached only No. 68 and disappeared from the *Billboard* Hot 100 after just five weeks. "That record should have done better than it did," Richard says.

"The image thing. I could be all wrong on this, but that's what I feel. And, of course, we're never going to know."

Before the Carpenters, "Touch Me When We're Dancing" was a minor *Billboard* Easy Listening and Hot 100 chart maker for a group of Muscle Shoals Sound Studio musicians called Bama.

"I just thought [the song] had potential," Richard says. "As it was taking shape, there was more to it than I expected. It's a case of a record being greater than the sum of its parts—although there are many parts in it."

Richard gave the tune first-class treatment, opening with an electric sitar line accompanied by a Fender Rhodes electric piano and acoustic and electric guitars. Enter Karen's lead solo, which builds to the first chorus, which Richard wrote for three-part harmony. She's doubled on three parts, making for six Karens, then given support from session singer Carolyn Dennis—"*nailing* the same parts," as per Richard. With this mix, he says, he found what he was seeking: a soulful "mocha" version of the Carpenters sound.

Karen, Richard, many radio programmers, and even some key players in A&M promotions had great faith in the record, which was the highest-debuting single the week it entered the *Billboard* Hot 100. What happened next is detailed in the prologue "The Image Problem."

CONTAINS THE HIT
"Touch Me When We're Dancing"
PLUS
"Those Good Old Dreams"
"(Want You) Back In My Life Again"
"Strength Of A Woman"

A&M SP-3723
Printed in U.S.A.

Single
"Beechwood 4-5789"

—

US release date
3/2/82

—

***Billboard* Hot 100**

Chart entry date (position)
4/24/82 (No. 83)

Peak date, position (weeks at peak)
5/8/82, No. 74 (2)

Total weeks on chart
4

—

***Billboard* Top 50 Adult Contemporary**

Chart entry date (position)
3/27/82 (No. 39)

Peak date, position (weeks at peak)
5/15/82, No. 16 (2)

Total weeks on chart
13

1981

Richard agrees that "(Want You) Back in My Life Again" is the closest the Carpenters ever got to disco, although that was never his intention. "I wasn't thinking about that," he says. "I simply liked it." It was just surprising to hear *the Carpenters* going there.

Looking back, "(Want You) Back in My Life Again" is no closer to disco than The Doobie Brothers' 1979 midtempo smash "What a Fool Believes." In fact the records somewhat resemble each other: a strong lead vocal, tight harmonies, just a touch of trendy synth, and, yes, you can *almost* dance to it.

The big difference between the two records? The Doobies had a great song. The Carpenters? Not so great. "It's kind of lightweight," Richard admits, noting that he did everything he could to make the track work, including that Hail Mary pass: Karen and Richard singing the tune-closing words "in my life" in breathtaking eight-part harmony.

"Those Good Old Dreams," co-written by Richard and John Bettis, took the songwriters—and the Carpenters—back to "Yesterday Once More" territory, with its theme of how happy memories can brighten dark days.

Richard says we shouldn't read too much into the lyric. "It's just a song that John and I came up with, a cross between pop and country. It was a perfect arranger's song. There's a lot going on in that song."

Indeed. There are acoustic, electric bass, and pedal steel guitars; Karen and Paulinho da Costa on percussion; drums, harp, mile-high harmonies. And yet the result is breezy, never busy.

Then there's that ending. "The flutes go up and it changes key," Richard says. "It opens up a whole new feeling of joy. There's a finger snap and then the changes with a steel guitar—really quite ethereal. A really good record."

"Another remake," Richard says, with a sigh. "I don't know what got into me. But those opening '*la-la*'s—they're glorious. The four-part, doubled, which is marvelous. But then it gets into the song itself. We were past this, and it's not a strong song. It never was. It wasn't for The Marvelettes, and it wasn't going to be for us as far as a hit. Ever."

Chapter 8

Karen Carpenter

1950–1983

Karen Carpenter

Karen Carpenter had been The Voice, The Icon, The Superstar Who Sang "Superstar." But by the time Richard was done telling the Carpenters' tale, we saw her as a human being: Karen wasn't perfect. She made bad decisions, could be stubborn to a fault, had moments of immaturity. For the most part, however, Richard's stories left us with images of a fun-loving woman who was also a tireless worker, a colleague who had your back, a true and thoughtful friend. She was a beloved daughter, niece, and, especially, sister.

Her spirit was so high and bright, she would light up a room, especially a recording studio filled with exhausted musicians and technicians. If you want a soundbite of the essential Karen, just listen to the first few seconds of "Make Believe It's Your First Time," where she is trying to pull her whimsical self together before the song begins:

"Uh, I have to get into a serious mood here."

In addition to being a musical treasure, Karen was personally cherished—making her sudden death all the more tragic. She died from a heart attack following complications of the eating disorder anorexia nervosa on February 4, 1983. She was just thirty-two years old.

While Karen's struggle with weight and her eating disorder have been mentioned briefly throughout this book, only now is it time to address them head-on. The whole point of this work is to celebrate and explore the Carpenters' musical legacy: their recordings. And Karen's problems never affected them; they never caused the delay of a Carpenters album—though they did have an impact on the other areas of the duo's career.

Nearly forty years after Karen's passing, Richard says he feels anorexia is as confounding to the medical profession today as it was in 1983, and he believes that it always will be. Karen's disorder certainly remains a mystery to Richard, who tries to shed some light on this part of his sister's story by offering benchmarks in her dieting and eating-disorder history.

In 1967, Karen went on the Stillman Diet, dropped some twenty-five pounds, "and she kept it there for the next eight years," he recalls. In mid-1973, Richard says Karen hired a personal trainer to keep fit. However, the program had the undesired effect of adding muscle and accentuating her hour-glass figure.

By early 1974, Karen began dieting again, approaching runway-model trim by November.

This was right at the time of the photo shoot for the *Horizon* album—its cover widely praised as the Carpenters' best. Karen's dieting continued.

In late summer 1975, the duo had a two-week engagement at the Riviera in Las Vegas, and Richard remembers audiences gasping at the sight of his rail-thin sister. "It had gotten so bad that she had to lie down between shows. It's meant as a testament to Karen's talent when he adds, "Nonetheless, she continued to sing as beautifully as ever."

Following the Las Vegas concerts, Richard cleared the Carpenters' itinerary through the rest of the year. Karen simply could not have endured tours of Japan, Europe, and the United Kingdom, which would have totaled seventy-eight engagements in just ten weeks.

"Karen needed rest," he says. And, on doctor's orders, she was confined to bed for the next two months. However, by the end of the year, Karen was feeling well enough to begin work on *A Kind of Hush*.

And so, Karen's story went on for five years. Personally, she battled what would eventually be diagnosed as anorexia nervosa. But after the fall-1975 concert cancellations, she fulfilled her professional commitments—all the way through the recording of *Made in America*.

It's understandably difficult for Richard to discuss Karen's passing. He gets angry when talking about the care she received. In early 1982, Karen began treatment in New York City under the supervision of a psychotherapist who, a few years earlier, had gained fame as a specialist in eating disorders. But Richard believes that "[the therapist] had done nothing to help her." As soon as a client's weight got down to eighty pounds or less, he turned them over to a medical doctor who admitted them to a hospital—in this instance Lenox Hill."

In early September, Karen checked into the hospital, and it was discovered that her digestive tract was so damaged that she would have to be fed via hyperalimentation. A stent was placed in her chest so that a tube could be inserted to get nutrition directly into her bloodstream.

But there was a complication. As the tube was inserted, it punctured one of Karen's lungs, much to her family's horror—which, Richard says, added to their belief that Karen's treatment was not in capable hands.

He recalls her being discharged from the hospital weighing approximately twenty pounds more than when she had checked in. By Thanksgiving, she was home, looking healthier and telling family that she was getting better.

"And perhaps she believed it, but *I* didn't believe it," Richard says. "I could see it in her eyes."

Photos of the Carpenter family's last Christmas together show Karen looking thin and tired, but happy.

Herb Alpert recalls his last meeting with Karen in January 1983, remembering her as "sparkling" and in typically high spirits, brimming with excitement about recording the new Carpenters album.

She was back on the A&M lot, back at her home away from home, and ready to get back to work.

Page 216:
Backstage at
Sahara Tahoe,
Lake Tahoe, 1973

Above: On the set
of *The Carpenters...
Space Encounters*,
Los Angeles, 1978

Chapter 9

Keeper of the Flame

1983–present

Album
Voice of the Heart

—

US release date
10/17/1983

—

Billboard Top LPs

Chart entry date (position)
11/19/1983 (No. 84)

Peak date, position (weeks at peak)
1/7/1984, No. 46 (2)

Total weeks on chart
19

Year-end chart rank
n/a

Single
"Make Believe It's Your First Time"

—

US release date
10/4/1983

—

Keeper of the Flame

"I didn't know what to do with myself."

Just weeks after Karen's death, Richard was back in the studio working on a new Carpenters album, *Voice of the Heart*. "I didn't know what to do with myself," he recalls. "I was under the impression that [A&M] wanted [the album] as soon as I could get it done.

"Of course, Karen would have had a fit at all of this [the release of another album] because, with the exception of 'Sailing on the Tide,' everything else on there is a work lead."

A work lead is a rough version of the lead vocal recorded to offer the musicians a guide as they play in the studio. Under usual circumstances, the work lead is replaced by a more polished, finished lead vocal. However, Karen's work leads were occasionally used in final recordings—usually due to lack of time to get her back in the studio.

Billboard Bubbling Under Hot 100

Chart entry date
11/26/1983 (No. 105)

Peak date, position (weeks at peak)
12/10/1983, No. 101 (1)

Total weeks on chart
4

Year-end chart rank
n/a

—

Billboard Top 50 Adult Contemporary

Chart entry date (position)
10/22/1983 (No. 40)

Peak date, position (weeks at peak)
12/24/1983, No. 7 (3)

Total weeks on chart
18

Year-end chart rank
n/a

Single
"Your Baby Doesn't Love You Anymore"

—

US release date
1/31/1984

—

Billboard Top 50 Adult Contemporary

Chart entry date (position)
2/11/1984 (No. 31)

Peak date, position (weeks at peak)
3/10/1984, No. 12 (2)

Total weeks on chart
13

Year-end chart rank
n/a

Page 220: 1980
Above: 1977

That her work leads were *ever* acceptable for any given release was a testament to Karen's talent. Richard says that even when she'd nail it the first time, she'd usually want to do additional takes to fix a little something here or there. But, unlike most singers, she was truly a one-take wonder.

Outside of the recently recorded work leads for "Now" and "You're Enough," which were intended for the new album, Karen also left behind a good number of work leads from outtakes: songs that the duo had decided not to release from years earlier. Richard says that many of those tracks "really needed to be built up from the beginning. All that we had that was acceptable were, like, the bass and the drums." It would be a lot of work. But Richard forged ahead anyway.

The unusually large quantity of Karen's unfinished work leads is what allowed *Voice of the Heart* to be an all-new Carpenters studio album. And, even after that release, Richard had enough work leads left over to supplement two more albums of unreleased material, *Lovelines* and *As Time Goes By*.

Richard says he has mixed feelings about all three releases. "I want to say now that just about everything I did the moment after Karen

Single
"Honolulu City Lights"

—

US release date
12/1986

The single did not chart in the US or any other countries tracked for this book.

passed away was wrong—I mean, concerning the Carpenters." (Richard eventually backtracked on that statement, praising select tracks on *Voice of the Heart* and calling *Lovelines* a "damned good album.")

To the average ear, Karen's work leads sound fine, but not to Richard, who notes that they would not be acceptable to Karen. "I can hear a couple of things where I know she would *really* not be happy about," he says. "Again, we're talking about small things. And then the other thing is that they were outtakes. I know a lot of people like them. But, yeah, she would not be happy."

However, the album proved the Carpenters were still in demand. Unlike *Made in America*, the previous Carpenters release, *Voice of the Heart* was certified Gold in the United States. It reached No. 46 on the *Billboard* Top LPs chart and had a nineteen-week run—peaking higher than any Carpenters album since *A Kind of Hush* and logging more weeks on the survey than any since *A Song for You* more than a decade earlier.

In 1989, Richard delivered another full album of unreleased material, *Lovelines*, half of which were outtakes recorded for Carpenters albums. *Lovelines* also includes four tracks gleaned from Karen's solo album. Richard made no secret of his fondness for the *Karen Carpenter* track "If I Had You," which he remixed to include veteran session bassist Joe Osborn.

Album
Lovelines

—

US release date
10/31/1989

Richard used four tracks from Karen's solo album for the Carpenters 1989 album *Lovelines*, right

Single
"If I Had You"

—

US release date
11/1989

—

Billboard Top 50 Adult Contemporary

Chart entry date (position)
11/25/1989 (No. 41)

Peak date, position (weeks at peak)
1/20/1990, No. 18 (1)

Total weeks on chart
11

Year-end chart rank
n/a

Album
As Time Goes By

—

Japan release date
8/1/2001

—

International release date
4/13/2004

Trade ad for
As Time Goes By,
2004

In 2001 in Japan (in 2004 internationally) came *As Time Goes By*. Its unreleased tracks date all the way back to "California Dreamin'," recorded in 1967 in Osborn's garage studio. Most material on the album originates from TV appearances, including the rarely heard "And When He Smiles" from a 1971 BBC concert special, a hits medley from *The Carpenters' Very First Television Special* (1976), and a Karen Carpenter/ Ella Fitzgerald medley from the 1980 *Music, Music, Music* TV special, with two of the century's greatest singers batting classic and contemporary pop standards back and forth for nearly six glorious minutes.

Trade ad for
*Yesterday Once
More* compilation,
1985

Critical
Compilations

Dozens of Carpenters compilation albums and boxed sets have been issued over the past five decades, dating back to the 1970 release of *Golden Double Deluxe* in Japan. We rank these among the most significant:

Yesterday Once More (1984, A&M Records/Silver Eagle Records, US and Canada)

This was the first major hits compilation released after Karen's death and supervised by Richard. Manufactured by A&M and distributed via mail order by TV-marketing company Silver Eagle Records, its biggest attraction for collectors is the "Superstar"/"Rainy Days and Mondays"/"Goodbye to Love" trilogy, which originally appeared on *The Singles 1969–1973*. Here, for the first time, it is slowed down to original playback speed.

Yesterday Once More (1984, A&M Records/EMI Records, UK)

Intrigued by the Silver Eagle release, A&M UK asked Richard to oversee a similar compilation it could sell in retail stores on a two-LP set as well as a limited-edition CD. For collectors: a number of tracks previously unavailable on CD at the time include the single mix of "Please Mr. Postman" and the original album mix of "Those Good Old Dreams," which includes a synth riff immediately following the last chorus that is not present in the single mix.

Anthology (1985, A&M/Pony Canyon, Japan)

At the time of its release, Richard said he considered *Anthology* the most "ambitious and thorough compilation to date." And it was. Introduced as a four-LP, limited-edition, numbered set, this album offered the first release of "Honolulu City Lights," which was released again as a single in 1986 and then on the *Lovelines* album in 1989. "Bacharach/David Medley (Live)," recorded at the Riviera Hotel in May 1974, was also included commercially for the first time, and would be rereleased in 1997 on the Reader's Digest set *Their Greatest Hits and Finest Performances*. The album introduced remixes of "Superstar,"

"Rainy Days and Mondays," and "Goodbye to Love" to the fold, marking the dawn of the Carpenters remix era.

Anthology was reissued in 1989 on CD and again in 1997. The latter issue includes remixes that were not in existence at the time of the album's debut.

Yesterday Once More (1985, A&M Records, US)

The first career-encompassing compilation made available at retail in the US includes numerous tracks updated with additional recording remixing and/or noise reduction. Three remixes previously released in Japan on the *Anthology* set appear here, along with an additional five remixes including "Yesterday Once More," "Bless the Beasts and Children," "There's a Kind of Hush," "I Need to Be in Love," and "We've Only Just Begun." It would be repackaged two years later under the title *Classics Volume 2* as part of A&M Records' twenty-fifth-anniversary series.

Only Yesterday: Richard and Karen Carpenter's Greatest Hits (1990, A&M Records, UK, South Africa, and Germany)

Rush-released in 1990 under Richard's supervision following the highly rated UK airing of *The Karen Carpenter Story* TV movie, this was a phenomenon—a multi-Platinum smash that marked the start of a massive resurgence in the Carpenters' popularity in the UK that has yet to abate.

Retitled *Their Greatest Hits* later in 1990, a slightly altered version containing a fewer number of tracks was released in South Africa. In 1993, *Their Greatest Hits* was released in Germany with the same cover photo, this time with a pinkish-red background instead of the white background used for the earlier releases.

Gold (A&M Records, 2000, 2001, 2004, and 2005, worldwide)

Sporting almost the same design and packaging as ABBA's *Gold: Greatest Hits*, the Carpenters' *Gold* has seen several reissues following its initial twenty-track, single-disc release in the UK in 2000.

In 2001, it was issued in Japan as a twenty-one-track, single-disc release, with different cover art and "Japanese Edition" at the top. The US, however, wouldn't see *Gold* until 2004, with the tagline *35th Anniversary Edition* added and packaged as a two-disc set. Many collectors purchased the US release upon learning that the single mix of "Solitaire" was included for the first time on the CD.

Gold was reissued in the US in 2005 with a different cover, featuring a 1974 photo by world-renowned photographer Annie Leibovitz. The photo was taken the same day that Leibovitz shot the famous *Rolling Stone* magazine cover portrait of the Carpenters. The UK saw a reissue of *Gold* in 2005, this time with a mirror-image version of the original photo.

From the Top (1991, A&M Records, US)

This expansive four-CD set, originally released in a twelve-by-twelve-inch box embossed with a copper-foil Carpenters logo, delivered a blast of rarities: demos, outtakes, interviews, and remixes, as well as a large booklet complete with never-published photos and liner notes by Richard. The first edition of *From the Top* is a collector's item. Later in 1991, it was reissued in a slimmer, book-style box following complaints by record stores that the original box design was difficult to display.

In 2002, an updated version of *From the Top* was released with a new title: *The Essential Collection: 1965–1997.* It included a couple of recordings not yet released in the US and reverted some of the remixes back to the original album mixes.

Sweet Memory (1994, A&M Records/Senshukai, Japan)

Released in a six-disc series by the Japanese mail-order company Senshukai, each disc had a different theme:

Disc 1: *All at Once*
Disc 2: *Those Days*
Disc 3: *On and Off*
Disc 4: *At Last*
Disc 5: *By and By*
Disc 6: *Someday*

This massive compilation contained non-Christmas studio recordings, with nothing much new on it. There is one major exception, however: a remix of "Another Song" (from the *Close to You*

One of the CD inserts for the six-disc Japanese *Sweet Memory* compilation

album). For this, Richard brought bassist Joe Osborn into the studio to replace the bass track originally played by a member of the Carpenters' road band, Dan Woodhams. Osborn's updated bassline brought a new edge and some attitude to the recording. "Make Believe It's Your First Time" and "Nowadays Clancy Can't Even Sing" are also included, this time without the studio chatter heard in the original mixes.

Sweet Memory was eventually repackaged as one complete set. It still manages to fetch several hundreds of dollars—assuming you're fortunate enough to find one.

Interpretations: A 25th Anniversary Celebration (1994, 1995, A&M Records, UK and US)
Including three previously unreleased recordings, *Interpretations* was issued in the UK in 1994 and followed by a truncated version (with five fewer tracks) in the US a year later.

Both releases open with an a cappella version of "Without a Song," originally recorded as the opener for the Carpenters' final ABC television special *Music Music Music* in 1980.

"From This Moment On," an outtake also recorded for *Music Music Music,* is included here as well. For the 1995 US release of *Interpretations*, the song is remixed, replacing Richard's original piano with an updated stereo version.

"Tryin' to Get the Feeling Again," an outtake from their 1975 *Horizon* album and completed in 1994, is also included in *Interpretations*. The sound of Karen turning one of the pages of her lead sheet can be heard immediately following the first chorus.

Japanese Single Box (2006, A&M Records, Japan)
This set contains thirty-three three-inch discs replicating the audio and the original artwork from Japanese-released 45 rpm singles. This limited-edition, numbered set marked the first time an exhaustive singles compilation became available on CD anywhere in the world. It was followed in 2015 with the release of *The Complete Singles* in the US.

30th Anniversary Collector's Edition (1998, A&M Records, Japan)
Considered one of the rarest and most sought-after Carpenters boxed sets, the *30th Anniversary Collector's Edition* is a studio-album anthology issued in CD format. It includes all eleven nonholiday Carpenters studio albums complete with their original mixes. Each disc is housed in a miniature replica of the original album cover (better-known as a mini LP) and inner sleeve. Additionally, each disc sports its original A&M label.

Housed in a black leather-bound flip-top box with the Carpenters logo embossed in gold foil on the front, it includes a black handkerchief (with Carpenters logo) as well as an extensive booklet with rare images and liner notes by Richard.

35th Anniversary Collector's Edition (2003, A&M Records, Japan)
Nearly identical to the *30th Anniversary Collector's Edition*, the *35th* includes both of the Carpenters' Christmas albums not included in the *30th* box. The *Christmas Portrait* disc, however, contains the remixed version of the album, as the original two-channel master that was pulled for the set was in poor shape and unsalvageable.

40th Anniversary Collector's Edition (2009, Universal Music Group/A&M Records, Japan)
Dubbed "The Breadbox," this white, rectangular, sixteen-disc boxed set is a larger, hybrid version of the earlier *30th* and *35th Anniversary* sets, with CDs replaced by supposedly superior SHM-CDs (Super High Material Compact Discs, although Richard is no fan of the medium). Individual discs are housed in hardback booklets, with liner notes and images coinciding with each studio album, and included the mini LP style replicated sleeves fastened inside.

Two additional audio discs are added: *As Time Goes By*, first released in 2001, and *Sweet Sixteen*, with a curiously curated mix of rare and widely available tracks.

A DVD version of *Gold* is also included. But it is like no other, including Richard's commentary on the secondary audio track. His hilarious comments on the "I Need to Be in Love" video are worth the price alone.

The Complete Singles (2015, Universal Music Special Markets/A&M Records, US)
Available exclusively as a premium to supporters of US public television stations, this three-disc set is a must-have for those looking to complete their Carpenters' collection with the original US 45 rpm single mixes. Most of the tracks were sourced from original two-channel tapes, with the exception of "Ticket to Ride," "Your Wonderful Parade," and "Calling Occupants of Interplanetary Craft (The Recognized Anthem of World Contact Day)," all of which were transferred digitally from the original vinyl. It is also worth noting that the album mix of "Flat Baroque" is included here, and not the single mix.

Album
Carpenters with the Royal Philharmonic Orchestra

—

US release date
12/7/2018

—

***Billboard* Classical Crossover Albums**
Chart entry date (position)
12/22/2018 (2)

Peak date, position (weeks at peak)
12/22/2018, No. 2 (6)

Total weeks on chart
56

Year-end chart ranking
No. 5

—

***Billboard* Classical Albums**
Chart entry date (position)
12/22/2018 (2)

Peak date, position (weeks at peak)
12/22/2018, No. 2 (6)

Total weeks on chart:
52

Year-end chart ranking
No. 5

—

***Billboard* Classical Crossover**
Artist for 2019
No. 5 (with the Royal Philharmonic)

***Billboard* Classical for 2019**
No. 5 (with the Royal Philharmonic)

Page 229:
Conducting the
Royal Philharmonic
Orchestra, London,
August, 2018

Carpenters Reimagined

Philharmonic and Surround Releases Offer Fresh Perspectives

In 2018, nearly 20 years after the previous album of unreleased Carpenters material, Richard was back in the studio—this time in London at the EMI/Abbey Road complex to record *Carpenters with the Royal Philharmonic Orchestra*.

While the result wasn't truly an all-new Carpenters album, it certainly sounded like one. And that was the point.

When asked to reflect on the release, Richard politely directed us to the liner notes he'd written for record just a couple years ago, noting that everything he had to say about it was there. After the countless words and hours he'd given us, we couldn't blame him for being talked out. And, frankly, the guy writes a hell of a liner note.

So, the floor is yours, Mr. Carpenter.

There have been countless times over many years when, after hearing one of our records, I would imagine how nice it would be to have another crack at an arrangement, or to correct various and sundry other things. So, it was a most pleasant surprise when I was asked to do just that, in addition to conducting the Royal Philharmonic Orchestra.

Carpenters with the Royal Philharmonic is more than a new "hits" collection, albeit with a larger orchestra. Much more.

To begin with, I selected songs that were not only well suited for Karen's voice, but also our multi-tracked harmonies, a contributing factor to the overall "Carpenter[s] sound," as it was soon to be labeled. Then it was on to revising my orchestral arrangements; applying the changes I'd been thinking of for years, such as the oboe line in the first chorus of "Ticket to Ride," the bassoon in the interlude of "Superstar," piccolo trumpet in "Goodbye to Love," and additional writing for the strings on virtually all the tracks.

The latest technology was employed to make right a number of blemishes and oversights in the original recordings that have been haunting me for years. To wit, key instruments in several of the songs were slightly out of tune and were not noticed by us until the records were either mixed or released; more than a few of our earlier recordings came to a close at a faster tempo than they had begun, and minor clicks, squeaks and creaks ultimately found their way into a completed record, much to our chagrin.

All have now been either expunged or corrected. Above all is the absence of the ambient noise, such as the A/C rumble, that made its way into Karen's lead vocals, among other things. This room noise was a bugaboo in the finest of studios, and by and large didn't seem that apparent until CDs came along. But now that it's gone (along with CDs), it seems it was only too apparent, and that, along with dialing back the amount of reverb used in our later recordings and remixes, makes Karen's leads sound cleaner, closer, warmer, and better than ever.

Album
Singles 1969–1981
Stereo Multichannel
Hybrid SACD

—

Release date
January 11, 2005

Carpenters with the Royal Philharmonic turned out to be not *only a monumental undertaking, but a labor of love, certainly for me, and I believe all who were instrumental in its making.*

In Surround

A&M's Stereo Multichannel Hybrid SACD (Super Audio Compact Disc) of the Carpenters' *Singles 1969–1981* ranks with Pink Floyd's *The Dark Side of the Moon*, Dire Straits' *Brothers in Arms*, and Roxy Music's *Avalon* as among SA-CD.net's top-rated releases—the ones that audiophiles are likely to use as go-to discs to show off their high-end systems.

An explanation for nonaudiophiles: a Stereo/Multichannel Hybrid SACD is a CD-size audio disc that can be played on a standard CD player and heard in stereo. The disc also contains a 5.1 mix that can be heard only by those with an SACD player connected to a special amplifier that extracts the disc's six channels: front-left, front-center, front-right, front-subwoofer, rear-left, and rear-right. (If you have a home theater with four speakers in front and two in the back, it's pretty much the same thing.)

Moving on... Just as Richard and associate producer Nick Patrick pushed the RPO series to new artistic heights, Richard and veteran audio engineer Al Schmitt did the same with the SACD. Again, Richard exercised restraint. There isn't a single sonic gimmick on the *Singles* SACD. With so much going on in every original Carpenters track, gimmicks weren't needed.

"Mixing in 5.1 was as natural as going from mono to stereo," Richard recalls, adding that the biggest challenge of the project was locating every bell and whistle tucked away on various tracks, given the lack of available track space due to all of the overdubbing required for a Carpenters recording.

The effort proved worthwhile. The *Singles* SACD places the listener dead-center of the musicians and makes even the album's earliest tracks sound as if they're being performed in the listener's living room—right now. As with the RPO release, the *Singles* SACD is like hearing a brand-new Carpenters album.

Now the bad news: even though the long-out-of-print SACD edition of *Singles* is still widely available on eBay (at one hundred dollars and up at the time of this writing), it isn't likely to play on your current home-theater DVD or Blu-ray machine. The SACD was embraced by audiophiles upon its introduction in 1999, but it failed to catch on with the general public. By 2009, most record companies dropped the format, and most electronics manufacturers began eliminating SACD players. However, a solid niche market for the format remains. And some record labels are now reissuing the 5.1 recordings produced for SACDs on Blu-ray discs that can be played on home-theater systems.

Lake Tahoe, 1973

Tom Nolan

Rolling Stone Reflections

Carpenters' Cover-Story Writer
Looks Back, and Forth

Left:
Tom Nolan

Page 233:
Rolling Stone
cover, July 4,
1974

In hindsight, it's easy to see how the Carpenters' debut album, *Offering*, fit into the abundantly creative popular music scene from which it sprang. Many talented record artists were expressing themselves to terrific effect in 1969, in Southern California and elsewhere, and Richard and Karen were responsive. *Offering*, to my ears, showed an appreciation of Buffalo Springfield, The Association, Burt Bacharach and Hal David, The Beatles (obviously), and even Frank Zappa. But all such influences were folded into the Carpenters' background in song and choral technique. They put their own spin on things, which is what the greats always do.

A few years later, when the Carpenters had won international success with their own distinctive style, the musical and personal differences between this mainstream duo and their more flamboyant pop-music contemporaries were more obvious than the similarities. Their well-crafted albums, with songs of everyday joy and melancholy (and often packaged like Hallmark cards) stood far apart from albums by the dangerous Doors and the bawdy Big Brother and the Holding Company. In the cultural context of their time, this duo seemed to have come from an earlier era. To many people their own age, Karen and Richard represented the establishment—hence, the enemy.

I was delighted, then, in 1974 to be asked to write a lengthy article on Richard and Karen Carpenter for

Rolling Stone magazine, the bible (or at least the *Daily Variety*) of the countercultural music scene. In the journal's early years, I'd done a brief piece for *Stone* about Tim Hardin (with a cameo appearance by Jim Morrison) and a feature on Phil Ochs, and then a long story on Brian Wilson and the Beach Boys (which was printed in two parts in 1971). But the magazine and I had had a falling-out over "artistic differences" surrounding that Beach Boys piece.

Our rift was healed when *Stone*'s new art director, Mike Salisbury, suggested I do this Carpenters piece. I'd known Mike and worked with him in the past at *West* magazine, the *Los Angeles Times* Sunday supplement, when he was its art director. It was Mike's suggestion that *Rolling Stone* feature the Carpenters; he was as much interested in them visually as musically, as was the magazine's rising-star photographer Annie Leibovitz. They both believed the Carpenters would look terrific on the cover of *Rolling Stone*. And Mike thought I would be the right person to tell the Carpenters' story, as an Angeleno with broad musical tastes.

If only from a selfish point of view, I thought this was a great idea; any freelance writer with half an ego wanted to do the cover piece. But more importantly, that slot gave you space to paint a more comprehensive picture, the chance to stretch out and do justice to an interesting subject. The cover slot also conveyed the magazine's imprimatur that this *was* an interesting and relevant subject, worth writing and reading about at length. And Annie's photo carried its own imperative; you *knew* the article had to be essential reading, in order to live up to her certain-to-be iconic image!

I benefited from the chance, in those access-generous days, to spend a good amount of time with the Carpenters, interviewing them in depth and spending a few days on tour with them. And they both seemed glad for the opportunity to tell their stories to a sympathetic listener. While the Carpenters had always received their appreciative due from entertainment-trade papers—after all, they were hugely

THE BOYS IN THE BAG BY HUNTER S. THOMPSON

ROLLING STONE

ISSUE NO. 164   JULY 4, 1974   75¢ UK25p

HEAVY METAL HALL OF FAME

JANE FONDA'S VIETNAM JOURNAL

FAREWELL TO THE DUKE BY RALPH J. GLEASON

THE CARPENTERS: THE FAMILY THAT PLAYS TOGETHER

talented and immensely popular, selling millions of records, doing a TV series and specials, headlining in Las Vegas and touring the world—they had not always gotten a fair shake from newspaper scribes. They were not, of course, bland pop dispensers. Neither were they the founts of solace and wisdom some of their fan correspondents assumed they would be. "We're just—normal people," an exasperated Karen said.

Their problems with reviewers had to do with the nature of music coverage in journals whose writers got their jobs because they knew something about the current scene, which at the time was largely countercultural. The Carpenters were not countercultural; they were a contemporary extension of outstanding American popular music, in the tradition of, say, Jo Stafford and Paul Weston. Karen had that beautiful voice; Richard wrote and picked fine songs, crafted excellent arrangements, and produced great singles; the two of them made wonderful records and put on good shows. The Carpenters were fresh and unique, but they had developed out of a tradition some people were determined to hate. If such critics were assigned to see a Carpenters event instead of something they'd rather attend, they didn't bother to consider the merits of artists coming from a different place than Jefferson Airplane; instead, they moaned about how uncool this all was, or made fun of these squares and their fans.

Young Americans had for decades used popular music as an occasion to express rebellious hedonism. Teens in the 1930s who jumped onto the stage and jitterbugged while the big bands tried to perform, kids who tore up theater seats to the '50s sounds of Bill Haley, young folk who tripped on acid while listening to the Grateful Dead—they were asserting their generational identity. As Artie Shaw once explained such acting-out: "You are going to a party, and Mommy and Daddy will not be invited." But the Carpenters' music did not promote hedonism; and Mommy and Daddy, if they wanted, *were* invited.

There was more than hedonism at play, though, in some customers' visceral rejection of the Carpenters. There was politics. Folk music, folk rock, and harder rock protested the ongoing carnage of the Vietnam War. Youth culture rallied to antiwar politicians and railed against the status quo. The Carpenters were hardly perceived as antiestablishment. Twice they went to the Nixon White House: once in recognition for Karen's work on behalf of cancer research, once to sing for West German Chancellor Willy Brandt. All quite apolitical; but for many citizens their own age, these visits seemed to prove how out of step Richard and Karen were.

I hoped my article might change some of those attitudes by showing the Carpenters as smart, authentic, complicated people coping with challenges any of us would find difficult—and as dedicated artists who deserved to be celebrated.

Annie certainly came through with a wonderful photograph. And she made a point of calling me, while I was writing, to describe her perceptions of Karen and Richard during her sessions with them; she wanted to give me the benefit of her eyewitness too—that's how seriously she also took the story.

How did other staff people feel about the Carpenters being on the cover of *Rolling Stone*? Some thought it smart and clever. Others thought it dopey: that it harmed the magazine's reputation as a "serious" rock journal and made it look pop, commercial, and frivolous. (Guess they hadn't yet *read* the story!) But those folks would have grumbled about anything that wasn't to their usual taste.

After covering the Carpenters, I was given *Stone* assignments to write about the Osmonds (cover piece, with another photo by Annie Leibovitz), Neil Sedaka, and Paul Anka. I had been quickly typecast as the go-to profiler of middle-of-the-road acts; it seemed I was the only writer around willing to take such performers seriously. For the sake of variety, then, I asked to profile a somewhat grittier artist and got to write about Rod Stewart and Faces (with Annie's cover photo of Rod and then-girlfriend Britt Ekland). After which came, once again, the assignment of documenting a mainstream duo: Loggins and Messina. I was in *Rolling Stone*'s modest L.A. office the day advance copies of that issue came in; a staff writer grabbed one and exclaimed in disgust: "Loggins and *Messina*? I can't *believe* they put those guys on the cover! Who *wrote* this? Oh—sorry, Tom…"

Pages 234–35:
Outside A&M
Studio C, 1975

Right: 1974

236

I don't know if being on the cover of the *Rolling Stone* won Karen and Richard more fans or increased their "credibility" with their peers. As time passed, though, such concerns seemed to fade. Excellence conquers the snide. The Carpenters became part of our zeitgeist. Theirs was a great career, one that ended due to circumstances beyond their control, as all careers do—even the Beatles'.

But miraculously, or predictably, their music survives. The 1994 revisionist cover-collection *If I Were a Carpenter* demonstrated the allure the Carpenters' music and mythos held for a flock of that now-already-bygone era's freethinking independent artists. The splendid *Carpenters with the Royal Philharmonic Orchestra* (2018) placed Richard and Karen's oeuvre in a lush and sophisticated context for a still later generation. Books are still being written about those extraordinary siblings. Their CDs are strong sellers nearly half a century after their original albums were made.

Several years ago, a critic scorned the idea that their music will live forever ("*Oh, really?*"). But in 2020—when you can be standing in line at the food market and hear the sound system play an eighty-three-year-old recording of Mildred Bailey (go ahead, Google her) covering an Irving Berlin song—the odds seem even, at least, that "Yesterday Once More" may have a place in all the world's tomorrows. Fifty years ago, lots of us couldn't get enough of Karen Carpenter's beguiling voice, its haunting mix of joy and sadness. Maybe we never will.

Mike Cidoni Lennox

Afterword: Last Call with Richard Carpenter

"Karen was more than my sibling and my creative partner. She was my best friend."

Richard Carpenter and I sit side by side in front of a computer that rests atop the large desk in his home office. We've been writing and editing and rewriting and fact-checking for so many months in this space that it feels like a second home. But now, it's back to life, back to reality. We need to button this thing up. We're past deadline. It's our last interview.

Mike Cidoni Lennox: I'm wondering what the process of working on this book has been like for you—all these interviews, all these months. For Chris and me, at times, it felt like being in therapy.

Richard Carpenter: It has. [Laughs.] I'm talking about myself as I would with a therapist. But it's with a therapist who knows—musically, at least, what the hell you're talking about.

Chris and I never wanted a single session to end. I loved it most when you and Chris got into musicology mode. I didn't understand a damned word. But it was so much fun watching the two of you slip away into your own world. I'll never hear that piano solo in "This Masquerade" the same way again. Tell me one of the most enjoyable parts of the process for you.

Probably going back to the beginning of the whole thing—as it all went down together and all leading up to "(They Long to Be) Close to You," and the first couple of years.

You speak in very visual terms, which I think will make this a really great read. You took us to the basement back in New Haven a number of times. You and Karen spent hours down there listening to music.

Oh, yes, when I should have been doing other things—like studying. [Chuckles.] You know, it's not just music that we loved. It was radio and records and everything about it. In New Haven, we had WINS out of New York "1010 on Your Dial." And, of course, that was the biggie at that

time. You'd get the Top 40 countdown every week and we would just listen to it.

You and Karen spent a lot of time together.

Many people asked us, "How do you do it? How *do* you guys do it? I'm always squabbling…" We were almost like male-female clones. The smiles were identical, and we liked and disliked the same things—and not just music: comedians, movies, just about everything. But Karen didn't like classical music the way I do.

A few weeks back you told me that there was one thing people needed to understand about your relationship to Karen. I'd prefer it come from you again. Do you recall what you said?

Yes. Karen was more than my sibling and my creative partner. She was my best friend.

One of the big takeaways of the Carpenters story is that your work ethic was so off the charts that it put you on the charts.

We were born with the gift of loving what we do for a living. Recording, performing—we were just meant to do it all. What are the odds? What would be the odds of a brother becoming a songwriter, arranger, and producer, and then having a sister who would become one of the greatest singers in history? What are the odds there? It's really something to think about. And then to sign with a major label [A&M] whose owners had the good sense to give them carte blanche and artistic license in the recording studio? It was one of the rare times where everything just went right.

The work ethic worked in your favor for a long time. You were driven.

It seemed like nothing could stop either of us.

The two of you just powered through the years as if your addiction to prescription sleeping aids and her eating disorder just weren't happening. That made them next to impossible to introduce those into this book. Here we were writing about the Carpenters' recordings, and those problems never technically affected the recordings—that is, until Karen's voice was finally silenced.

The whole thing was, we were both supremely gifted, but also seriously screwed up, the two of us. I was lucky enough to get through my problem, but Karen wasn't.

Finally, to the music: I'm curious if you're at all surprised that, fifty years later, many people still consider "(They Long to Be) Close to You" one of greatest pop records ever made.

No, I'm not surprised. Because it is. It's a quality song. A real song. It had been around for a few years, but it needed the right arrangement to make it work. Herb sensed this. And he brought it to me *not* just because I was the right arranger for it but because he knew that *Karen* and I were the right artists.

As I've said all along: it took two Carpenters to make "the Carpenters."

I know that Karen would be the first person to back you up on that. Individually, we were something. But, together, we were really something else.

Japan, 1974

Chris May

The Carpenters Studio Discography

In 1985, at the dawn of the digital media era, Richard Carpenter began the wholesale process of technically updating and preserving the Carpenters' recording catalog. This has been a labor of love...no, better yet, a self-imposed obligation on Richard's part to help maintain the legacy and success that he and his sister, Karen, built together as the Carpenters.

To be an A&M artist meant having carte blanche when it came to accessing the world-renowned A&M Recording Studios in Hollywood. Yet, despite the studio's state-of-the-art reputation, Richard and Karen were still much ahead of their time in the way they made their records. The multitracked layering of their vocal and instrumental sound throughout their careers would continue to push technical boundaries.

For example, the songs they recorded for their 1969 debut album, *Offering* (retitled *Ticket to Ride* in 1970), were done on eight-track, one-inch reel-to-reel tape. As Richard recalls, "We thought that was the end of the world...which it was, until 16 [-track] came along."

However, to record a rhythm section, sixteen-piece string section, horn section, woodwind section, a minimum of twelve to fifteen background vocals (all overdubbed by Richard and Karen), and lead vocals, which were sometimes doubled—all on a total of eight tracks, was a challenge, to say the least. Thankfully, A&M upgraded to sixteen-track, two-inch tape the following year. It was better...yet still not ideal.

In 1974, another upgrade resulted in the installation of several twenty-four-track, two-inch tape machines throughout Studios A, B, C—and now Studio D (which has long since been referred to as "the studio the Carpenters built"). It would also become their home for the remainder of their recording career. The duo's growing success, along with the advances in studio technology, also meant that Richard would increase the size of the orchestral ensembles he booked for the sessions.

By now, the strings were up to twenty-four pieces—which included sixteen violins, four violas,

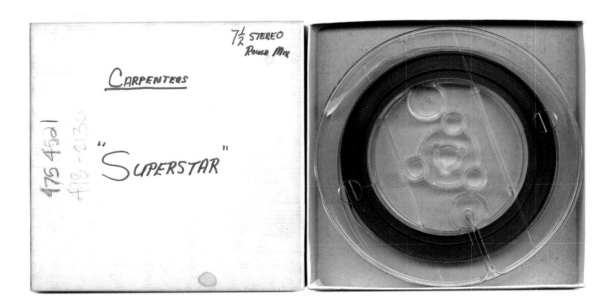

Reference mix tape of "Superstar"

and four cellos, unlike the prior 10-3-3 configuration. The piano and drums were now being recorded in stereo (as opposed to the first five albums, where these tracks had to be recorded in "mono" due to a lack of space on the master tape). And, of course, the outboard effects for mixing only got better over time.

Beyond the initial technical limitations, it was also common for Richard and Karen to struggle to find adequate time to dedicate to the recording studio, given that their management kept them overbooked elsewhere. This often pushed them to hasten an album's production, resulting in the overlooking of some of the minute details within the recordings.

Thanks to advances in digital technology, many of the tracks from the Carpenters catalog have been updated and remixed, under the strict, direct supervision of Richard. This, however, creates some confusion for fans, audiophiles, and completists seeking to track down a particular mix, outtake, or version of a recording.

Decades of research, along with countless hours spent with Richard, were poured into this resource, which reflects the body of work recorded in the studio by he and Karen together as the Carpenters.

On occasion, a solo recording made by either sibling is listed, *if* it was included on an official Carpenters compilation release. The same holds true for the live recordings, which, it is worth noting, Richard has never been particularly fond of. The "notes" included with many of the song entries contain either a bit of trivia, minutiae, or perhaps a detail that otherwise may not have been mentioned elsewhere in the book.

And finally: all of the original studio albums and only the major compilation releases that have been issued on some form of digital media have been included in the data below. However, box set releases that were designed to reproduce the original studio albums (and mixes) on compact disc (The *30th*, *35th*, and *40th Anniversary Collector's Edition* sets) are not referenced, for the sake of avoiding redundancy. Such is also the case for the *Remastered Classics* series discs released in the United States in 1998, which also replicated the original album mixes.

I hope that both the audiophile and casual listener alike will find something useful (and enjoyable) in this detailed, extensive listing.

Master-tape legend for "Superstar"

Foreign Country/ Region of Release:

Australia	AU
Brazil	BR
Canada	CA
Europe	EU
Germany	DE
Hong Kong	HK
Japan	JP
Netherlands	NL
South Africa	ZA
United Kingdom	UK

*If no country is listed next to release title, this indicates release in the United States.

Details	Notes	Versions

Song
1980 Medley (from the ABC TV special *Music, Music, Music*)

Written by
Sing (Joe Raposo), Knowing When to Leave (Burt Bacharach/Hal David), Make It Easy on Yourself (Burt Bacharach/Hal David), Someday (Richard Carpenter/John Bettis), We've Only Just Begun (Paul Williams/Roger Nichols)

Recorded at
A&M Studios—Studio D on 24-track, 2" tape

Instrumental Recording Date
1980

1980 "MUSIC, MUSIC, MUSIC" (ABC TV SPECIAL) (9:08)
From the Top (1991), *The Essential Collection—1965–1997* (2002), *Sweet Sixteen* (2009, *40th Anniversary Collector's Edition* bonus disc, JP)

Song
All I Can Do (Spectrum version)

Written by
Richard Carpenter
John Bettis

Recorded at
Home recording on Richard's Sony TC-200 reel-to-reel

Instrumental Recording Date
1967

Referred to as "The 5/4 Thing" in the early days, the first version, recorded by pre-Carpenters group Spectrum, was made in 1967 at the Carpenter home on Richard's Sony TC-200 reel-to-reel—the instrumentation laid down on one track and vocals overdubbed onto the other.

While recording several demos a year later at studio bassist Joe Osborn's garage studio, a more-refined version—this time with Richard and Karen singing all the vocal parts—was used for the Carpenters' demo tape that ultimately made it to Herb Alpert of A&M Records.

1967 SPECTRUM VERSION (1:50)
From the Top (1991), *The Essential Collection—1965–1997* (2002), *Sweet Sixteen* (2009, *40th Anniversary Collector's Edition* bonus disc, JP)

Song
All I Can Do (Carpenters version)

Written by
Richard Carpenter/John Bettis

Recorded at
Bassist Joe Osborn's garage studio, on 4-track tape

Instrumental Recording Date
1968

This definitive version found on *Offering* is the demo recorded at Joe Osborn's, albeit remixed for the album. There's no bass on it—just the electric piano, drums, and vocals.

1969 STUDIO ALBUM VERSION (1:42)
Offering (1969)/*Ticket to Ride* (1970 *Offering* retitled, repackaged reissue), *A&M Composers Series Vol. 2 Richard Carpenter & John Bettis* (1988, JP), *Japanese Single Box* (2006, JP)

Song
All of My Life

Written by
Richard Carpenter

Recorded at
A&M Studios—Studio B on 8-track, 1" tape

Instrumental Recording Date
June 2 and June 19, 1969 (rhythm tracks)

The electric bass on the original mix is played by none other than Karen—which she did on only one of the album's other tracks, "Eve." Played on a Hofner-like electric bass guitar given to her by studio bassist Joe Osborn, the original bass track was eventually replaced by Osborn in 1987 for the remix.

Other notable instrumental changes to the remix include Richard's replacement of the Wurlitzer 140B electric piano with a Yamaha DX7.

1969 STUDIO ALBUM VERSION (3:00)
Offering (1969)/*Ticket to Ride* (1970 *Offering* retitled, repackaged reissue), *The Complete Singles* (2015)
1987 REMIX (3:01)
Treasures (1987, JP), *From the Top* (1991), *Magical Memories of the Carpenters* (1993, UK), *Sweet Memory* (1994, JP), *Reflections* (1995, UK, EU, ZA, DE), *Sweet Sweet Smile* (2000, NL), *The Star Collection* (2000, NL), *The Essential Collection—1965–1997* (2002), *Carpenters Perform Carpenter* (2003), *Reflections—The Best 1200* (2005, JP), *The Best of the Carpenters* (2009, DE), *Sweet Sixteen* (2009, *40th Anniversary Collector's Edition* bonus disc, JP), *Best Songs* (2017, *Sweet Memory* repackaged, JP)

Details	Notes	Versions

Song
All You Get from Love Is a Love Song

Written by
Steve Eaton

Recorded at
A&M Studios—Studio D on 24-track, 2" tape

Instrumental Recording Date
April 1, 1977 (rhythm tracks, percussion, guitars, and horns), April 5 (guitars), April 6 (guitars and sax), April 12 (orchestra)

In an effort to take "the Carpenters sound" in a different direction for the *Passage* album, seasoned session vocalists Julia Tillman, Carlena Williams, and Maxine Willard were brought in to help complete the task. Their three-part harmony was recorded, then double tracked and blended in with Karen and Richard's. "I wanted to mix it up," Richard says. "It actually worked better than I thought it was going to."

He considers "All You Get from Love Is a Love Song" one of his favorite Carpenters recordings, calling it "a great piece of brain candy."

1977 STUDIO ALBUM VERSION (3:46)
Passage (1977), *The Singles 1974–1978* (1978, JP, CA, UK), *Yesterday Once More* (1984, UK), *Yesterday Once More* (1984, Silver Eagle Records, US and CA), *Yesterday Once More* (1985), *Classics Volume 2* (1987), *Reminiscing* (1988, CA), *Anthology* (1989, JP), *A&M New Gold Series Vol. 2* (1990, JP), *Only Yesterday: Richard and Karen Carpenter's Greatest Hits* (1990, UK), *Their Greatest Hits* (1990, UK, ZA), *From the Top* (1991), *Carpenters Collection* (1993, Time Life Music), *Magical Memories of the Carpenters* (1993, Reader's Digest, UK, AU, EU), *Their Greatest Hits* (1993, DE), *Carpenters Best Vol. 1* (1994, JP), *Sweet Memory* (1994, JP), *Anthology* (1997, remastered reissue, JP), *Love Songs* (1997), *Their Greatest Hits and Finest Performances* (1997, Reader's Digest), *Yesterday Once More* (1998), *Singles 1969–1981* (1999, JP), *Singles 1969–1981* (2000), *The Essential Collection—1965–1997* (2002), *Gold* (2004, 35th Anniversary Edition), *Gold* (2005), *Japanese Single Box* (2006, JP), *The Ultimate Collection* (2006, NL), *The Ultimate Collection* (2006, UK), *40/40* (2009), *40/40* (2009, EU, UK), *40/40 The Best Selection* (2009, JP), *Carpenters Collected* (2013), *Best Songs* (2017, *Sweet Memory* repackaged, JP)

Song
And When He Smiles

Written by
Alan C. Anderson

Recorded at
BBC Television Studios in London— Live for *Carpenters at the BBC*

Instrumental Recording Date
Sept. 25, 1971

For the 2001 Japanese release of *As Time Goes By*, this live recording is included as a "hidden," bonus track, which can be heard following approximately twenty seconds of silence at the end of the "'76 Hits Medley," track fourteen. The subsequent US reissue three years later, however, does list the song—assigning it to track fifteen.

2001 ALBUM VERSION (3:00)
As Time Goes By (2001, JP), *As Time Goes By* (2004)

Song
Another Song

Written by
Richard Carpenter/John Bettis

Recorded at
A&M Studios—Studios B and C on 16-track, 2" tape

Instrumental Recording Date
Nov. 1969 (rhythm tracks), July 28, 1970 (orchestra)

Preferred by some to the original mix, the 1994 remix features a rerecorded, more animated bassline by Joe Osborn, which replaces the original bass track played by Carpenters' bandmate Dan Woodhams. "Danny got mixed up in the whole thing and thrown off, but that album *had* to get done, so there was no time to fix it," Richard recalls.

The woodwind instrument in the instrumental section (1:51) was bandmate Doug Strawn's electric clarinet, played through the Gibson Maestro (sound system for woodwinds) while employing its "oboe" setting.

And the psychedelic "wah-wah" treatment heard a little later on (3:05) was Richard's Wurlitzer electric piano, played through a wah effects pedal.

1970 STUDIO ALBUM VERSION (4:22)
Close to You (1970)
1994 REMIX (4:24)
Sweet Memory (1994, JP), *Best Songs* (2017, *Sweet Memory* repackaged, JP)

Details	Notes	Versions
Song At the End of a Song **Written by** Richard Carpenter/John Bettis **Recorded at** A&M Studios—Studio D on 24-track, 2" tape **Instrumental Recording Dates** Nov. 20 and Nov. 22, 1980 (rhythm tracks, guitars, and percussion), March 7, 1983 (guitars), April 11, 1983 (horns) session 1, (strings) session 2		**1983 STUDIO ALBUM VERSION (3:42)** *Voice of the Heart* (1983), *Magical Memories of the Carpenters* (1993, Reader's Digest, UK, AU, EU), *Carpenters Perform Carpenter* (2003, JP)
Song Aurora **Written by** Richard Carpenter/John Bettis **Recorded at** A&M Studios—Studio D on 24-track, 2" tape **Instrumental Recording Dates** April 8, 1975 (piano), April 10 (orchestra)	"Aurora" is the opening bookend on the *Horizon* album, opposite "Eventide." Both share identical instrumental tracks, with differing lyrics (and lead vocal) by Karen.	**1975 STUDIO ALBUM VERSION (1:33)** *Horizon* (1975), *Sweet Memory* (1994, JP), *Best Songs* (2017, *Sweet Memory* repackaged, JP)
Song Ave Maria **Written by** Johann Sebastian Bach/Charles Gounod **Recorded at** A&M Studios—Studio D on 24-track, 2" tape **Instrumental Recording Dates** Feb. 9 and Feb. 13, 1978 (orchestra)	In addition to a full orchestra, "Ave Maria" was also intended to feature a large choir. Given the massive undertaking involved in the recording of *Christmas Portrait*, the original choral parts were misplaced, not to be discovered again until the album master was "in the can." In 1984, while production was underway for *An Old-Fashioned Christmas*, a forty-eight-voice choir was added, and the revised version included on *Christmas Portrait—The Special Edition* that same year. In 1990, "Ave Maria" was remixed, and an editing error fixed on Karen's lead vocal. Following the release of *Christmas Portrait*, the original Rhodes electric piano segue from "White Christmas" into "Ave Maria" was updated for Time Life's *Christmas with the Carpenters* in 1992, replacing it with a Yamaha DX7. And the DX7 was replaced with an acoustic piano for the 1996 *Christmas Collection* set.	**1978 STUDIO ALBUM VERSION (2:35)** *Christmas Portrait* (1978), *Christmas Portrait* (1984) *The only time the original mix appears on compact disc, DE. **1984 REMIX (2:33)** *Christmas Portrait—The Special Edition* (1984), *Anthology* (1989, JP) **1990 REMIX (2:35)** *From the Top* (1991, first edition version mastered incorrectly resulting in faster playback speed, second edition version returned to original speed), *Christmas with the Carpenters* (1992, Time Life Music), *Christmas Collection* (1996), *Anthology* (1997, remastered reissue, JP), *The Essential Collection—1965–1997* (2002), *Japanese Single Box* (2006, JP)
Song Baby It's You **Written by** Mack David/Burt Bacharach/Barney Williams **Recorded at** A&M Studios—Studio B on 16-track, 2" tape **Instrumental Recording Dates** July 13, 1970 (rhythm tracks), July 20 (orchestra)	The original "mono" acoustic piano recorded in 1970 was replaced in 1987 with the Yamaha DX7, and the track remixed for inclusion on the Japanese compilation set *Treasures*. Another alteration with the remix is the deletion of the bass track in the first verse, as it contained recorded static audible in the original mix.	**1970 STUDIO ALBUM VERSION (2:50)** *Close to You* (1970), *Japanese Single Box* (2006, JP) **1987 REMIX (2:50)** *Treasures* (1987, JP), *Treasures* (1990, UK), *Sweet Memory* (1994, JP), *Reflections* (1995, UK, EU, ZA, DE), *Sweet Sweet Smile* (2000, NL), *Reflections—The Best 1200* (2005, JP), *20/20 Best of the Best Selection* (2009, JP), *40/40* (2009), *40/40* (2009, EU, UK), *40/40 The Best Selection* (2009, JP), *The Best of the Carpenters* (2009, DE), *Best Songs* (2017, *Sweet Memory* repackaged, JP) **2018 ROYAL PHILHARMONIC VERSION (3:12)** *Carpenters with the Royal Philharmonic Orchestra* (2018)

Details	Notes	Versions

Song
Bacharach Medley (live)

Written by
Any Day Now (Burt Bacharach/Bob Hilliard), Baby It's You (Burt Bacharach/Hal David/Barney Williams), Knowing When to Leave (Burt Bacharach/Hal David), Make It Easy on Yourself (Burt Bacharach/Hal David)

Recorded at
The Riviera Hotel, Las Vegas

Instrumental Recording Dates
May 8–21, 1974

This live recording first surfaced in 1985 while the Japanese compilation package *Anthology* was being assembled. (It was reissued in 1989 and again in 1997.)

Due to an error in the recording, it was discovered that the kick drum, bass, piano, and male vocalists did not make it onto the tape. However, Karen's lead, the orchestra, and the rest of the drum kit did. For completion, Richard added a new kick, bass, piano, and background vocals, playing the kick and bass himself on a Kurzweil synthesizer.

1985 MIX (14:40)
Anthology (1989, JP), *Anthology* (1997, remastered reissue, JP), *Magical Memories of the Carpenters* (1993, Reader's Digest, UK, AU, EU),* *Their Greatest Hits and Finest Performances* (1997, Reader's Digest)

*The spoken intro is omitted on this release—total running time (13:09)

Song
Bacharach/David Medley

Written by
Burt Bacharach/Hal David
a. Knowing When to Leave
b. Make It Easy on Yourself
c. (There's) Always Something There to Remind Me
d. I'll Never Fall in Love Again
e. Walk on By
f. Do You Know the Way to San Jose?

Recorded at
A&M Studios—Studios A and C on 16-track, 2" tape

Instrumental Recording Dates
1971

Having been played live countless times in concert, the track for the "Bacharach/David Medley" was also recorded live at A&M's Studio C by the Carpenters and their road band, and all the vocals overdubbed later by Karen and Richard.

1971 STUDIO ALBUM VERSION (5:25)
Carpenters (1971)

Song
(Want You) Back in My Life Again

Written by
Kerry Chater/Chris Christian

Recorded at
A&M Studios—Studio D on 24-track, 2" tape

Instrumental Recording Dates
Oct. 21, 1980 (rhythm tracks, guitars, and percussion), Jan. 28, 1981 (sax), Jan. 29 and Feb. 2 (guitars), Feb. 5 (synthesizers), Feb. 26 (percussion), Feb. 11 (orchestra)

Daryl Dragon (of the acclaimed music duo Captain & Tennille) and Ian Underwood (of the Mothers of Invention) appear on this track for synthesizer programming.

Richard and Karen's background vocals peak near the end of the song (3:02), totaling eight parts doubled, sixteen voices.

Made in America became one of the Carpenters' most expensive albums to produce, as analog tape synchronization was in its infancy. This meant that two twenty-four-track tape machines could be paired, allowing a total of forty-eight tracks for recording. Ongoing errors in the syncing of the machines resulted in multiple delays, putting the album over budget.

1981 STUDIO ALBUM VERSION (3:40)
Made in America (1981), *Yesterday Once More* (1984, Silver Eagle Records, US and CA), *Yesterday Once More* (1984, UK), *Yesterday Once More* (1985), *Classics Volume 2* (1987), *Anthology* (1989, JP), *Magical Memories of the Carpenters* (1993, Reader's Digest, UK, AU, EU), *Sweet Memory* (1994, JP), *Anthology* (1997, remastered reissue, JP), *Their Greatest Hits and Finest Performances* (1997, Reader's Digest), *The Ultimate Collection* (2006, NL), *Carpenters Collected* (2013), *The Complete Singles* (2015), *Best Songs* (2017, *Sweet Memory* repackaged, JP)

Details	Notes	Versions
Song Because We Are in Love (The Wedding Song) **Written by** Richard Carpenter/John Bettis **Recorded at** A&M Studios—Studio D on 24-track, 2" tape Instrumental recording date: Aug. 26, 1980 (orchestra)	Written for Karen's wedding, which took place on Aug. 31, 1980, "The Wedding Song" was recorded five days beforehand, and Karen's lead vocal later rerecorded for inclusion on *Made in America*.	1981 STUDIO ALBUM VERSION (5:04) *Made in America* (1981), *Yesterday Once More* (1984, UK), *Yesterday Once More* (1984, Silver Eagle Records, US and CA), *Yesterday Once More* (1985), *Classics Volume 2* (1987), *Treasures* (1987, JP), *A&M Composers Series Vol. 2 Richard Carpenter & John Bettis* (1988, JP), *Anthology* (1989, JP), *Treasures* (1990, UK), *From the Top* (1991), *Magical Memories of the Carpenters* (1993, Reader's Digest, UK, AU, EU), *Carpenters Best Vol. 1* (1994, JP), *Sweet Memory* (1994, JP), *Reflections* (1995, UK, EU, ZA, DE), *Anthology* (1997, remastered reissue, JP), *Their Greatest Hits and Finest Performances* (1997, Reader's Digest), *Yesterday Once More* (1998), *Sweet Sweet Smile* (2000, NL), *The Essential Collection—1965–1997* (2002), *Carpenters Perform Carpenter* (2003), *Reflections—The Best 1200* (2005, JP), *Japanese Single Box* (2006, JP), *The Best of the Carpenters* (2009, DE), *The Complete Singles* (2015), *Best Songs* (2017, *Sweet Memory* repackaged, JP)
Song Beechwood 4-5789 **Written by** William Stevenson/Marvin Gaye/George Gordy **Recorded at** A&M Studios—Studio D on 24-track, 2" tape **Instrumental Recording Dates** Nov. 7, 1980 (rhythm tracks, guitars, and percussion), Jan. 28, 1981 (sax solo), Jan. 30 and Feb. 2 (guitars), Feb. 11 and Feb. 12 (orchestra)		1981 STUDIO ALBUM VERSION (3:06) *Made in America* (1981), *Yesterday Once More* (1984, Silver Eagle Records, US and CA), *Anthology* (1989, JP), *A&M New Gold Series Carpenters Vol. 2* (1990, JP), *Sweet Memory* (1994, JP), *Reflections* (1995, UK, EU, ZA, DE), *Anthology* (1997, remastered reissue, JP), *Their Greatest Hits and Finest Performances* (1997, Reader's Digest), *Sweet Sweet Smile* (2000, NL), *Reflections—The Best 1200* (2005, JP), *Japanese Single Box* (2006, JP), *The Ultimate Collection* (2006, NL), *The Best of the Carpenters* (2009, DE), *Carpenters Collected* (2013), *The Complete Singles* (2015), *Best Songs* (2017, *Sweet Memory* repackaged, JP)
Song Benediction **Written by** Richard Carpenter/John Bettis **Recorded at** A&M Studios—Studio B on 8-track, 1" tape **Instrumental Recording Dates** 1969		1969 STUDIO ALBUM VERSION (0:40) *Offering* (1969)/*Ticket to Ride* (1970 *Offering* retitled, repackaged reissue)

Details	Notes	Versions

Song
Bless the Beasts and Children

Written by
Barry De Vorzon/Perry Botkin Jr.

Recorded at
A&M Studios—Studio B on 16-track, 2" tape

Instrumental Recording Dates
April 16, 1971 (rhythm tracks), April 19 (orchestra)

There are three instrumental variations of the opening melody line in the song's introduction, depending on which album you own, featuring "Bless the Beasts."

On the motion picture soundtrack version—contrary to popular rumor that it was played on a vibraphone, it was actually played by Richard on a Wurlitzer electric piano, model 140B, with tremolo.

For the original *A Song for You* mix, Richard called on bandmate Doug Strawn to replace the line by playing his electric clarinet through a Gibson Maestro, using its "oboe" setting.

The line was replaced again for all future remixes in 1985 with an authentic oboe by Carpenters' regular studio woodwindist, Earle Dumler. Additional revisions were made to the master for the 1985 remix, including a complete rerecording of the entire rhythm section, notably Hal Blaine's drum track.

While recording the Hammond organ track, studio personnel mistakenly pushed open the door to the studio air lock. The squeak of the door made its way into the microphone, and thus onto the track, which was inadvertently left "unmuted" during mixdown. This can be heard in the first verse, underneath the lyric "for in this world they have no *voice*" in both the 1971 movie soundtrack and the 1972 *A Song for You* album mix. The mistake was caught after *A Song for You* was released, and later remedied in 1985 when Richard and engineer Roger Young remixed the song.

The drums were also rerecorded in stereo in 1985, once again played by original drummer Hal Blaine.

1971 MOVIE SOUNDTRACK VERSION (3:07)
Bless the Beasts & Children—Original Motion Picture Soundtrack Recording (1971), *Japanese Single Box* (2006, JP)
1972 STUDIO ALBUM VERSION (3:07)
A Song for You (1972), *The Ultimate Collection* (2006, NL), *Carpenters Collected* (2013), *The Complete Singles* (2015)
1985 REMIX (3:07)
Yesterday Once More (1985), *A&M Gold Series Vol. 2* (1986, JP), *Classics Volume 2* (1987), *Treasures* (1987, JP), *Anthology* (1989, JP), *A Song for You* (1989, Mobile Fidelity Sound Lab), *A&M New Gold Series Vol. 2* (1990, JP), *Treasures* (1990, UK), *From the Top* (1991), *Magical Memories of the Carpenters* (1993, UK), *Carpenters Best Vol. 2* (1994, JP), *The Best of Carpenters* (1994, BR), *Interpretations: A 25th Anniversary Celebration* (1994, UK), *Sweet Memory* (1994, JP), *Interpretations: A 25th Anniversary Celebration* (1995), *Anthology* (1997, remastered reissue, JP), *Their Greatest Hits and Finest Performances* (1997, Reader's Digest), *Yesterday Once More* (1998), *Best Songs* (2017, *Sweet Memory* repackaged, JP)
1991 REMIX (3:15)
Best of Best + Original Master Karaoke (1992, JP), *20th Century Masters Millennium Series* (2002), *The Essential Collection—1965–1997* (2002), *Gold* (2004, 35th Anniversary Edition), *Singles 1969–1981* SACD (2004, CD audio layer), *Gold* (2005), *The Ultimate Collection* (2006, UK), *20/20 Best of the Best Selection* (2009, JP), *40/40* (2009), *40/40* (2009, EU, UK), *40/40 The Best Selection* (2009, JP), *20th Century Masters Millennium Series* (2017, reissue, JP)
2004 SACD 5.1 + STEREO FOLD-DOWN MIX (3:15)
Singles 1969–1981 SACD (2004)

Song
Boat to Sail

Written by
Jackie DeShannon

Recorded at
A&M Studios—Studio D on 24-track, 2" tape

Instrumental Recording Dates
Jan. 24, 1976 (rhythm tracks), Feb. 16 (guitars), Feb. 26 (orchestra)

The line Karen ad-libs during the fade-out, "DeShannon is back," is a tip of the hat to the song's composer, Jackie DeShannon.

1976 STUDIO ALBUM VERSION (3:29)
A Kind of Hush (1976), *Magical Memories of the Carpenters* (1993, UK), *Sweet Memory* (1994, JP), *The Complete Singles* (2015), *Best Songs* (2017, *Sweet Memory* repackaged, JP)

Details	Notes	Versions

Song
Breaking Up Is Hard to Do

Written by
Neil Sedaka/Howard Greenfield

Recorded at
A&M Studios—Studio D on 24-track, 2" tape

Instrumental Recording Dates
Dec. 4, 1975 (rhythm tracks), Feb. 26, 1976 (orchestra), March 1 (percussion and sax), April 15 (percussion and guitars), April 20 (harp and sax)

The silly chatter heard during the song's fade-out was created in A&M's Studio C by a few of "the guys" (referring to the Carpenters' road band).

"There's that line from *The Return of the Pink Panther*, where [Inspector] Clouseau says to the beggar on the street with his monkey, '(Try to) do something about your filthy minkey.' That's what Doug Strawn is saying during the party bit in 'Breaking Up,' which you'll hear if you listen for it," Richard says.

1976 STUDIO ALBUM VERSION (2:35)
A Kind of Hush (1976), *A&M Gold Series Vol. 1* (1986, JP), *A&M New Gold Series Vol. 2* (1990, JP), *Japanese Single Box* (2006, JP)

Song
B'wana She No Home

Written by
Michael Franks

Recorded at
A&M Studios—Studio D on 24-track, 2" tape

Instrumental Recording Dates
April 13 and 15, 1977 (rhythm tracks, percussion, and sax)

Some audiophiles have pointed out that the mix on "B'wana She No Home" sounds a bit "midrange" in nature. In fact, several Carpenters album tracks recorded from around 1975 through 1978 sound this way.

According to Richard, veteran recording engineer Ray Gerhardt began suffering from hearing loss, affecting his full spectrum. "Listen to 'All You Get from Love Is a Love Song.' We asked Roger [Young] to record the tracks on that—you can hear the difference."

1977 STUDIO ALBUM VERSION (5:29)
Passage (1977), *Sweet Memory* (1994, JP), *Japanese Single Box* (2006, JP), *The Complete Singles* (2015), *Best Songs* (2017, *Sweet Memory* repackaged, JP)

Song
California Dreamin'

Written by
John Phillips/Michelle Phillips

Recorded at
Bassist Joe Osborn's garage studio, on 4-track tape

Instrumental Recording Dates
1967

Recorded in 1967, "California Dreamin'" features Karen on lead vocal and drums, Richard on keyboards, and college mate Bill Sissyoev on bass. Karen's lead ended up on its own track, unlike most of the instrumentation, which was "locked" together on another track, making it impossible to separate.

For inclusion on *As Time Goes By* in 2001, all the instrumentation was replaced, including Richard's Chamberlin Music Master, which was intended to create the effect of a real string section.

2001 ALBUM VERSION (4:35)
As Time Goes By (2001, JP), *As Time Goes By* (2004)

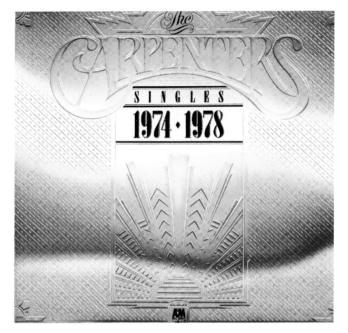

A revised version of "Can't Smile without You" made its debut on *The Singles 1974–1978*

Song
Calling Occupants of Interplanetary Craft (The Recognized Anthem of World Contact Day)

Written by
John Woloschuk/Terry Draper

Recorded at
A&M Soundstage and Studio D on 24-track, 2" tape

Instrumental Recording Dates
May 9, 1977 (rhythm tracks), May 16 (guitars), May 27 (orchestra and percussion)

The sound effect of the radio dial's "click" at the start of the track was created by staff engineer Ray Gerhardt. This was achieved by running a microphone and cable down the hallway from Studio D, out to the A&M Studios parking lot, and into Richard's Lincoln Mark IV. The scanning of airwaves was captured separately by Gerhardt from a radio and later edited.

All the space alien effects heard throughout the song were provided by Richard through a vocal effects processor.

On May 24, 1977, the orchestra was initially recorded on the A&M soundstage; however, this made the separation in the mix a problem due to leakage, particularly as a result of the trumpets. Parts of the orchestra were rerecorded in Studio D a few days later.

1977 STUDIO ALBUM VERSION (7:07)
Passage (1977), *The Singles 1974–1978* (1978, CA, JP, UK), *Yesterday Once More* (1984, UK), *Yesterday Once More* (1985), *A&M Gold Series Vol. 2* (1986, JP), *Classics Volume 2* (1987), *Reminiscing* (1988, CA), *Anthology* (1989, JP), *The Ultimate Collection* (2006, NL), *Carpenters Collected* (2013), *The Nation's Favourite Carpenters Songs* (2016, UK)
1978 SINGLE EDIT (clean intro, no DJ) (4:12)
Japanese Single Box (2006, JP), *The Complete Singles* (2015)
1989 REMIX (7:10)
Only Yesterday: Richard and Karen Carpenter's Greatest Hits (1990, UK), *Their Greatest Hits* (1990, UK, ZA), *From the Top* (1991), *Carpenters Collection* (1993, Time Life Music), *Magical Memories of the Carpenters* (1993, UK), *Their Greatest Hits* (1993, DE), *Carpenters Best Vol. 1* (1994, JP), *Interpretations: A 25th Anniversary Celebration* (1994, UK), *Interpretations: A 25th Anniversary Celebration* (1995), *Anthology* (1997, remastered reissue, JP), *Their Greatest Hits and Finest Performances* (1997, Reader's Digest), *Yesterday Once More* (1998), *The Essential Collection—1965–1997* (2002), *Gold* (2000, UK), *Singles 1969–1981* SACD (2004, CD audio layer), *Gold* (2005, UK), *The Ultimate Collection* (2006, UK), *40/40* (2009), *40/40* (2009, EU, UK), *40/40 The Best Selection* (2009, JP)
2004 SACD 5.1 + STEREO FOLD-DOWN MIX (7:07)
Singles 1969–1981 SACD (2004)

Song
Can't Smile without You

Written by
Chris Arnold/David Martin/Geoff Morrow

Recorded at
A&M Studios—Studio D on 24-track, 2" tape

Instrumental Recording Dates
Feb. 14, 1976 (rhythm tracks), Feb. 24 (orchestra), July 20 and July 22 (rhythm tracks and orchestra for the single version)

The album and single versions of this recording differ slightly.

The single version, released as the B-side to "Calling Occupants of Interplanetary Craft" fifteen months following the release of *Hush*, includes a rerecorded, slightly faster first verse, along with a revised lead vocal by Karen. The remainder of the original recording and lead vocal from the album version, starting from the second verse on, was spliced onto the newly recorded revision of the intro and verse one. Additional orchestration was added for the single mix.

1976 STUDIO ALBUM VERSION (3:26)
A Kind of Hush (1976), *A&M New Gold Series Vol. 1* (1990, JP)
1977 SINGLE VERSION (3:24)
The Singles 1974–1978 (1978, CA, JP, UK), *Sweet Memory* (1994, JP), *Reflections* (1995, UK, EU, ZA, DE), *Sweet Sweet Smile* (2000, NL), *Reflections—The Best* (2005, JP), *Japanese Single Box* (2006, JP), *The Best of the Carpenters* (2009, DE), *The Complete Singles* (2015), *Best Songs* (2017, *Sweet Memory* repackaged, JP)
1997 SINGLE VERSION REMIX (3:24)
Their Greatest Hits and Finest Performances (1997, Reader's Digest), *By Request* (2000, JP)

Song
Caravan (The Richard Carpenter Trio)

Written by
Irving Mills/Duke Ellington/Juan Tizol

Recorded at
Home recording on Richard's Sony TC-200 reel-to-reel

Instrumental Recording Dates
1965

This recording from 1965 by the Richard Carpenter Trio features Richard on piano, Karen on drums, and high school pal Wes Jacobs on tuba. It was recorded in the Carpenter family living room on Richard's Sony TC-200 reel-to-reel tape machine, in stereo.

1991 STUDIO ALBUM VERSION (3:37)
From the Top (1991), *The Essential Collection—1965–1997* (2002)

Details	Notes	Versions

Song
Carol of the Bells

Written by
Public Domain/Arranged by Richard Carpenter

Recorded at
A&M Studios—Studio D on 24-track, 2" tape

Instrumental Recording Dates
Feb. 9, 1978 (piano, rhythm tracks, and orchestra)

1978 STUDIO ALBUM VERSION (1:40)
   Christmas Portrait (1978), *Christmas Portrait* (1984, DE), *Christmas Portrait—The Special Edition* (1984)
1992 REMIX (1:40)
   Christmas Collection (1996)

Song
Carpenters/Como Medley

Written by
Yesterday Once More (Richard Carpenter/ John Bettis), Magic Moments (Burt Bacharach/Hal David), Sing (Joe Raposo), Catch a Falling Star (Lee Pockriss/Paul Vance), (They Long to Be) Close to You (Burt Bacharach/Hal David), It's Impossible (Armando Manzanero/Sid Wayne), We've Only Just Begun (Paul Williams/Roger Nichols), And I Love You So (Don McLean), Don't Let the Stars Get in Your Eyes (Slim Willet), Till the End of Time (Buddy Kaye/ Ted Mossman), No Other Love (Richard Rodgers/Oscar Hammerstein)

Recorded at
A&M Studios—Studio D on 24-track, 2" tape

Instrumental Recording Dates
1974

Notes: Recorded for *The Perry Como Christmas Show.*

2001 ALBUM VERSION (6:55)
   As Time Goes By (2001, JP), *As Time Goes By* (2004)

Song
Christ Is Born

Written by
Ray Charles/Domenico Bartolucci

Recorded at
A&M Studios—Studio D on 24-track, 2" tape

Instrumental Recording Dates
1977

Notes: The choral parts in the background of "Christ Is Born" were sung by the California State University, Long Beach, choir, then double tracked. The Tom Bähler Chorale was then added in order to help achieve a bigger sound.

1978 STUDIO ALBUM VERSION (3:13)
   Christmas Portrait (1978), *Christmas Portrait* (1984, DE), *Christmas Portrait—The Special Edition* (1984)
1990 REMIX (3:13)
   From the Top (1991), *Christmas with the Carpenters* (1992, Time Life Music), *Christmas Collection* (1996), *Their Greatest Hits and Finest Performances* (1997, Reader's Digest), *The Essential Collection—1965–1997* (2002)

Song
Christmas Song

Written by
Mel Tormé/Robert Wells

Recorded at
A&M Studios—Studio D on 24-track, 2" tape

Instrumental Recording Dates
1977

1977 SINGLE VERSION (clean open, no cross-fade) (3:39)
   Japanese Single Box (2006, JP), *The Complete Singles* (2015)
1978 STUDIO ALBUM VERSION (3:39)
   Christmas Portrait (1978), *Christmas Portrait* (1984, DE), *Christmas Portrait—The Special Edition* (1984)
1992 REMIX (3:39)
   Christmas with the Carpenters (1992, Time Life Music), *Christmas Collection* (1996)

Details	Notes	Versions

Song
Christmas Waltz

Written by
Jule Styne/Sammy Cahn

Recorded at
A&M Studios—Studio D on 24-track, 2" tape

Instrumental Recording Dates
Feb. 9, 1978 (rhythm tracks and orchestra), Feb. 12 (percussion and harp)

1978 STUDIO ALBUM VERSION (2:15)
Christmas Portrait (1978), *Christmas Portrait* (1984, DE), *Christmas Portrait—The Special Edition* (1984)
1992 REMIX (2:15)
Christmas with the Carpenters (1992, Time Life Music), *Christmas Collection* (1996)

Song
(They Long to Be) Close to You

Written by
Burt Bacharach/Hal David

Recorded at
A&M Studios—Studio B on 16-track, 2" tape

Instrumental Recording Dates
March 24, 1970 (rhythm tracks), April 13 (orchestra)

A&M Studios had several Steinway pianos in use during the Carpenters' career, according to Richard.

"Piano A," which was Richard's first choice and often referred to as the "Close to You" piano, was a Model B, and it is heard on most of the original Carpenters tracks. In "Close to You," a creak in the pedal assembly can be heard (0:30), which was removed during the "cleanup" efforts made during the mixing of the RPO album in 2018.

The harpsichord was recorded in "Mix One" at A&M Studios because none of the studios were available.

First-call session player Chuck Findley's trumpet solo was quadruple tracked. Richard says, "For years I thought it was tripled. But when we did the RPO album and had the tracks up, there were four of them. We put them on the string tracks where the strings weren't playing."

And, as mentioned elsewhere, Richard and Karen had difficulty "doubling" a vocal while listening back to the "single" on any given recording, as it would throw them off. In the case of "Close to You," however, Richard says, "If you listen to Karen's overdub going into the second bridge, it's doubled, which is the way I wanted it. But she listened to the [single lead] vibrato, so there's no clashing vibratos. Remarkable."

1970 STUDIO ALBUM VERSION (extended fade-out) (4:34)
Close to You (1970), *The Essential Collection—1965-1997* (2002), *The Ultimate Collection* (2006, NL), *Carpenters Collected* (2013), *The Nation's Favourite Carpenters Songs* (2016, UK)
1970 SINGLE VERSION (shortened fade-out) (3:41)
The Singles 1969-1973 (1973), *Yesterday Once More* (1984, Silver Eagle Records, US and CA), *Yesterday Once More* (1984, UK), *Yesterday Once More* (1985), *A&M Gold Series Vol. 2* (1986, JP), *Classics Volume 2* (1987), *Reminiscing* (1988, CA), *Anthology* (1989, JP), *A&M New Gold Series Vol. 1* (1990, JP), *Only Yesterday: Richard and Karen Carpenter's Greatest Hits* (1990, UK), *Their Greatest Hits* (1990, UK, ZA), *Treasures* (1990, UK), *A&M Gold Series* (1991, JP), *From the Top* (1991), *Startrax* (1991, EU, AU), *Their Greatest Hits* (1993, DE), *Singles 1969-1981* (1999, JP), *Singles 1969-1981* (2000), *Japanese Single Box* (2006), *The Complete Singles* (2015)
1991 REMIX (3:41)
Best of Best + Original Master Karaoke (1992, JP), *Carpenters Collection* (1993, Time Life Music), *Magical Memories of the Carpenters* (1993, UK), *Carpenters Best Vol. 2* (1994, JP), *The Best of Carpenters* (1994, BR), *Interpretations: A 25th Anniversary Celebration* (1994, UK), *Sweet Memory* (1994, JP), *Interpretations: A 25th Anniversary Celebration* (1995), *Anthology* (1997, remastered reissue, JP), *Love Songs* (1997), *Their Greatest Hits and Finest Performances* (1997, Reader's Digest), *By Request* (2000, JP), *Gold* (2000, UK), *Gold* (2001, JP), *Singles 1969-1981* SACD (2004, CD audio layer), *Gold* (2005, UK), *The Ultimate Collection* (2006, UK), *20/20 Best of the Best Selection* (2009, JP), *40/40* (2009), *40/40* (2009, EU, UK), *40/40 The Best Selection* (2009, JP), *Icon* (2014), *Best Songs* (2017, *Sweet Memory* repackaged, JP)
2004 SACD 5.1 + STEREO FOLD-DOWN MIX (3:40)
Singles 1969-1981 SACD (2004)
2018 ROYAL PHILHARMONIC VERSION (3:41)
Carpenters with the Royal Philharmonic Orchestra (2018)

Master tape legend for "(They Long to Be) Close to You"

Song
Crescent Noon

Written by
Richard Carpenter/John Bettis

Recorded at
A&M Studios—Studio B on 16-track, 2" tape

Instrumental Recording Dates
July 28, 1970 (orchestra)

1970 STUDIO ALBUM VERSION (4:09)
Close to You (1970), *Sweet Memory* (1994, JP), *Best Songs* (2017, *Sweet Memory* repackaged, JP)

Song
Crystal Lullaby

Written by
Richard Carpenter/John Bettis)

Recorded at
A&M Studios—Studio B on 16-track, 2" tape

Instrumental Recording Dates
March 23, 1972 (orchestra)

Notable differences between the original 1972 mix and the 1987 remix are the replacement of the original Wurlitzer electric piano track with a Yamaha DX7 as well as updated reverb effects and new mix assignment.

Another adjustment made in an attempt to fix a bad punch-in on Karen's lead vocal can be heard in the third verse, first word "Sometimes" (1:44), which sounds like "Tumtimes" on the original recording. Richard edited in his own "S" to correct the error for the remix.

1972 STUDIO ALBUM VERSION (3:58)
A Song for You (1972)
1987 REMIX (3:56)
A Song for You (1972), *Treasures* (1987, JP), *A&M Composers Series Vol. 2 Richard Carpenter & John Bettis* (1988, JP), *Magical Memories of the Carpenters* (1993, UK), *Sweet Memory* (1994, JP), *Carpenters Perform Carpenter* (2003), *Japanese Single Box* (2006, JP), *20/20 Best of the Best Selection* (2009, JP), *40/40* (2009), *40/40* (2009, EU, UK), *40/40 The Best Selection* (2009, JP), *The Complete Singles* (2015), *Best Songs* (2017, *Sweet Memory* repackaged, JP)

Song
Da Doo Ron Ron (When He Walked Me Home)

Written by
Ellie Greenwich/Jeff Barry/Phil Spector

Recorded at
A&M Studios—Studio B on 16-track, 2" tape

Instrumental Recording Dates
Jan. 9, 1973 (rhythm tracks), Feb. 7 (guitars)

1973 STUDIO ALBUM VERSION (found on "Oldies Medley") (1:46)
Now & Then (1973), *Anthology* (1989, JP)
1990 REMIX (found on "Oldies Medley") (1:46)
From the Top (1991), *Magical Memories of the Carpenters* (1993, UK), *Sweet Memory* (1994, JP), *Anthology* (1997, remastered reissue, JP), *The Essential Collection—1965–1997* (2002), *Best Songs* (2017, *Sweet Memory* repackaged, JP)

Song
Dancing in the Street

Written by
Ivy Hunter/Marvin Gaye/William Stevenson

Recorded at
A&M Studios—Studio D on 24-track, 2" tape

Instrumental Recording Dates
1978

Recorded for the ABC TV special *Space Encounters*

2001 ALBUM VERSION (2:00)
As Time Goes By (2001, JP), *As Time Goes By* (2004)

Song
Deadman's Curve

Written by
Jan Barry/Roger Christian/Artie Kornfeld/Brian Wilson

Recorded at
A&M Studios—Studio B on 16-track, 2" tape

Instrumental Recording Dates
Jan. 10, 1973 (rhythm tracks), Feb. 16 (orchestra)

The faint background vocals in "Deadman's Curve," otherwise difficult to make out, are "Ooh, slidin', slippin' and slidin', ooh slidin', slippin' and broadsidin'."

1973 STUDIO ALBUM VERSION (found on "Oldies Medley") (1:46)
Now & Then (1973), *Anthology* (1989, JP)
1990 REMIX (found on "Oldies Medley") (1:46)
From the Top (1991), *Magical Memories of the Carpenters* (1993, UK), *Sweet Memory* (1994, JP), *Anthology* (1997, remastered reissue, JP), *Their Greatest Hits and Finest Performances* (1997, Reader's Digest),* *The Essential Collection—1965–1997* (2002), *Best Songs* (2017, *Sweet Memory* repackaged, JP)
* The DJ chatter is omitted from the track for this release—total running time (1:37)

Details	Notes	Versions
Song Desperado **Written by** Don Henley/Glenn Frey **Recorded at** A&M Studios—Studio D on 24-track, 2" tape **Instrumental Recording Dates** Jan. 28–31, 1975 (rhythm tracks and guitars), Feb. 20 (harmonica), Feb. 21 (orchestra), March 14 (pedal steel guitar)	"Desperado" was remixed in 1994 to correct an issue with intermodular distortion related to Tommy Morgan's harmonica track. "This was a problem with the vinyl release in particular because with the way vinyls are pressed, the grooves would get tighter the further you get into the record. This would cause it to skip occasionally," Richard says.	1975 STUDIO ALBUM VERSION (3:37) *Horizon* (1975), *Anthology* (1989, JP), *A&M New Gold Series Vol. 1* (1990, JP), *Treasures* (1990, UK), *A&M Gold Series* (1991, JP), *Startrax* (1991, EU, AU), *Magical Memories of the Carpenters* (1993, UK), *Carpenters Best Vol. 1* (1994, JP), *Anthology* (1997, remastered reissue, JP), *The Ultimate Collection* (2006, NL), *The Ultimate Collection* (2006, UK), *Carpenters Collected* (2013) 1994 REMIX (3:37) *Interpretations: A 25th Anniversary Celebration* (1994, UK)
Song Dizzy Fingers **Written by** Edward E. "Zez" Confrey **Recorded at** A&M Studios—Studio D on 24-track, 2" tape **Instrumental Recording Dates** 1980	Richard insisted the arrangement to "Dizzy Fingers," recorded for the ABC TV special *Music, Music, Music*, be the Roger Van Epps version, played by Carmen Cavallaro in the 1956 biopic, *The Eddy Duchin Story*.	2001 ALBUM VERSION (2:26) *As Time Goes By* (2001, JP), *As Time Goes By* (2004)
Song Do You Hear What I Hear? **Written by** Noël Regney/Gloria Shayne **Recorded at** A&M Studios—Studio D on 24-track, 2" tape **Instrumental Recording Dates** Dec. 8, 1977 (rhythm tracks and orchestra)	Karen's lead vocal is a "work lead," which was taped while the orchestra was being recorded. However, she got distracted during the opening line, mumbling through the first couple of lyrics, rendering the take unusable. For release on *An Old-Fashioned Christmas* in 1984, Richard overdubbed his vocals. As for the conflicting call-and-response in verse one (0:15), Richard sings "Do you see what I see" followed by the chorale incorrectly echoing the line, "Do you hear what I hear?" Richard says, "Oh, that was a mistake…but I figured, what the hell."	1984 STUDIO ALBUM VERSION (2:53) *An Old-Fashioned Christmas* (1984), *Christmas Collection* (1996)
Song Don't Be Afraid (demo version) **Written by** Richard Carpenter **Recorded at** Bassist Joe Osborn's garage studio, on 4-track tape **Instrumental Recording Dates** 1968		1967 DEMO VERSION (2:06) *From the Top* (1991), *The Essential Collection—1965–1997* (2002), *Sweet Sixteen* (2009, 40th Anniversary Collector's Edition bonus disc, JP)
Song Don't Be Afraid (*Offering/Ticket to Ride* version) **Written by** Richard Carpenter **Recorded at** A&M Studios—Studio B on 8-track, 1" tape **Instrumental Recording Dates** June 19, 1969 (rhythm tracks)	The effect heard on the piano solo (1:07) was the result of slowing the master tape down during the recording. Richard played the solo to the slower playback—and once perfect, the tape was then returned to normal speed.	1969 STUDIO ALBUM VERSION (2:05) *Offering* (1969), *Ticket to Ride* (1970 *Offering* retitled, repackaged reissue), *Sweet Memory* (1994, JP), *The Complete Singles* (2015), *Best Songs* (2017, *Sweet Memory* repackaged, JP)

Details	Notes	Versions

Song
Druscilla Penny
 	
Written by
Richard Carpenter/John Bettis
 	
Recorded at
A&M Studios—Studio A on 16-track, 2" tape
 	
Instrumental Recording Dates
1971
	It has been a long-standing myth that the original vinyl pressing of *Carpenters* contains a glitch (in two places), causing the record to skip.
	    The first comes immediately following the lyric: "Your family's probably given up on you since you began to follow groups of long-haired rock and rollers…" (0:41). Then again a little later on, following the lyric: "I've seen your face at least a thousand times you're always standing there behind the stages at the concerts…" (1:27).
	    As it turns out, it is nothing more than a syncopated kick drum, played by Karen, which was pushed up in the mix.
		1971 STUDIO ALBUM VERSION (5:25)
		Carpenters (1971), *A&M Composers Series Vol. 2 Richard Carpenter & John Bettis* (1988, JP), *Japanese Single Box* (2006, JP), *The Complete Singles* (2015)

Song The End of the World **Written by** Arthur Kent/Sylvia Dee **Recorded at** A&M Studios—Studio B on 16-track, 2" tape **Instrumental Recording Dates** Jan. 9, 1973 (rhythm tracks), Feb. 16 (orchestra)		1973 STUDIO ALBUM VERSION (found on "Oldies Medley") (2:26) *Now & Then* (1973), *Anthology* (1989, JP) 1990 REMIX (found on "Oldies Medley") (2:26) *From the Top* (1991), *Magical Memories of the Carpenters* (1993, UK), *Sweet Memory* (1994, JP), *Anthology* (1997, remastered reissue, JP), *Their Greatest Hits and Finest Performances* (1997, Reader's Digest),* *The Essential Collection—1965–1997* (2002), *Best Songs* (2017, *Sweet Memory* repackaged, JP)
Song Eve **Written by** Richard Carpenter/John Bettis **Recorded at** A&M Studios—Studio B on 8-track, 1" tape **Instrumental Recording Dates** May 8, 1969 (rhythm tracks)	According to Richard, Karen's lead vocal in "Eve" is one of the rare instances where she sings slightly out of tune. This can be heard in the lyric, "Notice how the image saddens…how lonely she's *become*" the second time (2:13). Another issue with the recording is the clash between the cello and harpsichord in verse two (starting at 1:17). Richard hoped to fix it years later during the remixing. However, because of the limitations with 8-track recording, the cello was combined onto the same track with the harpsichord, making it impossible to separate.	1969 STUDIO ALBUM VERSION (2:51) *Offering* (1969)/*Ticket to Ride* (1970 retitled, repackaged reissue), *Japanese Single Box* (2006, JP) 1987 REMIX (2:52) *Treasures* (1987, JP), *From the Top* (1991), *Magical Memories of the Carpenters* (1993, UK), *Sweet Memory* (1994, JP), *Reflections* (1995, UK, EU, ZA, DE), *Sweet Sweet Smile* (2000, NL), *The Star Collection* (2000, NL), *The Essential Collection—1965–1997* (2002), *Carpenters Perform Carpenter* (2003), *Reflections—The Best 1200* (2005, JP), *The Best of the Carpenters* (2009, DE), *Sweet Sixteen* (2009, 40th Anniversary Collector's Edition bonus disc, JP), *Best Songs* (2017, *Sweet Memory* repackaged, JP)
Song Eventide **Written by** Richard Carpenter/John Bettis **Recorded at** A&M Studios—Studio D on 24-track, 2" tape Instrumental recording dates: April 8, 1975 (piano), April 10 (orchestra)	"Eventide" is the closing bookend on the *Horizon* album, opposite "Aurora." Both share identical instrumental tracks, with differing lyrics (and lead vocal) by Karen.	1975 STUDIO ALBUM VERSION (1:33) *Horizon* (1975), *Sweet Memory* (1994, JP), *Best Songs* (2017, *Sweet Memory* repackaged, JP)
Song The First Snowfall/Let It Snow, Let It Snow, Let It Snow **Written by** Paul Francis Webster/Jay Francis Burke (Sammy Cahn/Jule Styne) **Recorded at** A&M Studios—Studio D on 24-track, 2" tape Instrumental recording date: Dec. 10, 1977 (orchestra)		1978 STUDIO ALBUM VERSION (3:35) *Christmas Portrait* (1978), *Christmas Portrait* (1984, DE), *Christmas with the Carpenters* (1992, Time Life Music), *Christmas Collection* (1996) 1992 REMIX (3:35) *Christmas with the Carpenters* (1992, Time Life Music), *Christmas Collection* (1996)

254

Song
Flat Baroque

Written by
Richard Carpenter

Recorded at
A&M Studios—Studio B on 16-track, 2" tape

Instrumental Recording Dates
March 25, 1972 (piano and rhythm tracks),
March 27 (orchestra)

1972 STUDIO ALBUM VERSION (1:45)
A Song for You (1972), *Japanese Single Box* (2006, JP), *Sweet Sixteen* (2009, *40th Anniversary Collector's Edition* bonus disc, JP), *The Complete Singles* (2015)
1976 LIVE ALBUM VERSION (1:33)
Live at the Palladium (1976)

Song
For All We Know

Written by
Fred Karlin/Robb Wilson/Arthur James

Recorded at
A&M Studios—Studios B and C on 16-track, 2" tape—and Enterprise Studios, Burbank, CA

Instrumental Recording Dates
Nov. 11, 1970 (orchestra), Sep. 5, 1990 (oboe)

The original oboe track in the intro and re-intro of "For All We Know," played by popular session musician Jim Horn, was later replaced by Carpenters' veteran oboe and English horn virtuoso, Earle Dumler, in 1990. "Jim said, 'I'm really not an oboist ...' which he was not, actually. But Earle hadn't come into town yet," says Richard. "In my opinion, Earle is one of the top-five oboists in the world."

The recording of "For All We Know" is another rare instance where the rhythm tracks were recorded in Studio C—a room not meant for this type of use, as it had no air lock.

1971 STUDIO ALBUM VERSION (2:34)
Carpenters (1971), *The Singles 1969–1973* (1973), *Yesterday Once More* (1984, Silver Eagle Records, US and CA), *Yesterday Once More* (1984, UK), *Yesterday Once More* (1985), *A&M Gold Series Vol. 2* (1986, JP), *Classics Volume 2* (1987), *Reminiscing* (1988, CA), *Anthology* (1989, JP), *A&M New Gold Series Vol. 2* (1990, JP), *Only Yesterday: Richard and Karen Carpenter's Greatest Hits* (1990, UK), *Their Greatest Hits* (1990, UK, ZA), *Their Greatest Hits* (1993, DE), *The Essential Collection—1965–1997* (2002), *Japanese Single Box* (2006, JP), *The Ultimate Collection* (2006, NL), *Carpenters Collected* (2013), *The Complete Singles* (2015)
1990 REMIX (2:32)
From the Top (1991), *Best of Best + Original Master Karaoke* (1992, JP), *Carpenters Collection* (1993, Time Life Music), *Magical Memories of the Carpenters* (1993, UK), *Carpenters Best Vol. 2* (1994, JP), *Sweet Memory* (1994, JP), *The Best of Carpenters* (1994, BR), *Twenty-Two Hits of the Carpenters* (1995, HK), *Anthology* (1997, remastered reissue, JP), *Love Songs* (1997), *Their Greatest Hits and Finest Performances* (1997, Reader's Digest), *Yesterday Once More* (1998), *Singles 1969–1981* (1999, JP), *Gold* (2000, UK), *Singles 1969–1981* (2000), *Gold* (2001, JP), *Gold* (2004, 35th Anniversary Edition), *Gold* (2005), *Gold* (2005, UK), *Twenty-Two Hits of the Carpenters* (2005, The 10th Anniversary Edition, incl. karaoke disc, HK), *The Ultimate Collection* (2006, UK), *20/20 Best of the Best Selection* (2009, JP), *40/40* (2009), *40/40* (2009, EU, UK), *40/40 The Best Selection* (2009, JP), *The Nation's Favourite Carpenters Songs* (2016, UK), *Best Songs* (2017, *Sweet Memory* repackaged, JP)
2004 SACD 5.1 + STEREO FOLD-DOWN MIX (2:32)
Singles 1969–1981 SACD (2004)
2018 ROYAL PHILHARMONIC VERSION (2:56)
Carpenters with the Royal Philharmonic Orchestra (2018)

Trade ad for *Carpenters* [The Tan Album] which contained "For All We Know"

Details	Notes	Versions
Song From This Moment On (live version) **Written by** Cole Porter/Johann Sebastian Bach/Mitzie Welch/Ken Welch **Recorded at** The London Palladium **Instrumental Recording Dates** Nov. 27, 1976		1976 LIVE ALBUM VERSION (2:27) *Live at the Palladium* (1976), *From the Top* (1991),* *The Essential Collection—1965–1997* (2002)* * Shortened intro—total running time (2:13)

Song
From This Moment On (studio version)
 	
Written by
Cole Porter/Johann Sebastian Bach/Mitzie Welch/Ken Welch
 	
Recorded at
A&M Studios—Studio D on 24-track, 2" tape; Capitol Studios, Hollywood
 	
Instrumental Recording Dates
Feb. 1980
	Recorded in 1980 for their ABC TV special *Music, Music, Music*.
	    The recording first officially surfaced in 1994 on the UK release of *Interpretations: A 25th Anniversary Celebration*. The following year, Richard updated the recording's "mono" piano track by rerecording it in stereo.
	    The song was remixed, and the updated version included on 1995 US release of *Interpretations: A 25th Anniversary Celebration*.
		1994 COMPILATION ALBUM VERSION (1:57)
		Interpretations: A 25th Anniversary Celebration (1994, UK)
		1995 REMIX (1:57)
		Interpretations: A 25th Anniversary Celebration (1995)

Song Fun, Fun, Fun **Written by** Brian Wilson/Mike Love **Recorded at** A&M Studios—Studio B on 16-track, 2" tape **Instrumental Recording Dates** Jan. 9, 1973 (rhythm tracks)		1973 STUDIO ALBUM VERSION (found on "Oldies Medley") (1:32) *Now & Then* (1973), *Anthology* (1989, JP) 1990 REMIX (found on "Oldies Medley") (1:32) *From the Top* (1991), *Magical Memories of the Carpenters* (1993, UK), *Sweet Memory* (1994, JP), *Anthology* (1997, remastered reissue, JP), *Their Greatest Hits and Finest Performances* (1997, Reader's Digest),* *The Essential Collection—1965–1997* (2002), *Best Songs* (2017, *Sweet Memory* repackaged, JP) *Sound effects at intro omitted on this release—total running time (1:33)
Song Get Together (*Offering/Ticket to Ride* version) **Written by** Chet Powers **Recorded at** A&M Studios—Studio B on 8-track, 1" tape **Instrumental Recording Dates** 1969	The psychedelic effect on Richard's lead vocal was created by singing through his Baldwin keyboard amplifier, while activating its "tremolo" setting.	1969 STUDIO ALBUM VERSION (2:32) *Offering* (1969)/*Ticket to Ride* (1970 *Offering* retitled, repackaged reissue)
Song Get Together (*Your Navy Presents* version) **Written by** Chet Powers **Recorded at** A&M Studios—Studio C on 16-track, 2" tape **Instrumental Recording Dates** March 1970	*Your Navy Presents* (later retitled *Sounds Like the Navy*), a public service program, spanned the years 1967 to 1975 and was hosted by KHJ Los Angeles disc jockey Sam Riddle. It consisted of four fifteen-minute weekly segments, including live performances and interviews featuring popular musical guests, interspersed with announcements about the navy. In March 1970, the Carpenters and their road band recorded twelve songs live at A&M Studios for the program, which, along with two unsweetened master recordings, were later edited into Riddle's often factually incorrect, scripted Q and A with the duo.	1970 "YOUR NAVY PRESENTS" VERSION (2:40) *From the Top* (1991), *The Essential Collection—1965–1997* (2002)

Details	Notes	Versions

Song
Good Friends Are for Keeps

Written by
Jon Silberman

Recorded at
A&M Studios—Studio D on 24-track, 2" tape

Instrumental Recording Dates
1975

Recorded in 1975 for a "Ma Bell" telephone company campaign.

1990 REMIX (1:08)
From the Top (1991), *The Essential Collection—1965–1997* (2002), *Sweet Sixteen* (2009, *40th Anniversary Collector's Edition* bonus disc, JP)

Song
Goodnight

Written by
John Lennon/Paul McCartney

Recorded at
Radio Recorders, Los Angeles

Instrumental Recording Dates
May 9, 1969

Arranged and accompanied by Richard, and sung by Karen, for the California State University, Long Beach, choir.

1969 VINYL LP TRANSFER (2:31)
From the Top (1991)

Song
(I'm Caught Between) Goodbye and I Love You

Written by
Richard Carpenter/John Bettis

Recorded at
A&M Studios—Studio D on 24-track, 2" tape

Instrumental Recording Dates
Oct. 3, 1974 (rhythm tracks), March 31, 1975 (guitars and pedal steel guitar), April 10 (orchestra), May 2 (woodwinds)

1975 STUDIO ALBUM VERSION (4:04)
Horizon (1975), *A&M Composers Series Vol. 2 Richard Carpenter & John Bettis* (1988, JP), *Anthology* (1989, JP), *Magical Memories of the Carpenters* (1993, UK), *Sweet Memory* (1994, JP), *Anthology* (1997, remastered reissue, JP), *Japanese Single Box* (2006, JP), *The Complete Singles* (2015), *Best Songs* (2017, *Sweet Memory* repackaged, JP)

A tape reel containing a live version of "Get Together" for the radio program *Your Navy Presents*

257

Details

Song
Goodbye to Love

Written by
Richard Carpenter/John Bettis

Recorded at
A&M Studios—Studio B on 16-track, 2" tape

Instrumental Recording Dates
March 23, 1972 (orchestra)

Los Angeles, 1972

Notes

The track for "Goodbye to Love" has what is referred to as a "cold opening," which simply means no introduction. Perhaps a bit arcane, Karen's preliminary breath was edited out for the track's debut on *A Song for You*. This was due to the leakage caused by Richard's "1-2-3" count off, which made its way through Karen's headset and into her microphone, leaving the "3" slightly audible on her lead vocal track.

The first remix of the song appears in 1985 on the LP version of the Japanese *Anthology*—with the piano rerecorded, in stereo—and the count off intentionally left on. This particular remix has been used on various worldwide compilations over the years, most of which do not include the count off.

In an effort to keep it organic-sounding, Richard—calling it an "anecdote"—personally added in his own breath for the 1985 compilation set *Yesterday Once More*. However, several subsequent compilations containing a remix of "Goodbye to Love" keep Karen's original breath intact, thanks to the age of technology, and the ability to clean it up.

As for Tony Peluso's "fuzz" guitar solo, it was played on a 1957 vintage Gibson through an Electro-Harmonix Big Muff "fuzzbox." From there it went directly into the recording console in A&M's Studio B. Following several passes at the solo, the final edit was pieced together by Richard, who considers it to be one of the all-time best recorded guitar solos.

And despite both having overindulged in several glasses of house wine at their favorite local hot spot, Martoni's in Hollywood, prior to the session, a mildly intoxicated Richard and Karen managed to flawlessly overdub their four-part, triple-tracked "ahs" during the song's second guitar solo and fade-out.

The [original mix] version of "Goodbye to Love" found on *The Singles 1969–1973* was mastered at a slightly faster playback speed in order to match the album's two previous tracks—"Superstar" and "Rainy Days and Mondays" (both of which were also mastered at a faster playback speed). The songs were all linked together as part of a three-song sequence for that album.

Versions

1972 STUDIO ALBUM VERSION (3:50)
A Song for You (1972), *The Singles 1969–1973* (1973),* *Yesterday Once More* (1984, Silver Eagle Records, US and CA), *Yesterday Once More* (1984, UK),* *Japanese Single Box* (2006, JP), *The Ultimate Collection* (2006, NL), *Carpenters Collected* (2013), *The Complete Singles* (2015)
* Recording has been altered from original for faster playback speed

1985 REMIX (3:55)
Yesterday Once More (1985), *A&M Gold Series Vol. 2* (1986, JP), *Classics Volume 2* (1987), *Reminiscing* (1988, CA), *Anthology* (1989, JP),* *A Song for You* (1989, Mobile Fidelity Sound Lab), *A&M New Gold Series Vol. 1* (1990, JP), *Only Yesterday: Richard and Karen Carpenter's Greatest Hits* (1990, UK), *Their Greatest Hits* (1990, UK, ZA), *A&M Gold Series* (1991, JP), *From the Top* (1991),* *Startrax* (1991, EU, AU), *Their Greatest Hits* (1993, DE), *The Nation's Favourite Carpenters Songs* (2016, UK)*

1991 REMIX (3:58)
Best of Best + Original Master Karaoke (1992, JP), *Carpenters Collection* (1993, Time Life Music), *Magical Memories of the Carpenters* (1993, UK), *Carpenters Best Vol. 2* (1994, JP), *Sweet Memory* (1994, JP), *Twenty-Two Hits of the Carpenters* (1995, HK), *Anthology* (1997, remastered reissue, JP), *Love Songs* (1997), *Their Greatest Hits and Finest Performances* (1997, Reader's Digest), *Yesterday Once More* (1998), *Singles 1969–1981* (1999, JP), *Gold* (2000, UK), *Singles 1969–1981* (2000), *Gold* (2001, JP), *20th Century Masters Millennium Series* (2002), *The Essential Collection—1965–1997* (2002), *Carpenters Perform Carpenter* (2003), *Gold* (2004, 35th Anniversary Edition), *Singles 1969–1981* SACD (2004, CD audio layer), *Gold* (2005), *Gold* (2005, UK), *Twenty-Two Hits of the Carpenters* (2005, The 10th Anniversary Edition, incl. karaoke disc, HK), *The Ultimate Collection* (2006, UK), *40/40* (2009), *40/40* (2009, EU, UK), *40/40 The Best Selection* (2009, JP), *20th Century Masters Millennium Series* (2017, reissue, JP), *Best Songs* (2017, *Sweet Memory* repackaged, JP)

2004 SACD 5.1 + STEREO FOLD-DOWN MIX (3:55)
Singles 1969–1981 SACD (2004)

2018 ROYAL PHILHARMONIC VERSION (3:59)
Carpenters with the Royal Philharmonic Orchestra (2018)
* Richard's original count off left in—total running time (4:00)

Details	Notes	Versions

Song
Goofus

Written by
Gus Kahn/Wayne King/William Harold

Recorded at
A&M Studios—Studio D on 24-track, 2" tape

Instrumental Recording Dates
Dec. 9, 1975 (rhythm tracks), Jan. 6, 1976
(tuba), Jan. 8–9 (sax solo), Jan. 13 (guitars)

1976 STUDIO ALBUM VERSION (3:09)
A Kind of Hush (1976), *A&M New Gold Series Vol. 2* (1990, JP), *Sweet Memory* (1994, JP), *The Ultimate Collection* (2006, NL), *Carpenters Collected* (2013), *The Complete Singles* (2015), *Best Songs* (2017, *Sweet Memory* repackaged, JP)

Song
Happy

Written by
Tony Peluso/Diane Rubin/John Bettis

Recorded at
A&M Studios—Studio D on 24-track, 2" tape

Instrumental Recording Dates
Sep. 19, 1974 (rhythm tracks), Oct. 1
(orchestra), Oct. 5 (guitars), Feb. 20, 1975
(woodwinds)

1975 STUDIO ALBUM VERSION (3:50)
Horizon (1975), *The Singles 1974–1978* (1978, JP, CA, UK), *Treasures* (1987, JP), *Magical Memories of the Carpenters* (1993, UK), *Sweet Memory* (1994, JP), *By Request* (2000, JP), *Japanese Single Box* (2006, JP), *The Complete Singles* (2015), *Best Songs* (2017, *Sweet Memory* repackaged, JP)

Song
Have Yourself a Merry Little Christmas

Written by
Hugh Martin/Ralph Blane

Recorded at
A&M Studios—Studio D on 24-track, 2" tape

Instrumental Recording Dates
Nov. 13, 1977 (orchestra)

1978 STUDIO ALBUM VERSION (3:54)
Christmas Portrait (1978), *Christmas Portrait* (1984, DE), *Christmas Portrait—The Special Edition* (1984), *Christmas with the Carpenters* (1992, Time Life Music), *Christmas Collection* (1996)

Song
He Came Here for Me

Written by
Ron Nelson

Recorded at
A&M Studios—Studio D on 24-track, 2" tape

Instrumental Recording Dates
Feb. 12–13, 1978 (orchestra)

1984 STUDIO ALBUM VERSION (2:12)
An Old-Fashioned Christmas (1984), *Christmas with the Carpenters* (1992, Time Life Music), *Christmas Collection* (1996)

Song
Heather

Written by
John Pearson

Recorded at
A&M Studios—Studio B on 16-track, 2" tape

Instrumental Recording Dates
March 17, 1973 (rhythm tracks), March 20
(orchestra), May 9 (guitars)

Richard heard "Autumn Reverie" (the song's original title), written and recorded by British composer and orchestra leader John "Johnny" Pearson, in a television commercial for the popular vitamin supplement Geritol.

Upon asking writing partner and lyricist John Bettis what he "heard" as far as a new name for the title, Bettis replied, "Heather."

1973 STUDIO ALBUM VERSION (2:12)
Now & Then (1973), *Sweet Memory* (1994, JP), *Japanese Single Box* (2006, JP), *The Complete Singles* (2015), *Best Songs* (2017, *Sweet Memory* repackaged, JP)

Details	Notes	Versions
Song Help **Written by** John Lennon/Paul McCartney **Recorded at** A&M Studios—Studio B on 16-track, 2" tape **Instrumental Recording Dates** Jan. 8, 1970 (rhythm tracks), April 13 (orchestra)	When asked whether or not "Help!" (the song's title listing on all Carpenters releases mistakenly leaves the exclamation point off) was considered for release as a single, "Absolutely it was…" says Richard. "It was actually down to that and 'We've Only Just Begun.' This was my doing, because even though we were worried about a ballad on top of a ballad [following the release of 'Close to You'], I knew damn well that 'Begun' was going to be a hit."	1970 STUDIO ALBUM VERSION (3:03) *Close to You* (1970), *A&M Gold Series Vol. 1* (1986, JP), *Anthology* (1989, JP), *A&M New Gold Series Vol. 2* (1990, JP), *Treasures* (1990, UK), *Magical Memories of the Carpenters* (1993, UK), *Sweet Memory* (1994, JP), *Anthology* (1997, remastered reissue, JP), *Their Greatest Hits and Finest Performances* (1997, Reader's Digest), *Japanese Single Box* (2006, JP), *Best Songs* (2017, *Sweet Memory* repackaged, JP)
Song (A Place to) Hideaway **Written by** Randy Sparks **Recorded at** A&M Studios—Studio A on 16-track, 2" tape **Instrumental Recording Dates** 1971		1971 STUDIO ALBUM VERSION (3:39) *Carpenters* (1971), *Sweet Memory* (1994, JP), *Best Songs* (2017, *Sweet Memory* repackaged, JP)
Song Hits Medley '76 **Written by** a. Sing (Joe Raposo) b. (They Long to Be) Close to You (Burt Bacharach/Hal David) c. For All We Know (Fred Karlin/Robb Wilson/Arthur James) d. Ticket to Ride (John Lennon/Paul McCartney) e. Only Yesterday (Richard Carpenter/John Bettis) f. I Won't Last a Day without You (Paul Williams/Roger Nichols) g. Goodbye to Love (Richard Carpenter/John Bettis) **Recorded at** A&M Studios—Studio D on 24-track, 2" tape **Instrumental Recording Dates** 1976	Recorded for *The Carpenters Very First Television Special*, with additional recording and remix for inclusion on *As Time Goes By* in 2001.	2001 ALBUM VERSION (7:52) *As Time Goes By* (2001, JP), *As Time Goes By* (2004)
Song (There's No Place Like) Home for the Holidays **Written by** Robert Allen/Al Stillman **Recorded at** A&M Studios—Studio D on 24-track, 2" tape **Instrumental Recording Dates** Feb. 5, 1978 (rhythm tracks), Feb. 7 (orchestra), Feb. 12 (harp and percussion)		1984 STUDIO ALBUM VERSION (2:35) *An Old-Fashioned Christmas* (1984), *Christmas Portrait—The Special Edition* (1984), *Christmas with the Carpenters* (1992, Time Life Music), *Christmas Collection* (1996)

Song
Honolulu City Lights

Written by
Keola Beamer

Recorded at
A&M Studios—Studio D on 24-track, 2" tape

Instrumental Recording Dates
Aug. 13, 1978 (rhythm tracks and percussion), Aug. 24 (pedal steel guitar), April 14, 1983 (orchestra)

Song
Hurting Each Other

Written by
Peter Udell/Gary Geld

Recorded at
A&M Studios—Studio B on 16-track, 2" tape

Instrumental Recording Dates
Oct. 12, 1971 (rhythm tracks), Dec. 8 (orchestra)

There are a couple of differences between the 1972 album mix versus the 1973 remix, in that the tambourine track is deleted from the 1973 mix altogether, along with the timpani drum (first chorus only).

For inclusion on *From the Top* in 1990, additional recording and a remix were done on the song, with the replacement of the original "mono" piano track—now in stereo, as well as Joe Osborn's rerecorded bass track. "Hurting Each Other" would be remixed again the following year for the *Best of Best + Original Master Karaoke* album.

1989 STUDIO ALBUM VERSION (3:20)
Lovelines (1989), *Anthology* (1989, JP), *Sweet Memory* (1994, JP), *Anthology* (1997, remastered reissue, JP), *Japanese Single Box* (2006, JP), *The Complete Singles* (2015), *Best Songs* (2017, *Sweet Memory* repackaged, JP)

1972 STUDIO ALBUM VERSION (2:46)
A Song for You (1972), *Japanese Single Box* (2006, JP), *The Ultimate Collection* (2006, NL), *Carpenters Collected* (2013), *The Complete Singles* (2015)

1973 REMIX (2:46)
The Singles 1969–1973 (1973), *Yesterday Once More* (1984, Silver Eagle Records, US and CA), *Yesterday Once More* (1984, UK), *Yesterday Once More* (1985, A&M Gold Series Vol. 2* (1986, JP), *Classics Volume 2* (1987), *Reminiscing* (1988, CA), *A Song for You* (1989, Mobile Fidelity Sound Lab), *Anthology* (1989, JP), *A&M New Gold Series Vol. 2* (1990, JP), *Only Yesterday: Richard and Karen Carpenter's Greatest Hits* (1990, UK), *Their Greatest Hits* (1990, UK, ZA), *Their Greatest Hits* (1993, DE), *The Essential Collection—1965–1997* (2002)

1990 REMIX (2:45)
From the Top (1991), *Carpenters Collection* (1993, Time Life Music), *Magical Memories of the Carpenters* (1993, Reader's Digest, UK, AU, EU), *Carpenters Best Vol. 1* (1994, JP), *Sweet Memory* (1994, JP), *The Best of Carpenters* (1994, BR), *Twenty-Two Hits of the Carpenters* (1995, HK), *Anthology* (1997, remastered reissue, JP), *Their Greatest Hits and Finest Performances* (1997, Reader's Digest), *Twenty-Two Hits of the Carpenters* (2005, The 10th Anniversary Edition, incl. karaoke disc, HK), *Best Songs* (2017, *Sweet Memory* repackaged, JP)

1991 REMIX (2:47)
Best of Best + Original Master Karaoke (1992, JP), *Love Songs* (1997), *Yesterday Once More* (1998), *Singles 1969–1981* (1999, JP), *Singles 1969–1981* (2000), *Gold* (2004, 35th Anniversary Edition), *Singles 1969–1981* SACD (2004, CD audio layer), *Gold* (2005), *The Ultimate Collection* (2006, UK), *40/40* (2009), *40/40* (2009, EU, UK), *40/40 The Best Selection* (2009, JP), *The Nation's Favourite Carpenters Songs* (2016, UK)

2004 SACD 5.1 + STEREO FOLD-DOWN MIX (2:47)
Singles 1969–1981 SACD (2004)

2018 ROYAL PHILHARMONIC VERSION (3:58)
Carpenters with the Royal Philharmonic Orchestra (2018)

The singles duo of the year have a new single:

On A&M Records and Tapes   Produced by Jack Daugherty

Trade ad for "Hurting Each Other," 1971

Song
I Believe You

Written by
Dick Addrisi/Don Addrisi

Recorded at
A&M Studios—Studio D on 24-track, 2" tape

Instrumental Recording Dates
May 31, 1978 (rhythm tracks and orchestra),
Aug. 13 (rhythm, guitars, and percussion)

The *Singles 1969–1981* SACD (2004) and the *Carpenters with the Royal Philharmonic Orchestra* (2018) both feature mixes of "I Believe You" containing alternate lead vocal takes by Karen not heard in the original 1981 *Made in America* album mix.

1981 STUDIO ALBUM VERSION (3:54)
Made in America (1981), *Magical Memories of the Carpenters* (1993, Reader's Digest, UK, AU, EU), *Carpenters Best Vol. 2* (1994, JP), *Sweet Memory* (1994, JP), *Interpretations: A 25th Anniversary Celebration* (1995), *Singles 1969–1981* (1999, JP), *Singles 1969–1981* (2000), *20th Century Masters Millennium Series* (2002), *The Essential Collection—1965–1997* (2002), *Gold* (2004, 35th Anniversary Edition), *Singles 1969–1981* SACD (2004, CD audio layer), *Gold* (2005), *Japanese Single Box* (2006, JP), *The Ultimate Collection* (2006, UK), *Their Greatest Hits and Finest Performances* (1997, Reader's Digest), *20/20 Best of the Best Selection* (2009, JP), *40/40* (2009), *40/40* (2009, EU, UK), *40/40 The Best Selection* (2009, JP), *Carpenters Collected* (2013), *The Complete Singles* (2015), *20th Century Masters Millennium Series* (2017, reissue, JP), *Best Songs* (2017, *Sweet Memory* repackaged, JP)
2004 SACD 5.1 + STEREO FOLD-DOWN MIX (3:54)
Singles 1969–1981 SACD (2004)
2018 ROYAL PHILHARMONIC VERSION (3:54)
Carpenters with the Royal Philharmonic Orchestra (2018)

Song
I Can Dream, Can't I

Written by
Irving Kahal/Sammy Fain

Recorded at
A&M Studios—Studio D on 24-track, 2" tape

Instrumental Recording Dates
April 10, 1975 (orchestra)

1975 STUDIO ALBUM VERSION (4:58)
Horizon (1975), *Treasures* (1987, JP), *Magical Memories of the Carpenters* (1993, UK), *Sweet Memory* (1994, JP), *Best Songs* (2017, *Sweet Memory* repackaged, JP)

Song
I Can't Make Music

Written by
Randy Edelman

Recorded at
A&M Studios—Studio B on 16-track, 2" tape

Instrumental Recording Dates
Feb. 16, 1973 (orchestra), March 10 (harmonica)

Not included in the *Now & Then* album credits is first-chair session violinist Jimmy Getzoff, who played the solo violin in the outro of "I Can't Make Music."
The pipe organ was recorded at Whitney Recording Studio in Glendale, California.

1973 STUDIO ALBUM VERSION (3:17)
Now & Then (1973), *By Request* (2000, JP)
1987 REMIX (3:14)
Treasures (1987, JP), *Magical Memories of the Carpenters* (1993, UK)

Song
I Got Rhythm

Written by
George Gershwin/Ira Gershwin

Recorded at
A&M Studios—Studio D on 24-track, 2" tape

Instrumental Recording Dates
1980

Every now and again, certain songs would call for sound effects. The belch heard at the very end of "I Got Rhythm" was created by Richard.
"Although sometimes Karen would do them…because she burped better than I did," he says, with a chuckle.

2001 ALBUM VERSION (4:40)
As Time Goes By (2001, JP), *As Time Goes By* (2004)

Details	Notes	Versions

Song
I Have You

Written by
Richard Carpenter/John Bettis

Recorded at
A&M Studios—Studio D on 24-track, 2" tape

Instrumental Recording Dates
Jan. 30 and Feb. 13, 1976 (rhythm tracks), Feb. 17 (guitars), Feb. 24 (orchestra)

1976 STUDIO ALBUM VERSION (3:27)
A Kind of Hush (1976), *Sweet Memory* (1994, JP), *Japanese Single Box* (2006, JP), *The Complete Singles* (2015), *Best Songs* (2017, Sweet Memory* repackaged, JP)

Song
I Heard the Bells on Christmas Day

Written by
Johnny Marks/Henry Wadsworth Longfellow

Recorded at
A&M Studios—Studio D on 24-track, 2" tape

Instrumental Recording Dates
Dec. 11, 1977 (orchestra)

1984 STUDIO ALBUM VERSION (2:24)
An Old-Fashioned Christmas (1984), *Christmas with the Carpenters* (1992, Time Life Music), *Christmas Collection* (1996)

Song
I Just Fall in Love Again

Written by
Gloria Sklerov/Harry Lloyd/Larry Herbstritt/ Steve Dorff

Recorded at
A&M Soundstage and Studio D on 24-track, 2" tape

Instrumental Recording Dates
April 16, 1977 (rhythm tracks), May 24 and May 27 (orchestra), May 27 (percussion), June 1 (guitars, harp, and woodwinds)

1977 STUDIO ALBUM VERSION (4:02)
Passage (1977), *Treasures* (1987, JP), *Anthology* (1989, JP), *Treasures* (1990, UK), *Magical Memories of the Carpenters* (1993, UK), *Carpenters Best Vol. 2* (1994, JP), *Sweet Memory* (1994, JP), *Reflections* (1995, UK, EU, ZA, DE), *Anthology* (1997, remastered reissue, JP), *Love Songs* (1997), *Their Greatest Hits and Finest Performances* (1997, Reader's Digest), *Yesterday Once More* (1998), *Sweet Sweet Smile* (2000, NL), *20th Century Masters Millennium Series* (2002), *Gold* (2004, 35th Anniversary Edition), *Gold* (2005), *Reflections—The Best 1200* (2005, JP), *Japanese Single Box* (2006, JP), *The Best of the Carpenters* (2009, DE), *The Complete Singles* (2015), *20th Century Masters Millennium Series* (2017, reissue, JP), *Best Songs* (2017, Sweet Memory* repackaged, JP)
2018 ROYAL PHILHARMONIC VERSION (5:01)
Carpenters with the Royal Philharmonic Orchestra (2018)

Song
I Kept on Loving You

Written by
Paul Williams/Roger Nichols

Recorded at
A&M Studios—Studio B on 16-track, 2" tape

Instrumental Recording Dates
March 16 and March 24, 1970 (rhythm tracks), April 13 (orchestra)

1970 STUDIO ALBUM VERSION (2:14)
Close to You (1970), *Anthology* (1989, JP), *Anthology* (1997, remastered reissue, JP), *Japanese Single Box* (2006, JP), *The Complete Singles* (2015)

Details

Song
I Need to Be in Love

Written by
Richard Carpenter/John Bettis/Albert Hammond

Recorded at
A&M Studios—Studio D on 24-track, 2" tape

Instrumental Recording Dates
Jan. 23, 1976 (rhythm tracks), Feb. 24 and April 27 (orchestra), Feb. 27 (guitars and harp), April 23 (English horn and flute)

Notes

The rhythm tracks for "I Need to Be in Love" were first laid down by Richard (on piano), bassist Joe Osborn, and drummer Carl "Cubby" O'Brien in early December 1975. "Cubby was a better 'live' drummer, which worked well for television and all of that. So we only used him on *certain* things in the studio," Richard says.

Still needing a bit of finessing, Richard and Osborn returned to Studio D the following January with session drummer Jim Gordon to rerecord the rhythm tracks.

Versions

1976 STUDIO ALBUM VERSION (3:47)
A Kind of Hush (1976), *The Ultimate Collection* (2006, NL), *Carpenters Collected* (2013), *The Nation's Favourite Carpenters Songs* (2016, UK)

1976 SINGLE MIX (shorter intro) (3:25)
The Singles 1974–1978 (1978, JP, CA, UK), *Yesterday Once More* (1984, Silver Eagle Records, US and CA), *Yesterday Once More* (1984, UK), *Japanese Single Box* (2006, JP), *The Complete Singles* (2015)

1985 REMIX (shorter intro) (3:25)
Yesterday Once More (1985), *A&M Gold Series Vol. 2* (1986, JP), *Classics Volume 2* (1987), *A&M Composers Series Vol. 2 Richard Carpenter & John Bettis* (1988, JP), *Reminiscing* (1988, CA), *Anthology* (1989, JP), *A&M New Gold Series Vol. 1* (1990, JP), *A&M Gold Series* (1991, JP), *Startrax* (1991, EU, AU)

1990 REMIX (3:48)
Treasures (1990, UK), *From the Top* (1991), *Best of Best + Original Master Karaoke* (1992, JP), *Carpenters Collection* (1993, Time Life Music), *Magical Memories of the Carpenters* (1993, UK), *Carpenters Best Vol. 1* (1994, JP), *Sweet Memory* (1994, JP), *Reflections* (1995, UK, EU, ZA, DE), *Twenty-Two Hits of the Carpenters* (1995, HK), *Anthology* (1997, remastered reissue, JP), *Love Songs* (1997), *Their Greatest Hits and Finest Performances* (1997, Reader's Digest), *Yesterday Once More* (1998), *Singles 1969–1981* (1999, JP), *By Request* (2000, JP), *Gold* (2000, UK), *Singles 1969–1981* (2000), *Sweet Sweet Smile* (2000, NL), *Gold* (2001, JP), *20th Century Masters Millennium Series* (2002), *The Essential Collection—1965–1997* (2002), *Carpenters Perform Carpenter* (2003), *Gold* (2004, 35th Anniversary Edition), *Gold* (2005), *Gold* (2005, UK), *Reflections—The Best 1200* (2005, JP), *Twenty-Two Hits of the Carpenters* (2005, The 10th Anniversary Edition, incl. karaoke disc, HK), *The Ultimate Collection* (2006, UK), *20/20 Best of the Best Selection* (2009, JP), *40/40* (2009), *40/40* (2009, EU, UK), *40/40 The Best Selection* (2009, JP), *The Best of the Carpenters* (2009, DE), *Icon* (2014), *20th Century Masters Millennium Series* (2017, reissue, JP), *Best Songs* (2017, Sweet Memory repackaged, JP)

2018 ROYAL PHILHARMONIC VERSION (4:30)
Carpenters with the Royal Philharmonic Orchestra (2018)

Left: Master tape legend for "I Need to Be in Love"

Page 265: Trade ad for "I Won't Last a Day without You"

Song
I Won't Last a Day without You

Written by
Paul Williams/Roger Nichols

Recorded at
A&M Studios—Studio B on 16-track, 2"
tape

Instrumental Recording Dates
Dec. 28, 1971 (rhythm tracks), March 24, 1972
(orchestra)

The single mix adds electric guitar fills
played by Carpenters studio and road
guitarist Tony Peluso.

1972 STUDIO ALBUM VERSION (3:47)
A Song for You (1972), *The Singles 1974–1978*
(1978, JP, CA, UK),* *A&M Gold Series Vol.
2* (1986, JP),* *A Song for You* (1989, Mobile
Fidelity Sound Lab),* *A&M New Gold Series
Vol. 1* (1990, JP),* *Only Yesterday: Richard
and Karen Carpenter's Greatest Hits* (1990,
UK),* *Their Greatest Hits* (1990, UK, ZA),*
A&M Gold Series (1991, JP),* *Startrax* (1991,
EU, AU),* *Their Greatest Hits* (1993, DE),*
Japanese Single Box (2006, JP), *The Ultimate
Collection* (2006, NL), *Carpenters Collected*
(2013)

1974 SINGLE MIX (3:47)
Yesterday Once More (1984, Silver Eagle
Records, US and CA),* *Yesterday Once More*
(1984, UK), *Yesterday Once More* (1985),
Classics Volume 2 (1987), *Anthology* (1989, JP),
Japanese Single Box (2006, JP), *The Complete
Singles* (2015)*

1991 REMIX (3:54)
Best of Best + Original Master Karaoke (1992,
JP), *Carpenters Collection* (1993, Time Life
Music), *Magical Memories of the Carpenters*
(1993, UK), *Carpenters Best Vol. 2* (1994,
JP), *Sweet Memory* (1994, JP), *Twenty-Two
Hits of the Carpenters* (1995, HK), *Anthology*
(1997, remastered reissue, JP), *Their Greatest
Hits and Finest Performances* (1997, Reader's
Digest), *Love Songs* (1997), *Yesterday Once
More* (1998), *Singles 1969–1981* (1999,
JP),** *Gold* (2000, UK), *Singles 1969–1981*
(2000),** *Gold* (2001, JP), *The Essential
Collection—1965–1997* (2002), *Gold* (2004,
35th Anniversary Edition), *Singles 1969–1981*
SACD (2004, CD audio layer), *Gold* (2005),
Gold (2005, UK), *Twenty-Two Hits of the
Carpenters* (2005, The 10th Anniversary
Edition, incl. karaoke disc, HK), *The
Ultimate Collection* (2006, UK), *40/40*
(2009), *40/40* (2009, EU, UK), *40/40 The Best
Selection* (2009, JP), *The Nation's Favourite
Carpenters Songs* (2016, UK),** *Best Songs*
(2017, *Sweet Memory* repackaged, JP)

2004 SACD 5.1 + STEREO FOLD-DOWN MIX
(3:50)
Singles 1969–1981 SACD (2004)
*Recording has been altered from original
for faster playback speed
**Extended version, with piano tag at ending

Song
Iced Tea (The Richard Carpenter Trio)

Written by
Richard Carpenter

Recorded at
RCA Studios, Hollywood

Instrumental Recording Dates
September 1966

While under contract with RCA, the Richard
Carpenter Trio, which featured Richard on
piano, Karen on drums, and high school
pal Wes Jacobs on tuba, recorded this jazz
number, along with ten other sides.

1966 RCA RECORDING (2:36)
From the Top (1991), *The Essential
Collection—1965–1997* (2002)

Details	Notes	Versions
Song If I Had You **Written by** Steve Dorff/Gary Harju/Larry Herbstritt **Recorded at** A&R Studios, New York; A&M Studios, Hollywood; Kendun Recorders, Burbank, CA on 24-track, 2" tape **Instrumental Recording Dates** Jan. 4, 1980 (rhythm tracks)	Recorded by Karen for her solo album, released in 1996, "If I Had You" first debuted posthumously on the Carpenters album *Lovelines* in 1989. Several notable differences can be heard between the original solo album mix versus the 1989 remix for inclusion on *Lovelines*. The first involves the replacement of the bass guitar track in 1989 by Carpenters studio bassist Joe Osborn. Richard also chose to end the remix "cold," unlike the original mix, which faded out.	1989 (CARPENTERS) ALBUM MIX (3:58) *Lovelines* (1989), *From the Top* (1991), *Interpretations: A 25th Anniversary Celebration* (1994, UK), *The Essential Collection—1965–1997* (2002), *The Complete Singles* (2015)
Song If We Try **Written by** Rod Temperton **Recorded at** A&R Studios, New York; A&M Studios, Hollywood; Kendun Recorders, Burbank, CA on 24-track, 2" tape **Instrumental Recording Dates** Unknown	Recorded in 1979 and 1980 for Karen's solo album *Karen Carpenter* and later remixed for the Carpenters album *Lovelines* in 1989.	1989 (CARPENTERS) ALBUM MIX (3:42) *Lovelines* (1989)
Song I'll Be Home for Christmas **Written by** Kim Gannon/Walter Kent/Buck Ram **Recorded at** A&M Studios—Studio D on 24-track, 2" tape **Instrumental Recording Dates** Dec. 7, 1977 (orchestra)		1978 STUDIO ALBUM VERSION (3:48) *Christmas Portrait* (1978), *Christmas Portrait* (1984, DE), *Christmas Portrait—The Special Edition* (1984) 1992 REMIX (3:48) *Christmas with the Carpenters* (1992, Time Life Music), *Christmas Collection* (1996)
Song I'll Be Yours **Written by** Richard Carpenter **Recorded at** Bassist Joe Osborn's garage studio, on 4-track tape **Instrumental Recording Dates** 1966	The flip side of the Magic Lamp single "Looking for Love."	1966 KAREN CARPENTER SINGLE (2:27) *From the Top* (1991), *The Essential Collection—1965–1997* (2002)
Song I'll Never Fall in Love Again **Written by** Burt Bacharach/Hal David **Recorded at** A&M Studios—Studios B and C on 16-track, 2" tape **Instrumental Recording Dates** Nov. 8, 1969 (rhythm tracks), July 20, 1970 (orchestra)	"I'll Never Fall in Love Again" features a thirteen-part, triple-tracked, thirty-nine-voice chord on "...here to remind you."	1970 STUDIO ALBUM VERSION (2:56) *Close to You* (1970), *A&M Gold Series Vol. 1* (1986, JP), *A&M New Gold Series Vol. 2* (1990, JP), *Sweet Memory* (1994, JP), *Japanese Single Box* (2006, JP), *Best Songs* (2017, *Sweet Memory* repackaged, JP)

Acetate reference
disc for "I'll Be
Yours," B-side of
Karen's first single

Details	Notes	Versions
Song I'm Still Not Over You **Written by** Richard Carpenter/John Bettis **Recorded at** A&M Studios—Studio D on 24-track, 2" tape **Instrumental Recording Dates** June 26–28, 1985 (rhythm tracks and guitars), Sept. 5 (guitars), Nov. 4 (horns), Nov. 7 (strings)	Recorded for Richard's solo album *Time*, released in 1987.	1987 (RICHARD CARPENTER SOLO) ALBUM VERSION (3:15) *A&M Composers Series Vol. 2 Richard Carpenter & John Bettis* (1988, JP)
Song Intermission **Written by** Richard Carpenter, inspired by *Crucifixus*—Antonio Lotti **Recorded at** A&M Studios—Studio B on 16-track, 2" tape **Instrumental Recording Dates** Unknown	A vocal piece from the early days at Cal State Long Beach—Karen, Doug Strawn, and Richard would occasionally sing "Crucifixus" in the A&M studio hallways or on the soundstage. It was Richard who came up with the song's lyric "We'll be right back…after we go to the bathroom."	1972 STUDIO ALBUM VERSION (0:22) *A Song for You* (1972) 1989 REMIX (0:22) *A Song for You* (1989, Mobile Fidelity Sound Lab), *Sweet Sixteen* (2009, *40th Anniversary Collector's Edition* bonus disc, JP)
Song Invocation **Written by** Richard Carpenter/John Bettis **Recorded at** Bassist Joe Osborn's garage studio, on 4-track tape	The 1968 demo recording of "Invocation" was remixed in 1969 and serves as the definitive version on the Carpenters' debut album, *Offering*.	1968 DEMO VERSION (1:00) *From the Top* (1991), *The Essential Collection—1965–1997* (2002) 1969 STUDIO ALBUM VERSION (1:00) *Offering* (1969)/*Ticket to Ride* (1970 *Offering* retitled, repackaged reissue)
Song It Came Upon a Midnight Clear **Written by** Richard Willis/Edmund Sears **Recorded at** A&M Studios—Studio D on 24-track, 2" tape	Recorded in the vocal booth of Studio D, the nine-part, eighteen-voice a cappella opener for *An Old-Fashioned Christmas* was not created without a minor blunder. After laying down most of the overdubs, [recording engineer] Roger Young pointed out to Richard that one word in a recurring line in the song had been sung incorrectly. Instead of singing "To touch their harps of gold," Richard sang the word *hearts*. The corrections were made and the recording completed—albeit countless overdubs later.	1984 STUDIO ALBUM VERSION (0:43) *An Old-Fashioned Christmas* (1984), *Christmas Portrait—The Special Edition* (1984), *Christmas Collection* (1996)
Song It's Christmas Time/Sleep Well Little Children **Written by** Victor Young/Al Stillman) (Alan Bergman/Leon Klatzkin) **Recorded at** A&M Studios—Studio D on 24-track, 2" tape		1978 STUDIO ALBUM VERSION (2:53) *Christmas Portrait* (1978), *Christmas Portrait* (1984, DE), *Christmas Portrait—The Special Edition* (1984) 1992 REMIX (2:53) *Christmas with the Carpenters* (1992, Time Life Music), *Christmas Collection* (1996)

Details	Notes	Versions

Song
It's Going to Take Some Time

Written by
Carole King/Toni Stern

Recorded at
A&M Studios—Studio B on 16-track, 2" tape

Instrumental Recording Dates
Feb. 24, 1972 (flutes), March 22 (orchestra)

The notable difference between the 1972 and 1989 mix is the replacement of the original keyboards with the Yamaha DX7.

Carpenters studio and road bandmate Bob Messenger played the "upper" flute part and solo on the recording. And it was rock/jazz fusion pioneer Tim Weisberg who handled the "lower" alto flute part.

"Tim was in the hallway when we were recording the song. So I pulled him aside and said 'Tim, do you have a few minutes? Would you come in and play this?' I gave him the part and put 'Tim Weisberg appears courtesy of A&M Records' on the album credit," Richard says.

1972 STUDIO ALBUM VERSION (2:55)
A Song for You (1972), *The Singles 1969–1973* (1973), *Yesterday Once More* (1984, Silver Eagle Records, US and CA), *Yesterday Once More* (1985), *A&M Gold Series Vol. 2* (1986, JP), *Classics Volume 2* (1987), *Reminiscing* (1988, CA), *A&M New Gold Series Vol. 1* (1990, JP), *Carpenters Collection* (1993, Time Life Music), *Carpenters Best Vol. 1* (1994, JP), *The Essential Collection—1965–1997* (2002), *Japanese Single Box* (2006, JP), *The Ultimate Collection* (2006, NL), *Carpenters Collected* (2013), *The Complete Singles* (2015), *The Nation's Favourite Carpenters Songs* (2016, UK)

1989 REMIX (2:59)
A Song for You (1989, Mobile Fidelity Sound Lab), *A&M Gold Series* (1991, JP), *Startrax* (1991, EU, AU), *Magical Memories of the Carpenters* (1993, UK), *Sweet Memory* (1994, JP), *Twenty-Two Hits of the Carpenters* (1995, HK), *Their Greatest Hits and Finest Performances* (1997, Reader's Digest), *Yesterday Once More* (1998), *Singles 1969–1981* (1999, JP), *Gold* (2000, UK), *Gold* (2001, JP), *Singles 1969–1981* (2000), *Gold* (2004, 35th Anniversary Edition), *Singles 1969–1981* SACD (2004, CD audio layer), *Gold* (2005), *Gold* (2005, UK), *Twenty-Two Hits of the Carpenters* (2005, The 10th Anniversary Edition, incl. karaoke disc, HK), *The Ultimate Collection* (2006, UK), *40/40* (2009), *40/40* (2009, EU, UK), *40/40 The Best Selection* (2009, JP), *Best Songs* (2017, *Sweet Memory* repackaged, JP)

2004 SACD 5.1 + STEREO FOLD-DOWN MIX (3:00)
Singles 1969–1981 SACD (2004)

Song
Jambalaya (On the Bayou)

Written by
Hank Williams

Recorded at
A&M Studios—Studio B on 16-track, 2" tape

Instrumental Recording Dates
Dec. 28, 1972 (rhythm tracks), March 20, 1973 (orchestra)

Due to time constraints during the recording of *Now & Then*, the three-part harmony recorded in chorus two was "flown-in" to chorus three, much akin to the way vocals are recorded once, then copied and pasted digitally today. This was something Richard and Karen otherwise *never* did, as every overdub was always recorded authentically, regardless of repetition. "This was the first—and last—time we ever did it," says Richard.

1973 STUDIO ALBUM VERSION (3:40)
Now & Then (1973), *The Singles 1974–1978* (1978, JP, CA, UK),* *Yesterday Once More* (1984, UK),* *A&M Gold Series Vol. 1* (1986, JP), *Anthology* (1989, JP),* *A&M New Gold Series Vol. 2* (1990, JP), *Only Yesterday: Richard and Karen Carpenter's Greatest Hits* (1990, UK), *Their Greatest Hits* (1990, UK, ZA), *Their Greatest Hits* (1993, DE), *Japanese Single Box* (2006, JP), *The Ultimate Collection* (2006, NL), *Carpenters Collected* (2013), *The Nation's Favourite Carpenters Songs* (2016, UK)
* Stereo mix is inverted from its original

1991 REMIX (3:38)
Best of Best + Original Master Karaoke (1992, JP), *Magical Memories of the Carpenters* (1993, Reader's Digest, UK, AU, EU), *Carpenters Best Vol. 2* (1994, JP), *Sweet Memory* (1994, JP), *Twenty-Two Hits of the Carpenters* (1995, HK), *Anthology* (1997, remastered reissue, JP), *Their Greatest Hits and Finest Performances* (1997, Reader's Digest), *Gold* (2000, UK), *Gold* (2001, JP), *The Essential Collection—1965–1997* (2002), *Gold* (2004, 35th Anniversary Edition), *Gold* (2005), *Gold* (2005, UK), *Twenty-Two Hits of the Carpenters* (2005, The 10th Anniversary Edition, incl. karaoke disc, HK), *The Ultimate Collection* (2006, UK), *20/20 Best of the Best Selection* (2009, JP), *40/40* (2009), *40/40* (2009, EU, UK), *40/40 The Best Selection* (2009, JP), *Best Songs* (2017, *Sweet Memory* repackaged, JP)

Details	Notes	Versions

Song
Jingle Bells

Written by
James Lord Pierpont/adapted by Peter Knight

Recorded at
A&M Studios—Studio D on 24-track, 2" tape

Instrumental Recording Dates
Feb. 5, 1978 (rhythm tracks), Feb. 7 (orchestra),
Feb. 12 (harp and percussion)

1978 STUDIO ALBUM VERSION (1:10)
Christmas Portrait (1978), *Christmas Portrait*
(1984, DE)
1992 REMIX (1:10)
Christmas Collection (1996), *Japanese Single
Box* (2006, JP)

Song
Johnny Angel

Written by
Lyn Duddy/Lee Pockriss

Recorded at
A&M Studios—Studio B on 16-track, 2" tape

Instrumental Recording Dates
Jan. 10, 1973 (rhythm tracks), Jan. 18
(orchestra)

1973 STUDIO ALBUM VERSION (1:30)
Now & Then (1973), *Anthology* (1989, JP)
1990 REMIX (1:32)
From the Top (1991), *Magical Memories of
the Carpenters* (1993, UK), *Sweet Memory*
(1994, JP), *Their Greatest Hits and Finest
Performances* (1997, Reader's Digest),*
Anthology (1997, remastered reissue, JP), *The
Essential Collection—1965–1997* (2002), *Best
Songs* (2017, *Sweet Memory* repackaged, JP)
* The DJ chatter is omitted from the track for
this release—total running time (1:33)

Song
Karen/Ella Medley

Written by
a. This Masquerade (Leon Russell)
b. My Funny Valentine (Richard Rodgers/
Lorenz Hart)
c. I'll Be Seeing You (Sammy Fain/Irving
Kahal)
d. Someone to Watch Over Me (George
Gershwin/Ira Gershwin)
e. As Time Goes By (Herman Hupfeld)
f. Don't Get Around Much Anymore (Duke
Ellington/Bob Russell)
g. I Let a Song Go Out of My Heart (Duke
Ellington/Irving Mills/Henry Nemo/John
Redmond)

Recorded at
A&M Studios—Studio D on 24-track, 2" tape

Instrumental Recording Dates
1980

Karen and Ella Fitzgerald sing a medley of
standards together for the Carpenters' ABC
television special *Music, Music, Music*.

As with many of the television specials,
Karen prerecorded her lead vocals for this
medley, which also happened to be on her
thirtieth birthday: March 2, 1980.

2001 ALBUM VERSION (5:58)
As Time Goes By (2001, JP), *As Time Goes By*
(2004), *The Essential Collection—1965–1997*
(2002)

Song
Karen's Theme

Written by
Richard Carpenter

Recorded at
Capitol Studios—Studio A

Instrumental Recording Dates
Dec. 13, 1996 (piano and orchestra)

The melody, written for *The Karen
Carpenter Story* in 1989, was finished
and recorded in 1997 for Richard's solo
album titled *Pianist, Arranger, Composer,
Conductor*.

1997 (RICHARD CARPENTER SOLO) ALBUM
VERSION (2:40)
The Essential Collection—1965–1997 (2002),
Carpenters Perform Carpenter (2003), *Gold*
(2004, 35th Anniversary Edition), *Gold*
(2005), *The Ultimate Collection* (2006, NL),
Carpenters Collected (2013)

Details	Notes	Versions

Song
Kiss Me the Way You Did Last Night

Written by
Linda L. Lawley/Margaret Dorn

Recorded at
A&M Studios—Studio D on 24-track, 2" tape

Instrumental Recording Dates
July 27, Oct. 29, and Nov. 9, 1980 (rhythm tracks), Aug. 15 and Sept. 10 (guitars), April 14, 1983 (orchestra)

1989 STUDIO ALBUM VERSION (4:03)
Lovelines (1989)

Song
Leave Yesterday Behind

Written by
Fred Karlin

Recorded at
A&M Studios—Studio D on 24-track, 2" tape; Capitol Studios, Hollywood

Instrumental Recording Dates
May 28, 1978 (rhythm tracks)

"Leave Yesterday Behind" was an outtake that Richard completed, and included on *As Time Goes By* in 2001.

2001 ALBUM VERSION (3:31)
As Time Goes By (2001, JP), *As Time Goes By* (2004), *Gold* (2001, JP), *Gold* (2004, 35th Anniversary Edition), *Gold* (2005), *40/40 The Best Selection* (2009, JP)

Song
Let Me Be the One

Written by
Paul Williams/Roger Nichols

Recorded at
A&M Studios—Studio A on 16-track, 2" tape

Instrumental Recording Dates
1971

The notable difference between the 1971 album mix and the 1990 remix, instrumentally speaking, is Richard's replacement of the piano from "mono" to stereo, as well as the deletion of the Wurlitzer electric piano track.

The 1990 remix first surfaced on *From the Top* in 1991 and is a rare treat for listeners looking to hear drummer Hal Blaine's clicking of sticks leading into the downbeat. Karen's ad-lib during the count off and playfully sung chatter at the end are also worth noting, as these studio outtakes are muted on the original mix, which goes to a complete fade-out, as intended.

It is also worth mentioning that engineer Ray Gerhardt was known for his "clean" recording techniques, and not one to keep much studio chatter or outtakes on the master tapes, making this extended mix of "Let Me Be the One" a true rarity.

1971 STUDIO ALBUM VERSION (2:25)
Carpenters (1971), *Treasures* (1987, JP), *A&M New Gold Series Vol. 1* (1990, JP), *A&M Gold Series* (1991, JP), *Startrax* (1991, EU, AU), *By Request* (2000, JP), *The Essential Collection—1965–1997* (2002), *Gold* (2004, 35th Anniversary Edition), *Gold* (2005), *40/40 The Best Selection* (2009, JP)
1990 REMIX (2:49)
From the Top (1991),* *Magical Memories of the Carpenters* (1993, UK),** *Sweet Memory* (1994, JP),*** *Carpenters Best Vol. 2* (1994, JP),* *40/40* (2009),* *40/40* (2009, EU, UK),* *Sweet Sixteen* (2009, *40th Anniversary Collector's Edition* bonus disc, JP),* *Best Songs* (2017, *Sweet Memory* repackaged, JP)***
* Extended mix—starts with studio count off, playing through to end, no fade-out
** Limited extended mix—starts with cold opening, no studio count off, playing through to end, no fade-out
*** Album mix length—starts with cold opening, no studio count off, and ends with fade-out

---

Song
Little Altar Boy

Written by
Howlett Peter Smith

Recorded at
A&M Studios—Studio D on 24-track, 2" tape

Instrumental Recording Dates
Feb. 13, 1978 (orchestra)

1984 STUDIO ALBUM VERSION (3:43)
An Old-Fashioned Christmas (1984), *Christmas Portrait—The Special Edition* (1984), *From the Top* (1991), *Christmas with the Carpenters* (1992, Time Life Music), *Christmas Collection* (1996), *Their Greatest Hits and Finest Performances* (1997, Reader's Digest), *The Essential Collection—1965–1997* (2002)

Details	Notes	Versions

Song
Little Girl Blue

Written by
Richard Rodgers/Lorenz Hart

Recorded at
A&M Studios—Studio D on 24-track, 2" tape

Instrumental Recording Dates
1978

1989 STUDIO ALBUM VERSION (3:24)
Lovelines (1989), *From the Top* (1991), *Magical Memories of the Carpenters* (1993, UK), *Interpretations: A 25th Anniversary Celebration* (1994, UK), *Sweet Memory* (1994, JP), *Interpretations: A 25th Anniversary Celebration* (1995), *Their Greatest Hits and Finest Performances* (1997, Reader's Digest), *The Essential Collection—1965–1997* (2002), *Best Songs* (2017, *Sweet Memory* repackaged, JP)

Song
Little Girl Blue

Written by
Richard Rodgers/Lorenz Hart

Recorded at
A&M Studios—Studio D on 24-track, 2" tape

Instrumental Recording Dates
1978

1989 STUDIO ALBUM VERSION (3:24)
Lovelines (1989), *From the Top* (1991), *Magical Memories of the Carpenters* (1993, UK), *Interpretations: A 25th Anniversary Celebration* (1994, UK), *Sweet Memory* (1994, JP), *Interpretations: A 25th Anniversary Celebration* (1995), *Their Greatest Hits and Finest Performances* (1997, Reader's Digest), *The Essential Collection—1965–1997* (2002), *Best Songs* (2017, *Sweet Memory* repackaged, JP)

Song
Look to Your Dreams

Written by
Richard Carpenter/John Bettis

Recorded at
A&M Studios—Studio D on 24-track, 2" tape

Instrumental Recording Dates
Nov. 13 and Dec. 10, 1977 (orchestra), Nov. 15 (guitars)

Unlike the album version, the single does not include the piano tag fade-out. A few of the studio album reissues and compilation sets over the years mistakenly list the shorter, single version time code (4:28). However, it is the longer, album version that is included.

1983 STUDIO ALBUM VERSION (5:12)
Voice of the Heart (1983), *Treasures* (1987, JP), *Treasures* (1990, UK), *Magical Memories of the Carpenters* (1993, UK), *Sweet Memory* (1994, JP), *Their Greatest Hits and Finest Performances* (1997, Reader's Digest), *By Request* (2000, JP), *Carpenters Perform Carpenter* (2003), *Japanese Single Box* (2006, JP), *Best Songs* (2017, *Sweet Memory* repackaged, JP)
1983 SINGLE EDIT (4:28)
The Complete Singles (2015)

Song
Looking for Love

Written by
Richard Carpenter

Recorded at
Bassist Joe Osborn's garage studio, on 4-track tape

Instrumental Recording Dates
1966

Approximately five hundred copies of the Magic Lamp single (ML704) were pressed, with "Looking for Love" as the A-side, with "I'll Be Yours" as the flip.

1966 KAREN CARPENTER SINGLE (2:28)
From the Top (1991), *The Essential Collection—1965–1997* (2002)

Song
Love Is Surrender

Written by
Ralph Carmichael

Recorded at
A&M Studios—Studios B and C on 16-track, 2" tape

Instrumental Recording Dates
Nov. 5, 1969 (rhythm tracks), Nov. 21 (percussion), July 20, 1970 (orchestra)

1970 STUDIO ALBUM VERSION (1:59)
Close to You (1970), *A&M New Gold Series Vol. 1* (1990, JP)
1987 REMIX (1:58)
Treasures (1987, JP), *A&M Gold Series* (1991, JP), *Startrax* (1991, EU, AU), *Magical Memories of the Carpenters* (1993, UK), *Sweet Memory* (1994, JP), *Their Greatest Hits and Finest Performances* (1997, Reader's Digest), *20th Century Masters Millennium Series* (2002), *The Essential Collection—1965–1997* (2002), *20/20 Best of the Best Selection* (2009, JP), *40/40* (2009), *40/40* (2009, EU, UK), *40/40 The Best Selection* (2009, JP), *20th Century Masters Millennium Series* (2017, reissue, JP), *Best Songs* (2017, *Sweet Memory* repackaged, JP)

Details	Notes	Versions
Song Love Me for What I Am **Written by** John Bettis/Palma Pascale **Recorded at** A&M Studios—Studio D on 24-track, 2" tape **Instrumental Recording Dates** Sept. 10, 1974 (rhythm tracks), Sept. 11 (guitars), Sept. 30 (orchestra)		1975 STUDIO ALBUM VERSION (3:30) *Horizon* (1975), *Magical Memories of the Carpenters* (1993, UK), *Sweet Memory* (1994, JP), *Japanese Single Box* (2006, JP), *The Complete Singles* (2015), *Best Songs* (2017, *Sweet Memory* repackaged, JP)
Song Lovelines **Written by** Rod Temperton **Recorded at** A&R Studios, New York; A&M Studios, Hollywood; Kendun Recorders, Burbank, CA, on 24-track, 2" tape **Instrumental Recording Dates** Unknown	Recorded in 1979 and 1980 for Karen's solo album *Karen Carpenter* (posthumously released in 1996), and later remixed for the Carpenters album *Lovelines* in 1989.	1989 (CARPENTERS) ALBUM MIX (4:29) *Lovelines* (1989), *The Ultimate Collection* (2006, NL), *Carpenters Collected* (2013), *Best Songs* (2017, *Sweet Memory* repackaged, JP)
Song Make Believe It's Your First Time **Written by** Bob Morrison/Johnny Wilson **Recorded at** A&M Studios—Studio D on 24-track, 2" tape **Instrumental Recording Dates** Oct. 23, 1980 (rhythm tracks), March 8, 1983 (guitars), April 14 (orchestra)	The words "Uh, I have to get into a serious mood here" mumbled by Karen in the first two seconds of the recording are followed by a whimsical sound effect that she and the Carpenters' road group often did. This was achieved by pulling the cheek with the thumb and forefinger—three quick pulls, making a "tap dancing" sound.	1983 STUDIO ALBUM VERSION (4:07) *Voice of the Heart* (1983), *Yesterday Once More* (1984, UK), *A&M New Gold Series Vol. 1* (1990, JP), *Treasures* (1990, UK), *A&M Gold Series* (1991, JP), *Startrax* (1991, EU, AU), *Magical Memories of the Carpenters* (1993, UK), *Carpenters Best Vol. 2* (1994, JP), *Love Songs* (1997), *Their Greatest Hits and Finest Performances* (1997, Reader's Digest), *The Essential Collection—1965–1997* (2002), *Gold* (2004, 35th Anniversary Edition), *Gold* (2005), *The Ultimate Collection* (2006, NL), *Carpenters Collected* (2013) 1983 STUDIO SINGLE EDIT (spoken intro omitted) (4:07) *Yesterday Once More* (1985), *Classics Volume 2* (1987), *Sweet Memory* (1994, JP), *Yesterday Once More* (1998), *Japanese Single Box* (2006, JP), *The Complete Singles* (2015), *Best Songs* (2017, *Sweet Memory* repackaged, JP)
Song Man Smart, Woman Smarter **Written by** Norman Span **Recorded at** A&M Studios—Studio D on 24-track, 2" tape **Instrumental Recording Dates** March 29, 1977 (rhythm tracks, sax, and percussion)	The "burping" sound effect in the second chorus, following the lyric "That's right" (1:07), was created by Richard. And the spoken lyric "Wrong!" heard at the very end of the same chorus (1:12) was the voice of *Passage*'s third engineer Dave Iveland.	1977 STUDIO ALBUM VERSION (4:21) *Passage* (1977), *Magical Memories of the Carpenters* (1993, UK)

Details	Notes	Versions

Song
Maybe It's You

Written by
Richard Carpenter/John Bettis

Recorded at
A&M Studios—Studio B on 16-track, 2" tape

Instrumental Recording Dates
July 28, 1970 (orchestra)

Notable differences can be heard between the various mixes of "Maybe It's You."

For the 1987 remix, Richard replaces the original "mono" acoustic piano with the Yamaha DX7 synth.

In 1990, the DX7 was replaced by a stereo acoustic piano. This remix also includes an alternate take on Karen's lead vocal in verse one: "Maybe it's just that I've never been the kind who can pass a lucky penny by." Some of the compilation albums feature the 1990 remix with a clean introduction and no overlap from the previous track.

1970 STUDIO ALBUM VERSION (3:04)
Close to You (1970), *Japanese Single Box* (2006, JP), *The Complete Singles* (2015)
1987 REMIX (3:00)
Treasures (1987, JP), *A&M Composers Series Vol. 2 Richard Carpenter & John Bettis* (1988, JP)
1990 REMIX (3:06)
From the Top (1991),* *Magical Memories of the Carpenters* (1993, UK), *Sweet Memory* (1994, JP), *Reflections* (1995, UK, EU, ZA, DE),* *Sweet Sweet Smile* (2000, NL),* *20th Century Masters Millennium Series* (2002), *The Essential Collection—1965–1997* (2002), *Carpenters Perform Carpenter* (2003), *Gold* (2004, 35th Anniversary Edition), *Gold* (2005), *Reflections—The Best 1200* (2005, JP),* *20/20 Best of the Best Selection* (2009, JP), *40/40* (2009), *40/40* (2009, EU, UK), *40/40 The Best Selection* (2009, JP), *The Best of the Carpenters* (2009, DE),* *20th Century Masters Millennium Series* (2017, reissue, JP), *Best Songs* (2017, *Sweet Memory* repackaged, JP)
* The track opens clean, no cross-fade

Song
Medley (from the album *An Old-Fashioned Christmas*)

Written by
Here Comes Santa Claus (Gene Autry/Oakley Haldeman), Frosty the Snowman (Steve Nelson/Jack Rollins), Rudolph the Red-Nosed Reindeer (Johnny Marks), Good King Wenceslas (P.D. John Mason Neale/adapted by Richard Carpenter)

Recorded at
A&M Studios—Studio D; EMI Abbey Road Studios, London, on 24-track, 2" tape

Instrumental Recording Dates
1984

1984 STUDIO ALBUM VERSION (3:43)
An Old-Fashioned Christmas (1984), *Christmas Portrait—The Special Edition* (1984), *Christmas with the Carpenters* (1992, Time Life Music), *Christmas Collection* (1996)

Song
Medley: Close Encounters/Star Wars

Written by
John Williams

Recorded at
A&M Studios—Studio D on 24-track, 2" tape

Instrumental Recording Dates
1978

2001 ALBUM VERSION (6:00)
As Time Goes By (2001, JP), *As Time Goes By* (2004)

Song
Medley: "Superstar"/"Rainy Days and Mondays"

Written by
Bonnie Bramlett/Leon Russell, Paul Williams/Roger Nichols

Recorded at
A&M Studios—Studio D on 24-track, 2" tape

Instrumental Recording Dates
1977

2001 ALBUM VERSION (3:07)
As Time Goes By (2001, JP), *As Time Goes By* (2004)

Details	Notes	Versions
Song Merry Christmas, Darling **Written by** Richard Carpenter/Frank Pooler **Recorded at** A&M Studios—Studio B on 16-track, 2" tape **Instrumental Recording Dates** Nov. 11, 1970 (rhythm tracks), Nov. 13 (orchestra), Nov. 16 (sax solo)	Originally recorded in November 1970, Karen's lead vocal (only) was rerecorded in 1978, and the song remixed for inclusion on *Christmas Portrait*. For Time Life Music's *Christmas with the Carpenters* in 1992, Richard updated the original "mono" piano track with stereo, and gave the recording a remix, also giving the background vocals a push up, in, and throughout the mix. This is the only release containing the 1992 mix.	1970 SINGLE VERSION (3:05) *From the Top* (1991), *The Essential Collection—1965–1997* (2002), *Japanese Single Box* (2006, JP), *The Complete Singles* (2015) 1978 STUDIO ALBUM VERSION (3:05) *Christmas Portrait* (1978), *Christmas Portrait* (1984, DE), *Christmas Portrait—The Special Edition* (1984), *Christmas Collection* (1996), *Their Greatest Hits and Finest Performances* (1997, Reader's Digest), *Carpenters Perform Carpenter* (2003), *Gold* (2004, 35th Anniversary Edition), *Singles 1969–1981* SACD (2004, CD audio layer), *Gold* (2005) 1992 REMIX (3:05) *Christmas with the Carpenters* (1992, Time Life Music) 2004 SACD 5.1 + STEREO FOLD-DOWN MIX (3:05) *Singles 1969–1981* SACD (2004) 2018 ROYAL PHILHARMONIC VERSION (3:02) *Carpenters with the Royal Philharmonic Orchestra* (2018)
Song Morinaga Hi-Crown Chocolate Commercial **Written by** Koji Makaino **Recorded at** A&M Studios—Studio D on 24-track, 2" tape **Instrumental Recording Dates** 1974		1974 COMMERCIAL MIX (0:35) *The Essential Collection—1965–1997* (2002)
Song Mr. Guder **Written by** Richard Carpenter/John Bettis **Recorded at** A&M Studios—Studios B and C on 16-track, 2" tape **Instrumental Recording Dates** Nov. 8, 1969 (rhythm tracks), July 18, 1970 (orchestra)	On September 6, 1990, Richard invited Bob Messenger back into Enterprise Studios in Burbank to rerecord his flute parts and solo. This update can be heard in the remix from that same year.	1970 STUDIO ALBUM VERSION (3:15) *Close to You* (1970), *A&M Gold Series Vol. 2* (1986, JP), *A&M Composers Series Vol. 2 Richard Carpenter & John Bettis* (1988, JP), *Anthology* (1989, JP), *Japanese Single Box* (2006, JP), *The Complete Singles* (2015)* 1990 REMIX (3:22) *Magical Memories of the Carpenters* (1993, UK), *Carpenters Best Vol. 2* (1994, JP), *Anthology* (1997, remastered reissue, JP), *By Request* (2000, JP), *The Essential Collection—1965–1997* (2002), *Carpenters Perform Carpenter* (2003, JP), *Gold* (2004, 35th Anniversary Edition), *Gold* (2005) *Single edit—total running time (2:35)
Song My Body Keeps Changing My Mind **Written by** Leslie Pearl **Recorded at** A&R Studios, New York; A&M Studios, Hollywood; Kendun Recorders, Burbank, CA on 24-track, 2" tape **Instrumental Recording Dates** Nov. 8, 1979 (rhythm tracks)	Recorded for Karen's solo album and later remixed for the Carpenters 1991 compilation box set, *From the Top*.	1990 (CARPENTERS) ALBUM MIX (3:50) *From the Top* (1991)

Details	Notes	Versions

Song
My Favorite Things

Written by
Richard Rodgers/Oscar Hammerstein

Recorded at
A&M Studios—Studio D; EMI Abbey Road
Studios, London, on 24-track, 2" tape

Instrumental Recording Dates
1984

1984 STUDIO ALBUM VERSION (3:53)
An Old-Fashioned Christmas (1984),
Christmas Collection (1996)

Song
The Night Has a Thousand Eyes

Written by
Ben Wiseman/Dottie Wayne/Marilyn Garrett

Recorded at
A&M Studios—Studio B on 16-track, 2" tape

Instrumental Recording Dates
Jan. 10, 1973 (rhythm tracks), Jan. 18
(orchestra)

1973 STUDIO ALBUM VERSION (found on
"Oldies Medley") (1:45)
Now & Then (1973), *Anthology* (1989, JP)
1990 REMIX (found on "Oldies Medley") (2:23)
From the Top (1991), *Magical Memories of the
Carpenters* (1993, UK), *Sweet Memory* (1994,
JP), *Anthology* (1997, remastered reissue, JP),
Their Greatest Hits and Finest Performances
(1997, Reader's Digest),* *The Essential
Collection—1965–1997* (2002), *Best Songs*
(2017, *Sweet Memory* repackaged, JP)
* The DJ chatter is omitted from the track for
this release—track running time 1:50

Song
Now

Written by
Roger Nichols/Dean Pitchford

Recorded at
A&M Studios—Studio D on 24-track, 2" tape

Instrumental Recording Dates
April 25, 1982 (rhythm tracks), March 10,
1983 (pedal steel guitar), April 11 (woodwinds, horns, and sax solo), April 14
(orchestra)

1983 STUDIO ALBUM VERSION (3:46)
Voice of the Heart (1983), *Yesterday Once
More* (1984, UK), *Treasures* (1987, JP),
Anthology (1989, JP), *Treasures* (1990, UK),
From the Top (1991), *Magical Memories of the
Carpenters* (1993, Reader's Reader's Digest,
UK, AU, EU), *Carpenters Best Vol. 1* (1994,
JP), *Sweet Memory* (1994, JP), *Anthology*
(1997, remastered reissue, JP), *Their Greatest
Hits and Finest Performances* (1997, Reader's
Digest), *The Essential Collection—1965–1997*
(2002), *The Ultimate Collection* (2006, NL),
The Ultimate Collection (2006, UK), *40/40*
(2009), *40/40* (2009, EU, UK), *40/40 The
Best Selection* (2009, JP), *Carpenters Collected*
(2013), *Best Songs* (2017, *Sweet Memory*
repackaged, JP)

Song
Nowadays Clancy Can't Even Sing

Written by
Neil Young

Recorded at
A&M Studios—Studio B on 8-track, 1" tape

Instrumental Recording Dates
June 2, 1969 (rhythm tracks)

1969 STUDIO ALBUM VERSION (4:15)
Offering (1969)/*Ticket to Ride* (1970 retitled,
repackaged reissue), *Sweet Memory* (1994,
JP), *Best Songs* (2017, *Sweet Memory* repackaged, JP)

Song
Nowhere Man

Written by
John Lennon/Paul McCartney

Recorded at
Bassist Joe Osborn's garage studio, on
4-track tape

Instrumental Recording Dates
1967

One of several demo tapes destroyed in
a house fire at Joe Osborn's in 1974, this
recording was transferred from an acetate
reference disc, with additional recording
and remix done for inclusion on *As Time
Goes By* in 2001.

2001 ALBUM VERSION (2:53)
As Time Goes By (2001, JP), *As Time Goes By*
(2004)

Details	Notes	Versions
Song O Come, O Come, Emmanuel **Written by** P.D. John Mason Neale/adapted by Richard Carpenter **Recorded at** A&M Studios—Studio D on 24-track, 2" tape **Instrumental Recording Dates** 1978	The 1992 remix uses an alternate vocal take in the verse, replacing "…*and* ransom captive Israel" with, "…*shall* ransom captive Israel."	1978 STUDIO ALBUM VERSION (0:29) *Christmas Portrait* (1978), *Christmas Portrait* (1984, DE) 1992 REMIX (0:28) *Christmas with the Carpenters* (1992, Time Life Music), *Christmas Collection* (1996)
Song O Holy Night **Written by** Adolphe Adam/adapted by Richard Carpenter **Recorded at** A&M Studios—Studio D on 24-track, 2" tape **Instrumental Recording Dates** 1978 (orchestra), Aug. 17, 1984 (harp)	"O Holy Night" was arranged for, and intended to be sung by, Karen, for inclusion on *Christmas Portrait* in 1978. However, due to the plethora of material already recorded for the album, the orchestra track stayed "in the can," with no lead vocal. (It came down to a tossup between "O Holy Night" and "Christ Is Born," with the latter making the cut.) In 1984, Richard completed the recording by overdubbing his solo piano track in place of where Karen's lead vocal should have been and released it as an instrumental on *An Old-Fashioned Christmas*.	1984 STUDIO ALBUM VERSION (3:10) *An Old-Fashioned Christmas* (1984), *Christmas Portrait—The Special Edition* (1984), *Christmas with the Carpenters* (1992, Time Life Music), *Christmas Collection* (1996)
Song An Old-Fashioned Christmas **Written by** Richard Carpenter/John Bettis **Recorded at** A&M Studios—Studio D; EMI Abbey Road Studios, London, on 24-track, 2" tape **Instrumental Recording Dates** 1984		1984 STUDIO ALBUM VERSION (2:14) *An Old-Fashioned Christmas* (1984), *Christmas Portrait—The Special Edition* (1984), *Christmas with the Carpenters* (1992, Time Life Music), *Christmas Collection* (1996)
Song On the Balcony of the Casa Rosada/Don't Cry for Me Argentina **Written by** Andrew Lloyd Webber/Tim Rice **Recorded at** A&M Soundstage and Studio D on 24-track, 2" tape **Instrumental Recording Dates** May 24, 1977 (orchestra)	In May 1977, the Los Angeles Philharmonic was brought in to record the orchestral tracks for "Argentina," along with "Calling Occupants of Interplanetary Craft" and "I Just Fall in Love Again." Due to a contractual agreement, which did not allow for their name to be placed in the album credits, the hundred-member orchestra was credited instead as "The Overbudget Philharmonic."	1977 STUDIO ALBUM VERSION (7:45) *Passage* (1977), *Yesterday Once More* (1984, UK), *Anthology* (1989, JP),* *Treasures* (1990, UK),* *Magical Memories of the Carpenters* (1993, UK),* *Anthology* (1997, remastered reissue, JP), *Their Greatest Hits and Finest Performances* (1997, Reader's Digest),* *The Complete Singles* (2015)* * Edited down for length—total running time (5:54)
Song One Fine Day **Written by** Carole King/Gerry Goffin **Recorded at** A&M Studios—Studio B on 16-track, 2" tape **Instrumental Recording Dates** Feb. 18, 1973 (rhythm tracks), Feb. 21 (guitars)		1973 STUDIO ALBUM VERSION (found on "Oldies Medley") (1:39) *Now & Then* (1973), *Anthology* (1989, JP) 1990 REMIX (found on "Oldies Medley") (1:33) *From the Top* (1991), *Magical Memories of the Carpenters* (1993, UK), *Sweet Memory* (1994, JP), *Anthology* (1997, remastered reissue, JP), *Their Greatest Hits and Finest Performances* (1997, Reader's Digest), *The Essential Collection—1965–1997* (2002), *Best Songs* (2017, *Sweet Memory* repackaged, JP)

Details

Song
One Love

Written by
Richard Carpenter/John Bettis

Recorded at
A&M Studios—Studio A on 16-track, 2" tape

Instrumental Recording Dates
Jan. 27, 1971 (orchestra)

Song
One More Time

Written by
Lewis Anderson

Recorded at
A&M Studios—Studio D on 24-track, 2" tape

Instrumental Recording Dates
Feb. 14, 1976 (rhythm tracks), Feb. 24
(orchestra)

Notes

Versions

1971 STUDIO ALBUM VERSION (3:23)
Carpenters (1971), *Magical Memories of the Carpenters* (1993, UK), *Japanese Single Box* (2006, JP), *The Complete Singles* (2015)
1994 REMIX (3:23)
Sweet Memory (1994, JP), *By Request* (2000, JP), *Carpenters Perform Carpenter* (2003), *Best Songs* (2017, *Sweet Memory* repackaged, JP)

1976 STUDIO ALBUM VERSION (3:30)
A Kind of Hush (1976), *Treasures* (1987, JP), *Sweet Memory* (1994, JP), *Their Greatest Hits and Finest Performances* (1997, Reader's Digest), *40/40* (2009), *40/40* (2009, EU, UK), *40/40 The Best Selection* (2009, JP), *Best Songs* (2017, *Sweet Memory* repackaged, JP)

Left: The band with musician-bandleader-impresario Lawrence Welk (second from left)

Right: Lake Tahoe, 1973

Details

Song
Only Yesterday

Written by
Richard Carpenter/John Bettis

Recorded at
A&M Studios—Studio D on 24-track, 2" tape

Instrumental Recording Dates
Jan. 30, 1975 (rhythm tracks), Feb. 3 (guitars), Feb. 12 (guitars and sax solo), Feb. 20 (oboe), Feb. 21 (orchestra)

Notes

By 1975, the process of overdubbing background vocals (or "BGVs" as they're commonly called) had changed for Karen and Richard. In the earlier days, they would overdub their harmonies side by side, two parts at a time, then double, then triple them, before moving on to the next two parts. They now were each recording their vocals separately, while the other sat in the recording booth listening.

While recording the BGVs for "Only Yesterday," it was Karen's turn to lay down a number of overdubs to help complete the modulation that immediately follows the second chorus. Richard excused himself to use the bathroom while Karen and engineer Roger Young recorded her parts. By the time he returned, all of Karen's vocal overdubs had been laid down—flawlessly.

Versions

1975 STUDIO ALBUM VERSION (4:12)
Horizon (1975), *The Singles 1974–1978* (1978, JP, CA, UK), *Yesterday Once More* (1984, Silver Eagle Records, US and CA),** *Yesterday Once More* (1984, UK), *Yesterday Once More* (1985),** *A&M Gold Series Vol. 1* (1986, JP), *Classics Volume 2* (1987),** *A&M Composers Series Vol. 2 Richard Carpenter & John Bettis* (1988, JP), *Reminiscing* (1988, CA),** *Anthology* (1989, JP),* *A&M New Gold Series Vol. 2* (1990, JP), *Only Yesterday: Richard and Karen Carpenter's Greatest Hits* (1990, UK),** *Their Greatest Hits* (1990, UK, ZA),** *From the Top* (1991),* *Carpenters Collection* (1993, Time Life Music),* *Magical Memories of the Carpenters* (1993, UK),* *Their Greatest Hits* (1993, DE),** *Sweet Memory* (1994, JP), *The Best of Carpenters* (1994, BR),** *Twenty-Two Hits of the Carpenters* (1995, HK),* *Anthology* (1997, remastered reissue, JP),* *Their Greatest Hits and Finest Performances* (1997, Reader's Digest),* *Yesterday Once More* (1998),** *Singles 1969–1981* (1999, JP),** *Singles 1969–1981* (2000),** *Twenty-Two Hits of the Carpenters* (2005, The 10th Anniversary Edition, incl. karaoke disc, HK),* *Japanese Single Box* (2006, JP),** *The Ultimate Collection* (2006, NL), *Carpenters Collected* (2013), *The Complete Singles* (2015),** *Best Songs* (2017, *Sweet Memory* repackaged, JP)
* Early fade-out—total running time (3:58)
** Single release fade-out—total running time (3:47)

1991 REMIX (3:47)
Carpenters Best Vol. 2 (1994, JP), *Love Songs* (1997),* *By Request* (2000, JP), *Gold* (2000, UK), *Gold* (2001, JP), *20th Century Masters Millennium Series* (2002),* *The Essential Collection—1965–1997* (2002), *Carpenters Perform Carpenter* (2003),* *Gold* (2004, 35th Anniversary Edition), *Singles 1969–1981* SACD (2004, CD audio layer), *Gold* (2005), *Gold* (2005, UK), *The Ultimate Collection* (2006, UK), *20/20 Best of the Best Selection* (2009, JP), *40/40* (2009), *40/40* (2009, EU, UK), *40/40 The Best Selection* (2009, JP), *Icon* (2014), *The Nation's Favourite Carpenters Songs* (2016, UK), *20th Century Masters Millennium Series* (2017, reissue, JP)*
* Extended fade-out—total running time (3:57)

2004 SACD 5.1 + STEREO FOLD-DOWN MIX (3:37)
Singles 1969–1981 SACD (2004)

Details

Song
Ordinary Fool

Written by
Paul Williams

Recorded at
A&M Studios—Studio D on 24-track, 2" tape

Instrumental Recording Dates
Jan. 25, 1976 (rhythm tracks), April 11, 1983 (horns and sax solo), April 14 (orchestra)

Versions

1983 STUDIO ALBUM VERSION (3:40)
Voice of the Heart (1983), *From the Top* (1991), *Magical Memories of the Carpenters* (1993, UK), *Sweet Memory* (1994, JP), *The Essential Collection—1965–1997* (2002), *40/40* (2009), *40/40* (2009, EU, UK), *40/40 The Best Selection* (2009, JP), *Best Songs* (2017, *Sweet Memory* repackaged, JP)

Details	Notes	Versions

Song
Our Day Will Come

Written by
Bob Hilliard/Mort Garson

Recorded at
A&M Studios—Studio B on 16-track, 2" tape

Instrumental Recording Dates
Jan. 12, 1973 (rhythm tracks), Feb. 7 (guitars), Feb. 16 (orchestra)

1973 STUDIO ALBUM VERSION (found on "Oldies Medley") (2:00)
Now & Then (1973), *Anthology* (1989, JP)
1990 REMIX (found on "Oldies Medley") (2:01)
From the Top (1991), *Magical Memories of the Carpenters* (1993, UK), *Sweet Memory* (1994, JP), *Anthology* (1997, remastered reissue, JP), *Their Greatest Hits and Finest Performances* (1997, Reader's Digest),* *The Essential Collection—1965–1997* (2002), *Best Songs* (2017, *Sweet Memory* repackaged, JP)
* Sound effects at intro omitted on this release—total running time (1:57)

Song
Overture (from the album *Christmas Portrait*)

Written by
Deck the Halls (Traditional French Carol), I Saw Three Ships (Traditional Welsh Carol), Have Yourself a Merry Little Christmas (Hugh Martin/Ralph Blane), God Rest Ye Merry Gentlemen (Traditional English Carol), Away in a Manger (Martin Luther/C. F. Mueller), What Child Is This (William Chatterton Dix), Carol of the Bells (Traditional Ukranian Carol), O Come All Ye Faithful (John Francis Wade/Frederick Oakeley)

Recorded at
A&M Studios—Studio D on 24-track, 2" tape

Instrumental Recording Dates
Dec. 11, 1977 (orchestra)

1978 STUDIO ALBUM VERSION (4:38)
Christmas Portrait (1978), *Christmas Portrait* (1984, DE)
1992 REMIX (4:38)
Christmas with the Carpenters (1992, Time Life Music), *Christmas Collection* (1996)

Song
Overture (from the album *An Old-Fashioned Christmas*)

Written by
Happy Holiday (Irving Berlin), The First Noel (Traditional Old English Carol), March of the Toys (Victor Herbert), Little Jesus (Traditional Czech Carol/adapted by Richard Carpenter), I Saw Mommy Kissing Santa Claus (Tommie Connor), In Dulce Jubilo (Traditional German Carol/adapted by Richard Carpenter), Gesu Bambino (The Infant Jesus) (Pietro A. Yon), Angels We Have Heard on High (Traditional French Carol/adapted by Richard Carpenter)

Recorded at
A&M Studios—Studio D; EMI Abbey Road Studios, London, on 24-track, 2" tape

Instrumental Recording Dates
1984

1984 STUDIO ALBUM VERSION (8:13)
An Old-Fashioned Christmas (1984)
1992 REMIX (8:13)
Christmas with the Carpenters (1992, Time Life Music), *Christmas Collection* (1996)

Gift tag that was placed outside shrink wrap of Christmas Portrait album

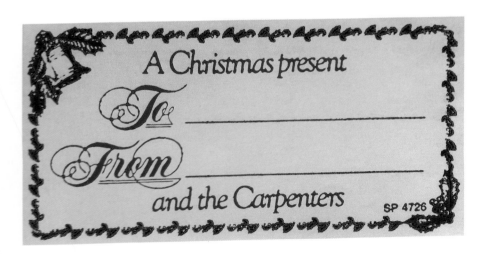

A Christmas present

To _____

From _____

and the Carpenters   SP 4726

Details	Notes	Versions

Song
Overture (from the album *Carpenters with the Royal Philharmonic Orchestra*)

Recorded at
(Formerly EMI) Abbey Road Studios, London

Instrumental Recording Dates
2018

2018 ROYAL PHILHARMONIC VERSION (1:30)
Carpenters with the Royal Philharmonic Orchestra (2018)

Song
The Parting of Our Ways
(Richard Carpenter)

Recorded at
Bassist Joe Osborn's garage studio, on 4-track tape

Instrumental Recording Dates
1966

Recorded along with several other tracks for the fledgling independent record label Magic Lamp.

1966 KAREN CARPENTER SINGLE (2:19)
From the Top (1991), *The Essential Collection—1965–1997* (2002)

Song
Piano Picker
(Randy Edelman)

Recorded at
A&M Studios—Studio B on 16-track, 2" tape

Instrumental Recording Dates
March 22, 1972 (strings), March 24 (horns)

The background vocal lyric Richard sings in the second chorus (1:31) is "Hanon, Czerny and Bach," referring to some of his early influences.

1972 STUDIO ALBUM VERSION (1:59)
A Song for You (1972), *A Song for You* (1989, Mobile Fidelity Sound Lab)
1987 REMIX (2:00)
Treasures (1987, JP), *Magical Memories of the Carpenters* (1993, UK)

1976

Page 283: Trade ad for "Please Mr. Postman"

Details	Notes	Versions

Song
Our Day Will Come

Written by
Bob Hilliard/Mort Garson

Recorded at
A&M Studios—Studio B on 16-track, 2" tape

Instrumental Recording Dates
Jan. 12, 1973 (rhythm tracks), Feb. 7 (guitars),
Feb. 16 (orchestra)

1973 STUDIO ALBUM VERSION (found on
"Oldies Medley") (2:00)
   Now & Then (1973), *Anthology* (1989, JP)
1990 REMIX (found on "Oldies Medley") (2:01)
   From the Top (1991), *Magical Memories of the
Carpenters* (1993, UK), *Sweet Memory* (1994,
JP), *Anthology* (1997, remastered reissue, JP),
Their Greatest Hits and Finest Performances
(1997, Reader's Digest),* *The Essential
Collection—1965–1997* (2002), *Best Songs*
(2017, *Sweet Memory* repackaged, JP)
* Sound effects at intro omitted on this
release—total running time (1:57)

Song
Overture (from the album *Christmas
Portrait*)

Written by
Deck the Halls (Traditional French Carol),
I Saw Three Ships (Traditional Welsh
Carol), Have Yourself a Merry Little
Christmas (Hugh Martin/Ralph Blane),
God Rest Ye Merry Gentlemen (Traditional
English Carol), Away in a Manger (Martin
Luther/C. F. Mueller), What Child Is This
(William Chatterton Dix), Carol of the Bells
(Traditional Ukranian Carol), O Come All
Ye Faithful (John Francis Wade/Frederick
Oakeley)

Recorded at
A&M Studios—Studio D on 24-track, 2" tape

Instrumental Recording Dates
Dec. 11, 1977 (orchestra)

1978 STUDIO ALBUM VERSION (4:38)
   Christmas Portrait (1978), *Christmas Portrait*
(1984, DE)
1992 REMIX (4:38)
   Christmas with the Carpenters (1992, Time
Life Music), *Christmas Collection* (1996)

Song
Overture (from the album *An Old-Fashioned
Christmas*)

Written by
Happy Holiday (Irving Berlin), The First
Noel (Traditional Old English Carol),
March of the Toys (Victor Herbert), Little
Jesus (Traditional Czech Carol/adapted by
Richard Carpenter), I Saw Mommy Kissing
Santa Claus (Tommie Connor), In Dulce
Jubilo (Traditional German Carol/adapted
by Richard Carpenter), Gesu Bambino (The
Infant Jesus) (Pietro A. Yon), Angels We
Have Heard on High (Traditional French
Carol/adapted by Richard Carpenter)

Recorded at
A&M Studios—Studio D; EMI Abbey Road
Studios, London, on 24-track, 2" tape

Instrumental Recording Dates
1984

1984 STUDIO ALBUM VERSION (8:13)
   An Old-Fashioned Christmas (1984)
1992 REMIX (8:13)
   Christmas with the Carpenters (1992, Time
Life Music), *Christmas Collection* (1996)

**Gift tag that was
placed outside
shrink wrap of
*Christmas
Portrait* album**

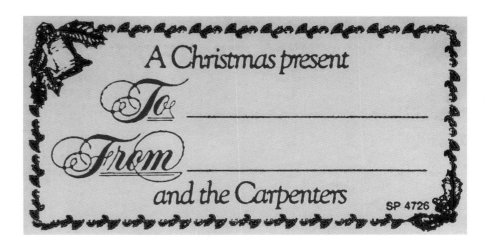

Details	Notes	Versions
Song Overture (from the album *Carpenters with the Royal Philharmonic Orchestra*) **Recorded at** (Formerly EMI) Abbey Road Studios, London **Instrumental Recording Dates** 2018		2018 ROYAL PHILHARMONIC VERSION (1:30) *Carpenters with the Royal Philharmonic Orchestra* (2018)
Song The Parting of Our Ways (Richard Carpenter) **Recorded at** Bassist Joe Osborn's garage studio, on 4-track tape **Instrumental Recording Dates** 1966	Recorded along with several other tracks for the fledgling independent record label Magic Lamp.	1966 KAREN CARPENTER SINGLE (2:19) *From the Top* (1991), *The Essential Collection—1965–1997* (2002)
Song Piano Picker (Randy Edelman) **Recorded at** A&M Studios—Studio B on 16-track, 2" tape **Instrumental Recording Dates** March 22, 1972 (strings), March 24 (horns)	The background vocal lyric Richard sings in the second chorus (1:31) is "Hanon, Czerny and Bach," referring to some of his early influences.	1972 STUDIO ALBUM VERSION (1:59) *A Song for You* (1972), *A Song for You* (1989, Mobile Fidelity Sound Lab) 1987 REMIX (2:00) *Treasures* (1987, JP), *Magical Memories of the Carpenters* (1993, UK)

1976

Page 283: Trade ad for "Please Mr. Postman"

Song
Please Mr. Postman

Written by
Please Mr. Postman
Brian Holland/Freddie Gorman/Georgia
Dobbins/Robert Bateman/William Garrett

Recorded at
A&M Studios—Studio D on 24-track, 2" tape

Instrumental Recording Dates
July 22, 1974 (rhythm tracks), July 23 (guitars
and sax solo), July 26 (baritone sax), July 31
(guitar solo)

1974 SINGLE MIX (2:49)
  The Singles 1974–1978 (1978, JP, CA, UK),*
  Yesterday Once More (1984, UK), *Japanese
  Single Box* (2006, JP), *Sweet Sixteen* (2009,
  40th Anniversary Collector's Edition bonus
  disc, JP), *The Complete Singles* (2015)
  * The single mix appears on LP version of
  this release
1975 STUDIO ALBUM VERSION (2:50)
  Horizon (1975), *The Singles 1974–1978*
  (1978, JP, CA, UK),* *Yesterday Once More*
  (1984, Silver Eagle Records, US and CA),
  Yesterday Once More (1985), *A&M Gold Series
  Vol. 1* (1986, JP), *Classics Volume 2* (1987),
  Reminiscing (1988, CA), *Anthology* (1989, JP),
  A&M New Gold Series Vol. 2 (1990, JP), *Only
  Yesterday: Richard and Karen Carpenter's
  Greatest Hits* (1990, UK), *Their Greatest
  Hits* (1990, UK, ZA), *From the Top* (1991),
  Their Greatest Hits (1993, DE), *The Ultimate
  Collection* (2006, NL), *The Ultimate Collection*
  (2006, UK), *Carpenters Collected* (2013)
  * The studio album mix appears on CD
  version of this release
1991 REMIX (2:49)
  Best of Best + Original Master Karaoke
  (1992, JP), *Carpenters Collection* (1993,
  Time Life Music), *Magical Memories of
  the Carpenters* (1993, UK), *Interpretations:
  A 25th Anniversary Celebration* (1994,
  UK), *Sweet Memory* (1994, JP), *The Best of
  Carpenters* (1994, BR), *Twenty-Two Hits of
  the Carpenters* (1995, HK), *Their Greatest
  Hits and Finest Performances* (1997, Reader's
  Digest), *Anthology* (1997, remastered reissue,
  JP), *Yesterday Once More* (1998), *Singles
  1969–1981* (1999, JP), *Singles 1969–1981*
  (2000), *Gold* (2000, UK), *Gold* (2001, JP),
  20th Century Masters Millennium Series
  (2002), *The Essential Collection—1965–1997*
  (2002), *Gold* (2004, 35th Anniversary
  Edition), *Singles 1969–1981* SACD (2004, CD
  audio layer), *Gold* (2005), *Gold* (2005, UK),
  Twenty-Two Hits of the Carpenters (2005,
  The 10th Anniversary Edition, incl. karaoke
  disc, HK), *40/40* (2009), *40/40* (2009, EU,
  UK), *40/40 The Best Selection* (2009, JP), *The
  Nation's Favourite Carpenters Songs* (2016,
  UK), *20th Century Masters Millennium Series*
  (2017, reissue, JP), *Best Songs* (2017, *Sweet
  Memory* repackaged, JP)
2004 SACD 5.1 + STEREO FOLD-DOWN MIX
(2:47)
  Singles 1969–1981 SACD (2004)
2018 ROYAL PHILHARMONIC VERSION
(2:56)
  *Carpenters with the Royal Philharmonic
  Orchestra* (2018)

Song
Prime Time Love

Written by
Mark Unobsky/Danny Ironstone

Recorded at
A&M Studios—Studio D on 24-track, 2" tape

Instrumental Recording Dates
July 25 and 26, 1980 (rhythm tracks), Jan. 28,
1981 (sax solo), April 11, 1983 (horns) session
1, (strings) session 2

1983 STUDIO ALBUM VERSION (3:10)
  Voice of the Heart (1983)

Song
Rainbow Connection

Written by
Paul Williams/Kenneth Ascher

Recorded at
A&M Studios—Studio D on 24-track, 2" tape

Instrumental Recording Dates
Oct. 24 and Oct. 29, 1980 (rhythm tracks)

2001 ALBUM VERSION (4:35)
As Time Goes By (2001, JP), *As Time Goes By* (2004), *Gold* (2001, JP), *Gold* (2004, 35th Anniversary Edition), *Gold* (2005)

Song
Rainy Days and Mondays

Written by
Paul Williams/Roger Nichols

Recorded at
A&M Studios—Studios A and B on 16-track, 2" tape

Instrumental Recording Dates
Jan. 25, 1971 (rhythm tracks and harmonica), Jan. 27 (orchestra)

All of [session musician] Tommy Morgan's harmonica parts on "Rainy Days" were recorded in Studio B in a total of fifteen minutes.

The strings during Bob Messenger's tenor sax solo were deleted from the 1991 and subsequent remixes, as Richard feels "they didn't work and weren't really necessary."

1971 STUDIO ALBUM VERSION (3:36)
Carpenters (1971), *Japanese Single Box* (2006, JP), *The Ultimate Collection* (2006, NL), *Carpenters Collected* (2013), *The Complete Singles* (2015), *The Nation's Favourite Carpenters Songs* (2016, UK)
1973 REMIX (3:40)
The Singles 1969–1973 (1973),* *Yesterday Once More* (1984, Silver Eagle Records, US and CA), *Yesterday Once More* (1984, UK)*
* Recording has been altered from original for faster playback speed
1985 REMIX (3:35)
Yesterday Once More (1985), *A&M Gold Series Vol. 1* (1986, JP), *Classics Volume 2* (1987), *Reminiscing* (1988, CA), *Anthology* (1989, JP), *A&M New Gold Series Vol. 1* (1990, JP), *Only Yesterday: Richard and Karen Carpenter's Greatest Hits* (1990, UK), *Their Greatest Hits* (1990, UK, ZA), *A&M Gold Series* (1991, JP), *From the Top* (1991), *Startrax* (1991, EU, AU), *Carpenters Collection* (1993, Time Life Music), *Their Greatest Hits* (1993, DE), *The Essential Collection—1965–1997* (2002)
1991 REMIX (3:36)
Best of Best + Original Master Karaoke (1992, JP), *Magical Memories of the Carpenters* (1993, UK), *Carpenters Best Vol. 1* (1994, JP), *Interpretations: A 25th Anniversary Celebration* (1994, UK), *Sweet Memory* (1994, JP), *The Best of Carpenters* (1994, BR), *Interpretations: A 25th Anniversary Celebration* (1995), *Twenty-Two Hits of the Carpenters* (1995, HK), *Anthology* (1997, remastered reissue, JP), *Love Songs* (1997), *Their Greatest Hits and Finest Performances* (1997, Reader's Digest), *Yesterday Once More* (1998), *Singles 1969–1981* (1999, JP), *By Request* (2000, JP), *Gold* (2000, UK), *Singles 1969–1981* (2000), *Gold* (2001, JP), *Gold* (2004, 35th Anniversary Edition), *Singles 1969–1981* SACD (2004, CD audio layer), *Gold* (2005), *Gold* (2005, UK), *Twenty-Two Hits of the Carpenters* (2005, The 10th Anniversary Edition, incl. karaoke disc, HK), *The Ultimate Collection* (2006, UK), *20/20 Best of the Best Selection* (2009, JP), *40/40* (2009), *40/40* (2009, EU, UK), *40/40 The Best Selection* (2009, JP), *Icon* (2014), *Best Songs* (2017, *Sweet Memory* repackaged, JP)
2004 SACD 5.1 + STEREO FOLD-DOWN MIX (3:33)
Singles 1969–1981 SACD (2004)
2018 ROYAL PHILHARMONIC VERSION (3:37)
Carpenters with the Royal Philharmonic Orchestra (2018)

The Carpenters Very First Television Special, 1976

Details	Notes	Versions
Song Reason to Believe **Written by** Tim Hardin **Recorded at** A&M Studios—Studio B on 16-track, 2" tape **Instrumental Recording Dates** July 13, 1970 (rhythm tracks), July 28 (orchestra)	The original Wurlitzer electric piano track was later replaced in 1987 by a synth sampled Wurlitzer, and remixed the same year.	1970 STUDIO ALBUM VERSION (3:02) *Close to You* (1970) 1987 REMIX (3:04) *Treasures* (1987, JP), *A&M New Gold Series Vol. 1* (1990, JP), *Treasures* (1990, UK), *A&M Gold Series* (1991, JP), *Startrax* (1991, EU, AU), *Carpenters Best Vol. 2* (1994, JP), *Sweet Memory* (1994, JP), *Interpretations: A 25th Anniversary Celebration* (1995), *Reflections* (1995, UK, EU, ZA, DE), *Their Greatest Hits and Finest Performances* (1997, Reader's Digest), *Sweet Sweet Smile* (2000, NL), *Gold* (2004, 35th Anniversary Edition), *Gold* (2005), *Reflections—The Best 1200* (2005, JP), *20/20 Best of the Best Selection* (2009, JP), *40/40* (2009), *40/40* (2009, EU, UK), *40/40 The Best Selection* (2009, JP), *The Best of the Carpenters* (2009, DE), *Best Songs* (2017, *Sweet Memory* repackaged, JP)
Song Remember When Lovin' Took All Night **Written by** John Farrar/Molly Ann Leike **Recorded at** A&R Studios, New York; A&M Studios, Hollywood; Kendun Recorders, Burbank, CA on 24-track, 2" tape **Instrumental Recording Dates** 1979–80	Recorded in 1979 and 1980 for Karen's solo album *Karen Carpenter* (posthumously released in 1996), it was later remixed for the Carpenters album *Lovelines* in 1989.	1989 (CARPENTERS) ALBUM MIX (3:47) *Lovelines* (1989)
Song Road Ode **Written by** Gary Sims/Dan Woodhams **Recorded at** A&M Studios—Studio B on 16-track, 2" tape **Instrumental Recording Dates** Dec. 17, 1971 (rhythm tracks), March 23, 1972 (strings), March 24 (horns)	The piano, bass, and flute (solo) were rerecorded in September 1990 at Enterprise Studios in Burbank for the remix.	1972 STUDIO ALBUM VERSION (3:50) *A Song for You* (1972), *A Song for You* (1989, Mobile Fidelity Sound Lab) 1990 REMIX (3:52) *Treasures* (1990, UK), *Magical Memories of the Carpenters* (1993, UK), *Sweet Memory* (1994, JP), *By Request* (2000, JP), *Japanese Single Box* (2006, JP), *The Complete Singles* (2015), *Best Songs* (2017, *Sweet Memory* repackaged, JP)
Song Sailing on the Tide **Written by** Tony Peluso/John Bettis **Recorded at** A&M Studios—Studio D on 24-track, 2" tape **Instrumental Recording Dates** April 2, 1977 (rhythm tracks), April 6 (guitars and woodwinds), April 12 (orchestra), April 29 (guitars), June 1 (woodwinds, harp, and guitars), July 18 (woodwinds)	An earlier iteration of the song was recorded starting late 1974 into the spring of 1975 but never released.	1983 STUDIO ALBUM VERSION (4:21) *Voice of the Heart* (1983), *Sweet Memory* (1994, JP), *The Complete Singles* (2015), *Best Songs* (2017, *Sweet Memory* repackaged, JP)

Details	Notes	Versions
Song Sandy **Written by** Richard Carpenter/John Bettis **Recorded at** A&M Studios—Studio D on 24-track, 2" tape **Instrumental Recording Dates** Dec. 9, 1975 (rhythm tracks), Jan. 20, 1976 (flute), Jan. 21 (flute and clarinet), Jan. 22 and 26 (guitars)	The Richard Carpenter solo version—featured on *Pianist, Arranger, Composer, Conductor*, uses the same rhythm and orchestration tracks recorded for the Carpenters' *A Kind of Hush* album, with Richard's solo piano replacing Karen's lead vocal. Additional instrumentation and choir were also added.	1976 STUDIO ALBUM VERSION (3:38) *A Kind of Hush* (1976), *Treasures* (1987, JP), *A&M Composers Series Vol. 2 Richard Carpenter & John Bettis* (1988, JP), *Magical Memories of the Carpenters* (1993, UK), *Carpenters Best Vol. 2* (1994, JP), *Sweet Memory* (1994, JP), *The Essential Collection—1965–1997* (2002), *Carpenters Perform Carpenter* (2003, JP), *Japanese Single Box* (2006, JP), *The Ultimate Collection* (2006, UK), *The Complete Singles* (2015), *Best Songs* (2017, *Sweet Memory* repackaged, JP) 1997 (RICHARD CARPENTER SOLO) ALBUM VERSION (3:52) *The Ultimate Collection* (2006, NL), *Carpenters Collected* (2013)
Song Santa Claus Is Coming to Town (single version found on *An Old-Fashioned Christmas*) **Written by** Haven Gillespie/J. Fred Coots **Recorded at** A&M Studios—Studios A, B, and D on 24-track, 2" tape **Instrumental Recording Dates** 1972 (rhythm tracks), Sept. 20, 1974 ([original] sax solo—"single" mix), Sept. 30 (orchestra), July 18, 1984 ([rerecorded] sax solo—"album" mix)	Karen recorded her lead vocal in Studio A in one take. The background vocal harmonies originally recorded in 1974 for the single mix were later discovered to be partially incomplete—with the "third" having been mistakenly omitted. When the master tape was pulled in 1984 during the recording of *An Old-Fashioned Christmas*, Richard overdubbed the part himself, completing the [vocal] arrangement.	1974 SINGLE VERSION (4:06) *Japanese Single Box* (2006, JP), *The Complete Singles* (2015) 1984 STUDIO ALBUM VERSION (4:04) *An Old-Fashioned Christmas* (1984), *From the Top* (1991), *Christmas with the Carpenters* (1992, Time Life Music), *Christmas Collection* (1996), *The Essential Collection—1965–1997* (2002), *Sweet Sixteen* (2009, *40th Anniversary Collector's Edition* bonus disc, JP)
Song Santa Claus Is Comin' to Town (*Christmas Portrait* version) **Written by** Haven Gillespie/J. Fred Coots **Recorded at** A&M Studios—Studio D on 24-track, 2" tape **Instrumental Recording Dates** Feb. 5, 1978 (rhythm tracks), Feb. 7 (orchestra)	This version is not to be confused with the full-length, single version found on the Carpenters' second Christmas album from 1984, *An Old-Fashioned Christmas*. The *Christmas Portrait* title listing also omits the "g" in "Coming," unlike the earlier single version, which includes the "g" as originally approved by Richard.	1978 STUDIO ALBUM VERSION (1:05) *Christmas Portrait* (1978), *Christmas Portrait* (1984, DE), *Christmas Portrait—The Special Edition* (1984) 1992 REMIX (1:05) *Christmas Collection* (1996)
Song Saturday **Written by** Richard Carpenter/John Bettis **Recorded at** A&M Studios—Studio A on 16-track, 2" tape **Instrumental Recording Dates** Jan. 27, 1971 (orchestra), March 9 (trumpet)		1971 STUDIO ALBUM VERSION (1:18) *Carpenters* (1971), *Treasures* (1987, JP), *A&M Composers Series Vol. 2 Richard Carpenter & John Bettis* (1988, JP), *Magical Memories of the Carpenters* (1993, UK), *Sweet Memory* (1994, JP), *Japanese Single Box* (2006, JP), *The Complete Singles* (2015), *Best Songs* (2017, *Sweet Memory* repackaged, JP)

Details	Notes	Versions

Song
Selections from "Nutcracker"
(Peter Illych Tchaikovsky/adapted by Richard
Carpenter)
a. Overture Miniature
b. Dance of the Sugar Plum Fairies
c. Trepak
d. Valse Des Fleurs

Recorded at
A&M Studios—Studio D; EMI Abbey Road
Studios, London, on 24-track, 2" tape

Instrumental Recording Dates
1984

1984 STUDIO ALBUM VERSION (6:15)
An Old-Fashioned Christmas (1984),
Christmas Portrait—The Special Edition
(1984),* *Christmas Collection* (1996)
* Third movement, "Trepak" omitted—total
running time (5:27)

Song
Silent Night

Written by
Franz Gruber/adapted by Peter Knight

Recorded at
A&M Studios—Studio D on 24-track, 2" tape

Instrumental Recording Dates
Feb. 14, 1978 (orchestra)

1978 STUDIO ALBUM VERSION (3:29)
Christmas Portrait (1978), *Christmas Portrait*
(1984, DE), *Christmas Portrait—The Special
Edition* (1984), *Japanese Single Box* (2006, JP)
1992 REMIX (3:19)
Christmas with the Carpenters (1992, Time
Life Music), *Christmas Collection* (1996),
Their Greatest Hits and Finest Performances
(1997, Reader's Digest)

Song
Sing

Written by
Joe Raposo

Recorded at
A&M Studios—Studio B on 16-track, 2" tape

Instrumental Recording Dates
Jan. 12, 1973 (rhythm tracks), Jan. 18
(orchestra)

Richard played the original piano track
using "piano B" (often referred to as "the
Carole King piano"—as it was the piano she
preferred when recording at A&M Studios).
"It was an older Steinway Model B, and not
my first choice," Richard says. "I always preferred 'piano A' whenever it was available."

A stereo piano replaced the original in
1994 when the recording was remixed.

Unlike the *Best of Best + Original Master
Karaoke* album in Japan, which does not
include an instrumental remix of "Sing,"
the karaoke disc included in the *Twenty-Two
Hits of the Carpenters* (The 10th Anniversary
Edition), released in 2005, *does* include the
1994 instrumental remix.

1973 STUDIO ALBUM VERSION (3:20)
Now & Then (1973), *The Singles 1969–1973*
(1973), *Yesterday Once More* (1984, Silver
Eagle Records, US and CA), *Yesterday
Once More* (1984, UK), *Yesterday Once More*
(1985), *A&M Gold Series Vol. 1* (1986, JP),
Classics Volume 2 (1987), *Reminiscing* (1988,
CA), *Anthology* (1989, JP), *A&M New Gold
Series Vol. 2* (1990, JP), *From the Top* (1991),*
Carpenters Collection (1993, Time Life
Music), *Magical Memories of the Carpenters*
(1993, UK), *Carpenters Best Vol. 2* (1994, JP),
The Best of Carpenters (1994, BR), *Japanese
Single Box* (2006, JP), *The Ultimate Collection*
(2006, NL), *Carpenters Collected* (2013),
The Complete Singles (2015), *The Nation's
Favourite Carpenters Songs* (2016, UK)
* Spanish single version with alternate lead
vocal
1994 REMIX (3:20)
*Interpretations: A 25th Anniversary
Celebration* (1994, UK), *Sweet Memory*
(1994, JP), *Twenty-Two Hits of the Carpenters*
(1995, HK), *Anthology* (1997, remastered
reissue, JP), *Their Greatest Hits and Finest
Performances* (1997, Reader's Digest), *Singles
1969–1981* (1999, JP), *Gold* (2000, UK),
By Request (2000, JP), *Gold* (2001, JP), *The
Essential Collection—1965–1997* (2002), *Gold*
(2004, 35th Anniversary Edition), *Singles
1969–1981 SACD* (2004, CD audio layer),
Gold (2005), *Gold* (2005, UK), *Twenty-
Two Hits of the Carpenters* (2005, The 10th
Anniversary Edition, incl. karaoke disc,
HK), *The Ultimate Collection* (2006, UK),
40/40 (2009), *40/40* (2009, EU, UK), *40/40*
The Best Selection (2009, JP), *Best Songs* (2017,
Sweet Memory repackaged, JP)
**2004 SACD 5.1 + STEREO FOLD-DOWN MIX
(3:18)**
Singles 1969–1981 SACD (2004)

Alternate picture
for "Santa Claus
Is Coming to
Town," 1974

Details	Notes	Versions

Song
Sleigh Ride

Written by
Mitchell Parish/Leroy Anderson

Recorded at
A&M Studios—Studio D on 24-track, 2" tape

Instrumental Recording Dates
1977

The first half of the first verse on the 1992 remix uses an alternate take on Karen's lead vocal.

1978 STUDIO ALBUM VERSION (2:39)
Christmas Portrait (1978), *Christmas Portrait* (1984, DE), *Christmas Portrait—The Special Edition* (1984)
1992 REMIX (2:39)
Christmas with the Carpenters (1992, Time Life Music), *Christmas Collection* (1996)

Song
Slow Dance

Written by
Mitch Margo

Recorded at
A&M Studios—Studio D on 24-track, 2" tape

Instrumental Recording Dates
Sept. 21, 1978 (rhythm tracks), Oct. 7, 1980 (woodwinds), April 11, 1983 (horns) session 1, (strings) session 2

1989 ALBUM MIX (3:33)
Lovelines (1989), *Sweet Memory* (1994, JP), *Best Songs* (2017, *Sweet Memory* repackaged, JP)

Song
Solitaire

Written by
Neil Sedaka/Phil Cody

Recorded at
A&M Studios—Studio D on 24-track, 2" tape

Instrumental Recording Dates
Jan. 28, 1975 (rhythm tracks), Feb. 20 (oboe), Feb. 21 (orchestra)

The electric guitar fills in "Solitaire" were created using a technique that Richard often utilized on many Carpenters recordings with session and road guitarist, Tony Peluso.

This was achieved by recording Tony's part on a track, then once perfect, recording the exact same part again [in unison] on a second track after slowing the master tape playback to a fraction of its original speed. This would cause the two guitars to fall slightly out of tune with each another. Once the second take was successfully recorded, the tape was then returned to normal speed, and the tracks were then placed opposite each other in the stereo mix assignment, creating a chorus effect in what is referred to as a "spread."

1975 STUDIO ALBUM VERSION (4:39)
Horizon (1975), *The Singles 1974–1978* (1978, JP, CA, UK), *Yesterday Once More* (1984, UK), *A&M Gold Series Vol. 2* (1986, JP), *Reminiscing* (1988, CA), *A&M New Gold Series Vol. 1* (1990, JP), *Only Yesterday: Richard and Karen Carpenter's Greatest Hits* (1990, UK), *Their Greatest Hits* (1990, UK, ZA), *A&M Gold Series* (1991, JP), *From the Top* (1991), *Startrax* (1991, EU, AU), *Their Greatest Hits* (1993, DE), *Interpretations: A 25th Anniversary Celebration* (1994, UK), *Sweet Memory* (1994, JP), *The Best of Carpenters* (1994, BR), *Interpretations: A 25th Anniversary Celebration* (1995), *Twenty-Two Hits of the Carpenters* (1995, HK), *Love Songs* (1997), *Their Greatest Hits and Finest Performances* (1997, Reader's Digest), *Gold* (2000, UK), *Gold* (2001, JP), *Gold* (2005, UK), *Twenty-Two Hits of the Carpenters* (2005, The 10th Anniversary Edition, incl. karaoke disc, HK), *The Ultimate Collection* (2006, NL), *Carpenters Collected* (2013), *The Nation's Favourite Carpenters Songs* (2016, UK), *Best Songs* (2017, *Sweet Memory* repackaged, JP)
1975 SINGLE MIX (4:41)
Gold (2004, 35th Anniversary Edition), *Gold* (2005), *Japanese Single Box* (2006, JP), *Sweet Sixteen* (2009, 40th Anniversary Collector's Edition* bonus disc, JP), *The Complete Singles* (2015)

Song
Somebody's Been Lyin'

Written by
Burt Bacharach/Carole Bayer Sager

Recorded at
A&M Studios—Studio D on 24-track, 2" tape

Instrumental Recording Dates
Aug. 26, 1980 (orchestra)

1981 STUDIO ALBUM VERSION (4:23)
Made in America (1981), *The Complete Singles* (2015)

Details	Notes	Versions
Song Someday **Written by** Richard Carpenter/John Bettis **Recorded at** A&M Studios—Studio B on 8-track, 1" tape **Instrumental Recording Dates** June 16, 1969 (piano)		1969 STUDIO ALBUM VERSION (5:13) *Offering* (1969)/*Ticket to Ride* (1970 *Offering* retitled, repackaged reissue)
Song Sometimes **Written by** Henry Mancini/Felice Mancini **Recorded at** A&M Studios—Studio B on 16-track, 2" tape **Instrumental Recording Dates** 1971		1971 STUDIO ALBUM VERSION (2:52) *Carpenters* (1971), *Anthology* (1989, JP), *Magical Memories of the Carpenters* (1993, UK), *Sweet Memory* (1994, JP), *Anthology* (1997, remastered reissue, JP), *By Request* (2000, JP), *Best Songs* (2017, *Sweet Memory* repackaged, JP)
Song A Song for You **Written by** Leon Russell **Recorded at** A&M Studios—Studio B on 16-track, 2" tape **Instrumental Recording Dates** Feb. 22, 1972 (rhythm tracks), March 22 (orchestra)	An alternate lead vocal take can be heard in the 1987 remix, second verse, where Karen sings the lyric "cause we're alone now and I'm singing this song for you" (0:55). Another bit of trivia relates to Bob Messenger's improvisational saxophone solo, where a total of four individual takes were recorded, each on a separate track. (In the days of analog recording, in order to create what sounded like a properly sequenced, single-take performance on the master tape, complete, individual takes had to be transferred to a separate tape. Then, the best sections from each take would be selected and placed in order, which was quite tedious and time-consuming.) Miraculously, the sections Richard liked best when editing Messenger's solo just happened to be played in order—across the four takes, which meant it was simply a matter of muting and unmuting tracks where necessary during mixdown, without any editing. When considering "A Song for You" for the *Carpenters with the Royal Philharmonic Orchestra* album in 2018, Richard recalls, "We had all four [sax solo] takes up and playing together at the same time…which was really something to hear."	1972 STUDIO ALBUM VERSION (4:42) *A Song for You* (1972), *A Song for You* (1989, Mobile Fidelity Sound Lab) 1987 REMIX (4:38) *A&M Gold Series Vol. 1* (1986, JP), *Treasures* (1987, JP), *Anthology* (1989, JP), *A&M New Gold Series Vol. 2* (1990, JP), *Magical Memories of the Carpenters* (1993, UK), *Carpenters Best Vol. 1* (1994, JP), *Sweet Memory* (1994, JP), *Reflections* (1995, UK, EU, ZA, DE), *Anthology* (1997, remastered reissue, JP), *Love Songs* (1997), *Their Greatest Hits and Finest Performances* (1997, Reader's Digest), *Sweet Sweet Smile* (2000, NL), *The Essential Collection—1965–1997* (2002), *Gold* (2004, 35th Anniversary Edition), *Gold* (2005), *Reflections—The Best 1200* (2005, JP), *40/40* (2009), *40/40* (2009, EU, UK), *40/40 The Best Selection* (2009, JP), *The Best of the Carpenters* (2009, DE), *Best Songs* (2017, *Sweet Memory* repackaged, JP)
Song A Song for You (reprise) **Written by** Leon Russell **Recorded at** A&M Studios—Studio B on 16-track, 2" tape **Instrumental Recording Dates** Feb. 22, 1972 (rhythm tracks), March 22 (orchestra)	This recording derives from the same master as "A Song for You," edited and remixed for the album's bookend.	1972 STUDIO ALBUM VERSION (0:53) *A Song for You* (1972), *A Song for You* (1989, Mobile Fidelity Sound Lab)

Details	Notes	Versions

Song
Still Crazy After all These Years

Written by
Paul Simon

Recorded at
A&R Studios, New York; A&M Studios, Hollywood; Kendun Recorders, Burbank, CA on 24-track, 2" tape

Instrumental Recording Dates
1979–80

Recorded in 1979 and 1980 for Karen's solo album *Karen Carpenter* (posthumously released in 1996), it was later remixed for the Carpenters compilation album *From the Top* in 1990.

1996 (KAREN CARPENTER) ALBUM MIX (4:17)
   The Ultimate Collection (2006, NL), *Carpenters Collected* (2013)
1990 (CARPENTERS) ALBUM MIX (4:17)
   From the Top (1991)

Song
Strength of a Woman

Written by
Phyllis Brown/Juanita Curiel

Recorded at
A&M Studios—Studio D on 24-track, 2" tape

Instrumental Recording Dates
Oct. 20, 1980 (rhythm tracks), Feb. 2, 1981 (guitars), Feb. 11 (horns), Feb. 26 (percussion), Feb. 12 (orchestra)

1981 STUDIO ALBUM VERSION (3:59)
   Made in America (1981), *Magical Memories of the Carpenters* (1993, UK), *Sweet Memory* (1994, JP), *Best Songs* (2017, *Sweet Memory* repackaged, JP)

Song
Suntory Pop (Jingle #1)

Written by
Hiromasa Suzuki/Yoko Narahashi

Recorded at
A&M Studios—Studio D on 24-track, 2" tape

Instrumental Recording Dates
1977

In 1977, the Japanese whiskey manufacturer Suntory introduced a carbonated grapefruit soft drink called "pop." Richard and Karen were asked to be spokespersons for its multimedia campaign. Two versions of the jingle were made—both remixed in 1990.

1990 REMIX (0:32)
   From the Top (1991), *The Essential Collection—1965–1997* (2002), *Sweet Sixteen* (2009, *40th Anniversary Collector's Edition* bonus disc, JP)

Song
Suntory Pop (Jingle #2)

Written by
Hiromasa Suzuki/Yoko Narahashi

Recorded at
A&M Studios—Studio D on 24-track, 2" tape

Instrumental Recording Dates
1977

1990 REMIX (0:33)
   From the Top (1991), *The Essential Collection—1965–1997* (2002), *Sweet Sixteen* (2009, *40th Anniversary Collector's Edition* bonus disc, JP)

1980

Details

Song
Superstar

Written by
Leon Russell/Bonnie Bramlett

Recorded at
A&M Studios—Studio A on 16-track, 2" tape

Instrumental Recording Dates
1971

Fresno, CA, 1976

Notes

"Superstar" has been remixed several times over the years, partly in an attempt to remedy the issue of "leakage" that transpired during the recording of the rhythm tracks [in Studio A]. Richard was also dissatisfied with the way the drums were originally recorded—sonically speaking, as a result of the lack of time the Carpenters were given to record their self-titled album, *Carpenters* aka The Tan Album.

While remixing several tracks in 1985 for the compilation set *Yesterday Once More*, Richard updated the keyboard tracks with the Fender Rhodes by adding an arpeggiated arrangement he'd begun playing years earlier on the road. Also added were three additional French horn parts to the existing three in the intro and re-intro of the recording (a suggested change made years earlier by the Carpenters' live orchestra conductor, Dick Palombi), by way of a Kurzweil synthesizer.

Additionally, it was suggested to Richard that he might consider bringing the song's original drummer, Hal Blaine, back into the studio to rerecord the drums. This allowed for not only an opportunity to improve the sonic quality, but the tom-toms could now be recorded in stereo as well.

There was one slight problem, however. During the song's original recording in 1971, Blaine's drums leaked in through the door of the studio's air lock where Karen was recording her "work lead" vocal (which ultimately became the "master lead"), making its way through her microphone and onto her vocal track. The drums also made their way into the microphone used on Joe Osborn's bass amplifier.

Although the updated drum track was able to mask much of the leakage caused by its predecessor, it didn't fully address the issue. This bothered Richard following the release of the 1985 remix. It was rarely pulled again for use in future compilations.

And for the karaoke enthusiast—the instrumental remix of "Superstar" also contains audible leakage from Karen's lead vocal, which made its way through Blaine's headset and onto the drum tracks, making Karen's lead slightly audible in the verses.

Versions

1971 STUDIO ALBUM VERSION (3:49)
Carpenters (1971), *By Request* (2000, JP), *The Essential Collection—1965-1997* (2002), *Japanese Single Box* (2006, JP), *The Ultimate Collection* (2006, NL), *Carpenters Collected* (2013), *The Complete Singles* (2015), *The Nation's Favourite Carpenters Songs* (2016, UK)

1973 REMIX (3:40)
The Singles 1969-1973 (1973),* *Yesterday Once More* (1984, Silver Eagle Records, US and CA), *Yesterday Once More* (1984, UK)*
* Recording has been altered from original for faster playback speed

1985 REMIX (3:46)
Yesterday Once More (1985), *A&M Gold Series Vol. 1* (1986, JP), *Classics Volume 2* (1987), *Reminiscing* (1988, CA), *Anthology* (1989, JP), *A&M New Gold Series Vol. 1* (1990, JP), *Only Yesterday: Richard and Karen Carpenter's Greatest Hits* (1990, UK), *Their Greatest Hits* (1990, UK, ZA), *A&M Gold Series* (1991, JP), *Startrax* (1991, EU, AU), *Their Greatest Hits* (1993, DE)

1990 REMIX (3:45)
From the Top (1991)

1991 REMIX (3:49)
Best of Best + Original Master Karaoke (1992, JP), *Carpenters Collection* (1993, Time Life Music), *Magical Memories of the Carpenters* (1993, UK), *Carpenters Best Vol. 1* (1994, JP), *Interpretations: A 25th Anniversary Celebration* (1994, UK), *Sweet Memory* (1994, JP), *The Best of Carpenters* (1994, BR), *Interpretations: A 25th Anniversary Celebration* (1995), *Twenty-Two Hits of the Carpenters* (1995, HK), *Anthology* (1997, remastered reissue, JP), *Love Songs* (1997), *Their Greatest Hits and Finest Performances* (1997, Reader's Digest), *Yesterday Once More* (1998), *Singles 1969-1981* (1999, JP), *Gold* (2000, UK), *Singles 1969-1981* (2000), *Gold* (2001, JP), *Gold* (2004, 35th Anniversary Edition), *Gold* (2005), *Gold* (2005, UK), *Twenty-Two Hits of the Carpenters* (2005, The 10th Anniversary Edition, incl. karaoke disc, HK), *Best Songs* (2017, *Sweet Memory* repackaged, JP)

2004 SACD 5.1 + STEREO FOLD-DOWN MIX (3:46)
Singles 1969-1981 SACD (2004)

2004 STEREO SACD FOLD-DOWN MIX (3:46)
Singles 1969-1981 SACD (2004, CD audio layer), *The Ultimate Collection* (2006, UK), *20/20 Best of the Best Selection* (2009, JP), *40/40* (2009), *40/40* (2009, EU, UK), *40/40 The Best Selection* (2009, JP), *Icon* (2014)

2018 ROYAL PHILHARMONIC VERSION (3:51)
Carpenters with the Royal Philharmonic Orchestra (2018)

Song
Sweet, Sweet Smile

Written by
Juice Newton/Otha Young

Recorded at
A&M Studios—Studio D on 24-track, 2" tape

Instrumental Recording Dates
May 8, 1977 (rhythm tracks)

1977 STUDIO ALBUM VERSION (3:02)
Passage (1977), *The Singles 1974–1978* (1978, JP, CA, UK), *Yesterday Once More* (1984, Silver Eagle Records, US and CA), *Yesterday Once More* (1984, UK), *Yesterday Once More* (1985), *A&M Gold Series Vol. 2* (1986, JP), *Classics Volume 2* (1987), *Reminiscing* (1988, CA), *Anthology* (1989, JP), *A&M New Gold Series Vol. 1* (1990, JP), *A&M Gold Series* (1991, JP), *Startrax* (1991, EU, AU), *Carpenters Collection* (1993, Time Life Music), *Magical Memories of the Carpenters* (1993, UK), *Sweet Memory* (1994, JP), *Reflections* (1995, UK, EU, ZA, DE), *Twenty-Two Hits of the Carpenters* (1995, HK), *Anthology* (1997, remastered reissue, JP), *Their Greatest Hits and Finest Performances* (1997, Reader's Digest), *Yesterday Once More* (1998), *The Essential Collection—1965–1997* (2002), *Gold* (2004, 35th Anniversary Edition), *Gold* (2005), *Reflections—The Best 1200* (2005, JP), *Twenty-Two Hits of the Carpenters* (2005, The 10th Anniversary Edition, incl. karaoke disc, HK), *Japanese Single Box* (2006, JP), *The Ultimate Collection* (2006, NL), *The Ultimate Collection* (2006, UK), *40/40* (2009), *40/40* (2009, EU, UK), *40/40 The Best Selection* (2009, JP), *The Best of the Carpenters* (2009, DE), *Carpenters Collected* (2013), *The Complete Singles* (2015), *Best Songs* (2017, *Sweet Memory* repackaged, JP)

Song
There's a Kind of Hush (All Over the World)

Written by
Les Reed/Geoff Stevens

Recorded at
A&M Studios—Studio D on 24-track, 2" tape

Instrumental Recording Dates
Jan. 30, 1976 (rhythm tracks), Feb. 3 (guitars), Feb. 5 (sax), Feb. 6 (orchestra), Feb. 7 (harp)

The ARP synthesizer track was removed from the 1985 remix, as Richard has much regretted having used it in any of the Carpenters recordings.

"'There's a Kind of Hush' was the first and only time Karen sang a doubled lead vocal, without fully singing out...like she did on 'Postman,'" says Richard.

1976 STUDIO ALBUM VERSION (2:57)
A Kind of Hush (1976), *The Singles 1974–1978* (1978, JP, CA, UK), *The Essential Collection—1965–1997* (2002), *Japanese Single Box* (2006, JP), *The Ultimate Collection* (2006, NL), *Carpenters Collected* (2013), *The Complete Singles* (2015)*
* Recording has been altered from original for faster playback speed
1985 REMIX (3:03)
Yesterday Once More (1985), *A&M Gold Series Vol. 1* (1986, JP), *Classics Volume 2* (1987), *Reminiscing* (1988, CA), *Anthology* (1989, JP), *A&M New Gold Series Vol. 2* (1990, JP), *Carpenters Collection* (1993, Time Life Music), *Magical Memories of the Carpenters* (1993, UK), *Carpenters Best Vol. 1* (1994, JP), *Sweet Memory* (1994, JP), *The Best of Carpenters* (1994, BR), *Twenty-Two Hits of the Carpenters* (1995, HK), *Anthology* (1997, remastered reissue, JP), *Their Greatest Hits and Finest Performances* (1997, Reader's Digest), *Gold* (2004, 35th Anniversary Edition), *Gold* (2005), *Twenty-Two Hits of the Carpenters* (2005, The 10th Anniversary Edition, incl. karaoke disc, HK), *The Ultimate Collection* (2006, UK), *The Nation's Favourite Carpenters Songs* (2016, UK), *Best Songs* (2017, *Sweet Memory* repackaged, JP)

1976

Details

Song
This Masquerade

Written by
Leon Russell

Recorded at
A&M Studios—Studio B on 16-track, 2" tape

Instrumental Recording Dates
March 12, 1973 (rhythm tracks), March 14 (flute solo), March 20 (orchestra)

Notes

Bob Messenger's flute solo was processed through an Eventide "Octaver" (an effect that electronically doubles a tone by adding the lower octave unison) for the 1973 album mix. This was a decision that Richard soon regretted, omitting the effect from all future remixes.

Richard's piano solo was played on the same piano—"piano A," and in the same location in Studio B, as the piano track to "(They Long to Be) Close to You."

Versions

1973 STUDIO ALBUM VERSION (4:50)
Now & Then (1973), *Yesterday Once More* (1984, Silver Eagle Records, US and CA), *Yesterday Once More* (1985), *A&M Gold Series Vol. 2* (1986, JP), *Classics Volume 2* (1987), *Treasures* (1987, JP), *Anthology* (1989, JP), *A&M New Gold Series Vol. 2* (1990, JP), *Only Yesterday: Richard and Karen Carpenter's Greatest Hits* (1990, UK), *Their Greatest Hits* (1990, UK, ZA), *Their Greatest Hits* (1993, DE), *20th Century Masters Millennium Series* (2002), *Japanese Single Box* (2006, JP), *The Ultimate Collection* (2006, NL), *Carpenters Collected* (2013), *The Complete Singles* (2015), *20th Century Masters Millennium Series* (2017, reissue, JP)

1990 REMIX (4:53)
From the Top (1991), *Magical Memories of the Carpenters* (1993, UK), *Carpenters Best Vol. 1* (1994, JP), *Interpretations: A 25th Anniversary Celebration* (1994, UK), *Sweet Memory* (1994, JP), *The Best of Carpenters* (1994, BR), *Interpretations: A 25th Anniversary Celebration* (1995), *Twenty-Two Hits of the Carpenters* (1995, HK), *Anthology* (1997, remastered reissue, JP), *Love Songs* (1997), *Their Greatest Hits and Finest Performances* (1997, Reader's Digest), *Gold* (2000, UK), *Gold* (2001, JP), *20th Century Masters Millennium Series* (2002), *The Essential Collection—1965–1997* (2002), *Gold* (2004, 35th Anniversary Edition), *Singles 1969–1981* SACD (2004, CD audio layer), *Gold* (2005), *Gold* (2005, UK), *Twenty-Two Hits of the Carpenters* (2005, The 10th Anniversary Edition, incl. karaoke disc, HK), *The Ultimate Collection* (2006, UK), *20/20 Best of the Best Selection* (2009, JP), *40/40* (2009), *40/40* (2009, EU, UK), *40/40 The Best Selection* (2009, JP), *Icon* (2014), *20th Century Masters Millennium Series* (2017, reissue, JP), *Best Songs* (2017, *Sweet Memory* repackaged, JP)

1991 REMIX (4:54)
Best of Best + Original Master Karaoke (1992, JP), *Yesterday Once More* (1998)

2004 SACD 5.1 + STEREO FOLD-DOWN MIX (4:53)
Singles 1969–1981 SACD (2004)

2018 ROYAL PHILHARMONIC VERSION (4:51)
Carpenters with the Royal Philharmonic Orchestra (2018)

Las Vegas, 1976

Song
Those Good Old Dreams

Written by
Richard Carpenter/John Bettis

Recorded at
A&M Studios—Studio D on 24-track, 2" tape

Instrumental Recording Dates
Nov. 20 and 22, 1980 (rhythm tracks), Jan. 30, 1981 (guitars), Feb. 11 (horns), Feb. 12 (orchestra), Feb. 26 and Oct. 16 (pedal steel guitar)

1981 STUDIO ALBUM VERSION (4:12)
   Made in America (1981, original LP only), *Yesterday Once More* (1984, UK)
1981 SINGLE MIX (4:12)
   Made in America (1981, CD reissues), *Yesterday Once More* (1984, Silver Eagle Records, US and CA), *Yesterday Once More* (1985), *Classics Volume 2* (1987), *Anthology* (1989, JP), *Only Yesterday: Richard and Karen Carpenter's Greatest Hits* (1990, UK), *Their Greatest Hits* (1990, UK, ZA), *A&M Gold Series* (1991, JP), *Startrax* (1991, EU, AU), *Magical Memories of the Carpenters* (1993, UK), *Their Greatest Hits* (1993, DE), *Carpenters Best Vol. 2* (1994, JP), *Sweet Memory* (1994, JP), *Anthology* (1997, remastered reissue, JP), *Their Greatest Hits and Finest Performances* (1997, Reader's Digest), *Yesterday Once More* (1998), *Singles 1969–1981* (1999, JP), *Singles 1969–1981* (2000), *The Essential Collection—1965–1997* (2002), *Carpenters Perform Carpenter* (2003), *Japanese Single Box* (2006, JP), *The Ultimate Collection* (2006, NL), *The Ultimate Collection* (2006, UK), *20/20 Best of the Best Selection* (2009, JP), *40/40* (2009), *40/40* (2009, EU, UK), *40/40 The Best Selection* (2009, JP), *Carpenters Collected* (2013), *Icon* (2014), *The Complete Singles* (2015), *Best Songs* (2017, *Sweet Memory* repackaged, JP)

Song
Ticket to Ride (*Offering/Ticket to Ride* album version)

Written by
John Lennon/Paul McCartney

Recorded at
A&M Studios—Studio B on 8-track, 1" tape

Instrumental Recording Dates
April 29, 1969 (rhythm tracks)

1969 STUDIO ALBUM VERSION (4:10)
   Offering (1969)/*Ticket to Ride* (1970 *Offering* retitled, repackaged reissue), *The Ultimate Collection* (2006, NL), *Japanese Single Box* (2006, JP), *Carpenters Collected* (2013)
1969 SINGLE VERSION (mono mix) (3:40)
   The Complete Singles (2015)

Lake Tahoe,
Nevada, 1970

Song
Ticket to Ride (*The Singles 1969–1973* single version)

Written by
John Lennon/Paul McCartney

Recorded at
A&M Studios—Studio B on 16-track, 2" tape

Instrumental Recording Dates
Sept. 18, 1973 (rhythm tracks)

August, 1969

1973 SINGLE VERSION (4:10)
The Singles 1969–1973 (1973), *Yesterday Once More* (1984, Silver Eagle Records, US and CA),† *Yesterday Once More* (1984, UK), *Yesterday Once More* (1985),*† *A&M Gold Series Vol. 1* (1986, JP), *Classics Volume 2* (1987),*† *Anthology* (1989, JP),*† *A&M New Gold Series Vol. 1* (1990, JP), *Only Yesterday: Richard and Karen Carpenter's Greatest Hits* (1990, UK), *Their Greatest Hits* (1990, UK, ZA), *A&M Gold Series* (1991, JP), *From the Top* (1991),* *Startrax* (1991, EU, AU), *Carpenters Collection* (1993, Time Life Music),* *Magical Memories of the Carpenters* (1993, UK),* *Their Greatest Hits* (1993, DE), *Carpenters Best Vol. 1* (1994, JP),* *Interpretations: A 25th Anniversary Celebration* (1994, UK),* *Sweet Memory* (1994, JP),* *Reflections* (1995, UK, EU, ZA, DE),* *Twenty-Two Hits of the Carpenters* (1995, HK),* *Anthology* (1997, remastered reissue, JP),*† *Their Greatest Hits and Finest Performances* (1997, Reader's Digest),*† *Yesterday Once More* (1998),*† *Singles 1969–1981* (1999, JP), *Singles 1969–1981* (2000), *By Request* (2000, JP), *Gold* (2000, UK), *Sweet Sweet Smile* (2000, NL),* *Gold* (2001, JP), *The Essential Collection—1965–1997* (2002), *Gold* (2004, 35th Anniversary Edition), *Singles 1969–1981* SACD (2004, CD audio layer), *Gold* (2005), *Gold* (2005, UK), *Twenty-Two Hits of the Carpenters* (2005, The 10th Anniversary Edition, incl. karaoke disc, HK),* *The Ultimate Collection* (2006, UK), *20/20 Best of the Best Selection* (2009, JP), *40/40* (2009), *40/40* (2009, EU, UK), *40/40 The Best Selection* (2009, JP), *The Best Of The Carpenters* (2009, DE),* *Best Songs* (2017, *Sweet Memory* repackaged, JP)*
* Stereo mix is inverted from its original
† Preceding track fade-out overlaps at start
2004 SACD 5.1 + STEREO FOLD-DOWN MIX (4:10)
Singles 1969–1981 SACD (2004)
2018 ROYAL PHILHARMONIC VERSION (4:11)
Carpenters with the Royal Philharmonic Orchestra (2018)

Song
Top of the World (*A Song for You* album version)

Written by
Richard Carpenter/John Bettis

Recorded at
A&M Studios—Studio B on 16-track, 2" tape

Instrumental Recording Dates
March 1, 1972 (rhythm tracks), March 22 (orchestra)

1972 STUDIO ALBUM VERSION (2:56)
A Song for You (1972), *From the Top* (1991), *The Essential Collection—1965–1997* (2002), *Japanese Single Box* (2006, JP), *The Ultimate Collection* (2006, NL), *Carpenters Collected* (2013), *The Nation's Favourite Carpenters Songs* (2016, UK)

Details

Song
Top of the World (*The Singles 1969–1973* single version)

Written by
Richard Carpenter/John Bettis

Recorded at
A&M Studios—Studios B and C on 16-track, 2" tape

Instrumental Recording Dates
March 1, 1972 (rhythm tracks), March 22 (orchestra), Aug. 15, 1973 (guitars), Aug. 16 (pedal steel guitar)

Notes

For its release as a single, a few things were added to the original master of "Top of the World": Richard's rerecorded Wurlitzer electric piano track, along with the addition of pedal steel guitar—played by the great Buddy Emmons—and an entirely new lead vocal by Karen.

As Richard points out, "She did the new lead in Studio C—which to the average listener, may not mean much. But all of the leads done in 'C' sounded the best."

Versions

1973 SINGLE VERSION (2:56)
  The Singles 1969–1973 (1973), *Yesterday Once More* (1984, UK), *A&M Composers Series Vol. 2 Richard Carpenter & John Bettis* (1988, JP), *Reminiscing* (1988, CA), *A Song for You* (1989, Mobile Fidelity Sound Lab), *Anthology* (1989, JP), *A&M New Gold Series Vol. 1* (1990, JP), *Only Yesterday: Richard and Karen Carpenter's Greatest Hits* (1990, UK), *Their Greatest Hits* (1990, UK, ZA), *A&M Gold Series* (1991, JP), *Startrax* (1991, EU, AU), *Their Greatest Hits* (1993, DE), *Gold* (2000, UK), *Gold* (2001, JP), *Gold* (2005, UK), *Japanese Single Box* (2006, JP), *20/20 Best of the Best Selection* (2009, JP), *40/40* (2009), *40/40* (2009, EU, UK), *40/40 The Best Selection* (2009, JP), *Icon* (2014), *The Complete Singles* (2015)

1991 REMIX (3:00)
  Best of Best + Original Master Karaoke (1992, JP), *Carpenters Collection* (1993, Time Life Music), *Magical Memories of the Carpenters* (1993, UK), *Sweet Memory* (1994, JP), *Twenty-Two Hits of the Carpenters* (1995, HK), *Anthology* (1997, remastered reissue, JP), *Love Songs* (1997), *Their Greatest Hits and Finest Performances* (1997, Reader's Digest), *Yesterday Once More* (1998), *Singles 1969–1981* (1999, JP), *By Request* (2000, JP), *Singles 1969–1981* (2000), *20th Century Masters Millennium Series* (2002), *Carpenters Perform Carpenter* (2003, JP), *Gold* (2004, 35th Anniversary Edition), *Gold* (2005), *Twenty-Two Hits of the Carpenters* (2005, The 10th Anniversary Edition, incl. karaoke disc, HK), *20th Century Masters Millennium Series* (2017, reissue, JP), *Best Songs* (2017, *Sweet Memory* repackaged, JP)

2004 SACD 5.1 + STEREO FOLD-DOWN MIX (3:01)
  Singles 1969–1981 SACD (2004)

2004 STEREO SACD FOLD-DOWN MIX (3:01)
  Singles 1969–1981 SACD (2004, CD audio layer), *The Ultimate Collection* (2006, UK)

2018 ROYAL PHILHARMONIC VERSION (2:59)
  Carpenters with the Royal Philharmonic Orchestra (2018)

ANNOUNCING A NEW CARPENTERS HIT:

TOP OF THE WORLD
CARPENTERS (AM 1468)
ON A&M RECORDS
Produced by Richard & Karen Carpenter & Jack Daugherty

Trade ad for "Top of the World," 1973

Song
Touch Me When We're Dancing

Written by
Terry Skinner/J. L. Wallace/Ken Bell

Recorded at
A&M Studios—Studio D on 24-track, 2" tape

Instrumental Recording Dates
June 15, 1980 (rhythm tracks), June 19 and
20 (guitars), Oct. 7 (sax solo), Feb. 11, 1981
(horns), Feb. 12 (orchestra)

Originally recorded for *Horizon* (1975), "Tryin' to Get the Feeling Again" was finally released in 1994 on *Interpretations: A 25th Anniversary Celebration*

1981 STUDIO ALBUM VERSION (3:20)
Made in America (1981), *Yesterday Once More* (1984, Silver Eagle Records, US and CA), *Yesterday Once More* (1984, UK), *Yesterday Once More* (1985), *Classics Volume 2* (1987), *Reminiscing* (1988, CA), *Anthology* (1989, JP), *A&M New Gold Series Vol. 1* (1990, JP), *Only Yesterday: Richard and Karen Carpenter's Greatest Hits* (1990, UK), *Their Greatest Hits* (1990, UK, ZA), *A&M Gold Series* (1991, JP), *From the Top* (1991), *Startrax* (1991, EU, AU), *Carpenters Collection* (1993, Time Life Music), *Magical Memories of the Carpenters* (1993, UK), *Their Greatest Hits* (1993, DE), *Carpenters Best Vol. 1* (1994, JP), *Sweet Memory* (1994, JP), *Twenty-Two Hits of the Carpenters* (1995, HK), *Anthology* (1997, remastered reissue, JP), *Their Greatest Hits and Finest Performances* (1997, Reader's Digest), *Yesterday Once More* (1998), *Singles 1969–1981* (1999, JP), *Singles 1969–1981* (2000), *Gold* (2000, UK), *Gold* (2001, JP), *The Essential Collection—1965–1997* (2002), *Gold* (2004, 35th Anniversary Edition), *Singles 1969–1981* SACD (2004, CD audio layer), *Gold* (2005), *Gold* (2005, UK), *Twenty-Two Hits of the Carpenters* (2005, The 10th Anniversary Edition, incl. karaoke disc, HK), *The Ultimate Collection* (2006, NL), *The Ultimate Collection* (2006, UK), *40/40* (2009), *Carpenters Collected* (2013), *Icon* (2014) *The Complete Singles* 2015), *The Nation's Favourite Carpenters Songs* (2016, UK), *Best Songs* (2017, *Sweet Memory* repackaged, JP)
2004 SACD 5.1 + STEREO FOLD-DOWN MIX (3:18)
Singles 1969–1981 SACD (2004)
2018 ROYAL PHILHARMONIC VERSION (3:16)
Carpenters with the Royal Philharmonic Orchestra (2018)

Song
Tryin' to Get the Feeling Again

Written by
David Pomeranz

Recorded at
A&M Studios—Studio D on 24-track, 2" tape;
Capitol Studios, Hollywood

Instrumental Recording Dates
Jan. 27, 1975 (rhythm tracks), May 31, 1994
(orchestra and guitar solo)

An outtake recorded in early 1975, the chart was finished and strings and background vocals (by Richard) added in 1994, for inclusion on *Interpretations: A 25th Anniversary Celebration.*

Because the vocal is a "work lead" and was never meant to be kept, Karen can be heard turning a page of the lead sheet at the end of the first chorus going into the second verse.

1994 COMPILATION ALBUM VERSION (4:21)
Interpretations: A 25th Anniversary Celebration (1994, UK), *Interpretations: A 25th Anniversary Celebration* (1995), *The Essential Collection—1965–1997* (2002), *Gold* (2004, 35th Anniversary Edition), *Gold* (2005), *The Ultimate Collection* (2006, NL), *The Ultimate Collection* (2006, UK), *Sweet Sixteen* (2009, *40th Anniversary Collector's Edition* bonus disc, JP), *Carpenters Collected* (2013)

Song
Turn Away

Written by
Richard Carpenter/John Bettis

Recorded at
A&M Studios—Studio B on 8-track, 1" tape

Instrumental Recording Dates
May 20, 1969 (rhythm tracks)

1969 STUDIO ALBUM VERSION (3:09)
Offering (1969)/*Ticket to Ride* (1970 *Offering* retitled, repackaged reissue), *Sweet Memory* (1994, JP), *Best Songs* (2017, *Sweet Memory* repackaged, JP)

Details	Notes	Versions

Song
Two Lives

Written by
Mark Jordan

Recorded at
A&M Studios—Studio D on 24-track,
2" tape

Instrumental Recording Dates
June 12, 1980 (rhythm tracks), April 11,
1983 (orchestra)

"Two Lives" is another outtake from the *Made in America* sessions.
    Richard says, "The only trouble with it, is that Karen's lead was a "work lead" and she was too far away from the microphone. If you listen to most of the other songs on that album, she's 'right there.' Whereas, in 'Two Lives,' she's further back. But I like the way she sings it."

1983 STUDIO ALBUM VERSION (4:32)
Voice of the Heart (1983), *Anthology* (1989, JP), *Sweet Memory* (1994, JP), *Anthology* (1997, remastered reissue, JP), *Best Songs* (2017, *Sweet Memory* repackaged, JP)

Song
Two Sides

Written by
Scott E. Davis

Recorded at
A&M Studios—Studio D on 24-track, 2" tape

Instrumental Recording Dates
March 31, 1977 (rhythm tracks), April 1 (orchestra), April 6 (guitars)

1977 STUDIO ALBUM VERSION (3:25)
Passage (1977), *Treasures* (1987, JP), *Magical Memories of the Carpenters* (1993, Reader's Digest, UK, AU, EU), *Sweet Memory* (1994, JP), *The Complete Singles* (2015), *Best Songs* (2017, *Sweet Memory* repackaged, JP)

Song
The Uninvited Guest

Written by
Buddy Kaye/Jeffrey Tweel

Recorded at
A&M Studios—Studio D on 24-track, 2" tape

Instrumental Recording Dates
Oct. 23, 1980 (rhythm tracks), April 14, 1983 (orchestra)

1989 STUDIO ALBUM VERSION (4:24)
Lovelines (1989), *The Complete Singles* (2015)

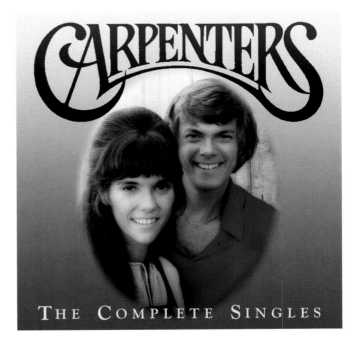

"The Uninvited Guest" appears on the rare compilation *The Complete Singles*

Details

Song
We've Only Just Begun

Written by
Paul Williams/Roger Nichols

Recorded at
A&M Studios—Studio B on 16-track, 2" tape

Instrumental Recording Dates
June 13, 1970 (rhythm tracks), July 17 (clarinet), July 20 (orchestra)

Misprint: Some picture sleeves for "We've Only Just Begun" erroneously list the B-side as "Maybe It's You"

Notes

In 1985, the original "mono" piano track was replaced by a stereo piano (with a few slight embellishments), and would be the piano track used on all subsequent remixes.

An alternate tom-tom fill on the drum track was also included in all the remixes from 1985, on, replacing the original fill heard just before the four-part, twelve-voice chord singing "We've only begun…" leading into the second verse.

Karen plays the tambourine track on "We've Only Just Begun," as she did on most of the Carpenters' recordings.

Versions

1970 STUDIO ALBUM VERSION (3:04)
Close to You (1970), *The Singles 1969–1973* (1973),* *Yesterday Once More* (1984, Silver Eagle Records, US and CA), *Yesterday Once More* (1984, UK), *A&M Gold Series Vol. 2* (1986, JP), *A&M New Gold Series Vol. 2* (1990, JP), *The Essential Collection—1965–1997* (2002), *Japanese Single Box* (2006, JP), *The Ultimate Collection* (2006, NL), *Carpenters Collected* (2013), *The Complete Singles* (2015)
* Starts with overture—total running time (4:09)

1985 REMIX (3:04)
Yesterday Once More (1985), *Classics Volume 2* (1987), *Reminiscing* (1988, CA), *Anthology* (1989, JP), *By Request* (2000, JP), *Only Yesterday: Richard and Karen Carpenter's Greatest Hits* (1990, UK), *Their Greatest Hits* (1990, UK, ZA), *From the Top* (1991), *Their Greatest Hits* (1993, DE), *Interpretations: A 25th Anniversary Celebration* (1994, UK), *Interpretations: A 25th Anniversary Celebration* (1995), *Twenty-Two Hits of the Carpenters* (1995, HK), *Yesterday Once More* (1998), *Singles 1969–1981* (1999, JP), *Gold* (2000, UK), *Singles 1969–1981* (2000), *Gold* (2001, JP), *Gold* (2004, 35th Anniversary Edition), *Singles 1969–1981* SACD (2004, CD audio layer), *Gold* (2005), *Gold* (2005, UK), *Twenty-Two Hits of the Carpenters* (2005, The 10th Anniversary Edition, incl. karaoke disc, HK), *The Ultimate Collection* (2006, UK), *20/20 Best of the Best Selection* (2009, JP), *40/40* (2009), *40/40* (2009, EU, UK), *40/40 The Best Selection* (2009, JP), *Icon* (2014), *The Nation's Favourite Carpenters Songs* (2016, UK)

1991 REMIX (3:04)
Best of Best + Original Master Karaoke (1992, JP), *Carpenters Collection* (1993, Time Life Music), *Magical Memories of the Carpenters* (1993, UK), *Carpenters Best Vol. 2* (1994, JP), *Sweet Memory* (1994, JP), *The Best of Carpenters* (1994, BR), *Anthology* (1997, remastered reissue, JP), *Love Songs* (1997), *Their Greatest Hits and Finest Performances* (1997, Reader's Digest), *Best Songs* (2017, *Sweet Memory* repackaged, JP)

2004 SACD 5.1 + STEREO FOLD-DOWN MIX (3:04)
Singles 1969–1981 SACD (2004)

2018 ROYAL PHILHARMONIC VERSION (4:00)
Carpenters with the Royal Philharmonic Orchestra (2018)

Song
What Are You Doing New Year's Eve?

Written by
Frank Loesser

Recorded at
A&M Studios—Studio D on 24-track, 2" tape

Instrumental Recording Dates
Dec. 8, 1977 (orchestra)

1984 STUDIO ALBUM VERSION (2:51)
An Old-Fashioned Christmas (1984), *Christmas with the Carpenters* (1992, Time Life Music), *Christmas Collection* (1996)

Details	Notes	Versions
Song What's the Use? **Written by** Richard Carpenter/John Bettis **Recorded at** A&M Studios—Studio B on 8-track, 1" tape **Instrumental Recording Dates** June 18, 1969 (rhythm tracks)	The background vocal lyric Richard sings during the second and third chorus is "I've a better life in mind."	1969 STUDIO ALBUM VERSION (2:43) *Offering* (1969)/*Ticket to Ride* (1970 *Offering* retitled, repackaged reissue)
Song When I Fall in Love **Written by** Edward Heyman/Victor Young **Recorded at** A&M Studios—Studio D on 24-track, 2" tape **Instrumental Recording Dates** Aug. 12, 1978 (rhythm tracks)		1989 STUDIO ALBUM VERSION (3:08) *Lovelines* (1989) 1990 REMIX (3:08) *Magical Memories of the Carpenters* (1993, UK), *Interpretations: A 25th Anniversary Celebration* (1994, UK), *Sweet Memory* (1994, JP), *Interpretations: A 25th Anniversary Celebration* (1995), *Love Songs* (1997), *Best Songs* (2017, *Sweet Memory* repackaged, JP)
Song When It's Gone (It's Just Gone) **Written by** Randy Handley **Recorded at** A&M Studios—Studio D on 24-track, 2" tape **Instrumental Recording Dates** June 12, 1980 (rhythm tracks), Jan. 27, 1981 (pedal steel guitar), Jan. 29 (guitars), Feb. 11 (horns), Feb. 12 (strings)		1981 STUDIO ALBUM VERSION (5:01) *Made in America* (1981), *Treasures* (1987, JP), *From the Top* (1991), *Magical Memories of the Carpenters* (1993, UK), *Interpretations: A 25th Anniversary Celebration* (1994, UK), *Sweet Memory* (1994, JP), *Interpretations: A 25th Anniversary Celebration* (1995), *Their Greatest Hits and Finest Performances* (1997, Reader's Digest), *The Essential Collection—1965–1997* (2002), *The Ultimate Collection* (2006, UK), *40/40* (2009), *40/40* (2009, EU, UK), *40/40 The Best Selection* (2009, JP), *The Complete Singles* (2015), *Best Songs* (2017, *Sweet Memory* repackaged, JP)
Song When Time Was All We Had **Written by** Richard Carpenter/Pamela Phillips Oland **Recorded at** A&M Studios—Studio D on 24-track, 2" tape **Instrumental Recording Dates** 1987	Recorded for Richard's solo album *Time*, released in 1987.	1987 (RICHARD CARPENTER SOLO) ALBUM VERSION (3:01) *The Ultimate Collection* (2006, NL), *Carpenters Collected* (2013)
Song When You've Got What It Takes **Written by** Roger Nichols/William Lane **Recorded at** A&M Studios—Studio D on 24-track, 2" tape **Instrumental Recording Dates** Aug. 20, 1980 (rhythm tracks), Feb. 11, 1981 (horns), Feb. 12 (strings), Feb. 26 (percussion)		1981 STUDIO ALBUM VERSION (3:41) *Made in America* (1981), *Treasures* (1987, JP), *Sweet Memory* (1994, JP), *Japanese Single Box* (2006, JP),* *40/40* (2009), *40/40* (2009, EU, UK), *40/40 The Best Selection* (2009, JP), *The Complete Singles* (2015), *Best Songs* (2017, *Sweet Memory* repackaged, JP) * Track starts with clean open, no cross-fade

Details	Notes	Versions
Song Where Do I Go From Here? **Written by** Parker McGee **Recorded at** A&M Studios—Studio D on 24-track, 2" tape **Instrumental Recording Dates** Aug. 11, 1978 (rhythm tracks), Aug. 17 and 21 (guitars)		**1989 STUDIO ALBUM VERSION (4:24)** *Lovelines* (1989), *From the Top* (1991), *Interpretations: A 25th Anniversary Celebration* (1994, UK), *Sweet Memory* (1994, JP), *Love Songs* (1997), *The Essential Collection—1965–1997* (2002), *40/40* (2009), *40/40* (2009, EU, UK), *40/40 The Best Selection* (2009, JP), *Best Songs* (2017, *Sweet Memory* repackaged, JP)
Song White Christmas **Written by** Irving Berlin **Recorded at** A&M Studios—Studio D on 24-track, 2" tape **Instrumental Recording Dates** Dec. 7, 1977 (orchestra)	This is the stand-alone track from the "Winter Wonderland"/"Silver Bells"/"White Christmas" medley on *Christmas Portrait*.	**1990 REMIX (2:29)** *From the Top* (1991), *Their Greatest Hits and Finest Performances* (1997, Reader's Digest), *The Essential Collection—1965–1997* (2002), *Christmas with the Carpenters* (1992, Time Life Music)* * Yamaha DX7 tag added to end—total running time (2:41)
Song Winter Wonderland/Silver Bells/White Christmas **Written by** Dick Smith/Felix Bernard/Jay Livingston/Ray Evans/Irving Berlin **Recorded at** A&M Studios—Studio D on 24-track, 2" tape **Instrumental Recording Dates** 1977–78		**1978 STUDIO ALBUM VERSION (5:31)** *Christmas Portrait* (1978), *Christmas Portrait* (1984, DE), *Christmas Portrait—The Special Edition* (1984) **1990 REMIX (5:31)** *Christmas Collection* (1996)* * Acoustic piano tag at end included in total running time
Song Without a Song (a cappella intro version) **Written by** Vincent Youmans/Billy Rose/Edward Eliscu **Recorded at** A&M Studios—Studio D on 24-track, 2" tape **Instrumental Recording Dates** 1980	To keep all of the vocals "in-time," Richard and Karen overdubbed them to a click track in 4/4 time, with the occasional measure of 6/4 interspersed, which allowed for a more "rubato" feel once the click was removed. Recorded for the opening of their ABC TV special *Music, Music, Music*.	**1994 COMPILATION ALBUM MIX (1:01)** *Interpretations: A 25th Anniversary Celebration* (1994, UK), *Interpretations: A 25th Anniversary Celebration* (1995)
Song Without a Song (full-length version) **Written by** Vincent Youmans/Billy Rose/Edward Eliscu **Recorded at** A&M Studios—Studio D on 24-track, 2" tape **Instrumental Recording Dates** 1980	Serving as the opener for the Carpenters' ABC TV special *Music, Music, Music*, special guests John Davidson and Ella Fitzgerald sang the original duet. Richard and Karen recorded the duet vocals for their personal collection, which is presented here.	**2001 ALBUM VERSION (1:58)** *As Time Goes By* (2001, JP), *As Time Goes By* (2004)

Details

Song
Yesterday Once More

Written by
Richard Carpenter/John Bettis

Recorded at
A&M Studios—Studio B on 16-track, 2" tape

Instrumental Recording Dates
Feb. 14, 1973 (rhythm tracks), Feb. 16
(orchestra)

Notes

The 1973 single mix includes additional
electric guitar fills, played by Tony Peluso.
  The 1985 remix replaces the original
"mono" piano track with stereo, adds an
arpeggiated Yamaha DX7 (doubling the
harp) in the second verse, and deletes the
tambourine from the choruses.

Versions

1973 STUDIO ALBUM VERSION (3:50)
  Now & Then (1973), *The Ultimate Collection*
  (2006, NL), *Carpenters Collected* (2013)
1973 SINGLE MIX (3:50)
  The Singles 1969–1973 (1973),* *Yesterday Once
  More* (1984, Silver Eagle Records, US and
  CA), *Yesterday Once More* (1984, UK), *A&M
  Gold Series Vol. 1* (1986, JP), *Anthology* (1989,
  JP), *A&M New Gold Series Vol. 2* (1990, JP),
  Japanese Single Box (2006, JP), *The Complete
  Singles* (2015)
  * The Canadian CD release of this title con-
  tains the 1985 remix
1985 REMIX (3:50)
  Yesterday Once More (1985), *Classics Volume 2*
  (1987), *A&M Composers Series Vol. 2 Richard
  Carpenter & John Bettis* (1988, JP), *Only Yesterday: Richard and
  Karen Carpenter's Greatest Hits* (1990, UK),
  Their Greatest Hits (1990, UK, ZA), *From the
  Top* (1991), *Carpenters Collection* (1993, Time
  Life Music), *Their Greatest Hits* (1993, DE),
  Magical Memories of the Carpenters (1993,
  UK), *Carpenters Best Vol. 2* (1994, JP), *Sweet
  Memory* (1994, JP), *The Best of Carpenters*
  (1994, BR), *Twenty-Two Hits of the Carpenters*
  (1995, HK), *Anthology* (1997, remastered
  reissue, JP), *Their Greatest Hits and Finest
  Performances* (1997, Reader's Digest), *20th
  Century Masters Millennium Series* (2002),
  The Essential Collection—1965–1997 (2002),
  Carpenters Perform Carpenter (2003), *Twenty-
  Two Hits of the Carpenters* (2005, The 10th
  Anniversary Edition, incl. karaoke disc,
  HK), *The Ultimate Collection* (2006, UK),
  20th Century Masters Millennium Series (2017,
  reissue, JP), *Best Songs* (2017, *Sweet Memory*
  repackaged, JP)
1991 REMIX (3:59)
  Best of Best + Original Master Karaoke (1992,
  JP), *Yesterday Once More* (1998), *Singles
  1969–1981* (1999, JP), *By Request* (2000, JP),
  Gold (2000, UK), *Singles 1969–1981* (2000),
  Gold (2001, JP), *Gold* (2004, 35th Anniversary
  Edition), *Singles 1969–1981* SACD (2004, CD
  audio layer), *Gold* (2005), *Gold* (2005, UK),
  20/20 Best of the Best Selection (2009, JP),
  40/40 (2009), *40/40* (2009, EU, UK), *40/40
  The Best Selection* (2009, JP), *Icon* (2014), *The
  Nation's Favourite Carpenters Songs* (2016,
  UK)
2004 SACD 5.1 + STEREO FOLD-DOWN MIX
(3:57)
  Singles 1969–1981 SACD (2004)
2018 ROYAL PHILHARMONIC VERSION
(3:57)
  *Carpenters with the Royal Philharmonic
  Orchestra* (2018)

Master tape legend
for "Yesterday
Once More"

Details	Notes	Versions
Song Yesterday Once More (reprise) **Written by** Richard Carpenter/John Bettis **Recorded at** A&M Studios—Studio B on 16-track, 2" tape **Instrumental Recording Dates** 1973	The background vocal lyric sung by Richard and Karen following "so fine" (0:31) is "Cumma cumma-oh, shoo bop, she down, down." Richard says, "This is followed by the mystery 'groan' that happened while mastering—to which [mastering engineer] Bernie [Grundman] had no answer." Bassist Joe Osborn was known for his unique style—which was achieved by playing on a fretted, 1960 Fender Jazz bass, strung with La Bella brand flat wound strings, using a guitar pick. The "Yesterday Once More" reprise was one of the rare instances where Richard requested that Osborn deviate from his original sound, using a fretless bass for the recording.	1973 STUDIO ALBUM VERSION (0:58) *Now & Then* (1973), *Anthology* (1989, JP) 1990 REMIX (1:01) *From the Top* (1991), *Sweet Memory* (1994, JP), *Anthology* (1997, remastered reissue, JP), *Their Greatest Hits and Finest Performances* (1997, Reader's Digest), *Best Songs* (2017, *Sweet Memory* repackaged, JP), *The Essential Collection—1965–1997* (2002)
Song You **Written by** Randy Edelman **Recorded at** A&M Studios—Studio D on 24-track, 2" tape **Instrumental Recording Dates** Jan. 24, 1976 (rhythm tracks), Jan. 26 and Feb. 3 (guitars), Feb. 6 (orchestra)	The playback speed on the original LP mix of "You" was increased slightly and also included on the 1993 UK compilation *Magical Memories of the Carpenters* and the 1994 Japanese compilation *Sweet Memory*. A few years later, however, the "Remastered Classics" version of *A Kind of Hush* on CD in the United States and the Japanese *By Request* both featured the recording returned to normal playback speed. The slower playback version is also included in the 30th, 35th, and 40th Anniversary Collector's Edition box sets.	1976 STUDIO ALBUM VERSION (3:45) *A Kind of Hush* (1976), *Magical Memories of the Carpenters* (1993, UK), *Sweet Memory* (1994, JP), *By Request* (2000, JP), *Best Songs* (2017, *Sweet Memory* repackaged, JP)
Song You'll Love Me (Summerchimes recording) **Written by** Richard Carpenter **Recorded at** United Audio—Orange County, CA **Instrumental Recording Dates** May 1967	A demo recorded by the Summerchimes (later renamed Spectrum) in 1967.	1967 DEMO (2:26) *From the Top* (1991), *The Essential Collection—1965–1997* (2002)
Song Your Baby Doesn't Love You Anymore **Written by** Larry Weiss **Recorded at** A&M Studios—Studio D on 24-track, 2" tape **Instrumental Recording Dates** Oct. 22, 1980 (rhythm tracks), April 11, 1983 (horns), April 14 (orchestra)		1983 STUDIO ALBUM VERSION (3:51) *Voice of the Heart* (1983), *Magical Memories of the Carpenters* (1993, UK), *Sweet Memory* (1994, JP), *Reflections* (1995, UK, EU, ZA, DE), *Their Greatest Hits and Finest Performances* (1997, Reader's Digest), *Sweet Sweet Smile* (2000, NL), *Gold* (2004, 35th Anniversary Edition), *Gold* (2005), *Reflections—The Best 1200* (2005, JP), *The Ultimate Collection* (2006, UK), *40/40* (2009), *40/40* (2009, EU, UK), *40/40 The Best Selection* (2009, JP), *The Complete Singles* (2015), *Best Songs* (2017, *Sweet Memory* repackaged, JP)

Details	Notes	Versions

Song
Your Wonderful Parade

Written by
Richard Carpenter/John Bettis

Recorded at
Bassist Joe Osborn's garage studio, on 4-track tape; A&M Studios—Studio B on 8-track, 1" tape

Instrumental Recording Dates
1968 (rhythm tracks)

One of several demos recorded at Joe Osborn's garage studio on four-track tape, the tracks for "Your Wonderful Parade" were eventually transferred over to eight-track tape at A&M Studios for inclusion on *Offering*. Real strings were added, Richard's vocals rerecorded, and the tape speed increased through variable speed oscillation (VSO) during mixdown.

In hindsight, Richard recalls that the song was already recorded "too fast" to begin with and regrets the decision to speed it up during mixdown.

The "phase" effect heard during the fade-out was the result of an unexplained glitch during mastering, remaining a mystery to Richard to this day.

1968 DEMO VERSION (2:22)
From the Top (1991), *The Essential Collection—1965–1997* (2002)
1969 STUDIO ALBUM VERSION (2:57)
Offering (1969)/*Ticket to Ride* (1970 retitled, repackaged reissue), *Treasures* (1987, JP), *A&M Composers Series Vol. 2 Richard Carpenter & John Bettis* (1988, JP)
1969 SINGLE VERSION (MONO MIX) (2:33)
The Complete Singles (2015)

Song
You're Enough

Written by
Richard Carpenter/John Bettis

Recorded at
A&M Studios—Studio D on 24-track, 2" tape

Instrumental Recording Dates
April 23, 1982 (rhythm tracks), April 11, 1983 (horns), April 14 (orchestra)

1983 STUDIO ALBUM VERSION (3:46)
Voice of the Heart (1983)

Song
You're Just in Love

Written by
Irving Berlin

Recorded at
A&M Studios—Studio D on 24-track, 2" tape

Instrumental Recording Dates
1980

2001 ALBUM VERSION (3:53)
As Time Goes By (2001, JP), *As Time Goes By* (2004)

Song
You're the One

Written by
Steve Ferguson

Recorded at
A&M Studios—Studio D on 24-track, 2" tape

Instrumental Recording Dates
April 2, 1977 (rhythm tracks), April 12 (orchestra), June 1 (harp)

1989 STUDIO ALBUM VERSION (4:14)
Lovelines (1989), *Interpretations: A 25th Anniversary Celebration* (1994, UK), *Sweet Memory* (1994, JP), *Love Songs* (1997), *The Ultimate Collection* (2006, UK), *Best Songs* (2017, *Sweet Memory* repackaged, JP)

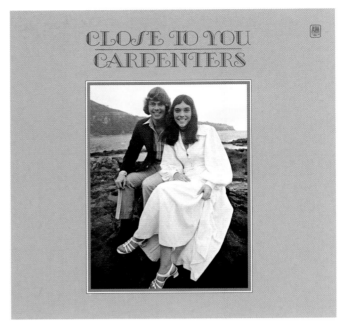
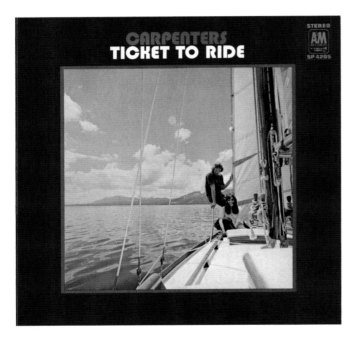
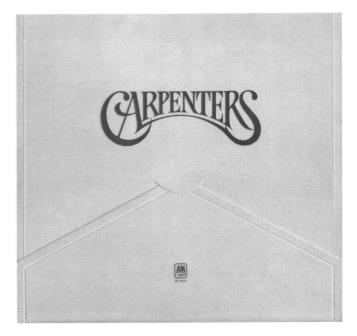

The US Studio Albums:

Offering (1969)
Close to You (Aug. 1970)
Ticket to Ride (Nov. 1970)
Carpenters [The Tan Album] (1971)

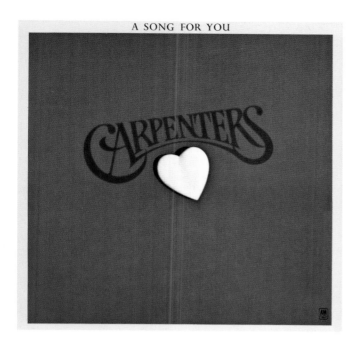

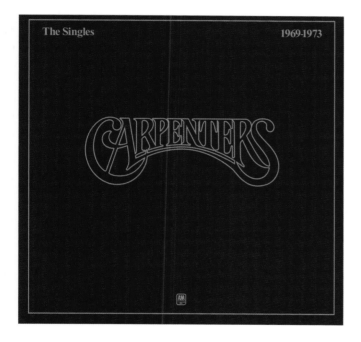

A Song for You (1972)
Now & Then (May 1973)
The Singles 1969–1973 (Nov. 1973)
Horizon (1975)

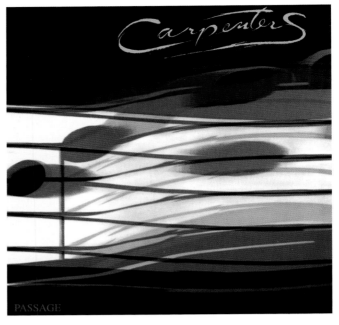

A Kind of Hush (1976)
Passage (1977)
Christmas Portrait (1978)
Made in America (1981)

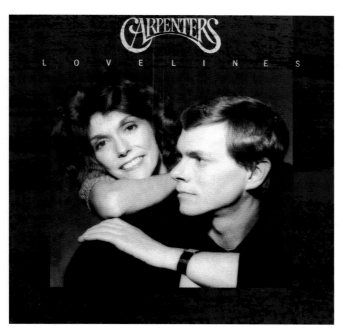

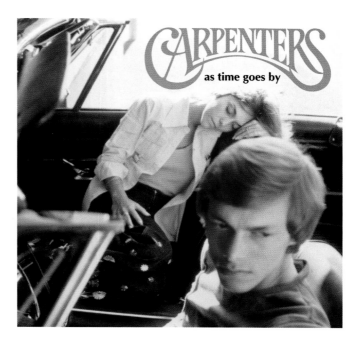

Voice of the Heart (1983)
An Old-Fashioned Christmas (1984)
Lovelines (1989)
As Time Goes By (2004)

On the Charts

The grid that follows documents peak positions for Carpenters recordings in the countries indicated. This is but a sampling of activity in the dozens of countries where the Carpenters charted. It is limited by both space and the challenges of obtaining reliable data from some territories and sources.

The figure in each listing indicates the title's highest chart position. Detailed information on chart sources is in this book's note section.

Works are broken into four categories: Studio Albums, Live Recordings, Compilations, and Singles. "Studio Albums" are defined as releases consisting solely of newly recorded or previously unreleased material. "Compilations" contain all or primarily previously released material.

Some recordings defy easy categorization. A note that although Richard used original Carpenters recordings as the foundation for *Carpenters with the Royal Philharmonic Orchestra* (2018), it is listed here as a studio album, as hundreds of hours went into preparing, recording, and postproduction of the project. Richard says he was "augmenting" the originals to deliver the recordings as he'd always intended but that budgets, technology, time, and experience did not allow for back in the day. *RPO* was a Herculean effort, and less time has been spent recording entirely new albums.

As for singles, in most cases they are listed as they appeared on the charts. An exception is "Superstar"/"Bless the Beasts and Children," which was listed as a double A-side for a portion of its *Billboard* Hot 100 run in the United States, but only as "Superstar" at its chart peak. Conversely, "Superstar" and "For All We Know" were listed together on the singles charts in the United Kingdom. And although the Carpenters never intended B-sides "Bless the Beasts and Children" and "Mr. Guder" to have respective solo pop-chart rides in the US and Canada, they did. Therefore, they get listings.

Though the single "If I Had You" is credited to Karen Carpenter, the CD- and cassette-single release listed here is the Carpenters' *Lovelines* version. It was substantially reworked—with original producer Phil Ramone's blessing—by Richard, starting with tracks from the *Karen Carpenter* album sessions.

Lack of space explains why digital-chart data was used for only the recently released *Carpenters with the Royal Philharmonic Orchestra* (2018) and the perennial chart hit *Christmas Portrait*. The breadth of countries covered by the iTunes/Amazon Music charts alone is incredible. And the complexities of the Spotify charts are worthy of their own book. Maybe it'll be our next one.

Finally, it's important to note that our chart researchers, Simon Worsley and Nancy Mescon, pored over thousands of archived pages of the publications cited to ensure the accuracy of data for each release. The researchers gathered, in addition to chart peak, figures including weeks at chart peak, total weeks on the charts, and year-end ranks. Space does not allow for inclusion of all that data here, but much of that information is cited throughout the book.

Given that this *is* a chapter titled "On the Charts," we just couldn't resist dropping a few of our favorite Carpenters chart achievements here.

· *The Close to You* album was on the US *Billboard* pop-album charts for an impressive eighty-seven consecutive weeks. And, according to Richard—meaning it's not mere record-company hype—the album sold more than five million copies in the US alone by the end of that first chart run.

· Starting February 2, 1974, *The Singles 1969–1973* was No. 1 for a jaw-dropping seventeen nonconsecutive weeks in the UK. The greatest-hits set spent 64 weeks in the Top 10 and a total 112 weeks in the Top 40. It was the No. 1 album of 1974 in the U.K.

· Also in 1974, a compilation, *Golden Prize Vol. 2*, spent eighteen weeks at the chart summit in Japan. Nearly twenty-two years later, another Japanese collection, *Twenty-Two Hits of the Carpenters* (1995) began a 121-week run on that country's charts.

· And, finally, perhaps our favorite: chart achievements for "Merry Christmas, Darling." When we include both the 1970 original single version and the 1978 rerecording and rereleases, as well as airplay of both versions, and log start-to-finish activity (nonconsecutive) on all US *Billboard* charts since the song's first appearance—whew!—that's a total forty-nine years and seventeen days. At the writing, the song's last appearance on any *Billboard* chart was at No. 40 on the Holiday 100 on January 4, 2020. However, we have no doubt it'll be back. That's what classics do.

Page 310:
The Chart Debut: *Billboard* Top 40 Easy Listening Chart, Dec. 27, 1969

Right: End of a run, but just the beginning

The Studio Albums

Year	Studio Album	Chart	Peak Position
1969	*Offering*	*United States/*Billboard* Top Pop Albums	150
		United Kingdom	20
		Australia	19
		Zimbabwe	18
		*While *Offering* failed to chart, a 1970 repackaged, retitled reissue, *Ticket to Ride*, debuted on the *Billboard* Top LPs survey in March 1971.	
1970	*Close to You*	United States/*Billboard* Top Pop Albums	2
		United States/*Cash Box* Top Pop Albums	1
		United States/*Record World* Top Pop Albums	3
		United Kingdom	23
		Japan	53
		Australia	16
		Canada	1
1971	*Carpenters* [The Tan Album]	United States/*Billboard* Top Pop Albums	2
		United States/*Cash Box* Top Pop Albums	2
		United States/*Record World* Top Pop Albums	2
		United Kingdom	11
		Japan	47
		Australia	16
		Canada	6
1972	*A Song for You*	United States/*Billboard* Top Pop Albums	4
		United States/*Cash Box* Top Pop Albums	4
		United States/*Record World* Top Pop Albums	3
		United Kingdom	13
		Japan	5
		Australia	6
		Canada	5
1973	*Now & Then*	United States/*Billboard* Top Pop Albums	2
		United States/*Cash Box* Top Pop Albums	1
		United States/*Record World* Top Pop Albums	1
		United Kingdom	2
		Japan	1
		Australia	3
		Canada	2
		Netherlands	2
		Norway	12
1975	*Horizon*	United States/*Billboard* Top Pop Albums	13
		United States/*Cash Box* Top Pop Albums	10
		United States/*Record World*	13
		United Kingdom	1
		Japan	1
		Australia	21
		Canada	4
		Germany	42
		New Zealand	3
		Norway	5
		Zimbabwe	1

Year	Studio Album	Chart	Peak Position
1976	*A Kind of Hush*	United States/*Billboard* Top Pop Albums	33
		United States/*Cash Box* Top Pop Albums	29
		United Kingdom	3
		Japan	5
		Australia	57
		Canada	22
		New Zealand	15
		Norway	17
		Zimbabwe	4
1977	*Passage*	United States/*Billboard* Top Pop Albums	49
		United States/*Cash Box* Top Pop Albums	53
		United States/*Record World*	55
		United Kingdom	12
		Japan	7
		Australia	48
		Canada	57
1978	*Christmas Portrait*	United States/*Billboard* Top Pop Albums	145
1981	*Made in America*	United States/*Billboard* Top Pop Albums	52
		United States/*Cash Box* Top Pop Albums	66
		United States/*Record World* Top Pop Albums	69
		United Kingdom	12
		Japan	44
		Australia	50
1983	*Voice of the Heart*	United States/*Billboard* Top Pop Albums	46
		United States/*Cash Box* Top Pop Albums	38
		United Kingdom	6
		Japan	41
		Australia	54
		New Zealand	10
1984	*Christmas Portrait: Special Edition*	United States/*Billboard* Top Pop Albums	56
		United States/*Billboard* Top Holiday Albums	5
		United Kingdom	104
1984	*An Old-Fashioned Christmas*	United States/*Billboard* Top Pop Albums	190
		United States/*Billboard* Top Holiday Albums	25
		Japan	42
1989	*Lovelines*	United Kingdom	73
2001	*As Time Goes By*	Japan	18
2018	*Carpenters with the Royal Philharmonic Orchestra*	United States/*Billboard* Top Classical Albums	2
		United Kingdom	8
		Japan	25
		Australia	29

The Live Albums

Year	Live Album	Chart	Peak Position
1975	*Live in Japan*	Japan	8
1977	*Live at the Palladium*	United Kingdom Japan	28 24

The Compilations

Year	Compilation	Chart	Peak Position
1971	*Golden Prize*	Japan	3
1972	*Golden Double Deluxe*	Japan	10
1972	*Great Hits of the Carpenters*	Australia	3
1972	*Gem of Carpenters*	Japan	13
1973	*Super Max 20*	Japan	26
1973	*Gem of Carpenters II*	Japan	3
1973	*The Singles 1969–1973*	United States/*Billboard* Top Pop Albums United States/*Cash Box* Top Pop Albums United States/*Record World* Top Pop Albums United Kingdom Canada France Netherlands Spain	1 1 1 1 1 2 2 8
1974	*Great Hits of the Carpenters Vol. II 1969–1973*	Australia	24
1974	*Golden Prize Vol. 2*	Japan	1
1974	*Gem of Carpenters III*	Japan	13
1975	*Gem of Carpenters IV*	Japan	16
1976	*Golden Prize Vol. 3: Solitaire*	Japan	8
1976	*Gem of Carpenters V*	Japan	42
1978	*The Singles 1974–1978*	United Kingdom	2

Year	Compilation	Chart	Peak Position
1980	*Beautiful Moments*	Germany	1
		Austria	2
1981	*Beautiful Lovesongs*	Netherlands	8
1982	*The Very Best of Carpenters*	Australia	1
		New Zealand	2
1984	*Yesterday Once More* (UK edition)	United Kingdom	10
1985	*Yesterday Once More* (US/International edition)	United States/*Billboard* Top Pop Albums	144
		Japan	25
1987	*The Carpenters Collection: Their Greatest Hits*	Netherlands	31
1990	*Only Yesterday: Richard & Karen Carpenter's Greatest Hits*	United Kingdom	1
		Australia	15
		Ireland	1
		Netherlands	3
		New Zealand	1
		Norway	8
		Spain	34
1994	*Interpretations: A 25th Anniversary Celebration*	United Kingdom	29
1995	*Twenty-Two Hits of the Carpenters*	Japan	3
1996	*Christmas Collection*	United States/*Billboard* Top Holiday Singles	40
1997	*Love Songs*	United States/*Billboard* Top Pop Albums	106
		United Kingdom	47
		Ireland	73
		Norway	34
2000	*Singles 1969–1981*	United States/*Billboard* Top Pop Albums	45
		United Kingdom	65
		Japan	73
		Ireland	12
2000	*Gold: Greatest Hits*	United Kingdom	4
		Japan	75
		DK	24
		Ireland	32
		New Zealand	17
2001	*Yesterday Once More: De Nederlandse Singles Collectie*	Netherlands	22

Year	Compilation	Chart	Peak Position
2004	*Gold: 35th Anniversary Edition*	United States/*Billboard* Top Pop Albums	106
2006	*The Ultimate Collection*	United Kingdom	53
		Netherlands	17
2009	*40/40*	United Kingdom	21
		Japan	3
		DK	7
		Norway	2
		Spain	92
2009	*20/20*	Japan	26
2013	*Collected*	Netherlands	25
2016	*The Nation's Favourite Carpenters Song*s	United Kingdom	2

The Singles

Year	Single	Chart	Peak Position
1969	"Ticket to Ride"	United States/*Billboard* Top Pop Singles	54
		United States/*Billboard* Adult Contemporary Singles	19
		United States/*Cash Box* Top Pop Singles	78
		United States/*Record World* Top Pop Singles	86
1970	"(They Long to Be) Close to You"	United States/*Billboard* Top Pop Singles	1
		United States/*Billboard* Adult Contemporary Singles	1
		United States/*Cash Box* Top Pop Singles	1
		United States/*Record World* Top Pop Singles	1
		United Kingdom	6
		Japan	71
		Australia	1
		Belgium	30
		Canada	1
		France	64
		Ireland	6
		Netherlands	30
		New Zealand	9
		Spain	8
		Zimbabwe	8
1970	"We've Only Just Begun"	United States/*Billboard* Top Pop Singles	2
		United States/*Billboard* Adult Contemporary Singles	1
		United States/*Cash Box* Top Pop Singles	1
		United States/*Record World* Top Pop Singles	1
		United Kingdom	28
		Japan	71
		Australia	6
		Canada	1
		Spain	26

Year	Single	Chart	Peak Position
1970	"Merry Christmas, Darling"	United States/*Billboard* Top Pop Singles	1
		United States/*Cash Box* Top Pop Singles	41
		United Kingdom	45
		Canada	50
		France	64
1970	"Mr. Guder"	Canada	78
1971	"For All We Know"	United States/*Billboard* Top Pop Singles	3
		United States/*Billboard* Adult Contemporary Singles	1
		United States/*Cash Box* Top Pop Singles	6
		United States/*Record World* Top Pop Singles	4
		Australia	10
		Canada	5
		New Zealand	6
1971	"Rainy Days and Mondays"	United States/*Billboard* Top Pop Singles	2
		United States/*Billboard* Adult Contemporary Singles	1
		United States/*Cash Box* Top Pop Singles	2
		United States/*Record World* Top Pop Singles	2
		United Kingdom	53
		Japan	72
		Australia	35
		Canada	3
		New Zealand	19
		Zimbabwe	19
1971	"Superstar"	United States/*Billboard* Top Pop Singles	2
		United States/*Billboard* Adult Contemporary Singles	1
		United States/*Cash Box* Top Pop Singles	2
		United States/*Record World* Top Pop Singles	1
		United Kingdom	18
		Japan	7
		Australia	35
		Canada	3
		Netherlands	19
		New Zealand	9
1971	"Superstar/For All We Know" (UK release)	United Kingdom	18
1971	"Bless the Beasts and Children"	United States/*Billboard* Top Pop Singles	67
		United States/*Billboard* Adult Contemporary Singles	28
		Japan	85
1971	"Hurting Each Other"	United States/*Billboard* Top Pop Singles	2
		United States/*Billboard* Adult Contemporary Singles	1
		United States/*Cash Box* Top Pop Singles	2
		United States/*Record World* Top Pop Singles	1
		Japan	56
		Australia	4
		Canada	2
		New Zealand	7
		Zimbabwe	17

Year	Single	Chart	Peak Position
1972	"It's Going to Take Some Time"	United States/*Billboard* Top Pop Singles	12
		United States/*Billboard* Adult Contemporary Singles	2
		United States/*Cash Box* Top Pop Singles	17
		United States/*Record World* Top Pop Singles	13
		Japan	48
		Australia	24
		Canada	14
		New Zealand	15
1972	"Goodbye to Love"	United States/*Billboard* Top Pop Singles	7
		United States/*Billboard* Adult Contemporary Singles	2
		United States/*Cash Box* Top Pop Singles	7
		United States/*Record World* Top Pop Singles	6
		United Kingdom	9
		Japan	55
		Australia	25
		Canada	4
		New Zealand	2
1972	"I Won't Last a Day without You" (album version)	United Kingdom	49
1972	"Top of the World" (album version)	Japan	21
		Australia	1
		New Zealand	1
1973	"Sing"	United States/*Billboard* Top Pop Singles	3
		United States/*Billboard* Adult Contemporary Singles	1
		United States/*Cash Box* Top Pop Singles	5
		United States/*Record World* Top Pop Singles	4
		United Kingdom	55
		Japan	18
		Australia	24
		Canada	4
		France	21
		New Zealand	7
1973	"Yesterday Once More"	United States/*Billboard* Top Pop Singles	2
		United States/*Billboard* Adult Contemporary Singles	1
		United States/*Cash Box* Top Pop Singles	1
		United States/*Record World* Top Pop Singles	1
		United Kingdom	2
		Japan	5
		Australia	9
		Belgium	5
		Canada	1
		Germany	21
		Ireland	8
		Netherlands	5
		New Zealand	2
		Norway	6
		Zimbabwe	6

Year	Single	Chart	Peak Position
1973	"Top of the World" (single version)	United States/*Billboard* Top Pop Singles	1
		United States/*Billboard* Adult Contemporary Singles	2
		United States/*Cash Box* Top Pop Singles	1
		United States/*Record World* Top Pop Singles	3
		United Kingdom	5
		Japan	52
		Belgium	27
		Canada	1
		Germany	38
		Ireland	3
		Netherlands	12
1974	"Jambalaya (On the Bayou)"	United Kingdom	12
		Japan	28
		Australia	95
		Austria	8
		Belgium	13
		Germany	50
		Ireland	12
		Netherlands	3
		New Zealand	13
1974	"I Won't Last a Day without You" (single version)	United States/*Billboard* Top Pop Singles	11
		United States/*Record World* Adult Contemporary Singles	1
		United States/*Cash Box* Top Pop Singles	9
		United States/*Record World* Top Pop Singles	9
		United Kingdom	32
		Japan	40
		Australia	63
		Canada	7
1974	"Santa Claus Is Coming to Town"	United Kingdom	37
1975	"Please Mr. Postman"	United States/*Billboard* Top Pop Singles	1
		United States/*Billboard* Adult Contemporary Singles	1
		United States/*Cash Box* Top Pop Singles	1
		United States/*Record World* Top Pop Singles	1
		United Kingdom	2
		Japan	11
		Australia	1
		Canada	1
		Germany	10
		Ireland	2
		Netherlands	29
		New Zealand	1
		Switzerland	5
		Zimbabwe	2

Year	Single	Chart	Peak Position
1975	"Only Yesterday"	United States/*Billboard* Top Pop Singles	4
		United States/*Billboard* Adult Contemporary Singles	1
		United States/*Cash Box* Top Pop Singles	8
		United States/*Record World* Top Pop Singles	6
		United Kingdom	7
		Japan	12
		Australia	16
		Canada	2
		Germany	43
		Ireland	5
		New Zealand	10
		Zimbabwe	1
1975	"Solitaire"	United States/*Billboard* Top Pop Singles	17
		United States/*Billboard* Adult Contemporary Singles	1
		United States/*Cash Box* Top Pop Singles	15
		United States/*Record World* Top Pop Singles	21
		United Kingdom	32
		Japan	44
		Australia	61
		Canada	12
		New Zealand	6
		Zimbabwe	13
1976	"There's a Kind of Hush (All Over the World)"	United States/*Billboard* Top Pop Singles	12
		United States/*Billboard* Adult Contemporary Singles	1
		United States/*Cash Box* Top Pop Singles	12
		United States/*Record World* Top Pop Singles	17
		United Kingdom	22
		Japan	27
		Australia	33
		Canada	8
		FR	47
		Ireland	7
		New Zealand	5
1976	"I Need to Be in Love"	United States/*Billboard* Top Pop Singles	25
		United States/*Billboard* Adult Contemporary Singles	1
		United States/*Cash Box* Top Pop Singles	32
		United States/*Record World* Top Pop Singles	n/a
		United Kingdom	36
		Japan	62
		Australia	47
		Canada	24
		Ireland	14
1976	"Breaking Up Is Hard to Do"	Japan	71
1976	Goofus	United States/*Billboard* Top Pop Singles	56
		United States/*Billboard* Adult Contemporary Singles	4
		United States/*Cash Box* Top Pop Singles	87
		Canada	82

Year	Single	Chart	Peak Position
1977	"All You Get from Love Is a Love Song"	United States/*Billboard* Top Pop Singles	35
		United States/*Billboard* Adult Contemporary Singles	4
		United States/*Cash Box* Top Pop Singles	43
		United States/*Record World* Top Pop Singles	63
		United Kingdom	54
		Japan	68
		Australia	89
		Canada	38
1977	"Calling Occupants of Interplanetary Craft (The Recognized Anthem of World Contact Day)"	United States/*Billboard* Top Pop Singles	32
		United States/*Billboard* Adult Contemporary Singles	18
		United States/*Cash Box* Top Pop Singles	24
		United States/*Record World* Top Pop Singles	37
		United Kingdom	9
		Australia	13
		Canada	18
		Ireland	1
		New Zealand	19
1978	"Sweet, Sweet Smile"	United States/*Billboard* Top Pop Singles	44
		United States/*Billboard* Adult Contemporary Singles	7
		United States/*Cash Box* Top Country Singles	8
		United States/*Cash Box* Top Pop Singles	42
		United States/*Cash Box* Top Country Singles	9
		United States/*Record World* Top Pop Singles	48
		United States/*Cash Box* Top Country Singles	7
		United Kingdom	40
		Japan	59
		Australia	100
		Belgium	19
		Canada	43
		Germany	22
		Netherlands	22
		Zimbabwe	10
1978	"I Believe You"	United States/*Billboard* Top Pop Singles	68
		United States/*Billboard* Adult Contemporary Singles	9
		United States/*Cash Box* Top Pop Singles	70
		United States/*Record World* Top Pop Singles	87
		Canada	81
1981	"Touch Me When We're Dancing"	United States/*Billboard* Top Pop Singles	16
		United States/*Billboard* Adult Contemporary Singles	1
		United States/*Cash Box* Top Pop Singles	17
		United States/*Record World* Top Pop Singles	19
		Australia	78
		New Zealand	22
1981	"(Want You) Back in My Life Again"	United States/*Billboard* Top Pop Singles	72
		United States/*Billboard* Adult Contemporary Singles	14
		United States/*Cash Box* Top Pop Singles	75
		United States/*Record World* Top Pop Singles	102

Year	Single	Chart	Peak Position
1981	"Those Good Old Dreams"	United States/*Billboard* Top Pop Singles United States/*Billboard* Adult Contemporary Singles United States/*Cash Box* Top Pop Singles	63 21 78
1982	"Beechwood 4-5789"	United States/*Billboard* Top Pop Singles United States/*Billboard* Adult Contemporary Singles United States/*Cash Box* Top Pop Singles United Kingdom New Zealand	74 16 88 78 10
1983	"Make Believe It's Your First Time"	United States/*Billboard* Top Pop Singles United States/*Billboard* Adult Contemporary Singles United Kingdom Australia Ireland	101 7 60 80 20
1984	"Your Baby Doesn't Love You Anymore"	United States/*Billboard* Adult Contemporary Singles	12
1987	"If I Had You"	United States/*Billboard* Adult Contemporary Singles	18
1990	"Merry Christmas, Darling" (1978 rere-cording)/"(They Long to Be) Close to You" (UK/Irish reissue)	United Kingdom Ireland	25 18
1993	"Rainy Days and Mondays" (UK, 1991 remix)	United Kingdom	63
1994	"Tryin' to Get the Feeling Again"	United Kingdom	44
1995	"I Need to Be in Love"/"Top of the World" (1990/1991 remixes)	Japan	5
2001	"The Rainbow Connection"	Japan	47

Charting US Success

One of "The Greatest of All Time Artists"

For all of the Carpenters' international successes, which are detailed throughout this book, it's their chart performances of US releases that steal the spotlight.

Some reasons for this are obvious: the US is the world's largest music market, and it is, after all, the Carpenters' homeland. Chart performances in the States also provide benchmarks on their career's timeline: their first chart hit, "Ticket to Ride"; their big breakthrough, when "(They Long to Be) Close to You" first reached No. 1; and their record-making and record-breaking string of hits throughout the 1970s and early 1980s.

Richard and Karen paid such close attention to the three major US music-trade magazine charts—in *Billboard*, *Cash Box*, and *Record World*—that they impressed even Herb Alpert, who notes, "They were in it more than I was." And Alpert was the cofounder of their record label, so he was in it to a large degree.

Like most in the music industry watching the charts in the 1970s, Richard says he and Karen were often baffled by the variations in their releases' rankings on the big three. For example, they scored three No. 1 pop-album chart hits in *Cash Box* (*Close to You*, *Now & Then*, and *The Singles 1969–1973*) but only one in *Billboard* (*The Singles 1969–1973*). They went to the top of the Record World pop-singles charts six times, but only three times in *Billboard*.

Little matter now, as Record World ceased publication in 1982 and *Cash Box* in 1996, leaving *Billboard* the gold standard, which is why its charts are most prominently featured in these pages.

Billboard Awards Editor Paul Grein, who originated the magazine's "Chart Beat" column in 1981, underscores and explains some of the Carpenters' most notable *Billboard* chart achievements:

· Greatest of All Time Artists: No. 54. The All Time Artist list, published at the end of 2019, includes chart performances for both singles and albums. It ranks the Beatles at No. 1. The Carpenters are the No. 2 duo on the list, bested only by Hall & Oates at No. 35.

· Greatest of All Time Hot 100 Artists: No. 36. Published in August 2018, this chart ranks only *Billboard* pop-

singles chart performance. Again, the Beatles are No. 1. The Carpenters are the No. 2 duo on the list, bested only by Hall & Oates at No. 35.

· Number One American Act of the 1970s: Grein says this oft-repeated statistic is gleaned from the book *Top Pop Singles* by Wisconsin-based chart researcher Joel Whitburn. The edition tabulated *Billboard* Hot 100 charts 1955–2018. Grein observes that the Carpenters "were the No. 4 act overall on the Hot 100 for the 1970s, per [Whitburn's] point system, behind Elton John (who is English), Paul McCartney (who is English) and Bee Gees ([whose members] were born on the Isle of Man to English parents and later moved to Australia)."

· Adult Contemporary Singles Artist: No. 2. "They notched fifteen No. 1 hits on the weekly Adult Contemporary chart," Grein says, explaining that's the most of any duo or group, and second overall only to Elton John, who led with sixteen.

· Adult Contemporary Singles Artist of the 1970s: No. 1. "Moreover, they are the only act to have two of the Top 10 AC hits of the 1970s," Grein adds. "'We've Only Just Begun' ranks No. 5. '(They Long to Be) Close to You' ranks No. 10. This list is based strictly on chart performance."

· The Top 20 Hot 100 Hit Streak: No. 6 (as of 2002). Grein says the Carpenters' run of sixteen consecutive A-sides to make the Top 20 on the Hot 100, from "(They Long to Be) Close to You" in 1970 to "There's a Kind of Hush" (All Over the World)" in 1976, was "extraordinary, but not unprecedented." Referring again to Whitburn's *Top Pop Singles* (2002 edition), Grein notes that Elvis Presley had thirty consecutive Top 10 hits 1956–62, the Beatles had twenty-four consecutive Top 10 hits 1964–76, Janet Jackson had twenty-three consecutive Top 10 hits 1989–2001, Michael Jackson had seventeen consecutive Top 10 hits 1979–88, and Madonna had seventeen consecutive Top 10 hits 1984–89.

On the Screen

The Carpenters
on TV and on Film

Above: On *The Perry Como Christmas Show*, 1974

Page 325: On *The Carol Burnett Show*, 1971

On Television

A select list of the Carpenters' appearances on broadcast television.

12/1/69
Your All-American College Show (US): This wasn't the first time the duo had enjoyed success on the national talent-competition program. But this was their first time performing as "the Carpenters." After host Arthur Godfrey mistakenly introduces them as "Ed and Karen Carpenter," Richard and Karen lip-sync "Ticket to Ride" to perfection. Showbiz-vet Godfrey and guest judge Ed Sullivan instantly get it: these kids got it.

7/2/70
The Dating Game (US) performance: "(They Long to Be) Close to You." Karen chooses. Richard is chosen.

9/15/70
The Don Knotts Show (US) performance: "(They Long to Be) Close to You."

9/18/70
The Tonight Show Starring Johnny Carson (US) performance: "(They Long to Be) Close To You," "We've Only Just Begun."

10/2/70
The David Frost Show (US). performance: "(They Long to Be) Close to You."

10/18/70
The Ed Sullivan Show (US) performance: "(They Long to Be) Close to You," "We've Only Just Begun."

11/8/70
The Ed Sullivan Show (US) performance: the "Bacharach/David Medley" for injured Vietnam soldiers in a special show recorded at Walter Reed Army Medical Center in Washington, D.C.

11/13/70
The Tonight Show Starring Johnny Carson (US).

1/24/71
Peggy Fleming at Sun Valley (US) performance: "Help." Fleming also skates to the Carpenters' recording of "(They Long to Be) Close to You."

2/13/71
The Andy Williams Show (US) performance: "For All We Know" and a medley with Williams: "Ticket to Ride," "I'll Never Fall in Love Again."

2/14/71
(syndicated throughout week): *This Is Your Life*. Karen and Richard honored.

3/16/71
The 13th Annual Grammy Awards (US) performance: "We've Only Just Begun."

3/24/71
The Johnny Cash Show (US) performance: "(They Long to Be) Close to You," "For All We Know," "Rainy Days and Mondays."

6/30/71
The Tonight Show Starring Johnny Carson (US)

7/20/71–9/7/71
Make Your Own Kind of Music (US), weekly summer-replacement musical-variety series cohosted by the Carpenters. Premiere-episode performance: "Make Your Own Kind of Music," "We've Only Just Begun," "Rainy Days and Mondays," "(They Long to Be) Close to You," "Good Day Sunshine."

7/22/71
The Mike Douglas Show (US) performance: "Rainy Days and Mondays," "Maybe It's You," "Love is Surrender."

7/27/71
Make Your Own Kind of Music (US) performance: "Help," "For All We Know," "Mr. Guder," "I Kept on Loving You," "Wishin' and Hopin.'"

8/3/71
Make Your Own Kind of Music (US) performance: "Bacharach/David Medley," "One Love," "Druscilla Penny," "A House is Not a Home."

8/10/71
Make Your Own Kind of Music (US) performance: "Don't Be Afraid," "(A Place to) Hideaway," "I Kept on Loving You," "What's the Use."

8/17/71
Make Your Own Kind of Music (US) performance: "Love Is Surrender," "Rainy Days and Mondays," "Baby It's You."

8/18/71
The 5th Dimension Traveling Sunshine Show (US) performance: "Superstar," "Reason to Believe."

8/19/71
The Tonight Show Starring Johnny Carson (US)

8/24/71
Make Your Own Kind of Music (US) performance: "All I Can Do," "Let Me Be the One," "Maybe It's You," "Trains and Boats and Planes."

8/31/71
Make Your Own Kind of Music (US) performance: "Your Wonderful Parade," "Bless the Beasts and Children," "Ticket to Ride," "I Want to Be Free."

9/7/71
Make Your Own Kind of Music (US) performance: "(They Long to Be) Close to You," "Reason to Believe," "We've Only Just Begun," "New World Coming," "Make Your Own Kind of Music."

9/22/71
The Carol Burnett Show (US) performance: "Superstar" and "Bacharach/David medley" with Burnett. Karen also joins the show's cast for "Who" and a few lines of "Smoke Gets in Your Eyes."

9/23/71
Top of the Pops (UK) performance: "Superstar" and "Help."

10/9/71
The Harry Secombe Show (UK) performance: "Bacharach/David Medley."

11/5/71
The Tonight Show Starring Johnny Carson (US)

11/6/71
The Carpenters (UK) In-studio concert recorded for broadcast on the BBC. Includes a rare, videotaped performance of "And When He Smiles."

1/19/72
The Carol Burnett Show (US) Performance: "Hurting Each Other" and medley with Carol Burnett of Paul Williams songs "An Old Fashioned Love Song," "We've Only Just Begun," "I Kept on Loving You," "Let Me Be the One."

2/17/72
Lulu's Party (UK): Special filmed in Berlin, Germany September 26, 1971, a few days following the Carpenter's successful first trip to the UK a few days earlier.

2/21/72
Jerry Visits the Carpenters (US): Popular Los Angeles television-news anchor interviews the duo in studio as they record "Hurting Each Other."

3/14/72
The 14th Annual Grammy Awards (US) performance: "Superstar."

4/10/72
The 44th Annual Academy Awards (US) performance: "Bless the Beasts and Children."

On *The Bob Hope Special*, 1972

5/7/72
The Special London Bridge Special starring Tom Jones (US) performance: "We've Only Just Begun," "For All We Know," "Love is Surrender." Includes a unique reprise of "For All We Know."

10/5/72
The Bob Hope Special (US) performance: "Top of the World" and "A Song For You."

6/1/73
Robert Young with the Young (US) performance: "Piano Picker," "Saturday," "Sometimes."

11/6/73
The Tonight Show Starring Johnny Carson (US) performance: "Superstar," "Rainy Days and Mondays," Goodbye to Love," "Mr. Guder."

11/13/73
The Bob Hope Special (US) performance: "We've Only Just Begun," "Top of the World."

3/2/74
The 16th Annual Grammy Awards (US) presentation: Best New Artist award to Bette Midler.

2/15/74
Grand Gala du Disque (NL): Live concert recorded in the RAI Amsterdam for TV broadcast.

3/3/74
Carpenters Live at the Talk of the Town (UK). Concert recorded for broadcast on the BBC.

3/10/74
Rock Concert: Tribute to Jim Croce (US): Karen and Richard share memories of the late folk-rock singer Jim Croce.

8/4/74
Evening at Pops (US): Live concert with The Boston Pops Orchestra conducted by Arthur Fiedler.

12/17/74
The Perry Como Christmas Show (US) performance: "Carol of the Bells" (Richard on piano), "Sleep Well, Little Children" (Karen and Perry duet), "Santa Claus Is Comin' to Town," and "Carpenters/Como Medley" (Richard, Karen, and Perry).

2/18/75
American Music Awards (US) Presentation: Favorite Pop Album.

12/3/76
A World of Music (UK): Live concert from The New London Theatre recorded for broadcast on the BBC.

12/8/76
The Carpenters Very First Television Special: The first of five hour-long specials for ABC, guests included pop star John Denver and musician-comic Victor Borge.

1/27/77
The Tonight Show Starring Johnny Carson (US) performance: "From This Moment On." Guest host Steve Martin.

2/4/77
American Bandstand's 25th Anniversary (US) performance: "We've Only Just Begun."

3/2/77
The Dorothy Hamill Winter Carnival Special (Canada) performance: "Make Me Laugh" and "From This Moment On."

12/9/77
The Carpenters at Christmas (US): The first of the duo's two holiday specials features guests Kristy McNichol, Harvey Korman, and famed puppeteer Burr Tillstrom with his beloved Kukla and Ollie.

2/5/78
ABC's Silver Anniversary Celebration (US) performance: Medley of "Silly Love Songs" and "We've Only Just Begun" (with Captain & Tennille and Ben Vereen).

3/16/78
Thank You, Rock 'N' Roll: A Tribute to Alan Freed (US) performance: "Yesterday Once More."

5/11/78
Starparade (Germany) performance: "Top of the World" and "Sweet, Sweet Smile."

5/17/78
The Carpenters... Space Encounters (US): A space-themed special on the heels of their success with "Calling Occupants of Interplanetary Craft (The Recognized Anthem of World Contact Day)," Karen and Richard are joined by guests Suzanne Somers, John Davidson, and Charlie Callas.

5/27/78
TopPop (Netherlands) performance: "Sweet, Sweet Smile."

6/27/78
The Tonight Show Starring Johnny Carson (US) performance: "Thank You for the Music" and "Superstar"/"Rainy Days and Mondays"/ Goodbye to Love" medley. Guest host John Davidson.

11/19/78
Disneyland: Mickey's 50 (US) performance: "We've Only Just Begun."

12/19/78
The Carpenters: A Christmas Portrait (US): The second of the duo's holiday specials includes highlights from their just-released smash holiday album, guest Gene Kelly, and a charming cameo appearance by Mom and Dad Carpenter.

12/24/78
Bruce Forsyth's Big Night (UK): Karen performs "Please Mr. Postman," "Merry Christmas, Darling," and "I Need to Be in Love." She also joins Forsyth for a medley of "Winter Wonderland" and "White Christmas."

3/13/80
20/20 (US): News segment on A&M cofounder Herb Alpert, with Karen singing a few lines of "Superstar" at A&M Studios.

5/16/80
The Carpenters: Music Music Music (US): The duo's fifth and final ABC special removes the "variety" from the "musical-variety" format for an elegant night of singing with guests John Davidson and Ella Fitzgerald.

5/20/80
Olivia Newton-John: Hollywood Nights (US) Karen joins Newton-John and guests for "Heartache Tonight."

8/10/81
Good Morning America (US): Interview promoting *Made in America*.

10/2/81
The Merv Griffin Show (US) Performance: "(Want You) Back in My Life Again."

10/22/81
Nationwide (UK): An interview promoting *Made in America*.

10/24/81
Multi-Coloured Swap Shop (UK): Karen is interviewed by host Noel Edmonds and answers call-in questions from viewers.

10/29/81
Show Express (Germany) performance: "Top of the World" and "Beechwood 4-5789."

1/11/83
Entertainment Tonight (US) A report on a photoshoot for the 25th anniversary of the Grammy Awards. Karen and Richard's final TV appearance together.

On Video and Film

A select list of Carpenters performances and appearances that have been authorized for sale on home video. Dates indicate DVD releases unless otherwise indicated:

Carpenters, *Yesterday Once More*
(release year: 1985, country of origin: US, distributor: A&M Video Beta, VHS, and LaserDisc) A collection of twelve selections gleaned from music videos, promotional films, and performances from TV shows.

The 5th Dimension Travelling Sunshine Show (2003, US, View Video)
An August 1971 TV special with the Carpenters performing "Superstar" and "Reason to Believe."

Carpenters, *Yesterday Once More* (1995, Japan, A&M Video)
As above, but including a previously unreleased promotional film for "I Need to Be in Love."

Carpenters, *Interpretations: A 25th Anniversary Celebration* (2003, US, A&M Records Chronicles)
A collection of eleven songs from 1970 to 1980 previously unreleased on home video, including "From This Moment On," an outtake from the duo's fifth television special, *Music Music Music.*

Carpenters, *Live at Budokan 1974* (1996, Japan, A&M Records)
A recording of the Carpenters' legendary 1974 concert at the Budokan arena in Tokyo, where they perform many of their top hits. Highlights include "Sing," which Karen performs in English and Japanese with a local children's chorus. Bonus footage includes airport arrival and concert setup.

Close to You: Remembering the Carpenters (1998, MPI Media Group)
An authorized biography includes memories from Richard, Carpenters bandmates, A&M cofounder Herb Alpert, singer Petula Clark, and more. Bonus features include radio

jingles, commercials, and TV promos, as well as footage from one of the duo's trips to the White House.

This is Your Life: '70s Music Icons—Richard & Karen Carpenter, Shirley Jones (2006, R2 Entertainment)
A 1971 episode pays tribute to Karen and Richard, with surprise appearances by their band, Herb Alpert, Burt Bacharach, and others. Includes new intro by host Ralph Edwards recorded in 1986.

Carpenters, *Gold: Greatest Hits* (2002, US, A&M Records)
A repackaged, retitled reissue of the original *Yesterday Once More.*

Perry Como's Christmas Show (2013, US, MPI Home Video)
Como's 1974 CBS Christmas special includes the Carpenters performing "Santa Claus Is Comin' to Town" as well as Como and the Carpenters in a medley of each other's hits including "(They Long to Be) Close to You," "Yesterday Once More," and "We've Only Just Begun."

Carpenters, *Gold: Greatest Hits* (2009, Japan, A&M Video/Universal Music Entertainment)
The 16th disc in the *Carpenters 40th Anniversary Collector's Edition* boxed set includes a limited-edition reissue of the 1995 Japan issue of *Yesterday Once More* including "I Need to Be in Love," with Richard offering commentary on a secondary audio track.

Ed Sullivan's Rock & Roll Classics (2012, US, Sofa Entertainment)
The Carpenters perform "We've Only Just Begun."

Close to You: Remembering the Carpenters (2015, US, MPI Media Group/TJL)
A revised version of the 1998 release with bonus features including an excerpt of "Dancing in the Street" from their early television appearance, and Petula Clark's performance of "For All We Know" in tribute to Karen shortly after her death.

The Wrecking Crew (2015, Magnolia Pictures)
A documentary about the legendary group of Los Angeles session players, many of whom Richard would hire to work with the Carpenters. The main feature includes a brief segment on "(They Long to Be) Close to You." The film's interview segments with Richard are in the bonus features. So, streamers and downloaders beware: The only way to see them is to buy the Blu-ray.

Hal David: What the World Needs Now (2018, John Paulson Productions)
A career retrospective of Burt Bacharach's longtime lyricist, including the Carpenters performing "(They Long to Be) Close to You."

Carpenters: Christmas Memories (2016, US, MPI Home Video/TCL)
Richard hosts a compilation of clips gleaned primarily from the duo's two ABC Christmas specials, including a performance of "Ave Maria," "Christmas Song (Chestnuts Roasting on an Open Fire)," and "Merry Christmas, Darling."

Herb Alpert Is… (2020, US Abramorama, various streaming services)
Richard is among the key interviewees in this documentary chronicling the career of trumpeter and A&M Records cofounder Alpert, including a segment on Alpert's role in the discovery and success of the Carpenters.

On the Soundtrack

A select list of movies and TV shows authorized to use Carpenters recordings on their soundtracks:

Bless the Beasts & Children (1971, Columbia Pictures)
The Carpenters perform the Oscar-nominated main-title tune, featuring the soundtrack version's alternate instrumental opening. A truncated version is played over the closing credits.

Tommy Boy (1995, Paramount Pictures)
A man-child (Chris Farley) and his irritated companion (David Spade) travel by car across the country. Excerpts of numerous popular tunes are heard as each character punches the radio's buttons, trying to find a song he can tolerate. Eventually, one of them lands on the Carpenters' "Superstar" and leaves it there. The men turn to each other and feign disinterest. The camera cuts away for a moment and then returns—to reveal the two joyfully (and hilariously) belting out the "Superstar" chorus. A classic comedy-film moment.

Starsky & Hutch (2004, Warner Bros.)
Ben Stiller and Owen Wilson head this tongue-in-cheek homage to the 1970s TV series. One verse of "We've Only Just Begun" plays under a poignant montage as the buddies break up.

Ghost Rider (2007, Columbia Pictures)
Nicolas Cage heads this Marvel adaptation, about a bounty hunter of the damned with a passion for the Carpenters. "Superstar" appears twice in the film, and both times is interrupted by someone attempting to turn off the music. To the first, Cage angrily responds, "You touch the Carpenters… again, and we're gonna have a scrap on our hands." To the second: "You're steppin' on Karen, man."

The Simpsons Movie (2007, 20th Century Fox)
Fed up at last, Marge leaves a VHS tape to tell Homer she's done with their relationship. "(They Long to Be) Close to You" plays during her farewell message, which she has recorded over their wedding video. That dissolves into more "Close to You," which is playing during their wedding reception. The song continues, as a heartbroken Homer wanders off into the wilderness.

1408 (2007, Weinstein)
John Cusack investigates a supposedly haunted hotel room where guests check in, but do not survive more than sixty minutes. About ten seconds of "We've Only Just Begun" blares out of a clock radio, alerting Cusack's character that his hour of terror has… only just begun.

Shrek Forever After (2010, DreamWorks Animation)
"Top of the World" plays under a montage as Shrek celebrates a return to his old self: a feared and hated ogre.

The Simpsons (2012, "Treehouse of Horror XXIII," FOX)
As Homer first gazes upon Marge, "(They Long to Be) Close to You" plays in his mind and becomes the musical theme of their courtship and, little do they know, their lifetime.

Dark Shadows (2012, Warner Bros.)
A feature adaptation of this favorite TV soap opera features "Top of the World" under a sequence where Johnny Depp's Barnabas leads the Collins family through a series of repairs and tasks at home and work. At one point, Barnabas discovers the song coming from a TV, which shows the Carpenters performing.

American Horror Story: Apocalypse (2018, "The End," FX)
As characters are trapped in a house together, trying try to survive the aftermath of nuclear war, "Calling Occupants of Interplanetary Craft (The Recognized Anthem of World Contact Day)" is played nonstop in the common room of the outpost, much to everyone's chagrin.

After Life (2020, episode 2.1, Netflix)
Season two of Ricky Gervais's divine dark dramedy opens with "Top of the World" playing at full volume, with a montage showing each principal character attempting to begin their day optimistically, in spite of their often grim circumstances.

Page 328: The Carpenters Very First Television Special, 1976

On the Road

No doubt, the Carpenters occasionally felt that all those rented cars and empty motel rooms led them everywhere but home.

But most of Richard's many memories of traveling and playing for concert audiences are happy ones. Richard says the Carpenters' song "Road Ode," written by bandmates Gary Sims and Dan Woodhams about the grind of touring life, is not autobiographical—at least as far as he and Karen were concerned.

If you've already read this far into the book, you know that the Carpenters' management's overbooking of concert dates was incredibly problematic for the Carpenters, especially when it came to limiting Richard's time to find strong content for albums.

But the concerts also, occasionally, provided content solutions.

Richard discovered "For All We Know" on a night off at the movies while on tour in Toronto. Without the crowds constantly shouting requests for "Top of the World," who knows if one of the Carpenters'

signature songs would have ever been released globally as a single? And it was the new summer 1972 tour highlight that provided the foundation for *Now & Then*'s oldies medley, which, in turn, inspired "Yesterday Once More."

Richard Carpenter was a master at finding hit records from the most unexpected places.

The list of (primarily) concert dates that follows is the most comprehensive we could compile and, arguably, is the most comprehensive ever compiled. Heretofore, the calendar for the duo's busy year following the release of "(They Long to Be) Close to You" had the most blanks. It's been the biggest mystery. That was solved for us by Richard himself, who went through the grueling process of thumbing through pages and pages of small notebooks and reading off concert dates and locations from handwritten itineraries. He also allowed us to go through a box of touring schedules containing invaluable concert itinerary data from 1971–1981.

We've done our best to double-check every entry against newspaper listings, photographs of handbills and programs, concert reviews, you name it. But, hard as we tried, not all dates could be paired with venues.

The Carpenters performed hundreds of shows from 1970–1981, with many dates added, canceled, and changed at the last minute. Therefore, even we have doubts that this list is completely accurate.

Finally, to those of you lucky enough to have attended even just one these dates:

We're more than a little jealous.

Left: The duo waits patiently during the taping of a Japanese pop music show, 1970

Right: Japan, 1974

1970

May 29–30: Westbury, NY, Westbury Music Fair
June 10–22: Lake Tahoe, NV, King's Castle Hotel and Casino
July 1–2: St. Louis, MO, The Muny
July 8–12: Los Angeles, CA, Greek Theatre
Aug. 6–19: Reno, NV, Harrah's Reno Hotel and Casino
Aug. 21: Twin Falls, ID, Fine Arts Center in the College of Southern Idaho
Aug. 22: Boise, ID, Capital High gymnasium
Sept. 6: Marshfield, WI, Central Wisconsin State Fair
Sept. 25–Oct. 8 Miami, FL, Hump Room, Eden Roc Hotel
Oct. 10: Kent, OH, Kent State University
Oct. 20–31: Toronto, Canada, O'Keefe Centre
Nov. 1: Ottawa, Canada, Ottawa Civic Center
Nov. 2–8: Chicago, IL, Mill Run Playhouse
Nov. 10: Dayton, OH, University of Dayton
Nov. 20–22: Tokyo, Japan, World Popular Song Festival
Nov. 23–25: Honolulu, HI, Cinerama Reef Towers Hotel's Polynesian Palace
Nov. 27: Montgomery, AL, Alabama State Coliseum
Nov. 28: Birmingham, AL
Nov. 29: Murray, KY
Dec. 1: Aberdeen, SD

Dec. 2: Minot, SD
Dec. 4: San Francisco, CA, San Francisco Civic Auditorium
Dec. 12: Long Beach, CA, Cal State Long Beach State gym

1971

Jan. 1–8: Reno, NV, Harrah's Reno Hotel and Casino
Jan. 15: Pasadena, CA, Pasadena Civic Center
Jan. 16: Santa Monica, CA, Santa Monica Civic Auditorium
Jan. 23: San Diego, CA, San Diego Civic Theatre
Jan. 30: Bakersfield, CA, Civic Auditorium,
Feb. 2: Davenport, IA, Davenport Masonic Auditorium
Feb. 3: Des Moines, IA, KRNT Theatre
Feb. 4: Cedar Falls, IA, Men's Gymnasium of State College
Feb. 5: Rochester, MN, Mayo Civic
Feb. 6: Mason City, IA, Mason City High School
Feb. 7: Vermillion, SD, University of South Dakota
Feb. 9: Kearney, NE, Kearney State College,
Feb. 10: Cedar Rapids, IA, Coe College
Feb. 11: Dayton, OH, Hara Arena

Feb. 13: Pittsburgh, PA, Syria Mosque
Feb. 14: Philadelphia, PA, Academy of Music
Feb. 19: Greencastle, IN, DePauw University
Feb. 20: Bloomington, IN, Indiana University
Feb. 22: Weatherford, OK, Southwestern Oklahoma State University
Feb. 23: Tulsa, OK
Feb. 24: Dallas, TX
Feb. 25: Little Rock, AR, Robinson Memorial Auditorium
Feb. 26: Athens, GA, Georgia Stegeman Coliseum
Feb. 27: Johnson City, TN, East Tennessee State University
Mar. 20–21: Honolulu, HI, Honolulu International Center
Mar. 23–Apr. 14: Las Vegas, NV, Sands Hotel
Apr. 21: Waco, TX, Baylor University
Apr. 22: Commerce, TX, East Texas State University
Apr. 23: Lubbock, TX, Texas State Technical College
Apr. 24: Abilene, TX, Taylor County Coliseum
Apr. 25: Houston, TX, Houston Music Hall
Apr. 27: New Orleans, LA, Loyola University

Apr. 28: Natchitoches, TX, Northwestern State University
Apr. 29: Monroe, LA, Monroe Civic Center
Apr. 30–May 1: Jackson, MS, Mississippi State Fair
May 2: Knoxville, TN, Stokely Athletic Center
May 4: Greenville, SC, Greenville Memorial Auditorium
May 5: Atlanta, GA, Municipal Auditorium
May 6: Columbia, SC, Carolina Coliseum
May 7: Roanoke, VA, Civic Center
May 8: Boone, NC, Appalachian State University
May 9: Charlotte, NC, Charlotte Coliseum
May 11: Boston, MA, Boston Music Hall
May 12: Providence, RI, Loew's State Theatre
May 14: New York, NY, Carnegie Hall
May 16: Detroit, MI, University of Detroit
May 18: Lansing, MI, Lansing Civic Center
May 20: Cincinnati, OH, Cincinnati Gardens
May 21: St Louis, MO, Kiel Opera House
May 22: Omaha, NE, Omaha Civic Auditorium
Jul. 8: Fresno, CA, Selland Arena
Jul. 9: Vancouver, BC, Canada, Queen Elizabeth Theatre
Jul. 10: Seattle, WA, Seattle Center Coliseum
Jul. 16: Los Angeles, CA, Hollywood Bowl
Jul. 17: Morrison, CO, Red Rocks Amphitheatre
Jul. 30: Salt Lake City, UT, Special Events Center
Aug. 1: Calgary, AB, Canada, Southern Alberta Jubilee Auditorium
Aug. 9: Saratoga Springs, NY, Saratoga Performing Arts Center
Aug. 11: Cuyahoga Falls, OH, Blossom Music Center
Aug. 15: Chicago, IL, Arie Crown Theater
Aug. 22: Toronto, ON, Canada, Canadian National Exhibition
Aug. 26–27: Columbus, OH, Ohio State Fairgrounds
Aug. 29: Falcon Heights, MN, Minnesota State Fair Grandstand
Sept. 24: London, England, Royal Albert Hall
Sept. 25: Manchester, England, BBC Studios
Oct. 9: Bussum, the Netherlands, Spant
Oct. 21: Stillwater, OK, Oklahoma State University
Oct. 22: College Station, TX, G. Rollie White Auditorium
Oct. 24: San Antonio, TX, San Antonio Municipal Auditorium
Nov. 10: Dayton, OH, University of Dayton Arena
Nov. 13: Nashville, TN, Nashville Municipal Auditorium
Nov. 16: Auburn, AL, Memorial Coliseum
Nov. 23: Rochester, NY, Rochester Community War Memorial
Nov. 24: Buffalo, NY, Buffalo Memorial Auditorium

Left: Fresno, CA, 1976

1972

Jan. 14: Provo, UT, Brigham Young University
Jan. 15: Logan, UT, Utah State University
Jan. 18: Albuquerque, NM, Albuquerque Civic Auditorium
Jan. 19: El Paso, TX, El Paso County Coliseum
Jan. 20: Tucson, AZ, Convention Center
Jan. 21: Phoenix, AZ, Arizona State University
Jan. 22: Anaheim, CA, Convention Center
Jan. 23: San Diego, CA, Convention Center
Feb. 1: Tempe, AZ, Arizona State University
Feb. 2: Tucson, AZ, Community Center Arena
Feb. 3: El Paso, TX, Civic Center
Mar. 17–19: Lake Tahoe, NV, Sahara Hotel
Mar. 31–Apr. 8: Miami Beach, FL, Eden Rock Hotel
Apr. 9: Gainesville, FL, University of Florida
Apr. 10: Atlanta, GA, Municipal Auditorium
Apr. 11: Savannah, GA, Coliseum
Apr. 12: Fayetteville, NC, Cumberland County Memorial Auditorium
Apr. 13: Greenville, NC, East Carolina University
Apr. 14: Richmond, VA, Richmond Coliseum
Apr. 15: Oxford, OH, Millett Assembly Hall
Apr. 16: Cincinnati, OH, Music Hall
Apr. 18: Bowling Green, KY, Western Kentucky University
Apr. 19: Pittsburgh, PA, Civic Arena
Apr. 20: Huntington, WV, Marshall University
Apr. 21: Philadelphia, PA, Academy of Music
Apr. 22: Syracuse, NY, Onondaga County War Memorial Auditorium
Apr. 23: College Park, MD, University of Maryland
Apr. 25: Washington, DC, Record Industry Annual Awards Dinner, Hilton Hotel
Apr. 29: Atlanta, GA, Municipal Auditorium
May 3: Honolulu, HI, International Center
May 8–20: Sydney, Australia, Chevron Hotel
May 22: Adelaide, Australia, Apollo Sports Center
May 24–25: Melbourne, Australia, Festival Hall
May 27: Brisbane, Australia, Festival Hall
May 30: Hong Kong
Jun. 1–11: Osaka, Nagoya, Kyoto, and Tokyo, Japan
Jul. 7: Houston, TX, University of Houston
Jul. 8: Shreveport, LA, Hirsch Memorial Coliseum
Jul. 9: Tulsa, OK, Assembly Center
Jul. 10: St. Louis, MO, The Muny
Jul. 11: Cuyahoga Falls, OH, Blossom Music Festival
Jul. 12: Johnstown, PA, Cambria County War Memorial
Jul. 13–15: Holmdel, NJ, Garden State Arts Center
Jul. 16: Saratoga, NY, Saratoga Performing Arts Center
Jul. 20: Indianapolis, IN, Convention Center
Jul. 21–23: Chicago, IL, McCormack Place
Jul. 26–29: Detroit, MI, Pine Knob Pavilion
Jul. 30: Saginaw, MI, Civic Auditorium

Aug. 1–3: Columbia, MD, Merriweather Post Pavilion
Aug. 4–5: Allentown, PA, State Fair
Aug. 9–15: Los Angeles, CA, Greek Theatre
Aug. 18: Morrison, CO, Red Rocks Amphitheater
Aug. 22–28: Lake Tahoe, NV, Sahara Hotel
Sept. 20–Oct. 3: Las Vegas, NV, Riviera Hotel
Oct. 4: Salt Lake City, UT, University of Utah Special Events Center
Oct. 5: Boise, ID, Boise State College
Oct. 6: Seattle, WA, Center Arena
Oct. 7: Spokane, WA, Coliseum
Oct. 8: Portland, OR, Coliseum
Oct. 11: Lincoln, NB, Pershing Center
Oct. 12: Sioux City, IA, Municipal Auditorium
Oct. 13: Omaha, NB, Civic Auditorium
Oct. 14: Fargo, ND, Civic Auditorium
Oct. 15: Bismarck, ND, Civic Arena
Oct. 16: Rochester, MN, Mayo Civic Center
Oct. 17: Green Bay, WI, Brown County Veteran's Memorial Arena
Oct. 18: Duluth, MN, Arena
Oct. 20: Sioux Falls, SD, Arena
Oct. 21: Waterloo, IA, McElroy Auditorium
Oct. 22: Davenport, IA, Masonic Center
Oct. 23: La Crosse, WI, Sawyer Auditorium
Oct. 24: Milwaukee, WI, Milwaukee Auditorium
Oct. 25: Charleston, IL, Eastern Illinois Gym
Oct. 26: Owensboro, KY, Sports Center
Oct. 27: Peoria, IL, Bradley University
Oct. 28: Terre Haute, IN, Indiana State College
Nov. 10: Ft. Wayne, IN, Allen County Memorial Coliseum
Nov. 11: Lafayette, IN, Purdue University Hall of Music
Nov. 12: Charleston, WV, Civic Center
Nov. 14: New Haven, CT, War Memorial
Nov. 15: Boston, MA, Boston Music Hall
Nov. 16: Utica, NY, Utica Memorial Auditorium
Nov. 17: Scranton, PA, Catholic Youth Center
Nov. 18: Norfolk, VA, Scope Arena
Nov. 19: Greensboro, NC, Greensboro Coliseum
Nov. 20: Charleston, SC, Gaillard Municipal Auditorium
Nov. 23: Jackson, MS, Memorial Auditorium
Nov. 24: Lake Charles, LA, Auditorium
Nov. 25: Shreveport, LA, Hirsch Memorial Coliseum
Nov. 26: Little Rock, AR, Robinson Theater

1973

Feb. 9: Sacramento, CA, Sacramento Memorial Auditorium
Feb. 11: Anaheim, CA, Anaheim Convention Center
Mar. 30: Albuquerque, NM, University of New Mexico
Mar. 31: Las Cruces, NM, New Mexico State
Apr. 1: Odessa, TX, Ector County Coliseum
Apr. 2: Wichita Falls, TX, Memorial Auditorium
Apr. 4: Austin, TX, Auditorium

Apr. 5: Waco, TX, Heart O' Texas Coliseum
Apr. 6: Dallas, TX, Southern Methodist University
Apr. 7: San Antonio, TX, Arena
Apr. 8: New Orleans, LA, Municipal Auditorium
Apr. 10: Corpus Christi, TX, Memorial Coliseum
Apr. 11: Brownsville, TX, Texas Southmost College
Apr. 12: Abilene, TX, Taylor County Coliseum
Apr. 13: Lubbock, TX, Municipal Coliseum
Apr. 14: Amarillo, TX, Civic Auditorium
Apr. 15: Oklahoma City, OK, Civic Center Music Hall
Apr. 19: Colombia, MO, University of Missouri
Apr. 20: Springfield, MO, Shrine Mosque
Apr. 21: Kansas City, MO, Municipal Auditorium
Apr. 22: Wichita, KS, Century II Convention Center
Apr. 27: Pocatello, ID, Idaho State University
Apr. 28: Laramie, WY, University of Wyoming
Apr. 29: Colorado Springs, CO, US Air Force Academy
May 1: Washington, DC, the White House
May 3: Tacoma, WA, Pacific Lutheran University
May 4: Corvallis, OR, Oregon State University
May 5: Pullman, WA, Washington State University
May 11: Bozeman, MT, Montana State University
May 12: Missoula, MT, University of Montana
May 13: Twin Falls, ID, University of Southern Idaho
May 18: San Diego, CA, Sports Arena
May 19: Claremont, CA, Claremont College
May 20: Bakersfield, CA, Civic Auditorium
May 23: Fresno, CA, Selland Arena
May 24–28: San Carlos, CA, Circle Star Theater
Jun. 22: Lake Charles, LA, Auditorium
Jun. 23: Shreveport, LA, Hirsch Memorial Coliseum
Jun. 24: Birmingham, AL, Boutwell Municipal Auditorium
Jun. 25: Atlanta, GA, Civic Center Auditorium
Jun. 26: Chattanooga, TN, Memorial Auditorium
Jun. 27: Knoxville, TN, Knoxville Civic Coliseum
Jun. 28: Roanoke, VA, Berglund Center
Jun. 29–Jul. 1: Columbia, MD, Merriweather Post Pavilion
Jul. 3–8: Valley Forge, PA, Valley Forge Music Fair
Jul. 10–15: Wallingford, CT, Oakdale Theatre
Jul. 16–21: Holmdel, NJ, Garden State Arts Center
Jul. 22: Saratoga Springs, NY, Saratoga Performing Arts Center
Jul. 24: Cuyahoga Falls, OH, Blossom Music Center
Jul. 25–29: Detroit, MI, Pine Knob Pavilion

Aug. 13–19: Universal City, CA, Universal Amphitheatre
Aug. 21–Sept. 3: Lake Tahoe, NV, Sahara Hotel
Sept. 26–Oct. 9: Las Vegas, NV, Riviera Hotel
Oct. 10: Ogden, UT, Weber State College
Oct. 11: Rexburg, ID, Ricks College
Oct. 12: Provo, UT, Brigham Young University
Oct. 17: Portland, ME, Exposition Building
Oct. 18: Bangor, ME, Bangor Auditorium
Oct. 19: Springfield, MA, Springfield Civic Center
Oct. 20: Troy, NY, Houston Fieldhouse
Oct. 21: Binghamton, NY, Broome County Veterans Memorial Arena
Oct. 22: Buffalo, NY, Kleinhans Music Hall
Oct. 23: Kitchener, ON, Canada, Kitchener Memorial Auditorium
Oct. 24: London, ON, Canada, Treasure Island Auditorium
Oct. 25: Kalamazoo, MI, Western Michigan University
Oct. 26: Muncie, IN, Ball State University
Oct. 27: South Bend, IN, University of Notre Dame
Oct. 28: Evansville, IN, Roberts Memorial Center
Nov. 9–10: Chicago, IL, Arie Crown Theater
Nov. 11: Rockford, IL, Rockford Valley College
Nov. 12: Oshkosh, WI, Wisconsin State University
Nov. 13: Macomb, IL, Western Illinois University
Nov. 14: Columbus, OH, Ohio State University, Mershon Auditorium
Nov. 15: Louisville, KY, Kentucky International Convention Center
Nov. 16: St. Louis, MO, Kiel Opera House
Nov. 17: Nashville, TN, Nashville Municipal Auditorium
Nov. 18: Memphis, TN, Mid-South College
Nov. 19: Starkville, MS, Mississippi State University
Nov. 20: Jackson, MS, Florence State Teachers College
Nov. 21: Mobile, AL, Municipal Auditorium
Nov. 22: Macon, GA, Macon Coliseum
Nov. 23: Savannah, GA, Convention Center
Nov. 24: Orlando, FL, Orlando Sports Stadium
Nov. 25: St. Petersburg, FL, Bayfront Center

1974

Feb. 1: Phoenix, AZ
Feb. 2: Tucson, AZ
Feb. 3: El Paso, TX
Feb. 10–11: Stockholm, Sweden, Stockholm Concert Hall
Feb. 12: Copenhagen, Denmark, Tivoli Concert Hall
Feb. 13: Hasselt, Belgium, Hasselt Cultural Center
Feb. 15: Amsterdam, Netherlands, RAI Amsterdam Convention Center, *Grand Gala du Disque* (TV show)

Feb. 16: Amsterdam, Netherlands, RAI Amsterdam Convention Center
Feb. 17: The Hague, Netherlands, Nederlands Congresgebouw
Feb. 18: Glasgow, Scotland, Apollo Centre
Feb. 19: Manchester, England, Free Trade Hall
Feb. 20: Liverpool, England, Empire Theatre
Feb. 21: Southport, England, Southport New Theatre
Feb. 22: London, England, Royal Festival Hall
Feb. 23: London, England, Hammersmith Odeon
Feb. 24: London, England, Talk of the Town
Feb. 25: Bristol, England, Colston Hall
Feb. 26: Bournemouth, England, Bournemouth Winter Gardens
Feb. 27: Birmingham, England, Birmingham Odeon
Mar. 2: Los Angeles, CA, Grammy Awards
Apr. 4: Bowling Green, KY
Apr. 5: Pittsburgh, PA
Apr. 6: Philadelphia, PA
Apr. 7: Utica, NY
Apr. 8–14: Westbury, NY, Westbury Music Fair
Apr. 15: Raleigh, NC
Apr. 16: Richmond, VA, The Mosque
Apr. 17: Beckley, WV
Apr. 18: Wheeling, WV
Apr. 19: Hershey, PA
Apr. 20: Syracuse, NY, Onondaga War Memorial
Apr. 21: Niagara Falls, NY, Niagara Falls Convention and Civic Center
Apr. 22–27 Toronto, ON, Canada, O'Keefe Center
Apr. 30: Boston, MA, Symphony Hall
May 8–21: Las Vegas, NV, Riviera Hotel
May 31: Tokyo, Japan, Budokan
Jun. 1: Shizuoka, Japan
Jun. 3: Kyoto, Japan, Kyoto Kaikan
Jun. 4: Osaka, Japan, Osaka Furitsu Taiikukan
Jun. 5: Fukuoka, Japan, Kyuden Taiikukan
Jun. 6–8: Osaka, Japan, Festival Hall
Jun. 9: Kobe, Japan, Chu Taiikukan
Jun. 10: Nagoya, Japan, Shimin Kaikan
Jun. 11: Yokohama, Japan, Yokohama Taiikukan
Jun. 12: Tokyo, Japan, Budokan
Jun. 14–15: Honolulu, HI
Jun. 25–Jul. 8: Lake Tahoe, NV, Sahara
Jul. 11: Eugene, OR, McArthur Court
Jul. 12: Seattle, WA, Arena
Jul. 13: Portland, OR, Auditorium
Jul. 14: Spokane, WA, Expo Opera House
Aug. 12–27: Lake Tahoe, NV, Sahara
Sept. 6: Los Angeles, CA, Hollywood Bowl
Oct. 9–22: Las Vegas, NV, Riviera Hotel
Oct. 24: Davenport, IA
Oct. 25: Minneapolis, MN
Oct. 26: Champaign, IL
Oct. 27: Carbondale, IL
Oct. 28: Indianapolis, IN
Oct. 29: Muskegon, MI
Oct. 30: Milwaukee, WI, Performing Arts Center
Oct. 31.: Naperville, IL, North Central College

Nov. 1–3: Chicago, IL, McCormick Place
Nov. 4: Lansing, MI, Lansing Civic Center
Nov. 5: Saginaw, MI, Civic Center
Nov. 6: Muskegon, MI, Elsie Walker Sports Arena
Nov. 7: New Castle, IN, Chrysler High School
Nov. 8: Ft. Wayne, IN, Coliseum
Nov. 9: Champaign, IL, University of Illinois
Nov. 10: Davenport, IA, Masonic Center
Nov. 15: Ft. Hays, KS, Kansas State College
Nov. 16: Denver, CO, Auditorium
Nov. 17: Colorado Springs, CO, Air Force Academy
Nov. 18: Colorado Springs, CO
Nov. 20: Boise, ID
Nov. 21: Pocatello, ID, Minidome
Nov. 22: Logan, UT, Dee Glen Smith Spectrum
Nov. 23: Salt Lake City, UT, Special Events Center
Nov. 24: Sacramento, CA
Nov. 25: Redding, CA
Nov. 26: Chico, CA
Nov. 27–Dec. 1: San Carlos, CA, Circle Star Theatre

1975

Apr. 3: Ames, IA, State University Hilton Coliseum
Apr. 4: Hays, KS, Gross Memorial Coliseum
Apr. 5: Denver, CO, Auditorium
Apr. 7: Colorado Springs, CO, Air Force Academy
Apr. 15: West Palm Beach, FL, Auditorium
Apr. 16: Lakeland, FL, Arena
Apr. 17: Jacksonville, FL, Auditorium
Apr. 18–19: Atlanta, GA, Civic Auditorium
Apr. 20: Columbia, SC, Coliseum
Apr. 21: Fayetteville, NC, Cumberland County Memorial Arena
Apr. 22–27: Valley Forge, PA, Music Theater
May 9: Topeka, KS, Municipal Auditorium
May 10–11: Kansas City, KS, Memorial Hall
May 12: Sioux City, IA, Municipal Auditorium
May 13: Bismarck, ND, Civic Arena
May 14: Jamestown, ND, Civic Center
May 15: Duluth, MN, Arena
May 16: Omaha, NE, Civic Auditorium
May 17: Minneapolis, MN, Auditorium

May 19: Westchester, NY, Premiere Theatre
May 29–Jun. 11: Las Vegas, NV, Riviera Hotel
Jun. 12–25: Las Vegas, NV, Riviera Hotel
Jul. 11–13: Toronto, ON, Canada, O'Keefe Center
Jul. 14–15: Cuyahoga Falls, OH, Blossom Music Center
Jul. 16–19: Detroit, MI, Pine Knob Pavilion
Jul. 20: Erie, PA, Erie County Field House
Jul. 21–26: Wallingford, CT, Oakdale Music Theatre
Jul. 27: Saratoga Springs, NY, Performing Arts Center
Jul. 28–Aug. 3: Warwick, RI, Music Theater
Aug. 4–9: Holmdel, NJ, Garden State Arts Center
Aug. 10–11: Columbia, MD, Merriweather Post Pavilion
Aug. 12–13: Chicago, IL, Ravinia Festival
Aug. 21–Sep. 3: Las Vegas, NV, Riviera Hotel

Concert program, Anaheim Convention Center, 1972

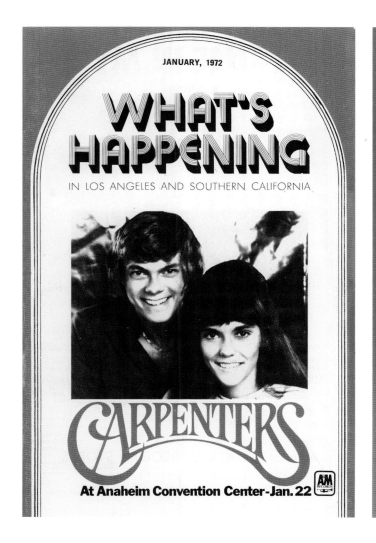

1976

Mar. 15–16: Tokyo, Japan, Budokan
Mar. 17: Shizuoka, Japan, Sunpu Kaikan
Mar. 18: Nagoya, Japan, Aichi-ken Taiikukan
Mar. 19: Kobe, Japan, Shiritsu Taiikukan
Mar. 20: Kyoto, Japan, Taiikukan
Mar. 21: Wakayama, Japan, Wakayama
  Kenritsu Taiikukan
Mar. 24–26: Osaka, Japan, Festival Hall
Mar. 28: Kanazawa, Japan, Taiikukan
Mar. 29: Okayama-shi, Japan, Taiikukan
Mar. 30: Yamaguchi, Japan, Kenritsu
  Taiikukan
Mar. 31: Fukuoka, Japan, Kuyden Taiikukan
Apr. 1: Kumamoto, Japan, Shiritsu Taiikukan
Apr. 2: Hiroshima, Japan, Kenritsu
  Taiikukan
Apr. 5: Sendai, Japan, Miyagi Sports Center
Apr. 7: Sapporo, Japan, Makomanai Ice
  Arena
Apr. 9: Tokyo, Japan, Budokan
Apr. 10: Yokohama, Japan, Kenmin Hall
Apr. 11: Mito, Japan, Kasamatsu Taiikukan
May 29: Fresno, CA, Selland Arena
Jun. 11–24: Lake Tahoe, NV, Sahara
Jul. 1–7: Las Vegas, NV, Riviera
Jul. 27: Edmonton, AB, Canada, Coliseum
Jul. 29: Minneapolis, MN, Northrop
  Auditorium
Jul. 30: Madison, WI, Dane County Coliseum
Jul. 31–Aug. 1: Chicago, IL, Arie Crown
  Theater
Aug. 2: Indianapolis, IA, Convention Center
Aug. 3: Fort Wayne, IN, Coliseum
Aug. 4: Kalamazoo, MI, Wings Stadium
Aug. 5–7: Toronto, ON, Canada, O'Keefe
  Center
Aug. 8: Binghamton, NY, Broome County
  Memorial Auditorium
Aug. 9: Fitchburg, MA, Wallace Civic Center
Aug. 10: Saratoga Springs, NY, Performing
  Arts Center
Aug. 11: Johnstown, PA
Aug. 12–13: Detroit, MI, Pine Knob Pavilion
Aug. 15: Philadelphia, PA, Robin Hood Dell
  West
Aug. 28–Sep. 8: Las Vegas, NV, Riviera
Oct. 13: Rexburg, ID, Ricks College
Oct. 14: Salt Lake City, UT, Special Events
  Center
Oct. 15: Logan, UT, Dee Glen Smith
  Spectrum
Oct. 16: Provo, UT, Brigham Young
  University
Oct. 19: Searcy, AK, Harding College
Oct. 20: Longview, TX, Longview High
  School Auditorium
Oct. 21: Nacogdoches, TX, William R.
  Johnson Coliseum
Oct. 22: Huntsville, TX, Sam Houston State
  University
Oct. 23: Norman, OK, Lloyd Noble Center
Oct. 24: Austin, TX, University of Texas
Oct. 25: Lake Charles, LA, Civic Auditorium
Nov. 10: Munich, Germany, Deutsches
  Museum
Nov. 12: Düsseldorf, Germany, Philipshalle
Nov. 13: Hamburg, Germany, Congress
  Centrum
Nov. 14: Amsterdam, Netherlands, Jaap
  Eden Hall
Nov. 15: Frankfurt, Germany,
  Jahrhunderthalle
Nov. 17: Edinburgh, Scotland
Nov. 18: Manchester, England, ABC Ardwick
Nov. 19: Blackpool, England, Opera House
Nov. 20: Birmingham, England,
  Hippodrome
Nov. 22–27: London, England, Palladium
Nov. 28: London, England, New London
  Theatre, *In Concert* (BBC TV special)

1977

Feb. 18–21: Lake Tahoe, NV, Harrah's
Apr. 19–24: Omaha, NE, Ak-Sar-Ben
  Coliseum
May 31–Jun. 5: Valley Forge, PA, Valley Forge
  Music Fair
Jun. 7–12: Owings, MD, Painters Mill Music
  Fair
Jun. 14–19: Gaithersburg, MD, Shady Grove
  Music Fair
Jun. 21–26: Westbury, NY, Westbury Music
  Fair
Jun. 30–Jul. 13: Las Vegas, NV, MGM Grand
  Hotel
Aug. 2–15: Lake Tahoe, NV, Harrah's
Dec. 24–Jan. 4: Las Vegas, NV, MGM Grand

1978

Feb. 16–23: Lake Tahoe, NV, Harrah's
Mar. 2–15: Las Vegas, NV, MGM Grand
May 11: Düsseldorf, Germany, *Starparade*
  (TV show)
Jun. 2–15: Lake Tahoe, NV, Harrah's
Jun. 29–Jul. 12: Las Vegas, NV, MGM Grand
Aug. 31–Sept. 4: Las Vegas, NV, MGM Grand
Dec. 3: Long Beach, CA, CSULB Terrace
  Theatre

1981

Oct. 14: Paris, France, *Palmarès des Chansons*
  (TV show)
Oct. 16: Paris, France, *Numéro Un* (TV show
  hosted by Julio Iglesias)
Oct. 20: Amsterdam, Netherlands, *Mies* (TV
  show)
Oct. 24: London, England, *Swap Shop* (BBC
  TV)
Oct. 29: Hamburg, Germany, *Show Express*
  (TV show)
Nov. 1: Rio de Janeiro, *Generation 1980s* (TV
  show)
Nov. 4: Rio de Janeiro, Brazil (two TV shows
  for the *Rede Globo* network)
Nov. 5: Rio de Janeiro, Brazil, *Fantastico* (TV
  show)
Nov. 6: Rio de Janeiro, Brazil, *Bandeirantes*
  (TV show)

The Awards Show

Color the Carpenters Silver, Gold, and Platinum

"We still can't believe we even *had* a record out!"

Standing alongside his *Partridge Family* TV mom (and real-life stepmother) Shirley Jones, David Cassidy struggles to open the envelope, adding just a bit more than the usual tension before the announcement of the next Grammy winner. This one is for 1970's Best Pop Vocal Performance by a Duo or Group.

"Carpenters, 'Close to You,'!" Cassidy exclaims, as both he and Jones smile. The audience applauds enthusiastically, and the camera cuts to Karen and Richard getting up from their front-row seats. Karen is beaming and Richard grins as they ascend the few stairs to the stage. Richard is handed the statuette as he joins Karen at the podium. Karen attempts to speak, but she is overwhelmed.

Richard approaches the mic: "We still can't believe we even *had* a record out!," he jokes, before graciously thanking producer Jack Daugherty, as well as A&M Records cofounders Jerry Moss and Herb Alpert. With an acceptance speech sincerely grateful, funny, and all of twelve seconds.

The Carpenters won another Grammy that night, for Best New Artist. But they lost the big honors,

Record of the Year and Album of the Year, to Simon & Garfunkel. Richard was also nominated on his own for arranging "(They Long to Be) Close to You," but "Bridge over Troubled Water" swept that statuette too.

Little matter, as the Carpenters would be back in Grammy's good graces just a year later, winning a 1971 award for their performances on *Carpenters* (The Tan Album).

Including Richard's arranging work, the Carpenters scored twelve nominations for their work between 1970 and 1978. By the time of that last nomination—an acknowledgment for Richard's epic treatment of Klaatu's cosmic cult hit "Calling Occupants of Interplanetary Craft (The Recognized Anthem of World Contact Day)"—the Carpenters knew the awards circuit well.

What follows is a list of Grammys and a mere sampling of a variety of other honors that came the Carpenters' way, including No. 1 year-end record-industry chart rankings and one way-cool space oddity.

Left: Presenting Bette Midler with the Best New Artist statuette at *The 16th Annual Grammy Awards*, 1974

Right: At *The 14th Annual Grammy Awards* with the statuette for Best Pop Vocal Performance by a Duo or Group, for *Carpenters* [The Tan Album], 1972

All-American College Show
1968: 1st Place Preliminary, The Richard Carpenter Trio
1968: 1st Place Semifinal, The Richard Carpenter Trio
1968: 1st Place Preliminary, Richard Carpenter (solo performance)

American Music Awards
1974: Favorite Duo or Group Pop/Rock

Billboard magazine
1970: Trendsetters Award, for leading "a trend toward the softer, melodic rock harmonies that influenced, in turn, many other groups."
1970: No. 1 New Artist
1970: No. 1 Easy Listening Artist
1970: No. 1 Easy Listening Single, "(They Long to Be) Close to You"
1971: No. 1 Easy Listening Artist
2019: No. 5 Classical Artist (w/RPO)
2019: No. 5 Classical Crossover Artist (w/RPO)

Cash Box magazine
1971: No. 1 Best Duo (Albums)
1971: No. 1 Best Duo (Singles)
1972: No. 1 Best Duo (Albums)
1972: No. 1 Best Duo (Singles)
1974: No. 1 International Artist of the Year
1974: No. 1 International Album of the Year, *The Singles 1969–1973*
1975: No. 1 Pop Singles Duo

Georgie Awards (American Guild of Variety Artists)
1971: Best Musical Group

Grammy Awards Wins
1970: Best New Artist of the Year
1970: Best Contemporary Vocal Performance by a Duo, Group or Chorus, *Close to You*
1971: Best Pop Vocal Performance by a Duo, Group or Chorus, *Carpenters*

Grammy Awards Nominations
1970: Album of the Year, *Close to You*
1970: Record of the Year, "(They Long to Be) Close to You"
1970: Best Arrangement Accompanying Vocalist(s), Richard Carpenter, "(They Long to Be) Close to You"
1971: Best Arrangement Accompanying Vocalist(s), Richard Carpenter, "Superstar"
1971: Album of the Year, *Carpenters*
1972: Best Instrumental Arrangement, Richard Carpenter, "Flat Baroque"
1973: Best Pop Vocal Performance by a Duo, Group or Chorus, "Sing"
1973: Best Arrangement Accompanying Vocalist(s), Richard Carpenter, "Sing"
1977: Best Arrangement Accompanying Vocalist(s), Richard Carpenter, "Calling Occupants of Interplanetary Craft (The Recognized Anthem of World Contact Day)"

Grammy Hall of Fame
1998: "We've Only Just Begun"
2000: "(They Long to Be) Close to You"

Hollywood Bowl Hall of Fame
2010: Carpenters
Richard conducted the Hollywood Bowl Philharmonic and performed "Superstar" with fellow inductee Donna Summer at the induction ceremony.

Hollywood Walk of Fame
1983: Carpenters
Richard, his parents, and Herb Alpert attended the ceremony on October 12 at 6931 Hollywood Boulevard.

Music Week/Record Mirror (UK)
1974: No. 1 Album of the Year, *The Singles 1969–1973*

County of Los Angeles Department of Parks & Recreation
1966: Hollywood Bowl Battle of the Bands, Sweepstakes Winner, The Richard Carpenter Trio
1966: Hollywood Bowl Battle of the Bands, Outstanding Instrumentalist, Richard Carpenter
1966: Hollywood Bowl Battle of the Bands, Combo Finalist, Richard Carpenter

NASA
1972: "We've Only Just Begun" provides wake-up call to Apollo 17 crew
1973–74: "Top of the World" provides wake-up call to Skylab 4 crew
1985: "Top of the World" provides wake-up call to Space Shuttle Challenger crew
2004: "Top of the World" provides wake-up call to Spirit, the robotic rover on Mars

Playboy magazine
1975: No. 1 Rock Drummer of the Year (Reader's Poll), Karen Carpenter

Radio Programmers of America
1975 (midyear): Favorite Duo or Group

Record World magazine
1971: No. 1 New Duo (Singles)
1971: No. 1 New Duo (Albums)
1972: No. 1 Top Duo (Singles)
1972: No. 1 Top Duo (Albums)
1973: No. 1 Top Duo (Singles)
1973: No. 1 Top Duo (Albums)

Ventura County
2007: Philanthropists of the Year, Richard and Mary Carpenter

World Disc Grand Prix (Japan)
1973: Artists of the Year
1973: Album of the Year, *Now & Then*
1973: Single of the Year, "Yesterday Once More"
1974: Artists of the Year
1974: Single of the Year, "I Won't Last a Day without You"
1975: Now Popular Award, "Only Yesterday"

Record Awards

The Carpenters have been awarded hundreds of Silver, Gold, and Platinum records over the years from all over the world, and they just keep coming. In fact, as this book was being written, news came that UK Silver awards had been issued for "(They Long to Be) Close to You" (March 2020) and "We've Only Just Begun" (November 2020). Some sixteen years after their first releases, the digital singles for each song passed the 200,000-sales mark in Britain. Given the strength of the Carpenters' catalog, more certifications are likely to be coming and coming.

To keep this list of Silver, Gold, and Platinum awards manageable, we limited the entries to sources we could confirm—primarily databases for music-trade organizations in the United States, Canada, the United Kingdom, and Japan.

The Singles

"(They Long to Be) Close to You"
Gold: United States, Australia, and Canada
Silver: United Kingdom

"We've Only Just Begun"
Gold: United States
Silver: United Kingdom

"For All We Know"
Gold: United States

"Rainy Days and Mondays"
Gold: United States

"Superstar"
Gold: United States and Japan

"Hurting Each Other"
Gold: United States

"Top of the World" (1972)
Platinum: Japan

"Sing"
Gold: United States

"Yesterday Once More"
4x Platinum: Japan
Gold: United States
Silver: United Kingdom

"Jambalaya (On the Bayou)"
Gold: Japan

"I Won't Last a Day without You"
Gold: Japan

"Top of the World" (1974)
Platinum: Japan
Gold: United States and Japan
Silver: United Kingdom

"Please Mr. Postman"
Gold: United States, Canada, and Japan
Silver: United Kingdom

"Only Yesterday"
Gold: Japan

"I Need to Be in Love"/"Top of the World" (1995 reissue)
4x Platinum: Japan

"I Need to Be in Love" (digital version)
Gold: Japan

"Top of the World" (digital version)
Platinum: Japan

The Albums

Close to You
2x multi-Platinum: United States
Platinum: United States
Gold: United States, Canada, Australia, and United Kingdom

Ticket to Ride
Silver: United Kingdom

Carpenters
4x multi-Platinum: United States
Platinum: United States
Gold: United States, Canada, Australia, and United Kingdom

Golden Prize
Gold: Japan

A Song for You
3x multi-Platinum: United States
Platinum: United States
Gold: United States, Canada, and United Kingdom

Now & Then
2x multi-Platinum: United States
Platinum: United States, The Netherlands, and Denmark
Gold: United States, Canada, The Netherlands, United Kingdom, and Japan
Silver: United Kingdom

The Singles 1969–1973
7x multi-Platinum: United States
4x multi-Platinum: United States
3x multi-Platinum: United States
Platinum: United States, Canada, United Kingdom, The Netherlands, and Denmark
Gold: United States, Canada, The Netherlands, South Africa, Hong Kong, and United Kingdom
Silver: United Kingdom

Golden Prize Vol. 2
Gold: Japan

Horizon
Platinum: United States
Gold: United States, Canada, United Kingdom, and Japan
Silver: United Kingdom

A Kind of Hush
Gold: United States and United Kingdom
Silver: United Kingdom

The Carpenters Collection: Their Greatest Hits
Silver: United Kingdom

Live at the Palladium
Gold: United Kingdom
Silver: United Kingdom

Christmas Portrait
Platinum: United States
Gold: United States, Canada

Passage
Gold: United Kingdom
Silver: United Kingdom

The Singles 1974–1978
Platinum: United Kingdom
Gold: United Kingdom
Silver: United Kingdom

Made in America
Silver: United Kingdom

Voice of the Heart
Gold: United States and United Kingdom
Silver: United Kingdom

An Old-Fashioned Christmas
Gold: United States

Yesterday Once More
2x multi-Platinum: United States
Platinum: United States and United Kingdom
Gold: United States and United Kingdom
Silver: United Kingdom

Only Yesterday: Richard & Karen Carpenter's Greatest Hits
5x Platinum: United Kingdom
4x Platinum: United Kingdom
3x Platinum: United Kingdom
2x Platinum: United Kingdom
Platinum: United Kingdom, Japan, and Australia
Gold: United Kingdom
Silver: United Kingdom

Live at the Palladium (1993 reissue)
Gold: United Kingdom
Silver: United Kingdom

Carpenters (1993, CD reissue)
Platinum: United Kingdom

Interpretations: A 25th Anniversary Celebration
Gold: United Kingdom
Silver: United Kingdom

Twenty-Two Hits of the Carpenters
12x Platinum: Japan

The Best of the Carpenters
Gold: United Kingdom
Silver: United Kingdom

Reflections
Silver: United Kingdom

Love Songs
Gold: United States and United Kingdom
Silver: United Kingdom

Gold: Greatest Hits
4x Platinum: United Kingdom
Platinum: United Kingdom
Gold: United Kingdom
Silver: United Kingdom

As Time Goes By
Gold: Japan

Gold: 35th Anniversary Edition
Gold: United States

The Singles 1969–1981
Gold: United Kingdom
Silver: United Kingdom

40/40
Gold: United Kingdom and Japan

The Ultimate Collection
Gold: United Kingdom

The Nation's Favourite Carpenters Songs
Silver: United Kingdom

Carpenters with the Royal Philharmonic Orchestra
Gold: United Kingdom
Silver: United Kingdom

The Videos

Close to You: Remembering the Carpenters
Gold: United States

Gold: Greatest Hits
Gold: United States and United Kingdom

Interpretations: A 25th Anniversary Celebration
Gold: United Kingdom

Acknowledgments

While we are grateful for the dozens who paved the way for *Carpenters: The Musical Legacy*, it was Sujata Murthy who ultimately got us, and the project, to Richard Carpenter. As senior vice president of Media + Artist Relations at Universal Music Enterprises, which distributes the Carpenters catalog, Sujata was painfully aware of our determination to write *the* Carpenters book. And, better yet, she shared our love for the duo's music, as well as our incredible respect for Richard.

Both authors had met Richard a number of times before, but neither we nor he had a clue where this book would take us. Within days of starting the project, Richard wasn't just our subject; he was our partner. And, over the months, we got to know him both as a musical genius and, much more importantly, as the most admirable of human beings. We pray that comes across in these pages.

Our gratitude also goes to Alan Nevins of Renaissance Literary and Talent, who "got" our vision for this project the instant he saw our proposal, and he knew exactly who should publish it: Lynn Grady, at Princeton Architectural Press. Lynn had us at "hello," as did executive editor Jennifer Thompson, who kept her cool, even though she was right there in the fire with us.

Just a few more among the many who worked so hard:

Thanks, Jozelle May, for being there from development through countless trips to scan images at Richard Carpenter's house to making sure the last image for the book's jacket didn't have a blemish. Your gorgeous design for the book proposal opened so many doors.

Thank you to contributing writer and editor Denise Quan, first-pass copy editors Sandy Cohen and Deborah Sprague, as well as Peter Desmond Dawe for photo acquisitions and Donavan Freberg for photo clearances. Thanks also to researchers Simon Worsley, Joe DiMaria, Stephen Richardson, Billy Rees, and Nancy Mescon.

And, at last, deepest gratitude to the design team at IN-FO.CO, Adam Michaels and Marina Kitchen, who worked fast and fabulously.

The authors would also like to thank Akira Tsukahara, Alana Voeller, Annie Leibovitz, Anthony Tran, Bob Messenger, Caroline Graham, Charles Hannah, Chris Cadman, Craig Braun, Craig Halstead, Deborah Shippen, Derek Green, Earle Dumler, Herb Alpert, Jim Pierson, Joan Messenger, John Bettis, Ken Silber, Kristen Ray, Kristine Krueger, Lisa Minnerly, Liska Yamada, Mark Taft, Morgan Ames, Norman Seeff, Paul Almond, Shun Okano, Stephen Richardson, Tom Nolan, and Yuka Ogura.

And our partners at Universal Music Enterprises: Bruce Resnikoff, Jane Ventom, Megan McLean Corso, Matt D'Amico, Mike Ruthig, Judah Joseph Vartan, Susan Lavoie, Beth Stempel, John Ray, Scott Ravine, Tom Rowland, Don Terbush, Xilonen Oreshnick, Ryan Null, Andrew Daw, Andrew Kronfeld, Sue Armstrong, Lucy Benbow, Richard Hinkley, Hirokazu Tanaka, Masaya Inokuchi.

Chris's personal acknowledgments: I must start off by thanking my Lord and Savior Jesus Christ for opening doors that otherwise would have been utterly unattainable, blessing me above and beyond my wildest dreams. *Delight yourself in the Lord, and He will give you the desires of your heart* (Psalm 37:4).

I want to thank my mother, Ann, and my stepfather, Syd, for their endless love and support, and for allowing my younger self to turn our rec room into a recording studio, where I picked apart all those records. To my father, Jeff, and stepmother, Cynthia, the demonstration of your faith has taught me that nothing is impossible. Thank you both for your unconditional love.

To my brother, Ryan, and sister, Devon, thank you for letting me replay the chorus to "Superstar" countless times on our trips around town. Oh, and for giving up the rec room!

To my "Zamora" family—Rose, Gerry, and Kris: Thank you for blessing me with my sweet, beautiful Jozelle, and for loving, supporting, and encouraging me like a true son and brother.

Thank you to Dan, Danielle, Alexis, and the rest of my extended family and friends for all your love and constant support and encouragement over the years.

A very special thanks to the gang at A&M Corner, especially Neil (Rudy) Rudish, Harry Neyhart, and Mike Blakesley.

And to my buddy Abe Faburada: I will never forget your love for the Carpenters, and your ability to take all of our musical chitter-chatter and make it a matter of the heart.

Mike's personal acknowledgments: To my family Cidoni: Mom, thanks for instilling in me a mad passion for music, movies, and theater from Day One, and insisting I chase my dream of becoming the next Bob Thomas. (I'm still working on it.) To Joanne: a sister and a best friend; and to Corey and Ben: thanks for keeping the music playing, kids.

For my family Lennox, I'll steal from Lou Grant in that last episode of *The Mary Tyler Moore Show*: "I cherish you people."

To colleagues at the Associated Press: your standards kept me reaching for the stars.

To my AP Entertainment sisters and brothers in Los Angeles, New York, Nashville, and London—especially Marcela Isaza, Jeff Turner, and Bruce Barton—for listening about this thing… *forever*. And to AP's Ryan Pearson, Anthony McCartney, and Vicki Cogliano for moving at the speed of light when the dream became reality.

To supportive friends, colleagues and champions in my two hometowns: Rochester, N.Y., and Los Angeles.

For being there: Chuck Perry, Bob and Elena Koenigsberg, Dr. Jim Seward, Nic and Randi Minetor, Dean Anthony La Barge, Cedric Herrera, Scott Mescon, Jim Mandell and Lisa Johnson Mandell, Natalie Kojen, Jodi Broitman, and Scott and Marla Fain.

Finally, to my brother, Stephan: the only way this journey would have been more incredible is if you had been here with us.